The Everyday Life Reader

The Everyday Life Reader brings together a wide range of thinkers from Freud to Baudrillard with primary sources on everyday life to provide a comprehensive resource on theories of everyday life. Ben Highmore's introduction surveys the development of thought about everyday life and discusses the issues raised. Each themed section opens with an essay outlining the debates and each article is prefaced with an editor's introduction. Sections include:

- Situating the everyday
- Everyday life and 'national' culture
- Ethnography near and far
- Reclamation work
- Everyday things

Contributors: Roland Barthes, Jean Baudrillard, Walter Benjamin, Pierre Bourdieu, Fernand Braudel, Steven Connor, Guy Debord, Michel de Certeau, Sigmund Freud, Betty Friedan, Luce Giard, Jean-Luc Godard, Erving Goffman, Stuart Hall, Harry Harootunian, Alice Kaplan, Mary Kelly, Siegfried Kracauer, Henri Lefebvre, Bronislaw Malinowski, Karal Ann Marling, Mass-Observation, Anne-Marie Miéville, Daniel Miller, Trinh T. Minh-ha, Edgar Morin, Georges Perec, Jacques Rancière, Kristin Ross, Georg Simmel, Dorothy E. Smith, Lynn Spigel, Carolyn Steedman, Xiaobing Tang, Leon Trotsky, Raymond Williams, Paul Willis.

The Editor: Ben Highmore is Senior Lecturer in Cultural and Media Studies at the University of the West of England. He is the author of *Everyday Life and Cultural Theory* (Routledge 2002).

The
Everyday Life
Reader

Edited by

Ben Highmore

  Routledge
Taylor & Francis Group

LONDON AND NEW YORK

First published 2002
by Routledge
2 Park Square, Milton Park, Abingdon, Oxon, OX14 4RN

Simultaneously published in the USA and Canada
by Routledge
270 Madison Ave, New York, NY 10016

Reprinted 2007 (twice)

Transferred to Digital Printing 2008

Routledge is an imprint of the Taylor & Francis Group, an informa business

© 2002 Ben Highmore for selection and editorial matter; individual chapters © the contributors

Typeset in Perpetua and Bell Gothic by RefineCatch Limited, Bungay, Suffolk

Printed and bound in Great Britain by TJI Digital, Padstow, Cornwall

British Library Cataloguing in Publication Data
A catalogue record for this book is available from the British Library

Library of Congress Cataloging in Publication Data
The everyday life reader / edited by Ben Highmore.
    p. cm.
    Includes bibliographical references and index.
    1. Life. 2. Civilization, Modern—20th century. 3. Culture—Philosophy. I. Highmore,
Ben, 1961–
BD431 .E94 2002
306—dc21   2001044194

ISBN13: 978–0–415–23024–7 (HB)
ISBN13: 978–0–415–23025–4 (PB)

For Angela and David Highmore

Contents

PART TWO
Everyday life and 'national' culture

PART THREE
Ethnography near and far

Illustrations

Preface

FIRST A SMALL WARNING: this is not a source book of everyday life materials. I cannot imagine what such a book would be like (where would it begin and end, what would it *not* include?). Instead this is a book featuring various approaches to different aspects of everyday life. Perhaps inevitably this means that something of the rich vernacular of actual lived everyday life gets sacrificed and replaced by the more formal diction of academic language. The trade-off, I hope, is a selection of texts, which, although particular in their address and content, have a more general application.

Putting together this *Reader* has mixed pleasure and pain. On the one hand it has encouraged an everyday pleasure shared by many adolescent boys and girls with time on their hands: the listing of favourites. But (and this is where the pain comes in) such a project seems to demand an ethics, a responsibility. The ethical tendency that this project first encountered was to try to be representative. Yet this sense of 'representation' (as has been pointed out in other contexts) is invariably burdensome. In this case it was also clearly impossible (think of the disciplines the 'everyday' impinges on, think of the internationally different cultural everydays that might serve as exemplification). Abandoning this approach, I opted instead for trying to bring together a range of texts that might fulfil a more modest ambition: to be used for imagining and practising the (future) study of everyday life. The texts would necessarily tend towards the theoretical (either implicitly or explicitly) but they would also need to be more 'work-a-day' (so to speak) and provide some examples of what everyday life studies might look like (if it chose to exist).

This collection aims to develop a cultural studies approach to everyday life and in doing so privileges two cultural perspectives: ethnography (including both anthropology and sociology) and historiography. It also takes these approaches to be pre-eminently practical and thereby open to any number of different actualisations. In constructing a book that might prove useful for someone wanting a practical outlet for some of the more theoretical resources on offer, I have included a few examples that demonstrate the possibilities of employing formally imaginative ways of registering everyday life. For the most part these are projects that are usually included in books about modern art and film. I would argue that everyday life studies demands the kind of attention to form that is usually reserved for art.

Inevitably any *Reader* ignores vast textual areas that clearly could (and should) contribute to the named field. Some of these seemed to demand their own anthology: for instance to do justice to the terrain of language and everyday life would mean including texts by the likes of Wittgenstein, Voloshinov, Austin and so on. To provide just a glimpse of such work here seemed not only inappropriate but also plain mean. Similarly, an anthology (or two) could be made of philosophical work that has set out by trying to apprehend the concrete lived-ness of everyday life (phenomenology and existentialism, for instance). Again I have chosen not to follow that particular path. The geographical scope of this selection is limited: its Euro-Americanism is continually evident. My only hope is that such limitations do not detract from the possibilities of everyday life finding a more global productivity in cross-cultural studies. As Anglophone academia is pulled puffing and stumbling to face the actuality of an international and global reality, its myopia is made increasingly vivid.

There is a danger that when a conceptual phrase gets its very own *Reader*, it has already entered into critical decline and is ready to be retired to the home for intellectual clichés. Optimistically I would argue that for the phrases 'everyday life' and 'the everyday', no such fate seems to be particularly imminent, ironically because these phrases are (precisely) already clichés. In a reversal of usual academic practice an *Everyday Life Reader* witnesses not the academic normalisation of some monstrous neologism (the *Ethnomethodology Reader*, the *Deconstructivist Reader* and so on) rather it takes an ordinary phrase (a phrase from everyday language) and seems to make it monstrous. Such a project is no doubt perverse; it certainly is not without its contradictions.

A number of people have encouraged this perversion and without them this *Reader* would not have been possible. First and foremost I would like to thank Michelle Henning, who has been a colleague and friend for a number of years. The idea of generating inventive ethnographic and historiographic approaches to everyday life first became a practical possibility in a course that we taught together. I would also like to thank Ian Buchanan, Gavin Butt, Stephen Clucas, Steven Connor, Barry Curtis, Michael E. Gardiner, Laura Marcus, Alan Read and Dorothy Sheridan, for encouragement and support. Friends and colleagues at the University of the West of England, Bristol, have found numerous ways of assisting this work on everyday life and I thank them for it. Rebecca Barden and Alistair Daniel at Routledge made this *Reader* happen. Espen Hauglid, Fred Orton, Griselda Pollock and especially Steven Connor introduced me to texts that now seem like old friends. While putting this collection together, I made contact with various people whose texts I have reproduced here; they were all encouraging and helpful. I would like to thank them all, and especially Ray Barrie and Mary Kelly, who have been particularly generous and helpful.

None of this could have happened without the continual everyday support of my partner Wendy Bonner. And it would have been less bearable without the distracting pleasures of our two children. Editing this collection with two small children in the wings made me recognise the importance of childhood for thinking about everyday life. For this reason (and for so many others) I dedicate this book to my parents.

Acknowledgements and permissions

1   Sigmund Freud, 'Parapraxes', by permission of A. W. Freud *et al.*, by arrangement with Mark Paterson & Associates.

2   Extract from Walter Benjamin, *Illuminations*, published by Jonathan Cape. Used by permission of the Random House Group Ltd. Extract from Walter Benjamin, *Illuminations*, copyright © 1955 Suhrkamp Verlag, Frankfurt a.M., English translation copyright © 1968 Harry Zohn and renewed © 1996 by Harcourt, Inc., reprinted by permission of Harcourt, Inc., Frankfurt a.M. 1968.

3   Fernand Braudel, 'Preface' to *The Mediterranean and the Mediterranean World in the Age of Philip II* [1946] published in English by Harper Row and William Collins Sons and Co. Ltd in 1972.

4   Erving Goffman, 'Front and Back Regions of Everyday Life', from Erving Goffman, *The Presentation of Self in Everyday Life*, copyright © 1959 Erving Goffman. Used by permission of Doubleday, a division of Random House. Reproduced by permission of Penguin Books Ltd.

5   Betty Friedan, 'The Problem that has No Name', from Betty Friedan, *The Feminine Mystique*, copyright © 1983, 1974, 1973, 1963 Betty Friedan. Used by permission of W. W. Norton & Company, Inc. and the Orion Publishing Group Ltd.

6   Michel de Certeau, 'General Introduction' to *The Practice of Everyday Life*, translated by Steven Rendall, copyright © 1984 the Regents of the University of California.

7   Alice Kaplan and Kristin Ross, 'Introduction' to *Everyday Life: Yale French Studies* [1987], with permission from Yale French Studies.

8   Leon Trotsky, 'Habit and Custom' copyright © 1973 by Pathfinder Press. Reprinted by permission.

9   Raymond Williams, 'Culture is Ordinary', from *Resources of Hope*, with permission from Verso, the imprint of New Left Books Ltd.

10   Karal Ann Marling, 'Nixon in Moscow', from Karal Ann Marling, *As Seen on TV*, pp. 243–50, 272–6, reprinted by permission of the publisher, Cambridge, Mass. and London: Harvard University Press, copyright © 1994 the President and Fellows of Harvard College.

11   Kristin Ross, 'Introduction' to *Fast Cars, Clean Bodies*, copyright © 1995 Massachusetts Institute of Technology.

12   Harry Harootunian, The Promise of 'Modern Life', from Harry Harootunian, *Overcome by Modernity: History, Culture, and Community in Interwar Japan*, copyright © 2000 Princeton University Press. Reprinted by permission of Princeton University Press.

13   Xiaobing Tang, 'The Anxiety of Everyday Life in Post-revolutionary China', is an edited version of Xiaobing Tang, 'New Urban Culture and the Anxiety of Everyday Life in Late-Twentieth-Century China', in *Chinese Modern: The Heroic and the Quotidian*, copyright © 2000 Duke University Press. All rights reserved. Printed with permission. This is a revised and expanded version of a chapter by the same title from *In Pursuit of Contemporary East Asian Culture* (copyright © 1996 Westview Press).

14   Bronislaw Malinowski, 'Proper Conditions for Ethnographic Work' [1922], with permission from Routledge.

15   Mass-Observation, 'Two Letters', copyright © 2000 New Statesman.

16   Edgar Morin, 'The Multidimensional Method', from Edgar Morin, *The Red and the White: Report from a French Village*, translated by A. M. Sheridan-Smith, copyright © 1970 Random House, Inc. Used by permission of Pantheon Books, a division of Random House, Inc.

17   Pierre Bourdieu, 'The Kabyle House or the World Reversed', with permission from Polity Press and Stanford University Press (www.sup.org).

18   Georges Perec, 'Approaches to What?', from *L'Infra-ordinaire*, copyright © 1989 Editions du Seuil, translation copyright © 1997 John Sturrock. Reproduced by permission of Penguin Books Ltd.

19   Mary Kelly, 'Documentation VI: Pre-writing alphabet, exerque and diary' [1977–8], by kind permission of the artist. Copyright © Mary Kelly 1983. Photo credit: Ray Barrie.

20   Jean-Luc Godard and Anne-Marie Miéville, 'France/Tour/Detour/Two/Children' [1978] produced by Institut National de l'Audiovisuel (Paris) and Sonimage (Rolle).

21   Trinh T. Minh-ha, 'Reassemblage', copyright © 1992, from Trinh T. Minh-ha, *Framer Framed*. Reproduced by permission of Routledge, Inc., part of the Taylor & Francis Group.

22   Henri Lefebvre, 'Work and Leisure in Everyday Life', from *Critique of Everyday Life*, translated by John Moore, with permission from Verso, the imprint of New Left Books Ltd.

23   Guy Debord, 'Perspectives for Conscious Alterations in Everyday Life', no copyright.

24   Jacques Rancière, 'Author's Preface' to *Proletarian Nights*. This translation, by Noel Parker, first appeared in *Radical Philosophy*, 31, summer, 1982, and is reprinted here with permission.

25   Stuart Hall, 'Reconstruction Work', by kind permission of the author.

26   Carolyn Steedman, 'Landscape for a Good Woman', with permission from Little, Brown and Co. Copyright © 1985 Carolyn Steedman.

27   Dorothy E. Smith, 'A Feminist Methodology', from Dorothy E. Smith, *The Everyday World as Problematic: A Feminist Sociology*, copyright © 1987 Dorothy E. Smith. Reprinted with the permission of Northeastern University Press.

28   Paul Willis, 'Symbolic Creativity', from Paul Willis, *Common Culture*, Open University Press 1990, with permission.

29   Georg Simmel, 'The Berlin Trade Exhibition', translated by Sam Whimster. Reprinted by permission of Sage Publications Ltd, from David Frisby and Mike Featherstone (eds) *Simmel on Culture*, copyright © 1991 Sage Ltd.

30   Siegfried Kracauer, 'Boredom', from Siegfried Kracauer, *The Mass Ornament*, translated by Thomas Y. Levin, pp. 331–4, reprinted by permission of the publisher, Cambridge, Mass.: Harvard University Press, copyright © 1995 the President and Fellows of Harvard College. With agreement from Suhrkamp Verlag, Frankfurt a.M.

31   Roland Barthes, 'Plastic', from *Mythologies*, translated by Annette Lavers. Translation copyright © 1972 by Jonathan Cape Ltd, with permission from The Random House Group Ltd. Reprinted by permission of Hill and Wang, a division of Farrar, Strauss and Giroux, LLC.

32   Jean Baudrillard, 'Structures of Interior Design', from *The System of Objects*, with permission from Verso, the imprint of New Left Books Ltd.

33   Luce Giard, 'Doing Cooking', from *The Practice of Everyday Life, Volume 2: Living and Cooking*, translated by Timothy J. Tomasik, published by the University of Minnesota Press. Copyright © 1998 the Regents of the University of Minnesota.

34   Lynn Spigel, 'Installing the Television Set: Popular Discourses on Television and Domestic Space, 1948–1955,' *Camera Obscura* (16:1, Winter 1998). Copyright 1998. All rights reserved. Reprinted by permission of Duke University Press.

35   Daniel Miller, 'Making Love in Supermarkets', copyright © Daniel Miller 1998. Used by permission of the publisher, Cornell University Press, and Blackwell Publishers Ltd.

36   Steven Connor, 'Rough Magic: Bags', by kind permission of the author.

Every effort has been made to obtain permission to reproduce copyright material. If any proper acknowledgement has not been made, or permission not received, we invite copyright holders to inform us of the oversight.

BEN HIGHMORE

INTRODUCTION
Questioning everyday life

EVERYDAY LIFE is a vague and problematic phrase. Any assumption that it is simply 'out there', as a palpable reality to be gathered up and described, should face an immediate question: whose everyday life? Often enough, however, such questions are purposefully ignored. To invoke the everyday can often be a sleight of hand that normalises and universalises particular values, specific world-views. Politicians, for instance, are often fond of using terms like 'everyday life' or 'ordinary people' as a way of hailing constituents to a common culture: people like us, lives like ours. The underside of this, of course, is that this everyday life is haunted by implicit 'others', who supposedly live outside the ordinary, the everyday. Claiming everyday life as self-evident and readily accessible becomes an operation for asserting the dominance of specific cultures and for particular understandings of such cultures.

Yet the term everyday life has also been used to side with the dominated against those that would dominate. Take, for example, the use of everyday life by social historians. To invoke everyday life can be to invoke precisely those practices and lives that have traditionally been left out of historical accounts, swept aside by the onslaught of events instigated by elites. It becomes shorthand for voices from 'below': women, children, migrants and so on. But while designed to challenge certain conventions, this can still maintain an unproblematic acceptance of everyday life as a transparent realm: now instead of looking at government records, attic rooms are plundered for diaries, letters and such like. This *Reader*, however, insists on questioning the transparency of the daily. It is dedicated to a less everyday use of the term everyday life. It explicitly and implicitly addresses the 'every-day' as a problematic, a contested and opaque terrain, where meanings are not to be found ready-made. Perhaps its starting point would be the idea that the everyday presents us with a recalcitrant object that does not give up its secrets too readily.

Everyday life is not simply the name that is given to a reality readily available for scrutiny; it is also the name for aspects of life that lie hidden. To invoke an ordinary culture

from below is to make the invisible visible, and as such has clear social and political reson-
ances. To summon-up a specific everyday, or to call a group of people together so as to
recognise a shared everyday life, has been an important step in bringing to visibility the
lives of those who have been sidelined by dominant accounts of social life. But this has
never been a simple act of calling on an already understood daily culture – in many
respects it has needed to produce that culture (as problematic) in the first place. Second-
wave feminism (for instance, Chapter 5) struggles to name an everydayness that was all
too readily seen at the time as both unproblematic and to a large degree simply invisible. It
was precisely the untroubled ease with which both men and women (but of course, mainly
men) understood the supposed naturalness of women's daily life as being organised around
the needs of children and husbands that made any alternative understanding seem counter-
intuitive or simply bizarre. The difficulty of bringing to light an alternative account of the
everyday life of middle-class women in 1950s and 1960s America is signalled by the title
of the first chapter of Betty Friedan's *The Feminine Mystique*: 'The Problem that has No
Name'. Of course, American women may well have experienced their lives as a domestic
straitjacket prior to Friedan's book (the massive sales could be seen as an index of this),
but even so, such an account of everyday life struggled to be seen as actuality. Feminism
had to actively register and name American women's everyday life, and as such the revolutionary agenda of second-wave feminism was to 'raise consciousness' about women's
daily life as an arena of domination. The project had to begin by actively producing
everyday life as an entity.

Everyday life can both hide and make vivid a range of social differences. But it should
be remembered that the production of recognisable difference initially required the manu-
facture of a sense of commonality (as in second-wave feminism). So the everyday (as a
theoretical and practical arena) has the potential ability of producing, not difference, but
commonality. It might be that this is where its generative ability lies. If 'everyday life' is
going to provide a re-imagining of the study of culture (and anything less would be to carry
on doing business-as-usual, thereby making a term like everyday life already obsolete) then
it might need to put on hold the *automatic* explanatory value placed on accepted cultural
differences. If cultural differences, such as gender, class, sexuality, ethnicity and so on, are
going to be useful for the understanding of everyday life (and I assume that they would be)
then their usefulness cannot be just presumed or taken for granted.

For example if I asked the question (with a nod towards psychoanalysis): 'Whose daily
life has been, on occasion, disturbed by the "uninvited" presence of a troubling memory?', I
might expect that most people would be familiar with such a scene even if their troubling
memories differed wildly. There is something of a radical commonality (which, now that
psychoanalysis has become part of our everyday life, might be less visible) to the suggestion that we all share a condition where our consciousness can be undermined by our
unconscious. Not only does this make visible an aspect of everyday life previously only
hinted at in literature (namely the unmanaged continuation of the past in the present), but
also it transforms our sense of the everyday (now the everyday becomes the unknowing
host for the return of traumatic material). That which transforms our sense of the everyday
in the guise of new commonalities (here memory, there a recognition of shared domination)
works to produce the everyday anew. If this is the goal of everyday life theory (and why
not?) then any preconstituted difference needs to be re-found in the job of producing the

everyday as an arena of study. As such we might move on from recognising a common condition (the persistence of the past) to seeing how the invasion of memories differs among people. It would seem likely that gender differences would register here, but what about other differences? How might other social and cultural conditions operate in relation to memory disturbances in everyday life? The traumas of migration and war might, for instance, affect everyday life in precisely this way.

If everyday life is going to challenge us into new ways of thinking and new ways of perceiving, then it will need to practise a kind of heuristic approach to social life that does not start out with predesignated outcomes. In its negotiation of difference and commonality it might, potentially, find new commonalities and breathe new life into old differences. But to do this will mean putting on hold some of the familiar conventions of contemporary studies of culture.

To question everyday life and to allow everyday life to question our understanding of the world is to specifically invite a theoretical articulation of everyday life. Theory is often a dense and abstruse form of writing, often designed to throw into crisis widely accepted and practised beliefs. Everyday life theory, while at times evidencing its share of obscurity, differs from this, at least potentially. Writing eight years after starting a project to study the practices of everyday life, Michel de Certeau and Luce Giard claimed: 'we know poorly the types of operations at stake in ordinary practices, their registers and their combinations, because our instruments of analysis, modeling and formalization were constructed for other objects and with other aims' (de Certeau *et al.* 1998: 256). Everyday life invites a kind of theorising that throws our most cherished *theoretical* values and practices into crisis. For instance, theorists often promote the values of 'rigorous' thought, 'systematic' elaboration and 'structured' argument: but what if rigour, system and structure were antithetical and deadening to aspects of everyday life? What if 'theory' was to be found elsewhere, in the pages of a novel, in a suggestive passage of description in an autobiography, or in the street games of children? What if theory (the kind that is designated as such) was beneficial for attending to the everyday, not via its systematic interrogations, but through its poetics, its ability to render the familiar strange? This is not to suggest that everyday life theory is anti-theoretical, far from it, but that in attending to the everyday such theory is never going to be a purely critical or deconstructive project. At the heart of the theoretical practices collected here is the desire for *constructive* and *inventive* thought, for a form of attention that struggles to articulate an intractable object (daily life) in the full knowledge that the everyday is always going to exceed the ability to register it.

No anthology of texts dedicated to a specific theme is going to be exhaustive, but if a *Reader* should provide a guide to the best that is on offer within a specific field, then an *Everyday Life Reader* is faced with a significant difficulty. For Henri Lefebvre, who spent his career working on the problem of the critique of everyday life, everyday life is 'defined by "what is left over" after all distinct, superior, specialized, structured activities have been singled out by analysis' (Lefebvre 1991: 97). If we assume that 'fields' constitute such distinct and specialised forms of knowledge, then clearly, for Lefebvre, the everyday is precisely what lies outside the disciplines of knowledge. However, Lefebvre goes on to insist that 'everyday life is profoundly related to *all* activities, and encompasses them with all their differences and their conflicts' (Lefebvre 1991: 97). If we look at the various fields that make up what is optimistically called the human sciences, we might draw the following conclusion: everyday life is both remaindered from fields of study as well as impacting on every single attempt to register human life. Cultural studies, sociology, social history, anthropology, ethnography, literary studies, psychology and so on would all, I guess, want to lay some claim to attending to the everyday – yet for the most part the tendency has been for specialised disciplines to invoke the everyday as a taken-for-granted aspect of social life. While these fields have made significant contributions to the productive problematic of everyday life (as both an indivisible singularity and overarching totality), they have rarely provided a space for putting such ideas at the centre of their inquiries. The potential of everyday life studies is not to unite disciplinary fields in some dream of multi-disciplinarity or interdisciplinarity; its potential is essentially anti-disciplinary. If as Lefebvre suggests the everyday lies both outside all the different fields of knowledge, while at the same time lying across them, then the everyday is not a field at all, more like a para-field, or a meta-field.

Thus an anthology of texts addressing the everyday cannot simply provide an overview of disciplinary approaches to everyday life, it cannot simply provide examples of how sociology (ethnomethodology, for instance) attends to the everyday, or how anthropology (participant observation, for instance) treats everyday life. If it is to do its job it will need to find those moments in disciplinary fields and outside them, when the everyday casts any disciplinary enterprise into doubt. Everyday life might therefore seem to constitute a field of doubt, but also, I would suggest, a field of experimentation, of possibility. In this introduction I want to set out something of an intellectual survey for thinking of the everyday as both problem and possibility. So if everyday life is, from here on in, going to stand in for a set of problems, for some productive stumbling blocks and detours, then we need to find a way of allowing these problems to surface. One way, the way chosen here, is to ask the most everyday of questions, the kind that 3-year olds ask in eager anticipation that a grown-up will be able to answer their curiosity ('where do clouds go to bed?' for instance). These are the blunt questions, driven by curiosity, the 'why, where, what, who, and how' that signal a frustration with nuanced interpretation.[1] Such questions want to cut to the chase. They necessarily require a broad brush. But unfortunately such questions rarely find satisfactory answers, inevitably generating more questions. So be warned – what follows does not provide much in the way of answers, and as a route-map to theories of everyday life it offers little in the way of short cuts.

What?

What is the everyday? Such a question leads us immediately into the realm of speculation. So much easier to be clear about what it is not. Lightning striking TV sets for instance, or your numbers winning the national lottery. But are not such things also part of everyday life? Is not the fear of lightning what might make you unplug your TV at night? And is not the unlikeliness of winning woven into the everydayness of the lottery? The problem with the everyday is that its contours might be so vague as to encompass almost everything (or certain aspects of everything). So on the one hand the national lottery points to the everyday as exceptional and singular (winning is exceptional, the choice of numbers nearly always particular, as are the dreams and aspirations that accompany playing the lottery). On the other hand the lottery can be seen as part of a vast number of people's everyday life in its ordinary generality (the majority of 'players' play each week, they share an understanding that they are more likely to be struck by lightning than win, yet still play). Here then might be a question facing the study of everyday life: is everyday life characterised by singular, individual acts (an accumulation of particularity, so to speak) or is it understandable as an overarching structure common to a large group of people?

If everyday life as an object of study sits uncertainly across these two perspectives (the particular and the general) we should also point out that this is merely one aspect of a range of dualities that can be seen to impact on everyday life studies. Here I want to suggest that these dualities can be provisionally grouped in interconnected ways that relate to a variety of perspectives on the everyday. So, in approaches that have privileged the particular we can find tendencies that have stressed other features of everyday life: the agency of individuals in daily life, forms of resistance or non-conformity to social structures, a stress on feelings and experience. Similarly, to approach everyday life as a realm of generality tends to privilege social structures, institutions and discourses, and to see these as a domain of power determining the everyday. Of course this is to oversimplify a complex history of the study of everyday life, and nearly all the writers and theorists who productively attend to the everyday evidence approaches that navigate across these poles (indeed this might be the very condition for attending to the everyday). However, it still might be useful to mark out these poles as *tendencies* with the understanding that we are not categorising approaches so much as getting a feel for certain (linked) orientations towards everyday life.

So if we sketch out a vector of these tendencies it might look something like this:

Particular	General
Agency	Structure
Experiences/Feelings	Institutions/Discourses
Resistance	Power
Micro-analysis	Macro-analysis

For shorthand these tendencies can be seen as forms of micro-analyses and macro-analyses. And if we cannot simply line up theorists of the everyday on one side or the other of this vector without losing something of the complexity of their thought, were we to do so we might at least uncover some partial truths. To list Michel de Certeau, say, under micro-analysis, and Michel Foucault, for instance, under macro-analysis, inevitably smoothes out contradictions and nuanced thought, but it does accord with *something* of the general drift of their work.

Perhaps the most central question for the recent history of cultural and social theory, and clearly a crucial question for the study of everyday life, is levelled at the duality resistance and/or power. Does the everyday provide the training ground for conformity, or is it rather the place where conformity is evaded? Or to put it slightly differently: is the everyday a realm of submission to relations of power or the space in which those relations are contested (or at least negotiated in relatively interesting ways)? Informing these questions (as I have already suggested) is a scepticism aimed at questioning the transparency of the everyday. Such scepticism is what makes any definite and simple answer to these questions problematic. Let me outline the form this scepticism takes.

Perhaps the two singular 'events' that lay the foundations for modern thought are to be found in the writing of Karl Marx and Sigmund Freud. What unites the very different work of Marx and Freud might be located at the level of the everyday. For Freud, as for Marx, the everyday is both real and unreal, both actuality and the disguise of actuality. To put it as simply as possible: the everyday is not as it appears. Or rather behind (or alongside, or underneath) the appearance of everyday life lies another actuality. For Freud what is bracketed out in the appearance of everyday life is a forceful realm of desire and fear that can, if unchecked, burst through the propriety of daily life. If you are lucky such interruptions will be confined to the occasional slip of the tongue (Chapter 1): if, on the other hand, the irruptions of the unconscious get the upper hand then the ability to function in daily life will be severely compromised. For the most part 'culture and society' can be understood as the name given to the checking and censorship that manages the troubling presence of these drives. Propriety and etiquette (the protocols of everyday life) instil a form of life 'safe' from untrammelled desires and murderous lusts.

Yet from another perspective what is presented as civilised conduct might constitute a seemly veil over a much more unseemly actuality. From the point of view of psychoanalysis, social propriety (morality, civilised behaviour, and so on) might be seen as a ritualistic and socially sanctioned re-presentation of desirous and fearful material. Thus, primeval desires could be seen as being re-coded into socially legitimate ones: in the place of blood-thirsty aggression lies 'healthy' competition and ambition; in the stead of unrestrained sexual appetites comes the complex and bizarre rigmarole of modern sexual mores. The everyday then, while it may give off a seemly appearance, never manages completely to bracket out the murky realm of the unconscious. Everyday life becomes the stage where the unconscious performs (individually via slips, dreams and neurotic symptoms, socially via accepted morality and the protocols of conventional behaviour), but never with its gloves off. Instead, the unconscious can be seen only in glimpses: in the oblique and devious forms of mistakes and fancy; in the circuitous routes it takes to fashion social protocols. As far as this goes we might suggest that Freud invites a contradictory understanding of everyday life. On the one hand the everyday becomes a repressive realm that censors the unconscious. On the other hand everyday life (or just as pertinently, every-night life) becomes the place where, however indirectly, the unconscious makes its presence felt. Whatever debates there are about the veracity of such an approach one thing remains clear; psychoanalysis undermines attempts to pass the everyday off as the accumulation of innocent habits and customs or as governed by fully conscious beings.

The idea of 'the actuality behind the actuality' is also a theme in Marx's understanding of everyday life. Perhaps the most explicit figuring of the everyday as an illusionistic yet 'real' reality is to be found in Marx and Engels' writing on ideology. In 1846, in *The German Ideology*, Marx and Engels (1985) argue that the self-understanding of a culture is produced from the 'material life-process' of society. Or to put it another way: ideology is a product of the relationships and processes of a society (rather than merely the result of thought). The way that the world appears (at first glance, so to speak) is the outcome of the particular material circumstances in which it is lived. This is Marx arguing for a form of materialist philosophy and against the prevailing inclination for idealist thought. The *actual everyday is life life lived upside down*

point for our purposes, however, is to note that for Marx, while there is a definite relationship between the material actuality of everyday life and the actual way it is perceived, this
relationship is distorted. Or in Marx and Engels' analogy, simply upside-down: 'if in all
ideology men and their circumstances appear upside-down as in a *camera obscura*, this
phenomenon arises just as much from their historical life-process as the inversion of
objects on the retina does from their physical life-process' (Marx and Engels [1846]
1985: 47). So for Marx and Engels the appearance of the everyday works to hide (distort)
the material circumstances (the division of labour, most crucially) that gives rise to this
distortion. Actual everyday life is life lived upside-down, where workers are paid a modest
but essentially fair wage, and where those that own property and people have only been
exercising their rights. But while Marx and Engels employ a language of illusion to
describe the ideological appearance of the world, it is clear that not only is this the outcome of real concrete processes, but also it describes a real *lived* actuality. We live this
upside-down-ness as reality. So if the *appearance* of the world it is not as fundamental as
the 'actuality behind the actuality', ideology has to be seen as a profound actuality rather
than an illusion that can simply be cast off by taking a second look.

This understanding of the ideology of the everyday as both illusory and profoundly real
is best seen historically. It is only when ideological forms are generally understood as
natural that the sense of ideology as being both illusion and actuality can be grasped. The
corollary of this is that by the time something is generally understood as ideological it is no
longer operating *as* ideology. It is only when the upside-down-ness of daily life is perceived
as right-way-up-ness (without a second thought) that ideology as a lived materiality can be
seen for the profound actuality that Marxism suggests. So when sexist ideologies are *not*
recognised as sexist by either the dominating sex or the dominated one, then ideology can
be seen as both illusion and lived actuality (rather than only illusion). So, for instance,
the moment of Friedan's *Feminine Mystique* might be seen as the moment when sexist
ideology is beginning to be recognised as such, when it is becoming visible as ideological.
Such a moment would have to be contrasted with a time when such an understanding of
everyday life could not even enter the imagination.

The difficulty here should be obvious: either ideology is both invisible and operative, or
visible and contested. If ideology is the alibi that allows exploitative divisions to appear
legitimate then the alibi needs to be believed. But perhaps this is overstating the case, after
all, in life ideology might be seen to operate unevenly with some people living their ideological beliefs in profound ways, while others hold on to the alibi of ideology as a form of
self-interest, and still others contesting ideology at every turn. It is also not hard to
imagine individuals living across these differences: fiercely contesting sexism, say, while
holding onto unexamined beliefs in the naturalness of heterosexual relations. Yet ideology
as a form that invisibly saturates a culture as nature (or second-nature) is ideology at is
most powerful and everyday.

This makes the analysis of ideology more difficult than at first it might seem because it
suggests that ideologies reside in precisely those places where they are not perceived to be
(or perceived at all). This is also why everyday life and ideology both overlap and have so
much in common – both 'suffer' from inattention. Both need to be seen as quasi-invisible
and surreptitious realms that require imaginative panache as much as straightforward
effort to make them visible.

So this brief description of Marxism and Freudianism begins to outline the sense of unease that a tradition of modern thought would have in confronting an everyday life that purported to be simply self-evident. It should also be clear that from this perspective the everyday does not supply happy endings or even happy beginnings. Both Marxism and Freudianism when applied to the everyday suggest an approach that in attempting to reveal the unconscious or non-apparent structures of everyday life uncover deep structures that are relentlessly gothic in their dimensions. For Freud it is the almost inevitable tragedy of loss, forbidden love, and death anxiety, which lurks bubbling under the everyday. For Marx everyday capitalism is a catastrophic engine devouring material and human resources and structured across class antagonisms.

Marx and Freud both attempt to reveal structures that might underpin (and undermine) the everyday reality of experience and to do this they both navigate across the poles of the particular and the general. If Marx and Freud set the scene for modern cultural theory they do so in a way that casts doubt on the veracity of perceived everyday actuality. But they do this contradictorily: on the one hand the surface of the everyday (its manifest content) needs to be given the closest of scrutiny (what you see is what there is), and on the other hand the project is precisely to go behind the scenes and reveal underlying structures and latent contents.

Macro tendencies

In certain ways Marx and Freud can be seen to approach modern everyday life from an anthropological perspective; they want to explain what it is to live as part of a culture. And it seems inevitable that anthropology (as a very loose catch-all term) will be productive for the study of everyday life. As the anthropologist Marc Augé suggests, traditional anthropology can be characterised as a 'concern for the qualitative, insistence on collecting direct testimony – lived experience', for the purpose of discerning what is 'permanent and unconscious' about a culture (Augé 1999a: 1). Of course the idea of permanent cultures is, as Augé is at pains to point out, tied to an idea that remote cultures (remote for western anthropologists that is), that have traditionally been anthropology's objects, are unchanging and socially 'backward'.[2] And it is this duality between empirical work in the everyday (in the field) that looks at the qualitative experience of culture, and the use of this information to construct an interpretation of culture as 'permanent and unconscious' that links us to the polar vector of micro- and macro-analyses.

Twentieth-century anthropology (like other disciplines in the social sciences) can be seen to hold out the goal of combining these tendencies. For Bronislaw Malinowski (see Chapter 14), writing in the 1920s about his work in the Trobriand Islands, anthropologists need first of all to immerse themselves in the daily life of the group of people they are studying:

> As I went on my morning walk through the village, I could see intimate details
> of family life, of toilet, cooking, taking of meals; I could see the arrangements
> of the day's work, people starting on their errands, or groups of men and
> women busy at some manufacturing tasks. Quarrels, jokes, family scenes, events

usually trivial, sometimes dramatic but always significant, formed the atmosphere of my daily life, as well as theirs.

(Malinowski 1922: 7)

Leaving aside the interesting question of Malinowski's *actual* relationship with the Trobri-
and Islanders (a theme eloquently explored in Clifford 1988 and Geertz 1993) his
declared intention is to ground his anthropological practice in a thorough familiarity with
the particularities of Trobriand daily life. Yet if Malinowski begins with the particular, his
(and other anthropologists') 'duty' is 'drawing up all the rules and regularities of tribal life;
all that is permanent and fixed' (Malinowski 1922: 11). The drift, therefore, of Malinowski's
approach is to move from the particular to the general, from the contingencies of the daily
to the permanent regularities of a culture seen as stable and fixed.

The explicit drive that starts out with the recording of everyday contingencies so as to
reveal what Ruth Benedict would later call the 'patterns of culture' (Benedict [1934]
1989) works to filter (and banish) exceptions from the mass of observed material so as to
leave only the customary. By observing and recording the routines of daily life (and the
non-everyday, but nonetheless regular, festivals and rituals) anthropologists can extract
custom from the merely haphazard or aberrant. To uncover underlying structures it
becomes necessary for ethnographers to search out the conventional, to be attuned to the
repetitious. As a contemporary ethnographer of western industrial cultures (particularly
labour unions) puts it:

I knew my job in the field was completed when I discovered the source of my
impatience. I had heard the stories, witnessed the exchanges, and observed the
events so many times that I knew how they would end when they began. I could
predict the process as well as the outcome. To paraphrase Anselm Strauss, my
research categories were saturated. To convince myself that saturation was not
simply an expedient excuse for fatigue, I tried to predict how the process would
unfold. When I succeeded, I knew the time to leave had come.

(Wellman 1994: 582)

Anthropological ethnography then is in many instances dedicated to looking for
behavioural and discursive repetitions, for the dominant forms of a culture. It is in this way
that the hard work of fieldwork gets used to underwrite interpretations of social structures, exchange networks, and so on.

A similar operation is evident in some traditions of western critical theory. For
instance Theodor Adorno's most ethnographic work was concerned with the detailed
analyses of mass cultural forms as a way of showing the prevalence of authoritarian
irrationalism in capitalist modernity (in itself a recognisably anthropological topic). In his
content analysis of the *Los Angeles Times* astrology column in the 1950s (Adorno 1994)
the 'field' of ethnographic investigation becomes the textual arena of astrological journalism in the form of predictions and advice for those born under the various astrological
signs. By looking at the insistent commands (voiced in the column) to follow the advice of
successful friends and colleagues, Adorno establishes an underlying authoritarianism that
promotes dependency on those with power, and urges submission to social norms. The fact

that Adorno's 'field' is textual makes it no less ethnographic; after all ethnographers are in the business of looking at culture as 'texts', whether those texts are spoken, gestured, performed or written. What Adorno is looking at is a number of particular instances of astrological culture as it is circulated on a daily basis (through a newspaper), and from which he can distil an authoritarian and conformist mode of address. Yet because Adorno's field is concerned only with the addressee as an imagined figure within the field of the *Los Angeles Times* we have no way of knowing what the impact of this mode of address is. This does not lessen the credibility of Adorno's analysis as Adorno is interested in cultural forms as a structure of dominance (and where better to find cultural dominance than in the pages of mass circulation newspapers?). What it does mean is that knowledge of the multiple singularities of reading the astrology column (on an occasional or daily basis) and the various modes of reading ('religiously', ironically and so on) are effectively bracketed out. In this sense the drift from the particularity of a field to the generality of interpretation bypasses the everyday as an arena of heterogeneous experience, and it does so in ways not dissimilar from anthropological practices of distillation and extraction.

Perhaps the most influential social and historical ethnographer of the West in contemporary critical theory is Michel Foucault. Although Foucault is concerned with the overarching governance of daily life, it is not at first clear how he stands in relation to the study of everyday life. On the one hand the kinds of institutional assemblages that he focuses on (hospitals, prisons and so on) clearly constitute elements of our everyday life, and at times simply become our everyday life. But if Lefebvre is right in suggesting that everyday life is what happens across and in-between these domains of specialised knowledges and practices then there is something clearly missing from Foucault's approach (for everyday life studies that is). In his accounts of the daily regimens and discursive practices of institutions like prisons (Foucault 1982) and asylums (Foucault 1971) Foucault offers a penetrating description of the way that power (or micro-power to use a specifically Foucauldian vocabulary) orchestrates daily life. For Foucault, power is never simply to be found in the legal rules governing an institution or in excessive displays of force, rather Foucault finds it in the repetitive practices that both produce and instil a sense of a disciplinary self.

Foucault is famous for an approach to culture that attends to networks of power observable within *discourses* on sexuality, health, crime and punishment, and so on. But his reliance on a specifically *written* archive of texts needs to be seen as a necessary condition of his historical orientation rather than as the object of investigation. In attempting to map the forms of power deployed in the nineteenth century under the banner of sexuality, for instance, he is necessarily limited to written documents. But it is his interest in the material *practices* of power that connects him to an ethnographic tradition of attending to culture and provides his most productive contribution to the study of everyday life. In this sense it is more accurate to see Foucault's object as an apparatus (*dispositif*) rather than a discourse. When asked what he meant by the term *dispositif* Foucault replied:

> What I'm trying to pick out with this term is, firstly, a thoroughly heterogeneous ensemble consisting of discourses, institutions, architectural forms, regulatory decisions, laws, administrative measures, scientific statements, philosophical, moral and philanthropic propositions – in short, the said as much

as the unsaid. . . . Secondly, what I am trying to identify in this apparatus is precisely the nature of the connection that can exist between these hetero-geneous elements.

(Foucault 1980a: 194)

It is this sense of particular practices (the bodily examination in the doctor's surgery for instance) linked with other practices (also based on a belief in the body's forensic ability to tell its own story) that suggests that power operates across a dispersed set of practices orchestrated by a ubiquitous understanding of the world. So here again we have an approach that starts out by scrutinising the particular and peculiar practices located at the level of the everyday, in order to arrive (through a concentrated attention to forms of repetition) at a general understanding of the operations of cultural apparatuses. In this way the everyday experience of prisoners becomes an unnecessary supplement to a story that sees the apparatus of disciplinarity as the production of a particular mentality. If this ends up describing an effective regularisation of everyday life then this is due to Foucault's attention to precisely those forms of governance that sought to regulate everyday life. Yet when his attention focuses on the particularity of one specific individual's experience of the apparatus of sexuality (in his presentation of the nineteenth-century hermaphrodite Herculine Barbin's diary and medical reports) the story that unfolds cannot be reduced to a tale of the generative power of discourse to produce subjects (Foucault 1980b). If Barbin's suicide is a direct result of the determining power of the contemporary medical regime (when Barbin was legally declared male) this tragic end is set against a story of daily life that seemed (for the most part) out of reach of medical governance.

For everyday life studies, Foucault could act as a kind of caution for any one claiming too hastily that the attention towards everyday life (academic, but also more broadly social scientific) is simply beneficial, and needs to be encouraged. What we cannot help but get out of Foucault (and this is an absolute crucial element in the study of everyday life) is the way that the everyday has been continually invaded by a certain scrutiny for the effective governance of social subjects. Thus any claim simply to suggest that the everyday evidences subtle and wily evasions to forms of domination would also need to recognise that the everyday has been the focus of scrutiny for centuries, and for the most part that scrutiny has accompanied the policing of everyday life. Sexual practices, hygiene, family life, work regimes, diet, have continually been seen as the province of governmental agents.

Micro tendencies

Perhaps the investigation of everyday life as both an accumulation of singular actions and (potentially at least) an arena for alternative and resistant practices is most easily associ-ated with a form of sociology that could be referred to as micro-sociology. Its most noted exponent is probably Erving Goffman (see Chapter 4). In his first book (written in 1956), Goffman argues that everyday life can be seen as an arena where the self performs in a number of different ways (Goffman 1990). For Goffman individuals (particularly, though not exclusively, those that perform subservient roles) act very differently according to the environment that they find themselves in. Thus the performance of polite deference that a waiter might enact on the restaurant floor (the 'front region' in Goffman's analysis) is reversed as the same waiter enters the kitchens (the 'back region') to perform a more unruly version of the self. In some ways then by concentrating on the micro-sociological spatiality of the everyday, Goffman finds activities that can be seen as resistant to the propriety of sanctioned social behaviour. And it is also by emphasising the *plural* performances of the self (or selves) that some form of resistant behaviour is to be found alongside more submissive activity.

A more explicit correlation between the particularity of everyday life and the theme of social resistance is provided by a range of ethnographic accounts of subcultures, most famously those associated with the Centre for Contemporary Cultural Studies at the University of Birmingham (UK). The Centre published a special issue of its journal *Working Papers in Cultural Studies* dedicated to research on subcultures (which was quickly republished as a book) with the evocative title *Resistance through Rituals: Youth Subcultures in Post-war Britain* (Hall and Jefferson 1976). In some respects work on subcultures (and what had previously been labelled 'deviancy' in mainstream sociology) has an ambivalent relationship to the everyday. Clearly subcultures exist *in* the everyday (although a number of people might be identified as 'weekend' punks, bikers and so on), yet subcultural activity might be seen as often setting its sights on the avoidance of anything that might smack of everydayness in its normative form. For the Birmingham ethnographers, though, it was the everydayness of subcultural activity that was most interesting. What was at stake in the everydayness of drug-taking, or the spectacular uses of clothes, or the practice of communal living, was the question of resistance. Recognising that subcultural activity could not be seen as a purposeful political critique of a social system accompanied by an organised programme of action, the Centre sought ways of understanding subcultural activity in its ritualistic and symbolic opposition to a dominant social order. To take one example: Dick Hebdige's work on mods shows how the appropriation and re-accentuation of social values and material (recoding negative values as positive ones, and vice versa, for instance) works as a form of symbolic defiance:

> The negative evaluations of their [mods'] capabilities imposed by the school and work were substituted by a positive assessment of their personal credentials in the world of play (i.e. the same qualities which were assessed negatively by their daytime controllers – e.g. laziness, arrogance, vanity etc. – were positively defined by themselves and their peers in leisure time).
>
> (Hebdige 1976: 93)

Thus disaffected working-class youths' fierce identification of subcultural codes in daily life positively values meanings and practices held up as negative by the various establishments that assess these young people. But what became one of the main areas of discussion was the extent to which this could be seen as resistance rather than a form of symbolic inventiveness, which had little or no social effectivity.

An approach to everyday life that emphasises its particularity and its peculiar tenacity in the face of powerful forces from 'above' is most vividly expressed in the work of Michel de Certeau (see Chapter 6). For de Certeau the everyday is a realm that is both practical and singular, and as such everyday studies would need to look at actions, use and ways of operating. While this follows Goffman in its emphasis on the live performativity of the everyday, and evidences some similarities with subcultural theory with its emphasis on resistance, it needs to be forcefully distinguished from these approaches as well. For one thing, de Certeau emphatically refuses to take identity as the locus for meaning in everyday life. For de Certeau the social individual is far too waywardly heterogeneous (too networked) to form the basis for an analysis of the everyday as practical life. After all, any one individual lives across a vast range of forces and relationships that, if taken as the basis for viewing the everyday, would obscure the singularity of any single action.

Perhaps as importantly we also need to qualify the term 'resistance' as it functions in de Certeau's work. Unlike many subcultural theorists, resistance in de Certeau's writing is not easily hitched to a cultural politics. In many ways resistance functions as a conservative force that is more easily associated with a slow tenacious refusal to adapt to the rhythms of modern capitalist culture than with the more flamboyant antagonisms performed by subcultures. And while de Certeau does see some of the practices of everyday life as inventively defiant, it would be more in keeping with de Certeau's position to compare everyday life to 'inner-speech'; that never-quite-heard rambling, conjuring up memories, and an uncensored response to life around us. In a weak sense the everyday (for de Certeau) is 'unconscious' in that it is not open to direct observation, or ever fully controllable.

De Certeau necessarily has to insist on a speculative response to the everyday: for him we have yet to describe and account for it. As such any political assessment of the everyday is simply premature. It may be then that all the talk about power and resistance that has preoccupied cultural studies obscures the attempt to ascertain what everyday life is and how it performs. While cultural studies has impatiently pronounced 'political' verdicts on the cultures of the daily, the work of attending to the everyday has yet to be done.

Negotiated territory

If my imaginary vector (that pits generality against particularity, power against resistance, discursive apparatuses against experience, and macro-analysis against micro-analysis) provides a perspective for making certain proclivities vivid, it start to break down irredeemably with any close examination of the practices we have been looking at. For instance, ethnographic tendencies that establish footholds in the everyday for the specific purpose of uncovering an order that transcends the everyday usually leave something of the material trace of this particularity (extracts from field journals, reported speech, and so on). Similarly those approaches that insist on the specificity of the micro-culture of everyday life also, and necessarily, provide more general schemas of understanding. In fact it is hard to imagine what the study of culture would look like if it did not at some point make general connections at a level that transcends the particularity of the everyday.

It is also clear that for those that explicitly address the everyday (Lefebvre, say, rather than Foucault) the difficulty and potential of navigating between the poles of particularity and generality becomes a specific focus. For Henri Lefebvre dialectics had to be at the centre of any engagement with the everyday. His explicit Marxism (both as a philosophy and as an activism) meant that his work gravitated towards stressing the general over the particular, but his dialectical approach understood the particular as saturated with the general in ways that were always particular (it was never simply subsumable within the general). For Lefebvre understanding the 'totality' (which was one of Lefebvre's names for the everyday) would mean not siding with the general against the particular, but weaving the two together. Thus the 'desire for totality' (or for a way of apprehending the logic of social practice) meant a form of attention that would reconcile the polarities of my binary oppositions without sacrificing one side or the other. Totality for Lefebvre could be an endless chain of everyday particularities and plural differences, linked in ways that neither obliterate them nor abandon them to isolation.

It might seem that these days the search for the totality of a culture is too easily associated with a totalitarian view of culture for it to sit easily in an academic culture nervously attuned to cultural differences. Yet while it is true that a desire for totality has often promoted universal values of culture and society (that have elided and suppressed cultural differences in the name of a privileged set of meanings) it is not a foregone conclusion that all ideas about totality will operate in this way. Indeed it may be that the idea of totality has not so much suffered from a lack of confidence, as from a lack of nerve (which might amount to the same thing).

Michel de Certeau also overcomes the opposition between particularity and generality. In an attempt to find the *logic* (or logics) of everyday practices he articulates what he calls a 'science of the singular'. The problem facing de Certeau is how to make sense of the everyday as a realm of practice that is always irreducibly specific (always only understandable within specific contexts). If this science is going to do something more than endlessly describe the specificity of countless practices it will need to overcome the duality of the particular and the general. The answer for de Certeau seems to be to address the everyday not at the level of content (to do this would be a Sisyphean task), but at the level of form. Thus one way of describing de Certeau's approach to the everyday is to see it as attempting to outline a *grammar* of everyday practices that will attempt to keep alive the specificity of operations while recognising formally similar modes of practice.

Lefebvre and de Certeau's very different solutions to the problem of combining micro and macro perspectives give them a central importance for everyday life studies. But rather than see them as having achieved an adequate understanding of everyday life, we need to see them as working projects that have yet to be completed.

Who and where?

The question of where to locate the everyday takes us in directions that are both local and global or, to put it another way, both micro-cultural and macro-cultural. The question of where to 'place' the everyday also determines *whose* everyday life will be the subject of attention. What does it mean, for instance, to suggest (as writers such as Maurice Blanchot have) that the privileged place for the everyday is the street (Blanchot 1987: 17)? What would it mean to shift the emphasis from the street to the home? Alternatively should we locate the everyday (after Foucault) in a series of institutional arrangements (schools, doctors, courts and so on) that might seem both to organise and (at times) to dominate our daily lives? Or is the everyday best seen as outside or between such arrangements?

Alongside such micro-cultural questions we need to ask about the global extensiveness of the everyday. Is everyday life, as a problematic constellation that informs the theorists we have been looking at so far, something peculiar to European and US society? What happens when everyday life is viewed from 'elsewhere'? How might we imagine globalising the study of everyday life?

Micro-cultural locations of the everyday

In an essay on representations of Paris in turn-of-the-century postcards (late nineteenth and early twentieth century), Naomi Schor (1992) begins by suggesting that theories of everyday life can be divided into two camps. On the one hand the everyday can be seen in a 'feminine or feminist' form that 'links the everyday with the daily rituals of private life carried out within the domestic sphere traditionally presided over by women' (Schor 1992: 188). On the other hand lies the 'masculine or masculinist' version, where the everyday exists in the 'public spaces and spheres dominated especially, but not exclusively, in modern Western societies by men':

> According to the one, the everyday is made up of the countless repetitive ges-
> tures and small practices that fall under the heading of what the existentialists
> called the contingent. According to the other, the everyday is made up of the
> chance encounters of the streets: its hero is not the housewife but the *flâneur*.
> (Schor 1992: 188)

For Schor (as for many other writers) such differences are marked by uneven attention: 'I think it would be safe to say that the street version of the everyday tends to prevail' (Schor 1992: 189). Such splitting of the outside and the inside, the street and the home, does not necessarily bracket-out actual lives (the house is occupied by both men and women, similarly the street is used by men and women). Rather the street and the home become synecdoches pointing to particular orientations and evaluations of everyday life. Put simply it can relate to the everyday as the realm of the repetitions, of habit, and the lack of value, or the everyday as the heroic realm of modernity, where 'we' parry the shocks of the new and encounter marvellous adventures on the street. As writers like Mike Featherstone (1995) and Xiaobing Tang (see Chapter 13) have argued, the 'heroic' is dedicated to overcoming everyday life, and in its connotations of masculinity might be seen to effectively accentuate the everyday (the non-heroic) as feminine. Perhaps then those well-known accounts of modernity, which evoke a heroism at the heart of the everyday, effectively shy away from the everydayness of the everyday (for instance Baudelaire 1964). Undoubtedly the privileging of 'the heroic life' has worked to exclude accounts of the everyday lives of women.

Schor's response to this non-symmetrical division is not simply to side with the (dominantly understood) feminine everyday (which might mean continuing a feminist historical examination of the domestic) but to explore a form where two everydays collide – postcards of Paris at the turn of the century. Schor not only works to restore women's position in the streets of Paris (her postcards picture women cab drivers, for instance) but by attending to the written message, she uncovers the registration of a domestic everyday as well. Looking at both sides of the postcard she finds a form that can be seen to negotiate between a *picturing* of Paris life on the one hand and a *writing* of everyday life on the other:

> From the backs of these cards emerges a murmur of small voices speaking of minor aches and pains, long-awaited engagements, obscure family feuds; reporting on safe arrivals and unexpected delays; ordering goat cheese; acknowledging receipt of a bouquet of violets, a bonnet; in short, carrying on the millions of minute transactions, the grain of everyday life.
>
> (Schor 1992: 239)

A project on postcard collecting that combines both recto and verso sides of the postcard is Tom Phillips' *The Postcard Century* (Phillips 2000). Significantly Phillips's collection of postcards which sweep chronologically across the twentieth century *show* a life 'less ordinary', so to speak, while the backs evidence a pressing need to articulate daily life. Where, then, we locate the everyday even at the most microscopic cultural level (which side of the postcard, for instance) is going to affect whose lives we talk about and how we can talk about them. It will come as no surprise to learn that some of the most productive work on the domestic everyday has emerged from feminist social historians and feminist design historians (see, for instance, Attfield and Kirkham 1995; Davidoff 1995). But it is interesting too that some of the most precisely *placed* discussions of everyday life street culture have also emerged from feminist studies (for instance, Pollock 1988b).

As we have already seen, Erving Goffman was attentive to the micro-spatiality of the daily, and it seems significant that in charting this terrain he made use of specifically feminist writing. For Goffman it is a writer like Simone de Beauvoir in her book *The Second Sex* (de Beauvoir [1949] 1993) who, by attending to the everydayness of women's lives, registers the particularity of location and space in the performance of gender. Earlier still we might want to suggest that a micro-cultural perspective is evident in the work of the psychoanalyst Joan Riviere writing about the daily lives of women in the 1920s:

> In everyday life one may observe the mask of femininity taking curious forms. One capable housewife of my acquaintance is a woman of great ability, and can herself attend to typically masculine matters. But when, e.g. any builder or upholsterer is called in, she has a compulsion to hide all her technical knowledge from him and show deference to the workman, making her suggestions in an innocent and artless manner, as if they were 'lucky guesses'.
>
> (Riviere 1986: 39)

What Riviere and others show by focusing on the everyday lives of women is not a series of *fixed* locations that require different performances of gender (or different masquerades in Riviere's description), but a spatiality that results from the everyday life context. Spaces that might be considered female oriented become open to a masculinisation when invaded by male professionals, just as those male professionals can find themselves feminised as they conduct their business in domestic settings.

The micro-location of the daily is clearly a productive arena for everyday life studies, but rather than simplifying our understanding of the everyday, it effectively complicates it. It might be that the spatiality of the daily (now more so than ever) evidences the multiplicity of 'everydaynesses' that congregate in the everyday environment. As Frank Mort puts it in writing about 'The Politics of Consumption':

> We are not in any simple sense 'black' or 'gay' or 'upwardly mobile'. Rather we carry a bewildering range of different, and at times conflicting, identities around with us in our heads at the same time. There is a continual smudging of personas and lifestyles, depending where we are (at work, on the high street) and the spaces we are moving between.
>
> (Mort 1989: 169)

The micro-geography of daily life provides a way of pluralising the self that a concentration on 'identity' in the singular would miss. But it also continually finds evidence for the way that identity categories animate such a geography. To make claims for everyday life being in one place rather than another will avoid attending to the 'movement of the daily', and it might be this movement, this continual drift of the daily, that is most difficult and most productive to register.

Macro-cultural location of the everyday

It will become clear to anyone looking at the contents and permission pages of this *Reader* that the vast majority of the chapters are European and North American in origin. Even those chapters that are about everyday life in Japan or China have been produced in US universities and publishing houses. Reflections on the problematics of everyday life are obviously not limited to such locations, yet the work of translating and disseminating a truly global perspective has yet to be done. So in thinking about the macro-cultural location of the everyday it is necessary to try to imagine what such a perspective might look like.

Returning for a moment to the work of the French philosopher Henri Lefebvre it would seem that he posits some form of 'neo'-colonialism at the heart of the everyday. In his 1958 'Foreword' to the *Critique of Everyday Life*, Lefebvre imagines an approach to everyday life that would move from the daily activities at the level of specifically individual experience (shopping, for instance) to the level of the supra-individual, for instance, global financial markets (Lefebvre 1991: 57). Importantly Lefebvre insists on the need to see the supra-individual *already* registered at the micro-cultural level of buying some sugar. Here the particularity of Lefebvre's example is significant: while sugar (in the 1950s at least) is the proverbial everyday commodity, to choose sugar over, say, a French cheese points to an important perspective for everyday life. The fact that sugar played a significant role in the history of western colonialism inflects the daily life of Parisian shoppers with the continued colonialism articulated by the global market. For Lefebvre the end of one stage of colonialism (marked by the successful liberation struggles of colonised people) does not end colonialism. Instead, new forms of colonialism find new spatial forms. For France this meant the concrete internalisation of colonial relations (as French urban environments increasingly became characterised by 'ethnic' enclaves) alongside economic developments that linked France to a transnational capitalism that was propped up by a proletariat now located in places like China and Korea. And, of course, France is not alone in this reconfiguring of colonial relations.

The insistence that non-western lives impact at the level of everyday life in the West is an important aspect of many recent forms of political culture. A 'politicisation of the everyday' (insisted on by environmentalist groups, anti-capitalist movements, and so on) takes as its source the understanding that what happens at the level of micro-culture also reverberates at a more global level. What to buy, throw away, what to eat and drink, and so on, echo across a global life-world, where the everydayness of one action (buying a pair of trainers or jeans, for instance) directly and indirectly affects and effects the everyday lives of others. To live in the West is to be connected to patterns of exploitation, environmental catastrophe, and poverty taking place in both the West and the non-West, even if those connections are hidden in the practices of big business. But while these approaches to everyday life importantly make connections between different nation-states, and make explicit the neo-colonialism at the heart of the everyday, they do so from a perspective that is still predominantly located in Europe and North America. What might happen if we actually change the location *from* which such questions about the everyday are asked?

Frank Mort's understanding of everyday life (mentioned above) is located in the urban centres of the UK, but is it pertinent to lives lived elsewhere? Does Mort's insistence that contemporary life is lived across a range of identities allow much purchase on the lives of those living their everyday lives in Beijing or Bangkok? The answer might be that the UK provides only a relatively weak version of such everyday phenomena, and that Mort's description of 'bewildering' and 'conflicting' identities is much more vivid elsewhere. For instance, the young Chinese adults walking the streets of Beijing, with dyed blonde hair, listening to Chinese and US pop on personal stereos, experiencing the conflicting tensions of school, then going home to eat a traditional meal in the family apartment, might fulfil Mort's claims about everyday identity more convincingly than any young adults in Europe and the USA ever could.

In this sense Maurice Blanchot's words, written in the 1950s, might suggest a perspective towards everyday life that will need to be taken globally. For Blanchot everyday life becomes recognisable at moments of revolutionary transformation:

> It will be a question of opening the everyday onto history, or even, of reducing its privileged sector: private life. This is what happens in moments of effervescence – those we call revolution – when existence is public through and through.
>
> (Blanchot [1959] 1987: 12)

While Blanchot's words might suggest that everyday life becomes public literally at the moment when people take to the streets, we would need to include other revolutionary processes as well. China's contemporary 'Cultural Revolution' (Mao being swapped for IKEA) brings the everyday to the surface vividly and problematically (see Chapter 13). What Mass-Observation were noticing in Britain in the 1930s (a series of symbolic crises that drive 'the everyday' out of hiding: see Chapter 15) is even more applicable in contemporary China. Kristin Ross's claim (extracted from Benjamin and Lefebvre) that 'the moments when everyday life becomes the most vivid or tangible are the moments when most people find themselves living more than one life' (Ross 1992: 63) could have been written for the blonde-haired youth of Beijing. It might be argued then that if everyday life studies is interested in everyday life at its most vivid and intense, it will need to 'travel' to those places where everyday life is at its most liminal.[3]

While these brief comments have hardly scratched the surface of the issues and potential surrounding the globalisation of an imagined everyday life studies project, it seems clear that an everyday life approach to culture has the capacity to orient itself in more global ways. How it will do this and what will happen when or if it does is the challenge posed by the present.

How?

If (as I argued right at the start of this survey) everyday life is not simply a quantifiable, transparent, palpable actuality to be straightforwardly mined for information, then the question of how to register it needs to be posed. But this is not simply a methodological question about how to eke out information from a shadowy and recalcitrant realm, it is also (and necessarily) a question of how to present and articulate the daily (how to write it, picture it and so on). Indeed the question of how to register the everyday might insist that issues of method take place simultaneously at the level of our attention to the everyday and in our representation of it. We have had a glimpse of the way that social science methodologies navigate across the dualities of relatively abstract categories (the particular and the general for instance), but the everyday is also an eminently practical realm that needs to pose the most practical questions to those who would try to present it. The everyday might suggest approaches that dialectically grasp daily life across a number of different registers, but the question of *how* these different registers will be practically knitted together (in a book, essay, film, etc.) is clearly crucial. The 'coherent narrative' and the 'rigorous argument' have been the dominant forms encouraged by social science approaches, but whether these forms of presentation fit the material world of everyday life is, I would argue, in need of questioning. This is to place the question of *form* at the forefront of everyday life theory. If it is not going continually to miss what it seeks, then everyday life studies will need to consider both the form of the everyday and the forms most adequate or productive for registering it.

Whether or not this is a question specific to everyday life, it seems clear that the everyday poses it in a particularly vivid way. For instance the anthropologist Michael Taussig asks:

> But what sort of sense is constitutive of this everydayness? Surely this sense includes much that is not sense so much as sensuousness, an embodied and somewhat automatic 'knowledge' that functions like peripheral vision, not studied contemplation, a knowledge that is imageric and sensate rather than ideational.
>
> (Taussig 1992: 141)

And if the everyday is not only, or dominantly, composed of ideas and 'knowledge', then does it make much 'sense' to talk and write about it only within such a frame? And if the everyday is something more like peripheral vision (or distraction) and is experienced as non-ideational sensation (tactile and odorous, for instance) then is not the challenge to find ways of writing and registering that are adequate to it or, perhaps more modestly, less inadequate?[4] For Taussig this 'calls for an understanding of the representation as contiguous with that being represented and not as something suspended above and distant from the represented' (Taussig 1992: 10).

How could the everyday be represented and articulated in such a contiguous manner that its qualities become both evident and productive? For example, if tiredness, boredom, distraction, daydreaming and so on are considered important aspects of daily life, then how would a 'study' (if that is the right word) present these elements as part of a felt experience of daily life? How would tiredness and boredom *register* in an account of daily life? Can we point to socio-cultural texts where a sense of the *feeling* of tiredness is recoverable? In this regard it might be that it has been the province of art and literature to provide experiential maps of the everyday. Literary traditions from nineteenth-century realism and naturalism, through to modernist novels (the writing of James Joyce and Virginia Woolf, for instance) and beyond, have insistently focused on the everydayness of life to mount what might be claimed as a literary phenomenology of modern life. I want to suggest here that the future of everyday life studies will necessitate a form of articulation built on the fault line that divides the social sciences and art. Or using another academic vernacular it will require an inventive 'blurring of genres' (Geertz 1993: 19–35): sociology and literature, for instance, but not the sociology of literature, rather a literary sociology (for example, Edgar Morin's suggestion in Chapter 16). Clearly there is much in the past that can be thought of in terms of genre blurring (the anthropologist Ruth Benedict, for instance, saw her work in terms of its literary standing: Benedict 1989) and many of the texts included here are examples of blurred practice. Yet it is also true that such blurring is never easy, particularly when more evidently expressive or poetic forms are brought into the arena of social and human science. Implicit and explicit 'poetic' approaches to the understanding of everyday life have found themselves easily dismissed as simply aestheticising social life.[5] But the anxiety that the foregrounding of 'style' could discredit certain kinds of knowledge can be based only on the search for a transparency of presentation. As Roland Barthes suggested in the 1960s such a desire for transparency does not dispense with the problem of style, rather it insists on the domination of a particular style (or styles) that are rendered invisible precisely because of their domination (Barthes [1966] 1987).

The examination of style has of course been a common enough project in art and literary criticism. And since the heady days of structuralism such a project has been aimed increasingly at the human sciences more generally. Anthropology, historiography, sociology, have all been examined as literary edifices that often work to veil the ubiquitous tools of their academic trade: namely the business of writing (see for instance the classic accounts offered by White 1973 and in Clifford and Marcus 1986). What such a perspective does is refuse the idea that any text is style-less, while admitting that certain forms (say narrative realism in history) have become so naturalised as effectively to appear invisible. Inquiring into the stylistics or poetics of a work regarded as simply factual or scientific performs the function of denaturalising it, making it strange and unfamiliar. As we will see, such procedures can be particularly useful in thinking about how to attend to the everyday.

But the project of inquiring into the poetics of the human sciences has usually been restricted to the descriptive and critical analyses of texts. Much less emphasis has been placed on the question of the generative potential of poetics for the human sciences.[6] Unsurprisingly perhaps, the theoretical debates that *were* primarily concerned with the generative potential of aesthetic procedures (as forms of inquiry, rather than simply 'expression') focused on practices of art production and filmmaking. These debates, particularly in the 1970s and 1980s concerning art and filmmaking, insisted on treating aesthetic procedures as forms of social practice and political engagement (particularly in regard to Marxism and Feminism). For a number of artists, filmmakers and theorists (such as Victor Burgin, Claire Johnston, Mary Kelly, Laura Mulvey, Griselda Pollock, Paul Willemen, Peter Wollen and so on), aesthetic forms became a crucial aspect of studying and articulating the social (see Pollock 1988a and Willemen 1994 for representative accounts). The dramatist Bertolt Brecht, in particular, provided some initial forms and procedures that could be adopted and adapted to articulate complex and provocative representations of the dynamics of sexuality and class. This is not the place to recount these various practices or to assess them in relation to everyday life, but it is worth considering how someone like Brecht might be a resource, not simply for the production of dramatic or artistic works, but for more prosaic attempts to register the daily. What might Brecht have to offer the practice of cultural studies, for instance, in its attempt to articulate the everyday? I want to suggest ways that Brechtianism might be a resource for articulating the everyday, but, as a qualification, I also want to suggest that Brechtianism (purposefully) ignores certain issues concerning an aesthetics of daily life.

As already hinted at, the question of 'making strange' or 'estrangement' is going to be a crucial tool for everyday life studies. Indeed as Fredric Jameson puts it in his book on Brecht's method: 'the theory of estrangement, which always takes off from the numbness and familiarity of everyday life, must always estrange us from the everyday' (Jameson 1998: 84). It is the everyday that receives our 'daily inattention' (Georges Bataille quoted in Hollier 1993: 14) and invites us to look elsewhere. It is to the everyday that we consign that which no longer holds our attention. Things become 'everyday' by becoming invisible, unnoticed, part of the furniture. And if familiarity does not always breed contempt, it does encourage neglect. As Brecht suggests:

> before familiarity can turn into awareness the familiar must be stripped of its inconspicuousness; we must give up assuming that the object in question needs no explanation. However frequently recurrent, modest, vulgar it may be it will now be labelled as something unusual.
>
> (Brecht 1964: 144)

How then do we strip the everyday of its inconspicuousness? By what means do we resuscitate something that fails to interest us?

The antidote to our negligence towards the everyday is a kind of purposefully alienating perspective that refuses to utilise ready-made descriptions (see for instance the kind of 'applied Brechtianism' evident in Chapters 19, 20 and 21). The example that Brecht gives suggests a way of transforming something as overly familiar and everyday as a car into something strange. By insisting on 'the Eskimo definition' that 'A car is a wingless aircraft that crawls along the ground' (Brecht 1964: 145) the car is momentarily rescued from naturalised inattention by being made 'strange' (denaturalised). It is worth noting that this 1940 example implies the usefulness of cross-cultural perspectives (in this case the importing of Inuit representation as a way of interrupting the 'inconspicuous' way that cars existed in certain non-Inuit cultures). Brecht, of course, recognised that what he was giving a name to had been the mainstay of literary production for centuries (after all it could be argued that the poetics of metaphor and allegory attempts to revivify the 'ordinary' world). He also argued that the 'making strange' that was performed by literature was a recognisable feature of the everyday landscape itself (when the inconspicuous seems to suddenly demand our attention). But by theorising the techniques and aim of defamiliarisation, he provides a useful platform for thinking about the methods for registering the everyday.

Cross-cultural estrangement (using the Inuit description of a car to 'view' traffic in Berlin or New York) provides an endless repertoire that could be used to show what is under your nose (there but not seen). But cross-cultural estrangement would not only mean viewing one (geographically distinct) culture from the point of view of another. Cross-cultural estrangement could also be thought of in terms of genre blurring. For instance the 'Critical Dictionary' that Georges Bataille edited and wrote (for the journal *Documents*) provides remarkable examples of cross-cultural estrangement performed as genre blurring. Something so simple as applying the language of chemistry and commerce to give account of 'the body' performs a dramatic estrangement:

> The bodily fat of a normally constituted man would suffice to manufacture seven cakes of toilet-soap. Enough iron is found in the organism to make a medium-sized nail, and sugar to sweeten a cup of coffee. The phosphorus would provide 2,200 matches. The magnesium would furnish the light needed to take a photograph. In addition, a little potassium and sulphur, but in an unusable quantity. These different raw materials, costed at current prices, represent an approximate sum of 25 francs.
>
> (Dr Charles Henry May quoted in Bataille *et al.* 1995: 56–7)

Such an 'estrangement' of the body (written in the 1920s) predicts the atrocious reality of Nazi death-camps in the 1930s and 1940s. As the entry 'Man' in the Critical Dictionary continues, Bataille shows how a certain literal facticity (albeit peppered with the rhetoric of conviction) can make the most naturalised and invisible of practices appear truly barbaric:

> If, taking the animals put to death in a single day in all the slaughterhouses of the Christian countries [in the 1920s], we set them walking head to tail, with only sufficient space between them that they do not tread on one another, they would stretch in Indian file for 1322 miles – more than thirteen hundred miles of warm, palpitating living bodies, dragged each day, as the years go by, to the Christians' bloody slaughterhouses, so that they might quench their thirst for blood at the red fountain gushing from the veins of their murdered victims. . . .

A calculation based on very modest figures shows that the quantity of blood shed each year in the slaughterhouses of Chicago is more than sufficient to float five transatlantic liners.

(Sir William Earnshaw Cooper quoted in Bataille, *et al.* 1995: 57–8)

For Bataille such 'base materialism' (the name he accorded such cross-cultural matter-of-fact-ness) brought out a dimension of western everyday life continually suppressed by the superimposition of 'reason' and 'civility'. To make vivid the everyday required a savage assault on notions of western decorum.

Estrangement for Brecht was intended to purposefully cut off the supply of pacifying intoxicants that he claimed the theatre supplied to its audiences. Brecht argued that the kinds of critical expertise voiced by audiences at sports events hardly ever came to the surface at theatrical events. For Brecht, theatre audiences were being emotionally bamboozled by the tricks of naturalist theatre that encouraged empathy rather than thought. He claimed that the theatre could perform such tricks only by systematically veiling its form of production (its trickery). As an example Brecht suggests that no one would ever think of hiding the light source for a sports event (an evening football match, for instance) but that such subterfuge is basic to the dominant theatrical effect (Brecht 1964: 141). Brecht's theatre would refuse such subterfuge, lights would be seen, actors would 'act' as actors (rather than pass themselves off as someone else) and the audience would be confronted with political and ethical problems.

To export Brechtianism into the human sciences might at first glance seem unnecessary; after all, could reading a work of philosophy really be described as a pacifying experience? In many ways then a certain Brechtianism is already at work in the human sciences as they set about questioning and making-strange the world we inhabit, while also revealing their bag of tricks (by declaring research methodologies, for instance). Yet Brecht encouraged a range of 'interruptive' strategies that would be set against the finality of many presentations of the real world. By using a range of media (film, writing, music and so on) and a range of genres (the Greek chorus, folk traditions, etc.) Brecht wove together a montage that was aimed at conflict rather than resolution. And it might be that in the practice of montage, whereby no single perspective or mode of presentation is ultimately privileged, that everyday life studies could undertake a more pronounced form of Brechtianism (purposefully offering plural and contradictory accounts of the everyday). In supplying the theatre with a plethora of forms, and multiple narratives stitched loosely together, Brecht provides a way of presenting complex accounts of the social and everyday world. By refusing the naturalism of the single narrative, and through techniques of interruption, Brecht leaves us with an account of the world decidedly unfinished and open to exploration.

But Brecht's orientation towards the use of different forms had an ultimately pragmatic purpose. For Brecht the use of forms had to entertain (albeit didactically) and had to become 'popular' with audiences (if they were not already) and if this did not happen they had to be abandoned (Brecht 1964: 110–12). Indeed Brecht set his hat against the kind of sensuous writing that might be thought most fitting to describe the everyday (Brecht 1964: 109). For Brecht the question that Taussig poses about a mode of writing contiguous with its object is avoided. Brecht's theatre is dedicated to a promiscuity of styles, in the belief that (a limited) aesthetic pluralism provided the set of tools necessary for attending to the complexities of the social. What Brechtianism offers everyday life studies is a vehicle more able to contain the multiple strands and complex interweavings of the everyday, while framing them in a way that acknowledges their constructedness and revivifies material that is continually slipping out of view.

The question that remains is still Michael Taussig's: are certain forms of expression particularly suited to the everyday, or contiguous with the everyday (stream of conscious-ness writing, perhaps)? Likewise are there other modes of registration that seem entirely inadequate to conveying the qualities of everyday life (the statistical survey, for instance)? The relationship between a form of registration and what is being registered is, for every-day life studies, an important question and one not easily resolved. Perhaps a short excur-sion into a particular moment in the history of art, when everyday life seemed (for some) to find an adequate form, will allow us to more accurately assess the problem.

The art of everyday life

Modern western art can be seen to exhibit an uneasy relation with everyday life. The cubist collages of Picasso and Braque employed the ephemera of daily life (cheap wallpaper, adverts, newspaper cuttings and such like) in a complex arrangement of forms. Duchamp's ready-mades (a urinal, a bottle rack, a hat-rack, a snow shovel and so on) polemically inserted the everyday into the bastions of high culture. Likewise Pop Art made the every-day commercial culture of its time (commodity packaging, Hollywood icons) its one true subject. The list could go on (see David Ross 2000 for an extensive listing of art's twentieth-century relationship with the quotidian). But does this work, which is clearly both *of* the everyday and *about* the everyday, exist *in* the everyday? Or to put it another way, does this engagement with the everyday ultimately perform some kind of transcend-ence of the everyday? For instance, to take some items, usually ones given only the most cursory of attention in daily life, and employ them for the business of art (where attention is never cursory, whatever the desire of the artist), might be understood as an act of salvation: to save the mundane from the negligence that surrounds it. The same argument could be made about sociological investigations of the everyday: in pursuing an everyday activity with the kind of attention brought to bear on it by sociology the activity is removed from the flow of daily life, transforming it (de-everyday-ing it) in the process. Perhaps this is simply the inevitable outcome of attending to the unattended, and perhaps the pay-off is the estrangement that relies on the recontextualisation of the everyday. To recognise the productivity of estrangement while continuing to seek the most adequate and contiguous mode of registration might then be seen as a contradictory and futile attempt. But unless all forms of estrangement are going to be viewed equally, it is at least worth *asking* questions about the appropriateness of specific *forms* for the everyday.

Art's truck with the everyday highlights this problem. This is not simply an abstract problem of form, but a question of how a *practice* of rendering an image or an object can be seen to coincide (or not) with its subject matter. Here I want to look very briefly at a style that has been dubbed impressionism.[7] What was radical about the artists associated with impressionism can be seen at the level of both subject matter and form, and (crucially) in how the two were combined. For example the work of Edouard Manet and Berthe Morisot (Figures I.1 and I.2) combined what might be thought of as a sketchy-ness in rendering, with a certain everydayness in terms of subject matter. While neither sketchyness nor everydayness was unfamiliar to the established world of Parisian art, the combination of both, for a practice that was designed to compete with the kind of highly accomplished historical painting (mainly of mythological subject matter) that dominated

Figure I.1 Edouard Manet, *Music in the Tuileries Gardens*, 1862 (76 × 119 cm) © National Gallery, London

Figure I.2 Berthe Morisot, *On a Summer's Day*, 1880 (46 × 75 cm) © National Gallery, London

the Paris Salon, was seen at the time as both a provocation and an absurdity (see Clark 1985a).

Tim Clark has written extensively on how paintings of 'modern' life can be seen to register *something* of the particular experience of everyday life in Paris during the Second Empire. In Clark's terms the peculiarity of Manet's work can be seen as 'a taste for the margins and vestiges of social life; a wish to celebrate the "insignificant" or disreputable in modernity' (Clark 1985b: 55). For Clark the everydayness of subject matter was both a characteristic of 'impressionist' work and a way of opposing dominant practices of art (his characterisation of this subject matter is part of an argument that claims that modern art should be seen as a 'practice of negation'). Clark goes on to suggest that what we are calling impressionism evidences 'deliberate displays of painterly awkwardness, or facility in kinds of painting that were not supposed to be worth perfecting' (Clark 1985b: 55). But the question that preoccupies Clark is how to make 'painterly awkwardness' or sketchy-ness relate to the historical experience of everyday living in late-nineteenth-century Paris.

The problem facing such an inquiry is the difficulty of translating the materiality of the representation (the way something is written or painted or filmed) into the experiential realm of the everyday. At first glance we might want to suggest that the connections between the sketchy-ness of a painting and the seemingly relaxed moments of sociability that are being depicted suggest the appropriateness of this manner of painting. But we also need to admit that the kinds of correspondence we are suggesting is being secured at the level of descriptive metaphor (how could we describe a particular manner of painting without recourse to metaphor?). For instance, 'sketchy' might be thought of as light, breezy, which suggests leisurely, and so on. Sketchy-ness or awkwardness are only a couple of the many metaphorical ways of describing the manner of the paintings' execution. In fact sketchy-ness (while an appropriate term for relating it to the business of making visual art) might be unhelpful in getting us from the style of painting to the everyday life being depicted. If instead we described Morisot and Manet's mark-making as 'impromptu' or 'improvised', we may find an easier route from the particularity of the rendition to the social life of its subject.

Second Empire Paris has come to be seen as an exemplary instance of modernity. At the level of everyday life, modernity can be seen as a disruption of the old certainties of previous generations (although how certain 'old certainties' were is never clear). In their place are not new traditions so much as the continued disruption of the new. To put it more broadly: everyday street life in Paris was beginning to be exemplified by the 'ephemeral, the fugitive, the contingent', as Baudelaire put it in 1863 (Baudelaire 1964: 13). How the new impacted on Parisian daily life was at once immediately material (the city itself was reconfigured) and strangely dislocating at the level of what we might call felt experience. Here is a Paris speeding up to the pace of rapid exchange, where relationships between people are becoming more and more governed by commodity exchange (department stores, for instance, allow for a new level of alienated communication between buyer and seller, as price tags are introduced). Would it therefore seem surprising if the deep illusionistic space of more traditional painting seemed unfitting for rendering the new and constantly changing everyday life of modern Paris? It would not be hard to make a leap between improvised paint marks and the kind of improvised behaviour that would be needed to navigate a modern everydayness in a perpetual state of transformation.

If modern everyday life can be described as an experiential realm that seemed more fleeting, less steady, than previous ways of life, then perhaps Manet and Morisot had found an adequate style for rendering it through a style that also seems more fleeting and less steady. But Clark is uneasy about making this leap too emphatically. Social historians of art, like Tim Clark, have taken a more circumspect route to try to historicise the particularity of impressionist paint-handling and its relation to its social (and everyday) moment. For instance the adoption and adaption of this quick-fire paint style should tell us first of all that traditional ways of painting no longer seemed available for picturing everyday modernity. This then is not to claim that impressionism was adequate to everyday life, merely that established ways of painting were terminally inadequate. If the impressionist project was to register the modern everyday as vividly as possible, it had to try to find a form that was at least not as inadequate as that which dominated the Salon. The mark-making that results, the impromptu, brash, hesitant, abbreviated, rough, stuttering, flowing paintwork, relates as much to the struggle to reimagine a painting practice as to the experience of everyday life. What Clark seems to suggest is that the very hesitancy of these paintings, their contradictory ambivalence between confident rendering and stuttering hesitancy, has parallels in everyday life. Rather than being wholly appropriate to a mode of daily life, Morisot and Manet's style registers the lack of possibility for there being a wholly appropriate and adequate style either in painting or in daily life. Everyday life (and by extension the business of getting it down on canvas) was just not settled enough for that.

Griselda Pollock has provided a feminist perspective for thinking about impressionism and has provided accounts of women's impressionist practice that offer something of a corrective to some of Clark's main preoccupations (Pollock 1988b). But in similar ways to Clark she is careful to suggest that a painting needs to be examined in terms of what it is not like, and what it does not include, as well as what it is like and what it does include. For Pollock the very subject matter (or more precisely the lack of subject matter) provides a trace of the conditions of everyday life. Because Morisot did not paint the kind of public displays of modernity (the café-theatre, the prostitutes and street scenes, and so on) we get a clue as to the limitations for women at this time (confirmed by looking at other forms of historical evidence). The coding of this spatial restriction though is not entirely absent from the paintings themselves, and might be glimpsed in the number of paintings by women impressionists that figure female subjects set in an environment that contains a barrier between them and the public spaces beyond. Balustrades, balconies, benches and fences reframe the female subjects within the frame of the painting. Again this is not a direct fit between the 'privacy' of middle-class women's everyday life and the materiality of the painting, but something of the particularity of this everydayness is registered in formal and structural ways.

So while we might not find in impressionist painting a perfectly adequate form we find *something* that in its hesitancy and provisional execution is more suited to registering the diverse everydayness of a moment of modernity. It is not surprising then that one of the first philosophical attempts to come to grips with everyday modernity (Georg Simmel's) was referred to (often disparagingly) as philosophical impressionism (see Chapter 29).

Perhaps then we are back in the territory of making strange: Manet and Morisot, in striving to reinvent painting, register the everyday in what seemed to be awkward and strange (non-traditional) ways. The vividness of impressionist registering of everyday life is probably more adequately explained by this strangeness than by the explanation that paint-ers like Morisot invented a form adequate to the daily. After all it might be said that the radical forms of collage practised by Berlin dada might be even more suited to articulating the daily. From the vantage point of the present though, the strangeness of Morisot's choppy paintwork, or Manet's abbreviated picturing, has been severely diminished, if not lost altogether. If these works look familiar it might very well be because they have entered the familiar terrain of everyday life, taking their place on biscuit tins and calendars.

If the everyday is poised on the edge of oblivion, suffering from sheer negligence and inattention, then it would need to be rescued from a habitual realm that might be respon-sible for sending it to oblivion in the first place (hence the importance of denaturalising everyday life). But the fate of impressionism would suggest that estrangement has a limited shelf-life, and that this shelf-life will be severely truncated by success. And if this is the case for artistic production, is it any different for more sociological or anthropological kinds of work? The historicity of form is clearly a crucial aspect of its performance, but if this would suggest a relativism in thinking about the forms for rendering the everyday, it should not suggest an absolute relativism. At any historical moment certain forms might seem to be particularly productive for looking at the overlooked. More importantly it should suggest that the business of finding adequate forms (or less inadequate ones) is not going to be completed: making strange, and inventively generating more productive forms for articulating the everyday, is the daily making and unmaking of cultural practice.

Why?

Two sets of related questions are relevant here. First: why is the everyday (as a problem) a useful approach to questions of social and cultural life? Why the everyday rather than culture, or society, or postmodernity, or globalisation? Second (and clearly connected to the first question): why does everyday life offer a productive perspective *now*? Why, for instance, is this *Reader* being produced at this moment and not another? What are the historical conditions that might give everyday life (as a form of attention) a contemporary value? What has the everyday (as it has emerged in its recent academic revival) responded to, reacted against and established a critical relationship with? I hope that by now the general question of why the everyday makes a productive problematic needs no further justification. The question, however, of why the everyday at this specific moment (a moment that could be seen to witness the re-emergence of theoretical and practical interest in the everyday) is something that might usefully be addressed.

Judging by the number of journals dedicating issues to the theme of everyday life, and the growing number of monographs that follow an explicitly quotidian orientation, we are witnessing something of an academic boom in everyday life.[8] Perhaps such an explosion of interest should be met with scepticism. Could this not be seen as another example of the commodity condition of academic production, where the everyday becomes simply a fash-ionable logo for repackaging familiar goods? But even if we grant this scepticism some purchase on the present-day fascination in the everyday, we would still need to suggest why it is everyday life that is of interest. It might be (to continue in a sceptical vein) that a quotidian turn is being used to reassert the contours of a disciplinarity that everyday life should purposefully negate. For instance, is it symptomatic that the titles of everyday life books seem to depend on the 'and' in their titles (photography *and* everyday life, film *and* everyday life, history *and* everyday life, and so on)? Is this enacting a disciplinary status quo, or does the everyday implicitly or explicitly disrupt the sense of stability that such titles might at first suggest? Here is not the place to review this growing body of writing, but it is the place to consider the potential of everyday life at this historical moment in academic writing.

Perhaps everyday life, instead of being a distinctive intervention in the human sciences, is best seen as a way of consolidating a number of symptomatic shifts in subject matter and focus that have been underway during the 1990s. Identifying such shifts might provide a way not just of indicating the potential of an everyday life perspective, but of situating such a perspective within both a continuum and a discontinuum of academic interests. Or to put it another way, it may begin to suggest how the ground was laid so that a renewal of interest in the everyday could take root.

There may be a way of grouping some recent work in the human sciences under the title 'the return of the real'. What the various forms of 'new historicism' (see Veeser 1989 as an example) share with work on 'the body' (for instance, Featherstone *et al.* 1991), despite all their genre differences, is an attempt to ground the study of culture more emphatically in concrete phenomena. But this does not assume that there is a 'truth' of the 'body' or 'history' that will suddenly emerge once the outer shell of representation has been pierced. In many ways what connects the disparate work signalled by these terms (body or historicism, or even the city, etc.) is a frustration with the opposition implied by a focus on *re-presentation*. It is, ironically, the refusal to assume that there is something else *there*, that is being *re*-presented, that would activate a return of the real. For instance, economics might suggest a form of attention that would escape the cultural domain of representation and access the real in more substantial and satisfying ways. Yet as Clark has written:

> It is one thing (and still necessary) to insist on the determinate weight in soci-
> ety of those arrangements we call economic; it is another to believe that in
> doing so we have poked through the texture of signs and conventions to the
> bedrock of matter and action upon it. Economic life – the 'economy', the eco-
> nomic realm, sphere, level, instance, or what-have-you – is in itself a realm of
> representations. How else are we to characterize money, for instance, or the
> commodity form, or the wage contract?
>
> (Clark 1985a: 6)

If this is drifting towards an understanding that there is no 'outside' to representation, then this is only half the story. If a provisional agreement is made about the extensiveness of representation and its saturation of the social, then it might seem to make little sense to assume implicitly that 'something' is still out there being re-presented. Instead it might seem more feasible to suggest that the social is a culture of *presentations* and *perform-ances*. And this in turn might mean that this world of presentations is the actual material reality of social and cultural life.

So this is not to argue that the unmanageable diversity of these presentations should simply be subsumed within an overarching schema of signification, or text (in that loose, promiscuous way). And neither does it suggest that we have exhausted the 'real' by attending to its textual traces. It is merely to claim that the duality, implied in the term re-presentation, has little hold on the actuality of culture. It should be noted that in sweeping aside the problematic of representation in this cavalier way, we have succeeded only in making a culture more complex, more unmanageable. How, for instance, could we approach a culture of presentations that would include both an intricately con-structed novel and an entirely personal experience in the world? There is no answer to this, and we should not expect one, but in letting go of the categories implied by repre-sentation we might have surreptitiously unleashed a curiosity that is well suited to the everyday.

For one thing, the very extensiveness of all those kinds of materials that designate and stipulate (the great archive of governmental decrees, for instance) could be looked at from the point-of-view of the everyday. Not just how they shape and reshape daily practices but how they might become (or not) the hard-wiring of experience. Foucault has suggested that the discursive assemblages that go by the name of sexuality or health (and so on) are not simply repressive regimes acting on preconstituted individuals. Instead he treats them as the material that constitutes the self and generates an ability to experience the world. But if we enter the world as something like empty vessels to be filled and shaped by culture, then this filling and shaping is itself likely to be heterogeneous right from the start. From the perspective of everyday life, the shape and content of culture would have to include everything from those early inchoate, and perhaps predominantly tactile experiences of babies (their groping, sucking and chewing of the world around them), to the extensive formal trainings we receive as we enter adulthood. And if such training extends throughout our lives, then does our less ideational involvement in the world not continue as well? How we experience our bodies, and how our bodies experience the world, cannot simply be adequately described by casting a critical eye over the discourses of the establishment. For one thing, the very form that such discourse takes is usually resolutely ideational and casts out-of-bounds the kinds of materials that might point to more amorphously sensate experiences.

This suggests that everyday life studies will require from the start more than one perspective. It also suggests that in looking for evidence of daily life, everyday life studies cannot simply supplement attention to the texture of the social 'from above' (by looking at those established and dominating assemblages of writings on health and sexuality, for instance) with more empirical ethnography. After all, the kinds of knowledge that can be accessed via observation, or solicited by questioning, are also likely to express what is most easily demonstrated and articulated. If everyday life includes those more hidden aspects of experience, then we might *also* need to look to those forms that have tried to attend to precisely this aspect of daily life. It might be that those attempts to try to grasp the texture of daily experience in art and literature need to be attended to as both evidential and theoretical. Just as Freud found that his immediate precursors were not other scientists but novelists and poets, so the study of everyday life might find that it has as much in common with Joyce and Woolf as it does with Garfinkel and Foucault.

When Alice Kaplan and Kristin Ross (Chapter 7) ask, 'what does it mean to approach cultural production from the vantage point of everyday life?' their answer suggests that everyday life studies is situated *between* the kinds of attention that would focus *either* on subjective experience *or* on the institutional frames of cultural life.

> It means attempting to grasp the everyday without relegating it either to insti-
> tutional codes and systems or to the private perceptions of a monadic subject.
> Between, for example, the traffic court and the angry driver who has received a
> moving violation, we would need to evoke a complex realm of social practice
> and to map out not merely a network of streets, but a conjunction of habit,
> desire and accident.
>
> (Kaplan and Ross 1987: 3)

It might be that, in trying to compose an archive of 'habit, desire and accident', we could do worse than take as a starting point those complex imaginary investigations that go by the name of 'art'. Rather than treating art as high culture, requiring connoisseurship and elaborate decoding, the everyday life archive would render relevant works as experimental studies in the experiential realm of the daily.

It might also be tha,t in attending to the everyday, studies of daily culture will need to look at those moments when everyday life breaks down, when everyday life becomes inter-rupted and dysfunctional. In the same way that studies of the body have focused on body modification (prosthetics, for example: see Stelarc 1997) or self-induced pain, everyday life studies might want to attend to daily life as it is wittingly and unwittingly disfigured. The purposeful interventions in daily life concocted by the Situationists (see Chapter 23) might serve as archetypes for experimental studies of daily life carried out in the field, so to speak. Or the psychoanalytic archive might be plundered for accounts of the impossibility of everyday life, when patients experience the everyday as a realm of obsession and horror. Edgar Morin's suggestions that ethnography should deal in extremes (rather than cultural norms) and should experimentally intervene in daily life, seem particularly appropriate for rethinking the study of everyday life (see Chapter 16).

But if everyday life studies might want to follow in the wake of some of the problems suggested by 'the body' or 'new historicism', it also becomes clear that it establishes itself in contradistinction to other tendencies within the human sciences.

Post-ism

Intellectual life in the human sciences during the 1980s and 1990s (predominantly, though not exclusively, in Europe and the USA) might be seen as characterised by posts: the most pervasive ones being the posts of poststructuralism and postmodernism. It is partly as a response to these posts that the historicity of contemporary interest in the everyday might be glimpsed most clearly. This is not to say that the everyday is necessarily a negation of the orientation that these posts represent (though I think in some cases this may be true), but that the everyday represents some kind of realignment of these loosely defined orienta-tions. The everyday then might operate as some kind of antidote or corrective to what are perceived to be the excesses of poststructuralism, without having to hand back all its (or their) accomplishments. The move towards more historically grounded work (especially in the case of literary studies and film studies) can be taken as a sign of a general frustration with the abstract and textual orientation of much poststructuralism (or with its various Anglophone imitators). To take only one example: if the star that was deconstruction began to wane (and for some has simply become a black hole) then partly this was due to the *perceived* unanchored uses that were made of its interpretative textual wizardry.

But such a straightforward account of the historicity of what might potentially be called everyday life studies is in danger of painting itself into a corner named 'a return to order' or 'back to basics'. Another way of historicising the appeal of everyday life studies, is to suggest that the general drift of poststructuralist thought might simply not be ambitious enough: it concedes, as unavailable, too much right from the start. By submitting the world to a form of textualisation, it renders the 'real' simply out of reach. Everyday life studies, in wanting to register the sensuous feel of culture, and wanting to have a go at weaving together the heterogeneity of the social, might simply find much that goes by the name of poststructuralism disappointing; at once too limited and too bombastic.

To see everyday life studies as a response to, and a critique of, postmodernism is perhaps more difficult. For one thing, many of the most influential formulations of the postmodern concentrated as much on the daily lived-ness of culture as on particular aesthetic objects that might or might not be designated as postmodern. In Jean-François Lyotard's account of postmodernism he makes a claim that the guarantors of knowledge have become delegitimised (knowledge for knowledge's sake, or knowledge for human betterment, no longer provide the alibis for research) as well as suggesting that postmodern life is defined by a hotchpotch of styles. It is not clear if the two are necessarily connected, but the lack of a singular style might be seen to relate both to the promiscuity of aesthetic forms and the delegitimation of knowledge (the former being a symptomatic expression of the latter, and both being symptomatic of more socially cataclysmic events). In an appendix to his book *The Postmodern Condition: A Report on Knowledge*, Lyotard argued that the postmodern is a form of stylistic eclecticism:

> Eclecticism is the degree zero of contemporary general culture: one listens to reggae, watches a western, eats McDonald's food for lunch and local cuisine for dinner, wears Paris perfume in Tokyo and 'retro' clothes in Hong Kong; knowledge is a matter for TV games.
>
> (Lyotard [1979] 1986: 76)

On the one hand, then, Lyotard grounds his argument (impressionistically) in 'ordinary' everyday culture, while on the other he seems to describe an experience of culture most available to the jet-setter or successful conference-hopping academic. It is worth noting, however, that Lyotard is aware that such a culture relates directly to economics and suggests that 'this realism of "anything goes" is in fact that of money' (Lyotard [1979] 1986: 76).

Where postmodernism connects with everyday life studies is in the ambition to provide a cognitive mapping of the contemporary world (although everyday life studies might want to map other ways of experiencing the world alongside the cognitive). And in this it tends to place the everyday as the context for its arguments. For instance in claiming that the postmodern can be seen as more spatial than temporal, Jameson (1991) insists on the context of daily life: 'I think it is at least empirically arguable that our daily life, our psychic experience, our cultural languages, are today dominated by categories of space rather than by categories of time' (Jameson 1991: 16). But everyday life departs from postmodernism in an insistence not on the latest cultural phenomena, but on the range of cultural experiences in circulation. In this it would want to argue that most people in the world do not live the kinds of lives that postmodernism describes, and even those that might seem to be in the thick of postmodernity would be unlikely to be full-time postmodernists. By concentrating on the literal day-to-day (work, food, washing and so on) an everyday life perspective can qualify the extensiveness of what goes by the name of the postmodern. In this Terry Eagleton's rejoinder to Lyotard is worth noting:

> It is not just that there are millions of other human subjects, less exotic than Lyotard's jet-setters, who educate their children, vote as responsible citizens, withdraw their labour and clock in for work; it is also that many subjects live more and more at the points of contradictory intersection between these two definitions.
>
> (Eagleton 1986: 146)

If postmodernism is interested in the plurality of cultural experiences on offer, everyday life studies need to pluralise this plurality, so to speak, by insisting on the persistence of more residual cultures.

Everyday life, then, as a specific theoretical orientation has not necessarily required a turning away from postmodernism and poststructuralism (although, for some, this might seem a very attractive proposition). What it has required is a regrounding of such interests in the materiality of culture. It might, however, be the case that when the question of everyday life is raised there is simply too much going on to spend time mounting stringent critiques of deconstruction (say) or other poststructuralist approaches. Everyday life studies might (it is hoped) get so wrapped up in its attempts to give account of the overlooked, that the conventional academic business of painstakingly arguing against intellectual positions you do not hold might itself get overlooked.

Notes

1   Perhaps there is a missing question here, namely the question of 'when'? Elsewhere (Highmore 2002, especially Chapter 1) I have argued that while everyday life is not limited to modernity in any essential way, the qualitative changes in time and space brought about by industrialisation constitute a shift in the patterns of daily life. These qualitative shifts and the emergent culture that proceeded them (such as leisure time, commuting and so on) make it problematic to think of everyday life as a category that can usefully be applied across history. As such, everyday life might best be reserved for naming the lived culture of modernity.

2   The idea that non-western cultures were backward or undeveloped turns on the belief that 'spatial distance' can be translated into 'historical distance'. In fact, Victorian anthropology was often practised as a form of archeology of past or residual cultures that anachronistically persist in the present. That such forms of anthropology were informed by a social Darwinian understanding of the evolution of cultures, and that this was linked to the bigger project of colonial domination of non-western cultures, is often the basis for critical investigation of anthropology's history (see Asad 1973; Augé 1999a; Fabian 1983).

3   The Subaltern Studies collective might provide a useful orientation for the historical extension of this attitude. Studying the histories of South Asian societies, specifically as they are poised at moments of colonial conflict and crises, Subaltern Studies looks to those whose lives are saturated by conflicting cultural cosmologies (see for instance Chatterjee 1993; Chaturvedi 2000).

4   This introductory essay, written in a style that this section would cast in doubt, is obviously not an attempt to answer this challenge. But here I am not attempting to register the everyday, merely to survey the problems and potentials for those (including myself) who might want to attempt this at some point.

5   For instance Michel de Certeau has been accused of 'an aestheticising strategy' that turns the study of everyday life into 'a poetics of the oppressed' (Bennett 1998: 174). Such a complaint is an old one; Simmel for instance suffered from it. It might be worth noting along with Michel Serres that 'what a sign of the times, when, to cruelly criticize a book, one says that it is only poetry!' (Serres and Latour 1995: 44).

6   A number of exceptions could be made here, particularly in the field of anthropology/ethnography. For one account of the various ethnographic filmmakers who have been interested in experimenting with the form of anthropology see Russell (1999). Clifford and Marcus (1986) also include attempts to rethink the practice of doing anthropology (including of course writing it) in both deconstructive and reconstructive ways.

7   The art historical literature on impressionism is of course vast and the problem of the category 'impressionism' has been the cause of much spilt ink. For those interested in the problems of desig-nating the who, what and when of impressionism, a good place to start is with the essays by Richard Shiff and Stephen Eisenman in Frascina and Harris (1992). It should be noted that I am playing fast and loose with the category 'impressionism'.

8   A record of this should be clear from the bibliography, but for journal special issues on everyday life, see: *XCP – Cross-cultural Poetics* 7, 2000, *Daidalos* 75, 2000, *Antithesis* 9, 1998 and *Current Sociology* 37(1), 1989.

PART ONE

Situating the everyday

INTRODUCTION TO PART ONE

HOW THE EVERYDAY IS SITUATED is of course a crucial issue for attending to it. The where and the when of the everyday is a problem that registers across the chapters in Part One and in this collection overall. Taken as an amorphous whole, work on everyday life might suggest that any fixing (especially in time and space) of the everyday is going to hamper discussion and perhaps limit the productivity of inquiry. Yet of course the downside of this is that the everyday can become a vague and at times vacuous term that points to everything and nothing.

Perhaps then situating the everyday is less about designating places and times of the everyday, and more about an orientation towards the social world. This would mean that it is not the everyday that requires situating but our attention to it. So, for instance, Freud's approach to the everyday sees it as an arena continually policed by forces of propriety (moral codes and the like) while also evidencing (through everyday so-called Freudian slips) a desirous realm that refuses to be held in check. The Freudian everyday then is never simply the world of routine conduct; it always bears the traces of desires and fears that cannot find a place in such routines. Such a split or double register is repeated for instance by Erving Goffman's micro-geographies of the everyday, or Michel de Certeau's understanding of the everyday as evidencing practices and beliefs that evade yet never vacate networks of power.

Such orientations seem to suggest an approach to the everyday that sees it as a realm where we can access the remainders and resistances to the social regimes that dominate us. Yet it is also clear that such orientations necessarily have to account for the everyday as (precisely) a form of domination. This perspective is bound to come to the fore when the description of everyday forms of domination is seen as a political task. Feminism, sexual liberation movements, antiracist studies and so on would necessarily need to show how the everyday could generate and perpetuate practices of domination. Yet even here the everyday needs to be thought of (at least potentially) as evidencing counter-practices. Thus an unanswerable but fundamental question hovers over the everyday and will determine how we orientate ourselves towards it: is the everyday an arena for the reproduction of power relations? Is it the training ground for business-as-usual, for the repetition of bigotries and ideologies? Or is the everyday a site of invention and resistance? Or perhaps it is a marginal arena for alternative practices that are left undisturbed due to their relative invisibility and low importance?

Perhaps another question needs posing here too. If Freud's understanding of parap- raxes required an approach that could call attention to the unremarkable and (more accurately) the unremarked-upon, it discovered within the moment-by-moment of the daily another temporality evidencing the tenacity of unconscious desires. Within the general hurly-burly of daily life was something like a geological seam that pointed to another 'time' of the everyday. To think about everyday life might be an invitation to consider the every- day, not as segments of discrete time, but as different *durations* or temporalities running simultaneously. In this way the question becomes how to weave together the surface dis- turbances that impact on our everyday environment (new building, new fashions, new fads) with slower and, perhaps, more structural forces. And if our attention to the everyday is normally attentive to those shifts and transformations that seem pre-eminently everyday (the introduction of electric lighting or the enforcement of compulsory education, for example) then how might you make a slower, more geological everyday come to light?

Chapter 1

Sigmund Freud

PARAPRAXES [1915–17]

(**Source**: Freud, Sigmund (1973) *Introductory Lectures on Psychoanalysis*, translated by James Strachey, Harmondsworth: Penguin, pp. 50–3, 57–62)

Editor's introduction

Sigmund Freud (1856–1939) wrote his *Introductory Lectures on Psychoanalysis* (from which this extract is taken) between 1915 and 1917. Written in a language designed for the interested reader (rather than the specialist psychoanalyst) the lectures can be seen as both an introduction and a stock-taking of psychoanalytic thought. The ideas of Freudian psychoanalysis, although always hotly disputed, rapidly entered everyday speech, particularly in regard to the most everyday phenomenon that Freud deals with here – namely 'parapraxes' or what have become known as Freudian slips. The extract relates to material that Freud had dealt with much more exhaustively in his *Psychopathology of Everyday Life* of 1901. While Freud does not rehearse the theoretical architecture that informs his attention to these slips, bungled actions and forms of forgetting, he does use this lecture to insist on the relationship between psychoanalysis and everyday life.

In *The Psychopathology of Everyday Life* he ends by declaring that all cases of parapraxes have something in common: '*the phenomena can be traced back to incompletely suppressed psychical material, which, although pushed away by conscious-ness, has nevertheless not been robbed of all capacity for expressing itself*' (Freud [1901] 1975: 344, emphasis in the original). For Freud, all forms of everyday parap-raxes register suppressed material. Following Freud we might say that while the sup-pressed material might be the traumatic material of early life (and thus not 'everyday' in the literal sense) it continues to live (to haunt us) in our everyday life (and of course, through dreams, in our every-night life). For Freud the project of psychoanalysis and its claim for cultural value was based on the ubiquity of the phenomena it was attending to. While in his case studies Freud deals with patients who find it almost impossible to live their everyday lives and are in need of some kind of help, his usual field of contemplation is the everyday world of the ordinarily troubled (himself, for instance).

Further reading: Ferguson 1996; Freud [1901] 1975; Pile 1996.

L ADIES AND GENTLEMEN, – We will not start with postulates but with an investigation. Let us choose as its subject certain phenomena which are very common and very familiar but which have been very little examined, and which, since they can be observed in any healthy person, have nothing to do with illnesses. They are what are known as 'parapraxes', to which everyone is liable.[1] It may happen, for instance, that a person who intends to say something may use another word instead (a *slip of the tongue* [*Versprechen*]), or he may do the same thing in writing, and may or may not notice what he has done. Or a person may read something, whether in print or manuscript, different from what is actually before his eyes (a *misreading* [*Verlesen*]), or he may hear wrongly something that has been said to him (a *mishearing* [*Verhören*]) – on the assumption, of course, that there is no organic disturbance of his powers of hearing. Another group of these phenomena has as its basis *forgetting* [*Vergessen*] – not, however, a permanent forgetting but only a temporary one. Thus a person may be unable to get hold of a *name* which he nevertheless knows and which he recognizes at once, or he may forget to carry out an *intention*, though he remembers it later and has thus only forgotten it at that particular moment. In a third group the temporary character is absent – for instance in the case of *mislaying* [*Verlegen*], when a person has put something somewhere and cannot find it again, or in the precisely analogous case of *losing* [*Verlieren*]. Here we have a forgetting which we treat differently from other kinds of forgetting, one at which we are surprised or annoyed instead of finding it understandable. In addition to all this there are particular sorts of *errors* [*Irrtümer*], in which the temporary character is present once more; for in their instance we believe for a time that something is the case which both before and afterwards we know is not so. And there are a number of other similar phenomena known by various names.

All these are occurrences whose internal affinity with one another is expressed in the fact that [in German] they begin with the syllable '*ver*'.[2] They are almost all of an unimportant kind, most of them are very transitory, and they are without much significance in human life. Only rarely does one of them, such as losing an object, attain some degree of practical importance. For that reason, too, they attract little attention, give rise to no more than feeble emotions, and so on.

It is to these phenomena, then, that I now propose to draw your attention. But you will protest with some annoyance: 'There are so many vast problems in the wide universe, as well as within the narrower confines of our minds, so many marvels in the field of mental disorders, which require and deserve to have light thrown upon them, that it does really seem gratuitous to waste labour and interest on such trivialities. If you could make us understand why a person with sound eyes and ears can see and hear in broad daylight things that are not there, why another person suddenly thinks he is being persecuted by the people of whom he has hitherto been most fond, or puts forward the cleverest arguments in support of delusional beliefs which any child could see were nonsensical, then we should have some opinion of psychoanalysis. But if it can do no more than ask us to consider why a speaker at a banquet uses one word instead of another or why a housewife has mislaid her keys, and similar futilities, then we shall know how to put our times and interest to better uses.'

I should reply: Patience, Ladies and Gentlemen! I think your criticism has gone astray. It is true that psychoanalysis cannot boast that it has never concerned itself with trivialities. On the contrary, the material for its observations is usually provided by the inconsiderable events which have been put aside by the other sciences as being too unimportant – the dregs, one might say, of the world of phenomena. But are you not making a confusion in your criticism between the vastness of the problems and the conspicuousness of what points to them? Are there not very important things which can only reveal themselves, under certain conditions and at certain times, by quite feeble indications? I should find no difficulty in giving you several examples of such situations. If you are a young man, for instance, will it not be from small pointers that you will conclude that you have won a girl's favour? Would you wait for an express declaration of love or a passionate embrace? Or would not a glance, scarcely noticed by other people, be enough? a slight movement, the lengthening by a second of the pressure of a hand? And if you were a detective engaged in tracing a murder, would you expect to find that the murderer had left his photograph behind at the place of the crime, with his address attached? or would you not necessarily have to be satisfied with comparatively slight and obscure traces of the person you were in search of? So do not let us under-estimate small indications; by their help we may succeed in getting on the track of something bigger. Furthermore, I think like you that the great problems of the universe and of science have the first claim on our interest. But it is as a rule of very little use to form an express intention of devoting oneself to research into this or that great problem. One is then often at a loss to know the first step to take. It is more promising in scientific work to attack whatever is immediately before one and offers an opportunity for research. If one does so really thoroughly and without prejudice or preconception, and if one has luck, then, since everything is related to everything, including small things to great, one may gain access even from such unpretentious work to a study of the great problems. That is what I should say in order to retain your interest, when we deal with such apparent trivialities as the parapraxes of healthy people.

[. . .]

No light is thrown on these small features of parapraxes by the theory of withdrawal of attention. The theory need not on that account be wrong, however; it may merely lack something, some addition, before it is entirely satisfying. But some of the parapraxes, too, can themselves be looked at from another point of view.

Let us take *slips of the tongue* as the most suitable sort of parapraxis for our purpose – though we might equally well have chosen slips of the pen or misreading.[3] We must bear in mind that so far we have only asked when – under what conditions – people make slips of the tongue, and it is only to that question that we have had an answer. But we might direct our interest elsewhere and inquire why it is that the slip occurred in this particular way and no other; and we might take into account what it is that emerges in the slip itself. You will observe that, so long as this question is unanswered and no light thrown on the product of the slip, the phenomenon remains a chance event from the psychological point of view, even though it may have been given a physiological explanation. If I make a slip of the tongue, I might obviously do so in an infinite number of ways, the right word might be replaced by any of a thousand others, it might be distorted in countless different directions. Is there something, then, that compels me in the particular case to make the slip in one special way, or does it remain a matter of chance, of arbitrary choice, and is the question perhaps one to which no sensible answer at all can be given?

[. . .]

After all, the commonest slips of the tongue are when, instead of saying one word, we say another very much like it; and this similarity is for many people a sufficient explanation of such slips. For instance, a Professor declared in his inaugural lecture: 'I am not '*geneigt* [inclined]' (instead of '*geeignet* [qualified]') to appreciate the services of my highly esteemed predecessor.' Or another Professor remarked: 'In the case of the female genitals, in spite of many *Versuchungen* [temptations] – I beg your pardon, *Versuche* [experiments]. . . .'

The most usual, and at the same time the most striking kind of slips of the tongue, however, are those in which one says the precise opposite of what one intended to say. Here, of course, we are very remote from relations between sounds and the effects of similarity; and instead we can appeal to the fact that contraries have a strong conceptual kinship with each other and stand in a particularly close psychological association with each other. There are historical examples of such occurrences. A President of the Lower House of our Parliament once opened the sitting with the words: 'Gentlemen, I take notice that a full quorum of members is present and herewith declare the sitting *closed*.'

[. . .]

The fact of the parapraxis having a sense of its own seems in certain cases evident and unmistakable. When the President of the Lower House with his first words *closed* the sitting instead of opening it, we feel inclined, in view of our knowledge of the circumstances in which the slip of the tongue occurred, to recognize that the parapraxis had a sense. The President expected nothing good of the sitting and would have been glad if he could have brought it to an immediate end. We have no difficulty in pointing to the sense of this slip of the tongue, or, in other words, in interpreting it. Or, let us suppose that one lady says to another in tones of apparent admiration: 'That smart new hat – I suppose you *aufgepatzt* [a non-existent word instead of *aufgeputzt* (trimmed)] it yourself?' Then no amount of scientific propriety will succeed in preventing our seeing behind this slip of the tongue the words: 'This hat is a *Patzerei* [botched-up affair].' Or, once more, we are told that a lady who was well-known for her energy remarked on one occasion: 'My husband asked his doctor what diet he ought to follow; but the doctor told him he had no need to diet: he could eat and drink what I want.' Here again the slip of the tongue has an unmistakable other side to it: it was giving expression to a consistently planned programme.

If it turned out, Ladies and Gentlemen, that not only *a few* instances of slips of the tongue and of parapraxes in general have a sense, but a considerable number of them, the *sense* of parapraxes, of which we have so far heard nothing, would inevitably become their most interesting feature and would push every other consideration into the background. We should then be able to leave all physiological or psychophysiological factors on one side and devote ourselves to purely psychological investigations into the sense – that is, the meaning or purpose – of parapraxes. We shall therefore make it our business to test this expectation on a considerable number of observations.

Notes

1   'Fehlleistungen', literally 'faulty acts' or 'faulty functions'. The general concept did not exist before Freud, and an English term was invented for its translation. The whole of The Psycho-pathology of Everyday Life (1901) is devoted to a discussion of them and a large number (over forty) of the examples and anecdotes [. . .] also appear in the various editions of that work. Freud often used parapraxes in his didactic writings (as he does here) as the most suitable material for an introduction to his theories. They were, indeed, among the earliest subjects of his own psycho-logical investigations.

2   The English syllable 'mis' has a similar sense.

3   It is most unfortunate from the point of view of the translator that Freud chose slips of the tongue as his most frequent examples of parapraxes [. . .] since they are from their very nature peculiarly resistant to translation. We have, however, followed our invariable practice in the Standard Edition and kept Freud's instances [. . .] rather than replace them by extraneous English ones. [. . .]

Chapter 2

Walter Benjamin

ON SOME MOTIFS IN BAUDELAIRE [1939]

(**Source**: Benjamin, Walter (1982) *Illuminations*, translated by Harry Zohn, London: Fontana, pp. 176–8)

Editor's introduction

Walter Benjamin (1892–1940) has emerged as perhaps the exemplary cultural historian of modernity. Between 1927 and his death in 1940, he embarked on a massive project of tracing the prehistory of modernity in the marginalia and trash of everyday life (Benjamin 1999b). While the *Arcades Project* remained an unfinished archive of scraps of information, it did generate a number of essays on Paris in the second half of the nineteenth century. This extract is from 'On Some Motifs in Baudelaire' first published in 1939. This is a wide-ranging essay that attempts to capture dialectically the emergence of a modern sensory consciousness and the problems and potentials that arise in the experiencing of modern everyday life.

In this very short extract he follows a line of thought that shows how modern everyday life is experienced as a series of operations analogous to the repetitive activity of the assembly line worker. Thus crossing the road, modern fun fairs, photography, film, matches and so on all offer a 'taste of the drill' – the militaristic experience of modern work. Yet Benjamin's work insists on a dialectic that will find redemption in the most unpromising of places. So if crossing the road 'has subjected the human sensorium to a complex kind of training' (in the same way that a couple of months on an assembly line effectively mechanises the body) this training can be rescued for a potentially critical understanding of modern life. In this Benjamin sees mass technological forms (film and photography in particular) as offering the potential *tools* for a new understanding of modern everyday life.

Benjamin's understanding of modern everyday life continues the work of Georg Simmel (see Chapter 29) but their different attitudes to everyday modernity might bear some scrutiny. The optimism that Benjamin continued to express (albeit against a gloomy assessment of capitalist modernity) is distinct from Simmel's more resigned desire to describe the dailiness of modernity. If for Simmel modern cultural forms were the only ones suited to the battered bodies and minds of modern life, it was because these forms (trade fairs, films, spectacular modern commerce) were partly responsible for the battering, and as such they were unlikely to become antidotes, merely temporary palliatives for modern life. For Benjamin there was always the hope that modern cultural forms would provide the tools that would allow for a historical awakening that would revolutionise everyday life.

Further reading: Benjamin 1996, 1999a, 1999b; Buck-Morss 1989; Cohen 1993; Gilloch 1996; Gary Smith 1989.

FEAR, REVULSION, AND HORROR were the emotions which the big-city crowd aroused in those who first observed it. For Poe it has something barbaric; discipline just barely manages to tame it. Later, James Ensor tirelessly confronted its discipline with its wildness; he liked to put military groups in his carnival mobs, and both got along splendidly – as the prototype of totalitarian states, in which the police make common cause with the looters. Valéry, who had a fine eye for the cluster of symptoms called 'civilization', has characterized one of the pertinent facts. 'The inhabitant of the great urban centers,' he writes, 'reverts to a state of savagery – that is, of isolation. The feeling of being dependent on others, which used to be kept alive by need, is gradually blunted in the smooth functioning of the social mechanism. Any improvement of this mechanism eliminates certain modes of behavior and emotions.' Comfort isolates; on the other hand, it brings those enjoying it closer to mechanization. The invention of the match around the middle of the nineteenth century brought forth a number of innovations which have one thing in common: one abrupt movement of the hand triggers a process of many steps. This development is taking place in many areas. One case in point is the telephone, where the lifting of a receiver has taken the place of the steady movement that used to be required to crank the older models. Of the countless movements of switching, inserting, pressing, and the like, the 'snapping' of the photographer has had the greatest consequences. A touch of the finger now sufficed to fix an event for an unlimited period of time. The camera gave the moment a posthumous shock, as it were. Haptic experiences of this kind were joined by optic ones, such as are supplied by the advertising pages of a newspaper or the traffic of a big city. Moving through this traffic involves the individual in a series of shocks and collisions. At dangerous intersections, nervous impulses flow through him in rapid succession, like the energy from a battery. Baudelaire speaks of a man who plunges into the crowd as into a reservoir of electric energy. Circumscribing the experience of the shock, he calls this man 'a *kaleidoscope* equipped with consciousness.' Whereas Poe's passers-by cast glances in all directions which still appeared to be aimless, today's pedestrians are obliged to do so in order to keep abreast of traffic signals. Thus technology has subjected the human sensorium to a complex kind of training. There came a day when a new and urgent need for stimuli was met by the film. In a film, perception in the form of shocks was established as a formal principle. That which determines the rhythm of production on a conveyor belt is the basis of the rhythm of reception in the film.

　　Marx had good reason to stress the great fluidity of the connection between segments in manual labor. This connection appears to the factory worker on an assembly line in an independent, objectified form. Independently of the worker's volition, the article being worked on comes within his range of action and moves away from him just as arbitrarily. 'It is a common characteristic of all capitalist production . . . ,' wrote Marx, 'that the worker does not make use of the working conditions. The working conditions make use of the worker; but it takes machinery to give this reversal a technically concrete form.' In working with machines, workers learn to coordinate 'their own movements with the uniformly constant movements of an automaton.' These words shed a peculiar light on the absurd kind of uniformity with which Poe wants to saddle the crowd – uniformities of attire and behavior, but also a uniformity of facial expression. Those smiles provide food for thought. They are probably the familiar kind, as expressed in the phrase 'keep smiling'; in that context they function as a mimetic shock absorber. 'All machine work,' it is said in the above context, 'requires early drilling of the worker.' This drill must be differentiated from practice. Practice, which was the sole determinant in craftsmanship, still had a function in manufacturing. With it as the basis, 'each particular area of production finds its appropriate technical form in *experience* and *slowly* perfects it.' To be sure, it quickly crystallizes it, 'as soon as a certain degree of maturity has been attained.' On the other hand, this same manufacturing produces 'in every handicraft it seizes a class of so-called unskilled laborers which the handicraft system strictly excluded. In developing the greatly simplified specialty to the point of virtuosity at the cost of the work capacity as a whole, it starts turning the lack of any development into a specialty. In addition to ranks we get the simple division of workers into the skilled and the unskilled.' The unskilled worker is the one most deeply degraded by the drill of the machines. His work has been sealed off from experience; practice counts for nothing there.[1] What the Fun Fair achieves with its Dodgem cars and other similar amusements is nothing but a taste of the drill to which the unskilled laborer is subjected in the factory – a sample which at times was for him the entire menu; for the art of being off center, in which the little man could acquire training in places like the Fun Fair, flourished concomitantly with unemployment. Poe's text makes us understand the true connection between wildness and discipline. His pedestrians act as if they had adapted themselves to the machines and could express themselves only automatically. Their behavior is a reaction to shocks. 'If jostled, they bowed profusely to the jostlers.'

Note

1   The shorter the training period of an industrial worker is, the longer that of a military man becomes. It may be part of society's preparation for total war that training is shifting from the practice of production to the practice of destruction.

Chapter 3

Fernand Braudel

PREFACE TO *THE MEDITERRANEAN AND THE MEDITERRANEAN WORLD IN THE AGE OF PHILIP II* [1946]

(**Source**: Braudel, Fernand (1995) *The Mediterranean and the Mediterranean World in the Age of Philip II*, translated by Siân Reynolds, Berkeley, Calif. and London: University of California Press, pp. 20–2)

Editor's introduction

Fernand Braudel (1902–1985) has been without doubt the most influential historian of the Annales School. His first major contribution to historical thought was a study of the Mediterranean basin during the second half of the sixteenth century. Yet such a description does not begin to suggest the vast scope of what Braudel was attempting, namely to set the social and political history of this moment within the long duration (*longue durée*) of geographical and geological time. Amazingly enough *The Mediterranean and the Mediterranean World in the Age of Philip II* was first drafted while Braudel was a prisoner of war in Germany, and without the aid of books or notes Braudel wrote it entirely from memory (Revel and Hunt 1995: 82).

Braudel's importance for the study of everyday life is ambiguous. On the one hand the notion of the *longue durée* might signal the sidelining of a more day-to-day social history – after all the kinds of historical shifts that Braudel saw as central were ones that stretched across centuries. Yet in giving space to the histories of such elements as fashion, furniture and food, Braudel (1985) clearly emphasised precisely those durational shifts that impacted at the level of everyday life. It might be that Braudel's usefulness for everyday life studies is not going to come from providing a paradigm for research; more likely it will come from his explicit *questioning* of historical time. In this extract from his preface to *The Mediterranean* Braudel divides historical time into three different temporalities (geo-time, social-time and event-time) and at first glance it might seem that everyday life should be located within social time. Yet if we follow Braudel's suggestion that history is lived *across* different temporalities (different durations) we might want to suggest that this will also be true of everyday life. Indeed we might want to go further than Braudel and ask why just stop at just three levels of historical time? Might there not also be generational-time, yearly-time, fashion-time and so on?

Braudel does not provide a definitive guide to the history of everyday life. In many ways he does something more important by asking us to think about history as a plurality of different *kinds* of time. If Braudel ends up by privileging one kind of historical time over another (the time of the *longue durée*), we are still left with the unfulfilled *potential* of writing the plural histories of everyday life, histories that weave together the different times of the everyday into a complex web.

Further reading: Braudel 1985; Burke 1990; Carrard 1995; Revel and Hunt 1995.

To its author, every work seems revolutionary, the result of a struggle for mastery. If the Mediterranean has done no more than force us out of our old habits it will already have done us a service.

This book is divided into three parts, each of which is itself an essay in general explanation.

The first part is devoted to a history whose passage is almost imperceptible, that of man in his relationship to the environment, a history in which all change is slow, a history of constant repetition, ever-recurring cycles. I could not neglect this almost timeless history, the story of man's contact with the inanimate, neither could I be satisfied with the traditional geographical introduction to history that often figures to little purpose at the beginning of so many books, with its descriptions of the mineral deposits, types of agriculture, and typical flora, briefly listed and never mentioned again, as if the flowers did not come back every spring, the flocks of sheep migrate every year, or the ships sail on a real sea that changes with the seasons.

On a different level from the first there can be distinguished another history, this time with slow but perceptible rhythms. If the expression had not been diverted from its full meaning, one could call it *social history*, the history of groups and group-ings. How did these swelling currents affect Mediterranean life in general – this was the question I asked myself in the second part of the book, studying in turn economic systems, states, societies, civilizations and finally, in order to convey more clearly my conception of history, attempting to show how all these deep-seated forces were at work in the complex arena of warfare. For war, as we know, is not an arena governed purely by individual responsibilities.

Lastly, the third part gives a hearing to traditional history – history, one might say, on the scale not of man, but of individual men, what Paul Lacombe and François Simiand called '*l'histoire événementielle*', that is, the history of events: surface disturb-ances, crests of foam that the tides of history carry on their strong backs. A history of brief, rapid, nervous fluctuations, by definition ultra-sensitive; the least tremor sets all its antennae quivering. But as such it is the most exciting of all, the richest in human interest, and also the most dangerous. We must learn to distrust this history with its still burning passions, as it was felt, described, and lived by contemporaries whose lives were as short and as short-sighted as ours. It has the dimensions of their anger, dreams, or illusions. In the sixteenth century, after the true Renaissance, came the Renaissance of the poor, the humble, eager to write, to talk of themselves and of others. This precious mass of paper distorts, filling up the lost hours and assuming a false importance. The historian who takes a seat in Philip II's chair and reads his papers finds himself transported into a strange one-dimensional world, a world of strong passions certainly, blind like any other living world, our own included, and unconscious of the deeper realities of history, of the running waters on which our frail barks are tossed like cockle-shells. A dangerous world, but one whose spells and enchantments we shall have exorcised by making sure first to chart those underlying currents, often noiseless, whose direction can only be discerned by watching them over long periods of time. Resounding events are often only momentary outbursts, surface manifestations of these larger movements and explicable only in terms of them.

The final effect then is to dissect history into various planes, or, to put it another way, to divide historical time into geographical time, social time, and individual time. Or, alternatively, to divide man into a multitude of selves. This is perhaps what I shall be least forgiven, even if I say in my defence that traditional divisions also cut across living history which is fundamentally *one*, even if I argue, against Ranke or Karl Brandi, that the historical narrative is not a method, or even the objective method *par excellence*, but quite simply a philosophy of history like any other; even if I say, and demonstrate hereafter, that these levels I have distinguished are only means of exposition, that I have felt it quite in order in the course of the book to move from one level to another. But I do not intend to plead my case further. If I am criticized for the method in which the book has been assembled, I hope the component parts will be found workmanlike by professional standards.

I hope too that I shall not be reproached for my excessive ambitions, for my desire and need to see on a grand scale. It will perhaps prove that history can do more than study walled gardens. If it were otherwise, it would surely be failing in one of its most immediate tasks which must be to relate to the painful problems of our times and to maintain contact with the youthful but imperialistic human sciences. Can there be any study of humanity, in 1946, without historians who are ambitious, conscious of their duties and of their immense powers? 'It is the fear of great history which has killed great history,' wrote Edmond Faral, in 1942. May it live again!

Chapter 4

Erving Goffman

FRONT AND BACK REGIONS OF EVERYDAY LIFE [1959]

(Source: Goffman, Erving (1990) *The Presentation of Self in Everyday Life*, Harmondsworth: Penguin, pp. 111–21)

Editor's introduction

Between 1949 and 1951 the sociologist Erving Goffman (1922–1983) worked in Scotland investigating the social structure of Shetland Islands communities. As can be seen in this extract from his first book *The Presentation of Self in Everyday Life*, Goffman seems more interested in what was going on in the kitchen of the hotel where he stayed than in mapping the general structures that governed the islands' communities. It is this attention to the micro-sociology of everyday life (rather than the macro-sociology of social structures) that characterises Goffman's contribution to sociology. And it is this focus on the everyday (along with a decidedly non-academic style of writing) that has made Goffman's books so popular both inside and outside the field of sociology. Goffman offers something like an investigation of what Tom Burns calls 'a rhetoric of conduct' (Burns 1992: 11): an attempt to trace the meanings of various ways of acting in different situations.

What Goffman ends up with is a version of the everyday self that is fundamentally plural (a theme that he also stressed in his book *Frame Analysis*: Goffman 1974). This is an understanding of the self (or the selves) that works to sidestep some of the pitfalls that can attend investigation of the everyday. Rather than approaching everyday life in the hope of distinguishing between the authentic and the inauthentic (separating the true self from the false self), Goffman recognises that the self is that collection of performances that take place in and across specific locations. By employing a set of tropes that are associated with theatre and gaming (play, stage, set and so on) Goffman's approach to the everyday suggests an inventory of performances spatially arranged across the geography of everyday life. In some ways this points to some shared concerns with a much more recent interest (or renewed interest) in performativity. In other ways it also shares some common ground with what Michel de Certeau will term the tactics of everyday life: that resistive or evasive creativity that takes place in the tears in the fabric of power (see Chapter 6). What it does not share with de Certeau's work is de Certeau's scepticism about the visibility and transparency of such actions. Anyone who has worked in a restaurant (rather than studied it) will know that the 'aggressive sampling' of a pudding is the very least of those inventively disgusting acts that are typical of everyday kitchen life. Is Goffman's tame version of Shetland kitchen life due to a certain propriety in crofter culture, or are more emphatically 'vulgar' actions invisible because Goffman is in the end resolutely marked out as a hotel guest?

Further reading: Burns 1992; Goffman 1974; Manning 1993.

IN THE STUDY OF SOCIAL ESTABLISHMENTS it is important to describe the prevailing standards of decorum; it is difficult to do so because informants and students tend to take many of these standards for granted, not realizing they have done so until an accident, or crisis, or peculiar circumstance occurs. It is known, for example, that different business offices have different standards as regards informal chatter among clerks, but it is only when we happen to study an office that has a sizeable number of foreign refugee employees that we suddenly appreciate that permission to engage in informal talk may not constitute permission to engage in informal talk in a foreign language.[1]

We are accustomed to assuming that the rules of decorum that prevail in sacred establishments, such as churches, will be much different from the ones that prevail in everyday places of work. We ought not to assume from this that the standards in sacred places are more numerous and more strict than those we find in work establishments. While in church, a woman may be permitted to sit, daydream, and even doze. However, as a saleswoman on the floor of a dress shop, she may be required to stand, keep alert, refrain from chewing gum, keep a fixed smile on her face even when not talking to anyone, and wear clothes she can ill afford.

One form of decorum that has been studied in social establishments is what is called 'make-work'. It is understood in many establishments that not only will workers be required to produce a certain amount after a certain length of time but also that they will be ready, when called upon, to give the impression that they are working hard at the moment. Of a shipyard we learn the following:

It was amusing to watch the sudden transformation whenever word got round that the foreman was on the hull or in the shop or that a front-office superintendent was coming by. Quartermen and leadermen would rush to their groups of workers and stir them to obvious activity. 'Don't let him catch you sitting down' was the universal admonition, and where no work existed a pipe was busily bent and threaded, or a bolt which was already firmly in place was subjected to further and unnecessary tightening. This was the formal tribute invariably attending a visitation by the boss, and its conventions were as familiar to both sides as those surrounding a five-star general's inspection. To have neglected any detail of the false and empty show would have been interpreted as a mark of singular disrespect.[2]

Similarly, of a hospital ward we learn:

> The observer was told very explicitly by other attendants on his first day of work on the wards not to 'get caught' striking a patient, to appear busy when the supervisor makes her rounds, and not to speak to her unless first spoken to. It was noted that some attendants watch for her approach and warn the other attendants so that no one will get caught doing undesirable acts. Some attendants will save work for when the supervisor is present so they will be busy and will not be given additional tasks. In most attendants the change is not so obvious, depending largely on the individual attendant, the supervisor, and the ward situation. However, with nearly all attendants there is some change in behavior when an official, such as a supervisor, is present. There is no open flouting of the rules and regulations.[3]

From a consideration of make-work it is only a step to consideration of other standards of work activity for which appearances must be maintained, such as pace, personal interest, economy, accuracy, etc.[4] And from a consideration of work standards in general it is only a step to consideration of other major aspects of decorum, instrumental and moral, in work places, such as: mode of dress; permissible sound levels; proscribed diversions, indulgences, and affective expressions.

Make-work, along with other aspects of decorum in work places, is usually seen as the particular burden of those of low estate. A dramaturgical approach, however, requires us to consider together with make-work the problem of staging its opposite, make-no-work. Thus, in a memoir written about life in the early nineteenth century among the barely genteel, we learn that:

> People were extremely punctilious on the subject of calls – one remembers the call in *The Mill on the Floss*. The call was due at regular intervals, so that even the day should almost be known in which it was paid or returned. It was a ceremonial which contained a great deal of ceremony and make-believe. No one, for instance, was to be surprised in doing any kind of work. There was a fiction in genteel families that the ladies of the house never did anything serious or serviceable after dinner; the afternoon was supposed to be devoted either to walking, or to making calls, or to elegant trifling at home. Therefore if the girls were at the moment engaged upon any useful work – they crammed it under the sofa, and pretended to be reading a book, or painting, or knitting, or to be engaged in easy and fashionable conversation. Why they went through this elaborate pretence I have not the least idea, because everybody knew that every girl in the place was always making, mending, cutting out, basting, gussetting, trimming, turning and contriving. How do you suppose that the solicitor's daughters made so brave a show on Sunday if they were not clever enough to make up things for themselves? Everybody, of course, knew it, and why the girls would not own up at once one cannot now understand. Perhaps it was a

sort of suspicion, or a faint hope, or a wild dream, that a reputation for ladylike uselessness might enable them to cross the line at the county Ball, and mingle with the Country people.[5]

It should be plain that while persons who are obliged to make-work and make-no-work are likely to be on the opposite sides of the track, they must yet adapt themselves to the same side of the footlights.

It was suggested earlier that when one's activity occurs in the presence of other persons, some aspects of the activity are expressively accentuated and other aspects, which might discredit the fostered impression, are suppressed. It is clear that accentuated facts make their appearance in what I have called a front region; it should be just as clear that there may be another region – a 'back region' or 'backstage' – where the suppressed facts make an appearance.

A back region or backstage may be defined as a place, relative to a given performance, where the impression fostered by the performance is knowingly contradicted as a matter of course. There are, of course, many characteristic functions of such places. It is here that the capacity of a performance to express something beyond itself may be painstakingly fabricated; it is here that illusions and impressions are openly constructed. Here stage props and items of personal front can be stored in a kind of compact collapsing of whole repertoires of actions and characters.[6] Here grades of ceremonial equipment, such as different types of liquor or clothes, can be hidden so that the audience will not be able to see the treatment accorded them in comparison with the treatment that could have been accorded them. Here devices such as the telephone are sequestered so that they can be used 'privately'. Here costumes and other parts of personal front may be adjusted and scrutinized for flaws. Here the team can run through its performance, checking for offending expressions when no audience is present to be affronted by them; here poor members of the team, who are expressively inept, can be schooled or dropped from the performance. Here the performer can relax; he can drop his front, forgo speaking his lines, and step out of character. Simone de Beauvoir provides a rather vivid picture of this backstage activity in describing situations from which the male audience is absent.

> What gives value to such relations among women is the truthfulness they imply. Confronting man woman is always play-acting; she lies when she makes believe that she accepts her status as the inessential other, she lies when she presents to him an imaginary personage through mimicry, costumery, studied phrases. These histrionics require a constant tension: when with her husband, or with her lover, every woman is more or less conscious of the thought: 'I am not being myself': the male world is harsh, sharp edged, its voices are too resounding, the lights are too crude, the contacts rough. With other women, a woman is behind the scenes; she is polishing her equipment, but not in battle; she is getting her costume together, preparing her make-up, laying out her tactics; she is lingering in dressing-gown and slippers in the wings before making her entrance on the stage; she likes this warm, easy, relaxed atmosphere . . .
>
> For some women this warm and frivolous intimacy is dearer than the serious pomp of relations with men.[7]

Very commonly the back region of a performance is located at one end of the place where the performance is presented, being cut off from it by a partition and guarded passageway. By having the front and back regions adjacent in this way, a performer out in front can receive backstage assistance while the performance is in progress and can interrupt his performance momentarily for brief periods of relaxation. In general, of course, the back region will be the place where the performer can reliably expect that no member of the audience will intrude.

Since the vital secrets of a show are visible backstage and since performers behave out of character while there, it is natural to expect that the passage from the front region to the back region will be kept closed to members of the audience or that the entire back region will be kept hidden from them. This is a widely practised technique of impression management, and requires further discussion.

Obviously, control of backstage plays a significant role in the process of 'work control' whereby individuals attempt to buffer themselves from the deterministic demands that surround them. If a factory worker is to succeed in giving the appearance of working hard all day, then he must have a safe place to hide the jig that enables him to turn out a day's work with less than a full day's effort.[8] If the bereaved are to be given the illusion that the dead one is really in a deep and tranquil sleep, then the undertaker must be able to keep the bereaved from the workroom where the corpses are drained, stuffed, and painted in preparation for their final performance.[9] If a mental hospital staff is to give a good impression of the hospital to those who come to visit their committed kinfolk, then it will be important to be able to bar visitors from the wards, especially the chronic wards, restricting the outsiders to special visiting-rooms where it will be practicable to have relatively nice furnishings and to ensure that all patients present are well dressed, well washed, well handled and relatively well behaved. So, too, in many service trades, the customer is asked to leave the thing that needs service and to go away so that the tradesman can work in private. When the customer returns for his automobile – or watch, or trousers, or radio – it is presented to him in good working order, an order that incidentally conceals the amount and kind of work that had to be done, the number of mistakes that were first made before getting it fixed, and other details the client would have to know before being able to judge the reasonableness of the fee that is asked of him.

Service personnel so commonly take for granted the right to keep the audience away from the back region that attention is drawn more to cases where this common strategy cannot be applied than to cases where it can. For example, the American filling-station manager has numerous troubles in this regard.[10] If a repair is needed, customers often refuse to leave their automobile overnight or all day, in trust of the establishment, as they would do had they taken their automobile to a garage. Further, when the mechanic makes repairs and adjustments, customers often feel they have the right to watch him as he does his work. If an illusionary service is to be rendered and charged for, it must, therefore, be rendered before the very person who is to be taken in by it. Customers, in fact, not only disregard the right of the station personnel to their own back region but often also define the whole station as a kind of open city for males, a place where an individual runs the risk of getting his clothes dirty and therefore has the right to demand full backstage privileges. Male motorists will saunter in, tip back their hats, spit, swear, and ask for free service or free travel advice. They will barge in to make familiar use of the toilet, the station's tools, the office telephone, or to search in the stockroom for their own supplies.[11] In order to avoid traffic lights, motorists will cut right across the station driveway, oblivious to the manager's proprietary rights.

Shetland Hotel provides another example of the problems workers face when they have insufficient control of their backstage. Within the hotel kitchen, where the guests' food was prepared and where the staff ate and spent their day, crofters' culture tended to prevail. It will be useful to suggest some of the details of this culture here.

In the kitchen, crofter employer–employee relations prevailed. Reciprocal first-naming was employed, although the scullery boy was fourteen and the male owner over thirty. The owning couple and employees ate together, participating with relative equality in meal-time small talk and gossip. When the owners held informal kitchen parties for friends and extended kin, the hotel workers participated. This pattern of intimacy and equality between management and employees was inconsistent with the appearance both elements of the staff gave when guests were present, as it was inconsistent with the guests' notions of the social distance which ought to obtain between the official with whom they corresponded when arranging for their stay, and the porters and maids who carried luggage upstairs, polished the guests' shoes each night, and emptied their chamber pots.

Similarly, in the hotel kitchen, island eating-patterns were employed. Meat, when available, tended to be boiled. Fish, often eaten, tended to be boiled or salted. Potatoes, an inevitable item in the day's one big meal, were almost always boiled in their jackets and eaten in the island manner: each eater selects a potato by hand from the central bowl, then pierces it with his fork and skins it with his knife, keeping the peels in a neat pile alongside his place, to be scooped in with his knife after the meal is finished. Oilcloth was used as a cover for the table. Almost every meal was preceded by a bowl of soup, and soup bowls, instead of plates, tended to be used for the courses that came after. (Since most of the food was boiled anyway, this was a practical usage.) Forks and knives were sometimes grasped fist-like, and tea was served in cups without saucers. While the island diet in many ways seemed to be adequate, and while island table manners could be executed with great delicacy and circumspection – and often were – the whole eating complex was well understood by islanders to be not only different from the British middle-class pattern, but somehow a violation of it. Perhaps this difference in pattern was most evident on occasions when food given to guests was also eaten in the kitchen. (This was not uncommon and was not more common because the staff often preferred island food to what the guests were given.) At such times the kitchen portion of the food was prepared and served in the island manner, with little stress on individual pieces and cuts, and more stress on a common source of servings. Often the remains of a joint of meat or the broken remains of a batch of tarts would be served – the same food as appeared in the guest dining-hall but in a slightly different condition, yet one not offensive by island kitchen standards. And if a pudding made from stale bread and cake did not pass the test of what was good enough for guests, it was eaten in the kitchen.

Crofter clothing and postural patterns also tended to appear in the hotel kitchen. Thus, the manager would sometimes follow local custom and leave his cap on; the scullery boys would use the coal bucket as a target for the well-aimed expulsion of mucus; and the women on the staff would rest sitting with their legs up in unladylike positions.

In addition to these differences due to culture, there were other sources of discrepancy between kitchen ways and parlour ways in the hotel, for some of the standards of hotel service that were shown or implied in the guests' regions were not fully adhered to in the kitchen. In the scullery wing of the kitchen region, mould would sometimes form on soup yet to be used. Over the kitchen stove, wet socks would be dried on the steaming kettle – a standard practice on the island. Tea, when guests had asked for it newly infused, would be brewed in a pot encrusted at the bottom with tea leaves that were weeks old. Fresh herrings would be cleaned by splitting them and then scraping out the innards with newspaper. Pats of butter, softened, misshapen, and partly used during their sojourn in the dining-hall, would be rerolled to look fresh, and sent out to do duty again. Rich puddings, too good for kitchen consumption, would be sampled aggressively by the fingerful before distribution to the guests. During the mealtime rush hour, once-used drinking glasses would sometimes be merely emptied and wiped instead of being rewashed, thus allowing them to be put back into circulation quickly.[12]

Given, then, the various ways in which activity in the kitchen contradicted the impression fostered in the guests' region of the hotel, one can appreciate why the doors leading from the kitchen to the other parts of the hotel were a constant sore spot in the organization of work. The maids wanted to keep the doors open to make it easier to carry food trays back and forth, to gather information about whether guests were ready or not for the service which was to be performed for them, and to retain as much contact as possible with the persons they had come to work to learn about. Since the maids played a servant role before the guests, they felt they did not have too much to lose by being observed in their own milieu by guests who glanced into the kitchen when passing the open doors. The managers, on the other hand, wanted to keep the door closed so that the middle-class role imputed to them by the guests would not be discredited by a disclosure of their kitchen habits. Hardly a day passed when these doors were not angrily banged shut and angrily pushed open. A kick-door of the kind modern restaurants use would have provided a partial solution for this staging problem. A small glass window in the doors that could act as a peephole – a stage device used by many small places of business – would also have been helpful.

Notes

1   See Edward Gross (1949) 'Informal Relations and the Social Organization of Work in an Industrial Office', unpublished PhD dissertation, Department of Sociology, University of Chicago, page 186.

2   Katherine Archibald (1947) *Wartime Shipyard*, Berkeley, Calif: University of California Press, page 159.

3   Robert H. Willoughby (1953) 'The Attendant in the State Mental Hospital', unpublished Master's thesis, Department of Sociology, University of Chicago, page 43.

4   An analysis of some major work standards may be found in Gross, op. cit., from which the above examples of such standards are taken.

5   Sir Walter Besant (1887) 'Fifty Years Ago', *The Graphic Jubilee Number*, quoted in James Laver (1954) *Victorian Vista*, London: Hulton Press.

6   As Alfred Métraux [no date] 'Dramatic Elements in Ritual Possession', *Diogenes* 11, page 24, suggests, even the practice of voodoo cults will require such facilities:

Every case of possession has its theatrical side, as shown in the matter of disguises. The rooms of the sanctuary are not unlike the wings of a theater where the possessed find the necessary accessories. Unlike the hysteric, who reveals his anguish and his desires through symptoms – a personal means of expression – the ritual of possession must conform to the classic image of a mythical personage.

7   Simone de Beauvoir (1953) *The Second Sex*, London: Cape.
8   See Orvis Collins, Melville Dalton and Donald Roy [no date] 'Restriction of Output and Social Cleavage in Industry', *Applied Anthropology* (now *Human Organization*), 4: 1–14, especially page 9.
9   Mr Habenstein has suggested in seminar that in some states the undertaker has a legal right to prevent relatives of the deceased from entering the workroom where the corpse is in preparation. Presumably the sight of what has to be done to the dead to make them look attractive would be too great a shock for non-professionals and especially for kinfolk of the deceased. Mr Habenstein also suggests that kinfolk may want to be kept from the undertaker's workroom because of their own fear of their own morbid curiosity.
10   The statements which follow are taken from a study by Social Research, Inc., of two hundred small-business managers.
11   At a sports car garage the following scene was reported to me by the manager regarding a customer who went into the storeroom himself to obtain a gasket, presenting it to the manager from behind the storeroom counter:

Customer: 'How much?'
Manager: 'Sir, where did you get in and what would happen if you went behind the counter in a bank and got a roll of nickels and brought them to the teller?'
Customer: 'But this ain't a bank.'
Manager: 'Well, those are my nickels. Now, what did you want, sir?'
Customer: 'If that's the way you feel about it, O.K. That's your privilege. I want a gasket for a '51 Anglia.'
Manager: 'That's for a '54.'

While the manager's anecdote may not be a faithful reproduction of the words and actions that were actually interchanged, it does tell us something faithful about his situation and his feelings in it.
12   These illustrations of the discrepancy between the reality and appearances of standards should not be considered extreme. Close observation of the backstage of any middle-class home in Western cities would be likely to disclose discrepancies between reality and appearance that were equally as great. And wherever there is some degree of commercialization, discrepancies no doubt are often greater.

Chapter 5

Betty Friedan

THE PROBLEM THAT HAS NO NAME [1963]

(**Source**: Friedan, Betty (1965) *The Feminine Mystique*, Harmondsworth: Penguin, pp. 13–18)

Editor's introduction

Betty Friedan's 1963 book *The Feminine Mystique* has become synonymous with the emergence of second-wave feminism in the USA. What is distinctive about Friedan's assessment of women's social position in postwar America is that it insists that within the heart of an economically affluent society is a gendered poverty of experience. The everyday landscape of Friedan's book is for the most part resolutely suburban and middle class. Yet while this has been an aspect of her writing that has come in for criticism, it might be that this message of anger, anxiety and dissatisfaction from those supposedly in receipt of all the spoils of economic success, tactically found the Achilles heel of the American Dream. The rhetoric of entrepreneurial capitalism could always argue that economic poverty and social injustice could be overcome by hard work and invention, but what could it say to those who when offered the rewards claimed they were a poisoned chalice? For Friedan the everydayness of women's lives evidences an emptiness of value. Her social psychology of women's everyday life traces the symptoms of female anomie, and diagnoses a society trapped in an iron-cage of gender norms.

Friedan's writing crossed the world of academia and the (perhaps more everyday) world of popular journalism. Perhaps her experience as a labour activist in the 1940s and 1950s necessarily gave her writing a vibrancy that both suited the world of magazine journalism and spoke to those who were the subjects of her analysis. *The Feminine Mystique* was an immediate and unqualified success, and did much to put the women's movement at the forefront of social issues. The notoriety of Friedan made her a natural spokesperson for the emerging feminist movement and Friedan was one of the founders (and first president) of the National Organisation for Women (NOW).

Further reading: Bassnett 1986; Horowitz 1998; Pulin and Colebrook 1993.

T HE PROBLEM LAY BURIED, unspoken, for many years in the minds of American women. It was a strange stirring, a sense of dissatisfaction, a yearning that women suffered in the middle of the twentieth century in the United States. Each suburban wife struggled with it alone. As she made the beds, shopped for groceries, matched slipcover material, ate peanut butter sandwiches with her children, chauffeured Cub Scouts and Brownies, lay beside her husband at night, she was afraid to ask even of herself the silent question: 'Is this all?'

For over fifteen years there was no word of this yearning in the millions of words written about women, for women, in all the columns, books and articles by experts telling women their role was to seek fulfilment as wives and mothers. Over and over women heard in voices of tradition and of Freudian sophistication that they could desire no greater destiny than to glory in their own femininity. Experts told them how to catch a man and keep him, how to breastfeed children and handle their toilet training, how to cope with sibling rivalry and adolescent rebellion; how to buy a dishwasher, bake bread, cook gourmet snails, and build a swimming pool with their own hands; how to dress, look, and act more feminine and make marriage more exciting; how to keep their husbands from dying young and their sons from growing into delinquents. They were taught to pity the neurotic, unfeminine, unhappy women who wanted to be poets or physicists or presidents. They learned that truly feminine women do not want careers, higher education, political rights – the independence and the opportunities that the old-fashioned feminists fought for. Some women, in their forties and fifties, still remembered painfully giving up those dreams, but most of the younger women no longer even thought about them. A thousand expert voices applauded their femininity, their adjustment, their new maturity. All they had to do was devote their lives from earliest girlhood to finding a husband and bearing children.

By the end of the 1950s, the average marriage age of women in America dropped to 20, and was still dropping, into the teens. Fourteen million girls were engaged by 17. The proportion of women attending college in comparison with men dropped from 47 per cent in 1920 to 35 per cent in 1958. A century earlier, women had fought for higher education; now girls went to college to get a husband. By the mid 1950s, 60 per cent dropped out of college to marry, or because they were afraid too much education would be a marriage bar. Colleges built dormitories for 'married students', but the students were almost always the husbands. A new degree was instituted for the wives – 'Ph.T.' (Putting Husband Through).

Then American girls began getting married in high school. And the women's magazines, deploring the unhappy statistics about these young marriages, urged that courses on marriage, and marriage counsellors, be installed in the high schools. Girls started going steady at twelve and thirteen, in junior high. Manufacturers put out brassières with false bosoms of foam rubber for little girls of ten. And an advertisement for a child's dress, sizes 3–6x, in the *New York Times* in the fall of 1960, said: 'She Too Can Join the Man-Trap Set.'

By the end of the 1950s, the United States birthrate was overtaking India's. Statisticians were especially astounded at the fantastic increase in the number of babies among college women. Where once they had two children, now they had four, five, six. Women who had once wanted careers were now making careers out of having babies. So rejoiced *Life* magazine in a 1956 paean to the movement of American women back to the home.

In a New York hospital, a woman had a nervous breakdown when she found she could not breastfeed her baby. In other hospitals, women dying of cancer refused a drug which research had proved might save their lives: its side effects were said to be unfeminine. 'If I have only one life, let me live it as a blonde', a larger-than-life-sized picture of a pretty, vacuous woman proclaimed from newspaper, magazine, and drug-store ads. And across America, three out of every ten women dyed their hair blonde. They ate a chalk called Metrecal, instead of food, to shrink to the size of the thin young models. Department-store buyers reported that American women, since 1939, had become three and four sizes smaller. 'Women are out to fit the clothes, instead of vice versa,' one buyer said.

Interior decorators were designing kitchens with mosaic murals and original paint-ings, for kitchens were once again the centre of women's lives. Home sewing became a million-dollar industry. Many women no longer left their homes, except to shop, chauffeur their children, or attend a social engagement with their husbands. Girls were growing up in America without ever having jobs outside the home. In the late 1950s, a sociological phenomenon was suddenly remarked: a third of American women now worked, but most were no longer young and very few were pursuing careers. They were married women who held part-time jobs, selling or secretarial, to put their husbands through school, their sons through college, or to help pay the mortgage. Or they were widows supporting families. Fewer and fewer women were entering profes-sional work. The shortages in the nursing, social work, and teaching professions caused crises in almost every American city. Concerned over the Soviet Union's lead in the space race, scientists noted that America's greatest source of unused brainpower was women. But girls would not study physics: it was 'unfeminine'. A girl refused a science fellowship at Johns Hopkins to take a job in a real-estate office. All she wanted, she said, was what every other American girl wanted – to get married, have four children, and live in a nice house in a nice suburb.

The suburban housewife – she was the dream image of the young American women and the envy, it was said, of women all over the world. The American housewife – freed by science and labour-saving appliances from the drudgery, the dangers of childbirth, and the illnesses of her grandmother. She was healthy, beautiful, educated, concerned only about her husband, her children, her home. She had found true feminine fulfillment. As a housewife and mother, she was respected as a full and equal partner to man in his world. She was free to choose automobiles, clothes, appliances, supermarkets; she had everything that women ever dreamed of.

In the fifteen years after the Second World War, this mystique of feminine fulfill-ment became the cherished and self-perpetuating core of contemporary American culture. Millions of women lived their lives in the image of those pretty pictures of the American suburban housewife, kissing their husbands good-bye in front of the picture window, depositing their stationwagonsful of children at school, and smiling as they ran the new electric waxer over the spotless kitchen floor. They baked their own bread, sewed their own and their children's clothes, kept their new washing machines and dryers running all day. They changed the sheets on the beds twice a week instead of once, took the rug-hooking class in adult education, and pitied their poor frustrated mothers, who had dreamed of having a career. They gloried in their role as women, and wrote proudly on the census blank: 'Occupation: housewife'.

For over fifteen years, the words written for women, and the words women used when they talked to each other, while their husbands sat on the other side of the room and talked shop or politics or septic tanks, were about problems with their children, or how to keep their husbands happy, or improve their children's school, or cook chicken, or make slipcovers. Nobody argued whether women were inferior or superior to men; they were simply different. Words like 'emancipation' and 'career' sounded strange and embarrassing; no one had used them for years. When a French-woman named Simon de Beauvoir wrote a book called *The Second Sex*, an American critic commented that she obviously 'didn't know what life was all about', and besides, she was talking about French women. The 'woman problem' in America no longer existed.

If a woman had a problem in the 1950s and 1960s, she knew that something must be wrong with her marriage, or with herself. Other women were satisfied with their lives, she thought. What kind of a woman was she if she did not feel this mysterious fulfilment waxing the kitchen floor? She was so ashamed to admit her dissatisfaction that she never knew how many other women shared it. If she tried to tell her husband, he didn't understand what she was talking about. She did not really understand it herself. For over fifteen years women in America found it harder to talk about this problem than about sex. 'I don't know what's wrong with women today,' a suburban psychiatrist said uneasily. 'I only know something is wrong because most of my patients happen to be women. And their problem isn't sexual.' Most women with this problem did not go to see a psychoanalyst, however. 'There's nothing wrong really,' they kept telling themselves. 'There isn't any problem.'

But on an April morning in 1959, I heard a mother of four, having coffee with four other mothers in a suburban development fifteen miles from New York, say in a tone of quiet desperation, 'the problem'. And the others knew, without words, that she was not talking about a problem with her husband, or her children, or her home. Suddenly they realized they all shared the same problem, the problem that has no name. They began, hesitantly, to talk about it. Later, after they had picked up their children at nursery school and taken them home to nap, two of the women cried, in sheer relief, just to know they were not alone.

Gradually I came to realize that the problem that has no name was shared by countless women in America. As a magazine writer I often interviewed women about problems with their children, or their marriages, or their houses, or their communities. But after a while I began to recognize the telltale signs of this other problem. I saw the same signs in suburban ranch houses and split-levels on Long Island and in New Jersey and Westchester County; in colonial houses in a small Massachusetts town; on patios in Memphis; in suburban and city apartments; in living-rooms in the Midwest. Some-times I sensed the problem, not as a reporter, but as a suburban housewife, for during this time I was also bringing up my own three children in Rockland Country, New York. The groping words I heard from other women, on quiet afternoons when children were at school or on quiet evenings when husbands worked late, I think I understood first as a woman long before I understood their larger social and psychological implications.

Just what was this problem that has no name? What were the words women used when they tried to express it? Sometimes a woman would say 'I feel empty somehow . . . incomplete.' Or she would say, 'I feel as if I don't exist.' Sometimes she blotted out the feeling with a tranquillizer. Sometimes she thought the problem was with her husband, or her children, or that what she really needed was to redecorate her house, or move to a better neighbourhood, or have an affair, or another baby. Sometimes, she went to a doctor with symptoms she could hardly describe: 'A tired feeling . . . I get so angry with the children it scares me . . . I feel like crying without any reason.' (A Cleveland doctor called it 'the housewife's syndrome'.) A number of women told me about great bleeding blisters that break out on their hands and arms. 'I call it the housewife's blight,' said a family doctor in Pennsylvania. 'I see it so often lately in these young women with four, five, and six children, who bury themselves in their dishpans. But it isn't caused by detergent and it isn't cured by cortisone.'

Sometimes a woman would tell me that the feeling gets so strong she runs out of the house and walks through the streets. Or she stays inside her house and cries. Or her children tell her a joke, and she doesn't laugh because she doesn't hear it. I talked to women who had spent years on the analyst's couch, working out their 'adjustment to the feminine role', their blocks to 'fulfilment as a wife and mother'. But the desperate tone in these women's voices, and the look in their eyes, was the same as the tone and the look of other women, who were sure they had no problem, even though they did have a strange feeling of desperation.

Chapter 6

Michel de Certeau

GENERAL INTRODUCTION TO *THE PRACTICE OF EVERYDAY LIFE* [1980]

(**Source**: de Certeau, Michel (1984) *The Practice of Everyday Life,* translated by Steven Rendall, Berkeley, Calif.: University of California Press, pp. xi–xxiv)

Editor's introduction

Michel de Certeau (1925–1986) was a polymath who practised an interdisciplinarity that is often espoused but rarely performed. His wide range of interests and expertise covered religious history, ethnography, psychoanalysis, the history of colonial encounters, and the history of popular culture. His academic homes were similarly diverse, moving between Paris, California (San Diego, University of California, from 1978 to 1984), various European universities and a range of Latin American countries (Brazil, Argentina and Chile).

A preoccupation with everyday life can be seen to increasingly animate his work after the events in Paris of May 1968 (events on which de Certeau was a significant commentator). In 1974 he started work with a team of researchers on a project for the governmental agency Délégation Générale à la Recherche Scientifique et Technique. The project involved

> sketching a *theory of everyday practices* in order to bring out of their murmuring the 'ways of operating' that, as a majority in social life, often only figure as 'resistances' or as apathies in relation to the development of sociocultural production.
>
> (de Certeau, *et al.* 1998: xx)

While de Certeau might at times be considered an obscure and quixotic theorist, his rhetorical panache (and seemingly effortless erudition) is continually marshalled to the job of finding new ways of articulating the opaque realm of the everyday. Never simply a 'critical' theorist, de Certeau seeks to invent new ways of bringing into the light (and thereby actually producing) the inventiveness of the everyday.

This extract is from the first volume of *The Practice of Everyday Life* and is the

General Introduction to the project. In lots of ways this intricate piece of writing is a condensed version of the entire book and repays multiple readings.

Further reading: Ahearne 1995; Buchanan 2000; de Certeau 1997a, 1997b; Highmore 2000a, 2002; Poster 1997.

T HIS ESSAY is part of a continuing investigation of the ways in which users – commonly assumed to be passive and guided by established rules – operate. The point is not so much to discuss this elusive yet fundamental subject as to make such a discussion possible; that is, by means of inquiries and hypotheses, to indicate pathways for further research. This goal will be achieved if everyday practices, 'ways of operating' or doing things, no longer appear as merely the obscure background of social activity, and if a body of theoretical questions, methods, categories, and perspectives, by penetrating this obscurity, make it possible to articulate them.

The examination of such practices does not imply a return to individuality. The social atomism which over the past three centuries has served as the historical axiom of social analysis posits an elementary unit – the individual – on the basis of which groups are supposed to be formed and to which they are supposed to be always reducible. This axiom, which has been challenged by more than a century of sociological, economic, anthropological, and psychoanalytic research (although in history that is perhaps no argument) plays no part in this study. Analysis shows that a relation (always social) determines its terms, and not the reverse, and that each individual is a locus in which an incoherent (and often contradictory) plurality of such relational determinations interact. Moreover, the question at hand concerns modes of operation or schemata of action, and not directly the subjects (or persons) who are their authors or vehicles. It concerns an operational logic whose models may go as far back as the age-old ruses of fishes and insects that disguise or transform themselves in order to survive, and which has in any case been concealed by the form of rationality currently dominant in Western culture. The purpose of this work is to make explicit the systems of operational combination (*les combinatoires d'opérations*) which also compose a 'culture', and to bring to light the models of action characteristic of users whose status as the dominated element in society (a status that does not mean that they are either passive or docile) is concealed by the euphemistic term 'consumers'. Everyday life invents itself by *poaching* in countless ways on the property of others.

1 Consumer production

Since this work grew out of studies of 'popular culture' or marginal groups,[1] the investigation of everyday practices was first delimited negatively by the necessity of not locating cultural *difference* in groups associated with the 'counter-culture' – groups that were already singled out, often privileged, and already partly absorbed into folklore – and that were no more than symptoms or indexes. Three further, positive determinations were particularly important in articulating our research.

Usage, or consumption

Many, often remarkable, works have sought to study the representations of a society, on the one hand, and its modes of behavior, on the other. Building on our knowledge of these social phenomena, it seems both possible and necessary to determine the *use* to which they are put by groups or individuals. For example, the analysis of the images broadcast by television (representation) and of the time spent watching television (behavior) should be complemented by a study of what the cultural consumer 'makes' or 'does' during this time and with these images. The same goes for the use of urban space, the products purchased in the supermarket, the stories and legends distributed by the newspapers, and só on.

The 'making' in question is a production, a *poiēsis*[2] – but a hidden one, because it is scattered over areas defined and occupied by systems of 'production' (television, urban development, commerce, etc.), and because the steadily increasing expansion of these systems no longer leaves 'consumers' any *place* in which they can indicate what they *make* or *do* with the products of these systems. To a rationalized, expansionist and at the same time centralized, clamorous, and spectacular production corresponds *another* production, called 'consumption'. The latter is devious, it is dispersed, but it insinuates itself everywhere, silently and almost invisibly, because it does not manifest itself through its own products, but rather through its *ways of using* the products imposed by a dominant economic order.

For instance, the ambiguity that subverted from within the Spanish colonizers' 'success' in imposing their own culture on the indigenous Indians is well known. Submissive, and even consenting to their subjection, the Indians nevertheless often *made of* the rituals, representations, and laws imposed on them something quite different from what their conquerors had in mind; they subverted them not by rejecting or altering them, but by using them with respect to ends and references foreign to the system they had no choice but to accept. They were *other* within the very colonization that outwardly assimilated them; their use of the dominant social order deflected its power, which they lacked the means to challenge; they escaped it without leaving it. The strength of their difference lay in procedures of 'consumption'. To a lesser degree, a similar ambiguity creeps into our societies through the use made by the 'common people' of the culture disseminated and imposed by the 'elites' producing the language.

The presence and circulation of a representation (taught by preachers, educators, and popularizers as the key to socioeconomic advancement) tells us nothing about what it is for its users. We must first analyze its manipulation by users who are not its makers. Only then can we gauge the difference or similarity between the production of the image and the secondary production hidden in the process of its utilization.

Our investigation is concerned with this difference. It can use as its theoretical model the *construction* of individual sentences with an *established* vocabulary and syntax. In linguistics, 'performance' and 'competence' are different: the act of speaking (with all the enunciative strategies that implies) is not reducible to a knowledge of the language. By adopting the point of view of enunciation – which is the subject of our study – we privilege the act of speaking; according to that point of view, speaking operates within the field of a linguistic system; it effects an appropriation, or reappropriation, of language by its speakers; it establishes a *present* relative to a time and place;

and it posits a *contract with the other* (the interlocutor) in a network of places and relations. These four characteristics of the speech act[3] can be found in many other practices (walking, cooking, etc.). An objective is at least adumbrated by this parallel, which is, as we shall see, only partly valid. Such an objective assumes that (like the Indians mentioned above) users make (*bricolent*) innumerable and infinitesimal trans-formations of and within the dominant cultural economy in order to adapt it to their own interests and their own rules. We must determine the procedures, bases, effects, and possibilities of this collective activity.

The procedures of everyday creativity

A second orientation of our investigation can be explained by reference to Michel Foucault's *Discipline and Punish*. In this work, instead of analyzing the apparatus exercis-ing power (i.e., the localizable, expansionist, repressive, and legal institutions), Foucault analyzes the mechanisms (*dispositifs*) that have sapped the strength of these institutions and surreptitiously reorganized the functioning of power: 'miniscule' technical procedures acting on and with details, redistributing a discursive space in order to make it the means of a generalized 'discipline' (*surveillance*).[4] This approach raises a new and different set of problems to be investigated. Once again, however, this 'microphysics of power' privileges the productive apparatus (which produces the 'discipline'), even though it discerns in 'education' a system of 'repression' and shows how, from the wings as it were, silent technologies determine or short-circuit insti-tutional stage directions. If it is true that the grid of 'discipline' is everywhere becom-ing clearer and more extensive, it is all the more urgent to discover how an entire society resists being reduced to it, what popular procedures (also 'miniscule' and quotidian) manipulate the mechanisms of discipline and conform to them only in order to evade them, and finally, what 'ways of operating' form the counterpart, on the consumer's (or 'dominee's'?) side, of the mute processes that organize the establishment of socioeconomic order.

These 'ways of operating' constitute the innumerable practices by means of which users reappropriate the space organized by techniques of sociocultural production. They pose questions at once analogous and contrary to those dealt with in Foucault's book: analogous, in that the goal is to perceive and analyze the microbe-like operations proliferating within technocratic structures and deflecting their functioning by means of a multitude of 'tactics' articulated in the details of everyday life; contrary, in that the goal is not to make clearer how the violence of order is transmuted into a disciplinary technology, but rather to bring to light the clandestine forms taken by the dispersed, tactical, and make-shift creativity of groups or individuals already caught in the nets of 'discipline.' Pushed to their ideal limits, these procedures and ruses of consumers compose the network of an antidiscipline[5] which is the subject of this book.

The formal structure of practice

It may be supposed that these operations — multiform and fragmentary, relative to situations and details, insinuated into and concealed within devices whose mode of usage they constitute, and thus lacking their own ideologies or institutions – conform to certain rules. In other words, there must be a logic of these practices. We are thus confronted once again by the ancient problem: What is an *art* or 'way of making'? From the Greeks to Durkheim, a long tradition has sought to describe with precision the complex (and not at all simple or 'impoverished') rules that could account for these operations.[6] From this point of view, 'popular culture,' as well as a whole literature called 'popular',[7] take on a different aspect: they present themselves essentially as 'arts of making' this or that, i.e., as combinatory or utilizing modes of consumption. These practices bring into play a 'popular' *ratio*, a way of thinking invested in a way of acting, an art of combination which cannot be dissociated from an art of using.

In order to grasp the formal structure of these practices, I have carried out two sorts of investigations. The first, more descriptive in nature, has concerned certain ways of making that were selected according to their value for the strategy of the analysis, and with a view to obtaining fairly differentiated variants: readers' practices, practices related to urban spaces, utilizations of everyday rituals, re-uses and functions of the memory through the 'authorities' that make possible (or permit) everyday practices, etc. In addition, two related investigations have tried to trace the intricate forms of the operations proper to the recomposition of a space (the Croix-Rousse quarter in Lyons) by familial practices, on the one hand, and on the other, to the tactics of the art of cooking, which simultaneously organizes a network of relations, poetic ways of 'making do' (*bricolage*), and a re-use of marketing structures.[8]

The second series of investigations has concerned the scientific literature that might furnish hypotheses allowing the logic of unselfconscious thought to be taken seriously. Three areas are of special interest. First, sociologists, anthropologists, and indeed historians (from E. Goffman to P. Bourdieu, from Mauss to M. Détienne, from J. Boissevain to E. O. Laumann) have elaborated a theory of such practices, mixtures of rituals and makeshifts (*bricolages*), manipulations of spaces, operators of networks.[9] Second, in the wake of J. Fishman's work, the ethnomethodological and sociolinguistic investigations of H. Garfinkel, W. Labov, H. Sachs, E. A. Schegloff, and others have described the procedures of everyday interactions relative to structures of expectation, negotiation, and improvisation proper to ordinary language.[10]

Finally, in addition to the semiotics and philosophies of 'convention' (from O. Ducrot to D. Lewis),[11] we must look into the ponderous formal logics and their extension, in the field of analytical philosophy, into the domains of action (G. H. von Wright, A. C. Danto, R. J. Bernstein),[12] time (A. N. Prior, N. Rescher and J. Urquhart),[13] and modalisation (G. E. Hughes and M. J. Cresswell, A. R. White).[14] These extensions yield a weighty apparatus seeking to grasp the delicate layering and plasticity of ordinary language, with its almost orchestral combinations of logical elements (temporalization, modalization, injunctions, predicates of action, etc.) whose dominants are determined in turn by circumstances and conjunctural demands. An investigation analogous to Chomsky's study of the oral uses of language must seek to restore to everyday practices their logical and cultural legitimacy, at least in the sectors – still very limited – in which we have at our disposal the instruments necessary to account for them.[15] This kind of research is complicated by the fact that these practices themselves alternately exacerbate and disrupt our logics. Its regrets are like those of the poet, and like him, it struggles against oblivion:

And I forgot the element of chance introduced by circumstances, calm or haste, sun or cold, dawn or dusk, the taste of strawberries or abandonment, the half-understood message, the front page of newspapers, the voice on the telephone, the most anodyne conversation, the most anonymous man or woman, everything that speaks, makes noise, passes by, touches us lightly, meets us head on.[16]

The marginality of a majority

These three determinations make possible an exploration of the cultural field, an exploration defined by an investigative problematics and punctuated by more detailed inquiries located by reference to hypotheses that remain to be verified. Such an exploration will seek to situate the types of *operations* characterizing consumption in the framework of an economy, and to discern in these practices of appropriation indexes of the creativity that flourishes at the very point where practice ceases to have its own language.

Marginality is today no longer limited to minority groups, but is rather massive and pervasive; this cultural activity of the non-producers of culture, an activity that is unsigned, unreadable, and unsymbolized, remains the only one possible for all those who nevertheless buy and pay for the showy products through which a productivist economy articulates itself. Marginality is becoming universal. A marginal group has now become a silent majority.

That does not mean the group is homogeneous. The procedures allowing the re-use of products are linked together in a kind of obligatory language, and their function-ing is related to social situations and power relationships. Confronted by images on television, the immigrant worker does not have the same critical or creative elbow-room as the average citizen. On the same terrain, his inferior access to information, financial means, and compensations of all kinds elicits an increased deviousness, fan-tasy, or laughter. Similar strategic deployments, when acting on different relationships of force, do not produce identical effects. Hence the necessity of differentiating both the 'actions' or 'engagements' (in the military sense) that the system of products effects within the consumer grid, *and* the various kinds of room to maneuver left for consumers by the situations in which they exercise their 'art'.

The relation of procedures to the fields of force in which they act must therefore lead to a *polemological* analysis of culture. Like law (one of its models), culture articu-lates conflicts and alternately legitimizes, displaces, or controls the superior force. It develops in an atmosphere of tensions, and often of violence, for which it provides symbolic balances, contracts of compatibility and compromises, all more or less tem-porary. The tactics of consumption, the ingenious ways in which the weak make use of the strong, thus lend a political dimension to everyday practices.

2 The tactics of practice

In the course of our research, the scheme, rather too neatly dichotomized, of the relations between consumers and the mechanisms of production has been diversified in relation to three kinds of concerns: the search for a problematics that could articulate the material collected; the description of a limited number of practices (reading, talking, walking, dwelling, cooking, etc.) considered to be particularly significant; and the extension of the analysis of these everyday operations to scientific fields apparently governed by another kind of logic. Through the presentation of our investigation along these three lines, the overly schematic character of the general statement can be somewhat nuanced.

Trajectories, tactics, and rhetorics

As unrecognized producers, poets of their own acts, silent discovers of their own paths in the jungle of functionalist rationality, consumers produce through their signifying practices something that might be considered similar to the 'wandering lines' ('*lignes d'erre*') drawn by the autistic children studied by F. Deligny:[17] 'indirect' or 'errant' trajectories obeying their own logic. In the technocratically constructed, written, and functionalized space in which the consumers move about, their trajectories form unforeseeable sentences, partly unreadable paths across a space. Although they are composed with the vocabularies of established languages (those of television, newspapers, supermarkets, or museum sequences) and although they remain subordinated to the prescribed syntactical forms (temporal modes of schedules, paradigmatic orders of spaces, etc.), the trajectories trace out the ruses of other interests and desires that are neither determined nor captured by the systems in which they develop.[18]

Even statistical investigation remains virtually ignorant of these trajectories, since it is satisfied with classifying, calculating, and putting into tables the 'lexical' units which compose them but to which they cannot be reduced, and with doing this in reference to its own categories and taxonomies. Statistical investigation grasps the material of these practices, but not their *form*; it determines the elements used, but not the 'phrasing' produced by the *bricolage* (the artisan-like inventiveness) and the discursiveness that combine these elements, which are all in general circulation and rather drab. Statistical inquiry, in breaking down these 'efficacious meanderings' into units that it defines itself, in reorganizing the results of its analyses according to its own codes, 'finds' only the homogeneous. The power of its calculations lies in its ability to divide, but it is precisely through this ana-lytic fragmentation that it loses sight of what it claims to seek and to represent.[19]

'Trajectory' suggests a movement, but it also involves a plane projection, a flattening out. It is a transcription. A graph (which the eye can master) is substituted for an operation; a line which can be reversed (i.e., read in both directions) does duty for an irreversible temporal series, a tracing for acts. To avoid this reduction, I resort to a distinction between *tactics* and *strategies*.

I call a 'strategy' the calculus of force-relationships which becomes possible when a subject of will and power (a proprietor, an enterprise, a city, a scientific institution) can be isolated from an 'environment'. A strategy assumes a place that can be circumscribed as *proper* (*propre*) and thus serve as the basis for generating relations with an exterior distinct from it (competitors, adversaries, 'clientèles', 'targets', or 'objects' of research). Political, economic, and scientific rationality has been constructed on this strategic model.

I call a 'tactic', on the other hand, a calculus which cannot count on a 'proper' (a spatial or institutional localization), nor thus on a borderline distinguishing the other as a visible totality. The place of a tactic belongs to the other.[20] A tactic insinuates itself into the other's place, fragmentarily, without taking it over in its entirety, without being able to keep it at a distance. It has at its disposal no base where it can capitalize on its advantages, prepare its expansions, and secure independence with respect to circumstances. The 'proper' is a victory of space over time. On the contrary, because it does not have a place, a tactic depends on time – it is always on the watch for opportunities that must be seized 'on the wing'. Whatever it wins, it does not keep. It must constantly manipulate events in order to turn them into 'opportunities'. The weak must continually turn to their own ends forces alien to them. This is achieved in the propitious moments when they are able to combine heterogeneous elements (thus, in the supermarket, the housewife confronts heterogeneous and mobile data – what she has in the refrigerator, the tastes, appetites, and moods of her guests, the best buys and their possible combinations with what she already has on hand at home, etc.); the intellectual synthesis of these given elements takes the form, however, not of a discourse, but of the decision itself, the act and manner in which the opportunity is 'seized'.

Many everyday practices (talking, reading, moving about, shopping, cooking, etc.) are tactical in character. And so are, more generally, many 'ways of operating'; victories of the 'weak' over the 'strong' (whether the strength be that of powerful people or the violence of things or of an imposed order, etc.), clever tricks, knowing how to get away with things, 'hunter's cunning', maneuvers, polymorphic simulations, joyful discoveries, poetic as well as warlike. The Greeks called these 'ways of operating' *mētis*.[21] But they go much further back, to the immemorial intelligence displayed in the tricks and imitations of plants and fishes. From the depths of the ocean to the streets of modern megalopolises, there is a continuity and permanence in these tactics.

In our societies, as local stabilities break down, it is as if, no longer fixed by a circumscribed community, tactics wander out of orbit, making consumers into immigrants in a system too vast to be their own, too tightly woven for them to escape from it. But these tactics introduce a Brownian movement into the system. They also show the extent to which intelligence is inseparable from the everyday struggles and pleasures that it articulates. Strategies, in contrast, conceal beneath objective calculations their connection with the power that sustains them from within the stronghold of its own 'proper' place or institution.

The discipline of rhetoric offers models for differentiating among the types of tactics. This is not surprising, since, on the one hand, it describes the 'turns' or tropes of which language can be both the site and the object, and, on the other hand, these manipulations are related to the ways of changing (seducing, persuading, making use of) the will of another (the audience).[22] For these two reasons, rhetoric, the science of the 'ways of speaking', offers an array of figure-types for the analysis of everyday ways of acting even though such analysis is in theory excluded from scientific discourse. Two logics of action (the one tactical, the other strategic) arise from these two facets of practicing language. In the space of a language (as in that of games), a society makes more explicit the formal rules of action and the operations that differentiate them.

In the enormous rhetorical corpus devoted to the art of speaking or operating, the Sophists have a privileged place, from the point of view of tactics. Their principle was, according to the Greek rhetorician Corax, to make the weaker position seem the stronger, and they claimed to have the power of turning the tables on the powerful by the way in which they made use of the opportunities offered by the particular situation.[23] Moreover, their theories inscribe tactics in a long tradition of reflection on the relationships between reason and particular actions and situations. Passing by way of *The Art of War* by the Chinese author Sun Tzu[24] or the Arabic anthology, *The Book of Tricks*,[25] this tradition of a logic articulated on situations and the will of others continues into contemporary sociolinguistics.

Reading, talking, dwelling, cooking, etc.

To describe these everyday practices that produce without capitalizing, that is, without taking control over time, one starting point seemed inevitable because it is the 'exorbitant' focus of contemporary culture and its consumption: *reading*. From TV to newspapers, from advertising to all sorts of mercantile epiphanies, our society is characterized by a cancerous growth of vision, measuring everything by its ability to show or be shown and transmuting communication into a visual journey. It is a sort of *epic* of the eye and of the impulse to read. The economy itself, transformed into a 'semeiocracy',[26] encourages a hypertrophic development of reading. Thus, for the binary set production-consumption, one would substitute its more general equivalent: writing-reading. Reading (an image or a text), moreover, seems to constitute the maximal development of the passivity assumed to characterize the consumer, who is conceived of as a voyeur (whether troglodytic or itinerant) in a 'show biz society.'[27]

In reality, the activity of reading has on the contrary all the characteristics of a silent production: the drift across the page, the metamorphosis of the text effected by the wandering eyes of the reader, the improvisation and expectation of meanings inferred from a few words, leaps over written spaces in an ephemeral dance. But since he is incapable of stockpiling (unless he writes or records), the reader cannot protect himself against the erosion of time (while reading, he forgets himself and he forgets what he has read) unless he buys the object (book, image) which is no more than a substitute (the spoor or promise) of moments 'lost' in reading. He insinuates into another person's text the ruses of pleasure and appropriation: he poaches on it, is transported into it, pluralizes himself in it like the internal rumblings of one's body. Ruse, metaphor, arrangement, this production is also an 'invention' of the memory. Words become the outlet or product of silent histories. The readable transforms itself into the memorable: Barthes reads Proust in Stendhal's text;[28] the viewer reads the landscape of his childhood in the evening news. The thin film of writing becomes a movement of strata, a play of spaces. A different world (the reader's) slips into the author's place.

This mutation makes the text habitable, like a rented apartment. It transforms another person's property into a space borrowed for a moment by a transient. Renters make comparable changes in an apartment they furnish with their acts and memories; as do speakers, in the language into which they insert both the messages of their native tongue and, through their accent, through their own 'turns of phrase,' etc., their own history; as do pedestrians, in the streets they fill with the forests of their desires and goals. In the same way the users of social codes turn them into metaphors and ellipses of their own quests. The ruling order serves as a support for innumerable productive activities, while at the same time blinding its proprietors to this creativity (like those 'bosses' who simply *can't* see what is being created within their own enterprises).[29] Carried to its limit, this order would be the equivalent of the rules of meter and rhyme for poets of earlier times: a body of constraints stimulating new discoveries, a set of rules with which improvisation plays.

Reading thus introduces an 'art' which is anything but passive. It resembles rather that art whose theory was developed by medieval poets and romancers: an innovation infiltrated into the text and even into the terms of a tradition. Imbricated within the strategies of modernity (which identify creation with the invention of a personal language, whether cultural or scientific), the procedures of contemporary consumption appear to constitute a subtle art of 'renters' who know how to insinuate their countless differences into the dominant text. In the Middle Ages, the text was framed by the four, or seven, interpretations of which it was held to be susceptible. And it was a book. Today, this text no longer comes from a tradition. It is imposed by the generation of a productivist technocracy. It is no longer a referential book, but a whole society made into a book, into the writing of the anonymous law of production.

It is useful to compare other arts with this art of readers. For example, the art of conversationalists: the rhetoric of ordinary conversation consists of practices which transform 'speech situations', verbal productions in which the interlacing of speaking positions weaves an oral fabric without individual owners, creations of a communication that belongs to no one. Conversation is a provisional and collective effect of competence in the art of manipulating 'commonplaces' and the inevitability of events in such a way as to make them 'habitable'.[30]

But our research has concentrated above all on the uses of space,[31] on the ways of frequenting or dwelling in a place, on the complex processes of the art of cooking, and on the many ways of establishing a kind of reliability within the situations imposed on an individual, that is, of making it possible to live in them by reintroducing into them the plural mobility of goals and desires – an art of manipulating and enjoying.[32]

Extensions: prospects and politics

The analysis of these tactics was extended to two areas marked out for study, although our approach to them changed as the research proceeded: the first concerns prospects, or futurology, and the second, the individual subject in political life.

The 'scientific' character of futurology poses a problem from the very start. If the objective of such research is ultimately to establish the intelligibility of present reality, and its rules as they reflect a concern for coherence, we must recognize, on the one hand, the nonfunctional status of an increasing number of concepts, and on the other, the inadequacy of procedures for thinking about, in our case, space. Chosen here as an object of study, space is not really accessible through the usual political and economic determinations; besides, futurology provides no theory of space.[33] The metaphorization of the concepts employed, the gap between the atomization characteristic of research and the generalization required in reporting it, etc., suggest that we take as a definition of futurological discourse the 'simulation' that characterizes its method.

Thus in futurology we must consider: (1) the relations between a certain kind of *rationality* and an imagination (which is in discourse the mark of the locus of its production); (2) the difference between, on the one hand, the tentative moves, pragmatic ruses, and successive *tactics* that mark the stages of practical investigation and, on the other hand, the *strategic* representations offered to the public as the product of these operations.[34]

In current discussions, one can discern the surreptitious return of a rhetoric that metaphorizes the fields 'proper' to scientific analysis, while, in research laboratories, one finds an increasing distance between actual everyday practices (practices of the same order as the art of cooking) and the 'scenarios' that punctuate with utopian images the hum of operations in every laboratory: on the one hand, mixtures of science and fiction; on the other, a disparity between the spectacle of overall strategies and the opaque reality of local tactics. We are thus led to inquire into the 'underside' of scientific activity and to ask whether it does not function as a collage — juxtaposing, but linking less and less effectively, the theoretical ambitions of the discourse with the stubborn persistence of ancient tricks in the everyday work of agencies and laboratories. In any event, this split structure, observable in so many administrations and companies, requires us to rethink all the tactics which have so far been neglected by the epistemology of science.

The question bears on more than the procedures of production: in a different form, it concerns as well the *status of the individual* in technical systems, since the involvement of the subject diminishes in proportion to the technocratic expansion of these systems. Increasingly constrained, yet less and less concerned with these vast frameworks, the individual detaches himself from them without being able to escape them and can henceforth only try to outwit them, to pull tricks on them, to rediscover, within an electronicized and computerized megalopolis, the 'art' of the hunters and rural folk of earlier days. The fragmentation of the social fabric today lends a *political* dimension to the problem of the subject. In support of this claim can be adduced the symptoms represented by individual conflicts and local operations, and even by ecological organizations, though these are preoccupied primarily with the effort to control relations with the environment collectively. These ways of reappropriating the product-system, ways created by consumers, have as their goal a *therapeutics for deteriorating social relations* and make use of techniques of re-employment in which we can recognize the procedures of everyday practices. A politics of such ploys should be developed. In the perspective opened up by Freud's *Civilization and Its Discontents*, such a politics should also inquire into the public ('democratic') image of the microscopic, multiform, and innumerable connections between *manipulating* and *enjoying*, the fleeting and massive reality of a social activity at play with the order that contains it.

Witold Gombrowicz, an acute visionary, gave this politics its hero — the anti-hero who haunts our research — when he gave a voice to the small-time official (Musil's 'man without qualities' or that ordinary man to whom Freud dedicated *Civilization and Its Discontents*) whose refrain is 'When one does not have what one wants, one must want what one has': 'I have had, you see, to resort more and more to very small, almost invisible pleasures, little extras. . . . You've no idea how great one becomes with these little details, it's incredible how one grows.'[35]

Notes

1   See M. de Certeau, *La Prise de parole* (Paris: DDB, 1968); *La Possession de Loudun* (Paris: Julliard-Gallimard, 1970); *L'Absent de l'histoire* (Paris: Mame, 1973): *La Culture au pluriel* (Paris: UGE 10/18, 1974); *Une politique de la langue* (with D. Julia and J. Revel) (Paris: Gallimard, 1975); etc.

2   From the Greek *poiein* 'to create, invent, generate'.

3   See Emile Benveniste, *Problèmes de linguistique générale* (Paris: Gallimard, 1966), 1, 251–266.

4   Michel Foucault, *Surveiller et punir* (Paris: Gallimard, 1975); *Discipline and Punish*, trans. A. Sheridan (New York: Pantheon, 1977).

5   From this point of view as well, the works of Henri Lefebvre on everyday life constitute a fundamental source.

6   On art, from the *Encyclopédie* to Durkheim, see pp. 66–68 [in de Certeau 1984].

7   For this literature, see the booklets mentioned in *Le Livre dans la vie quotidienne* (Paris: Bibliothèque Nationale, 1975) and in Geneviève Bollème, *La Bible bleue, Anthologie d'une littérature 'populaire'* (Paris: Flammarion, 1975), 141–379.

8   The first of these two monographs was written by Pierre Mayol, the second by Luce Giard (on the basis of interviews made by Marie Ferrier). See *L'Invention du quotidien*, II, Luce Giard and Pierre Mayol, *Habiter, cuisiner* (Paris: UGE 10/18, 1980).

9   By Erving Goffman, see especially *Interaction Rituals* (Garden City, NY: Anchor Books, 1976); *The Presentation of Self in Everyday Life* (Woodstock, NY: The Overlook Press, 1973); *Frame Analysis* (New York: Harper & Row, 1974). By Pierre Bourdieu, see *Esquisse d'une théorie de la pratique. Précédée de trois études d'ethnologie kabyle* (Genève: Droz, 1972); 'Les Stratégies matrimoniales', *Annales: économies, sociétés, civilisations* 27 (1972), 1105–1127; 'Le Langage autorisé', *Actes de la recherche en sciences sociales*, No. 5–6 (November 1975), 184–190; 'Le Sens pratique', *Actes de la recherche en sciences sociales*, No. 1 (February 1976), 43–86. By Marcel Mauss, see especially 'Techniques du corps', in *Sociologie et anthropologie* (Paris: PUF, 1950). By Marcel Détienne and Jean-Pierre Vernant, *Les Ruses de l'intelligence. La mètis des Grecs* (Paris: Flammarion, 1974). By Jeremy Boissevain, *Friends of Friends. Networks, Manipulators and Coalitions* (Oxford: Blackwell, 1974). By Edward O. Laumann, *Bonds of Pluralism. The Form and Substance of Urban Social Networks* (New York: John Wiley, 1973).

10 Joshua A. Fishman, *The Sociology of Language* (Rowley, Mass.: Newbury, 1972). See also the essays in *Studies in Social Interaction*, ed. David Sudnow (New York: The Free Press, 1972); William Labov, *Sociolinguistic Patterns* (Philadelphia: University of Pennsylvania Press, 1973); etc.

11 Oswald Ducrot, *Dire et ne pas dire* (Paris: Hermann, 1972); and David K. Lewis, *Convention: a Philosophical Study* (Cambridge, Mass.: Harvard University Press, 1974), and *Counterfactuals* (Cambridge, Mass.: Harvard University Press, 1973).

12 Georg H. von Wright, *Norm and Action* (London: Routledge & Kegan Paul, 1963); *Essay in Deontic Logic and the General Theory of Action* (Amsterdam: North Holland, 1968); *Explanation and Understanding* (Ithaca, NY: Cornell University Press, 1971). And A. C. Danto, *Analytical Philosophy of Action* (Cambridge: Cambridge University Press, 1973); Richard J. Bernstein, *Praxis and Action* (London: Duckworth, 1972); and *La Sémantique de l'action*, ed. Paul Ricoeur and Doriane Tiffeneau (Paris: CNRS, 1977).

13 A. N. Prior, *Past, Present and Future: a Study of 'Tense Logic'* (Oxford: Oxford University Press, 1967) and *Papers on Tense and Time* (Oxford: Oxford University Press, 1968). N. Rescher and A. Urquhart, *Temporal Logic* (Oxford: Oxford University Press, 1975).

14 Alan R. White, *Modal Thinking* (Ithaca, NY: Cornell University Press, 1975); G. E. Hughes and M. J. Cresswell, *An Introduction to Modal Logic* (Oxford: Oxford University Press, 1973); I. R. Zeeman, *Modal Logic* (Oxford: Oxford University Press, 1975); S. Haacker, *Deviant Logic* (Cambridge: Cambridge University Press, 1976); *Discussing Language with Chomsky, Halliday, etc.*, ed. H. Parret (The Hague: Mouton, 1975).

15 As it is more technical, the study concerning the logics of action and time, as well as modalization, will be published elsewhere.

16 Jacques Sojcher, *La Démarche poétique* (Paris: UGE 10/18, 1976), 145.

17 See Fernand Deligny, *Les Vagabonds efficaces* (Paris: Maspero, 1970); *Nous et l'innocent* (Paris: Maspero, 1977); etc.

18   See M. de Certeau, *La Culture au pluriel*, 283–308; and 'Actions culturelles et stratégies politiques', *La Revue nouvelle*, April 1974, 351–360.

19   The analysis of the principles of isolation allows us to make this criticism both more nuanced and more precise. See *Pour une histoire de la statistique* (Paris: INSEE, 1978), 1, in particular Alain Desrosières, 'Eléments pour l'histoire des nomenclatures socio-professionnelles', 155–231.

20   The works of P. Bourdieu and those of M. Détienne and J.-P. Vernant make possible the notion of 'tactic' more precise, but the socio-linguistic investigations of H. Garfinkel, H. Sacks, et al. also contribute to this clarification. See notes 9 and 10.

21   M. Détienne and J.-P. Vernant, *Les Ruses de l'intelligence*.

22   See S. Toulmin, *The Uses of Argument* (Cambridge: Cambridge University Press, 1958); Ch. Perelman and L. Ollbrechts-Tyteca, *Traité de l'argumentation* (Brussels: Université libre, 1970); J. Dubois, et al., *Rhétorique générale* (Paris: Larousse, 1970); etc.

23   The works of Corax, said to be the author of the earliest Greek text on rhetoric, are lost; on this point, see Aristotle, *Rhetoric*, 11, 24, 1402a. See W. K. C. Guthrie, *The Sophists* (Cambridge: Cambridge University Press, 1971), 178–179.

24   Sun Tzu, *The Art of War*, trans. S. B. Griffith (Oxford: Clarendon Press, 1963). Sun Tzu (Sun Zi) should not be confused with the later military theorist Hsün Tzu (Xun Zi).

25   *Le Livre des ruses. La Stratégie politique des Arabes*, ed. R. K. Khawam (Paris: Phébus, 1976).

26   See Jean Baudrillard, *Le Système des objets* (Paris: Gallimard, 1968): *La Société de consommation* (Paris: Denoël, 1970); *Pour une critique de l'économie politique du signe* (Paris: Gallimard, 1972).

27   Guy Debord, *La Société du spectacle* (Paris: Buchet-Chastel, 1967).

28   Roland Barthes, *Le Plaisir du texte* (Paris: Seuil, 1973), 58; *The Pleasure of the Text*, trans. R. Miller (New York: Hill & Wang, 1975).

29   See Gérard Mordillat and Nicolas Philibert, *Ces patrons éclairés qui craignent la lumière* (Paris: Albatros, 1979).

30   See the essays of H. Sacks, E. A. Schegloff, etc., quoted above. This analysis, entitled *Arts de dire*, will be published separately.

31   See Part III, Chapters VII to IX [in de Certeau 1984].

32   We have devoted monographs to these practices in which the proliferating and disseminated bibliography on the subject will be found (see *L'Invention du quotidien*, II, *Habiter, cuisiner*, by Luce Giard and Pierre Mayol).

33   See, for example, A. Lipietz, 'Structuration de l'espace foncier et aménagement du territoire', *Environment and Planning*, A, 7 (1975), 415–425, and 'Approche théorique des transformations de l'espace français', *Espaces et Sociétés*, No. 16 (1975), 3–14.

34   The analyses found in *Travaux et recherches de prospective* published by the Documentation Française, in particular in volumes 14, 59, 65 and 66, and notably the studies by Yves Barel and Jacques Durand have served as the basis for this investigation into futurology. It will be published separately.

35   W. Gombrowicz, *Cosmos* (Paris: Gallimard Folio, 1971), 165–168: originally *Kosmos* (1965); *Cosmos*, trans. E. Mosbacker (London: Macgibbon & Kee, 1967).

Chapter 7

Alice Kaplan and Kristin Ross

INTRODUCTION TO *EVERYDAY LIFE: YALE FRENCH STUDIES* [1987]

(Source: Kaplan, Alice and Ross, Kristin eds (1987) *Everyday Life: Yale French Studies*, 73, pp. 1–4)

Editor's introduction

In 1987 Alice Kaplan and Kristin Ross edited an issue of the journal *Yale French Studies* devoted to everyday life. This collection can be seen as marking a concerted engagement with continental theories of everyday life within Anglophone intellectual culture. Kaplan and Ross convincingly argue that the successful incorporation of French structuralist thought into US universities in the 1960s and 1970s has to be seen in relation to the lack of interest shown towards theorists and theories of everyday life. Structuralism is thereby seen as evidencing a purposeful blindness towards the kinds of social and political questions that relate most strongly to the daily experiences of modern life. In their view 'everyday life theory' offers the possibility of re-engaging the study of culture with the lived experience of social agents.

For Kaplan and Ross the writings of Henri Lefebvre (see Chapter 22) and the Situationists (see Chapter 23) productively intervene between the subjectivism of phenomenology and the 'reified institutions' often described by structuralists. In this edition of *Yale French Studies* the work of Lefebvre and the Situationists is combined with explorations of such diverse topics as street lighting, television weather forecasts, popular music in Paris in the 1930s, and constructions of French culture in American promotion of fashion, food and housing. What these texts have in common is clearly not to be found at the level of manifest content. Their shared orientation becomes more obvious though when contrasted with another body of texts that can be seen to foreground the everyday, namely the work that has famously been associated with British Cultural Studies (Chapter 28 for instance). If British Cultural Studies gravitated towards contemporary subcultures, with an interest in finding cultures of resistance, then these texts offer a more historical orientation and a much more undecided approach to the question of 'power' and 'resistance'. They also continue to engage with the canons of high culture (Rimbaud and Flaubert for instance) albeit in decidedly anti-canonical ways.

Further reading: Kaplan 1993; Rifkin 1993; Kristin Ross 1988; Schivelbusch 1988.

T O   A D V A N C E   A   T H E O R Y of everyday life is to elevate lived experience to the status of a critical concept – not merely in order to describe lived experience, but in order to change it. One of the purposes of this issue is to bring to the attention of an American readership new work informed by such a transformative project: a critique of everyday life elaborated in France in the 1950s and 1960s which remains underacknowledged and little translated in [the United States].

The strain of French thought produced in the 1950s and 1960s which *did* come to be known in American universities with enormous speed and authority was, of course, structuralism and its various derivatives. One of the reasons for the eventual institutional success of structuralism in America was undoubtedly its pedagogical efficiency: techniques of textual analysis could be smoothly transmitted to students who had grown up isolated from French cultural or historical referents. In France the dazzling technical innovations of structuralism were produced during the same decades that saw an intense intellectual and political critique – both inside and outside academic institutions – of consumer society. This questioning was to culminate in the events surrounding May 1968.

Thought so intimately tied up with lived experience and political struggle would obviously not find the same American audience as structuralist discourse, which viewed its arena as textual. Postwar American academics still preoccupied with questions of lived experience and ideological debate tended to formulate those questions within dated existentialist categories involving authenticity and inauthenticity, good faith or bad faith. The critique of everyday life was to concern itself rather with extramoral perceptions; it was to find a small audience in the United States, as in England, Italy and West Germany, primarily among student activists and anarchist groups.

The critique of everyday life in France achieved notoriety with the activities of a fringe group called the Situationists. In the mid-1950s the Situationists formed themselves out of the shards of a number of avantgarde groups, including the dada-inspired International Lettrists, the antifunctionalist Society for an Imaginist Bauhaus, and the Scandinavian COBRA movement. They proclaimed their own era to be 'The Society of the Spectacle' – the historical moment in which the logic of commodities had successfully seized and colonized all social and cultural relations, the totality of everyday life. They took their concept of everyday life from the one first substantially developed in the first volume of Henri Lefebvre's *Critique de la vie quotidienne*, published in 1947 (two more volumes would follow in subsequent decades). Everyday life, defined elliptically as 'whatever remains after one has eliminated all specialized activities', is, Lefebvre argues, a limited historical phenomenon. It is inextricably tied to two parallel developments: first, to the rise of a middle class and the demise of the great 'styles' formerly imposed in western societies by Church and Monarch; second, to the vast migration of those middle classes to urban centers, spaces where their everyday activities would become increasingly organized – hence perceptible.

Cultural interventionists rather than academics, the Situationists interpreted Lefe-bvre's concept of everyday life in an essentially spatial way. They initiated a series of empirico-utopian experiments under the general rubric *psychogeography*: the active study of mental states and spatial ambiances produced by the material organization of the urban terrain. They proposed a division of the city into affective zones or micro-climates; in more or less organized and only carelessly documented traipses through Paris, they surveyed the city for what might be salvaged and used in a utopian reconstruction of social space. To link them to a French utopian/spatial tradition, we might mention several ghost intellectual figures hovering about Situationist activities: the Fourier of a *Nouveau Monde amoureux*; the Lafargue of a *Droit à la paresse*; the Reclus of a radical anticolonialist geography.

Perhaps the best way to appreciate the force of situationist activities is to compare them to traditional Marxist blueprints for action. We can outline two interrelated areas of difference. In their attempts to disrupt the dominant organization of social space, that is, in their essentially synchronic sensibility, the Situationists mark a signifi-cant departure from the diachronically oriented Marxist of the nineteenth century. Staying within a specifically Marxist vocabulary, we might say that the Situationists shifted their attention from the relations of production within the factory to that basic yet undertheorized problem of *social reproduction* – the myriad activities and conditions for existence that must be satisfied in order for relations of production to take place at all. Social reproduction – what we are calling here everyday life – has, of course, become in our own time the urgent issue on a host of political and cultural agendas, most significantly on that of feminism. For everyday life has always weighed heavily on the shoulders of women.

Quotidie: how many times a day? How many days? The quotidian is on the one hand the realm of routine, repetition, reiteration: the space/time where constraints and bore-dom are produced. Far from being an escape from this realm, segmented leisure time such as the weekend is rather a final cog permitting the smooth functioning of the routine. Even at its most degraded, however, the everyday harbors the possibility of its own transformation; it gives rise, in other words, to desires which cannot be satisifed within a weekly cycle of production/consumption. The Political, like the purloined letter, is hidden in the everyday, exactly where it is most obvious: in the contradictions of lived experience, in the most banal and repetitive gestures of everyday life – the commute, the errand, the appointment. It is in the midst of the utterly ordinary, in the space where the dominant relations of production are tirelessly and relentlessly reproduced, that we must look for utopian and political aspirations to crystallize.

At this point it should be clear how our conception of everyday life differs from that great accumulation and inventory of detail undertaken by the Annales School of historiography. Like that of the Annales School, the critique of everyday life we represent here veers away from canonical events and personages. But while the dis-course of permanence produced by the Annales School would recenter history in an immutable village life or in climatic durée, we would insist on the mutable, and specifically on the power of the city both to constrain and to alter consciousness. For this reason, the articles we have included here bear little resemblance to the mimetic effort of cataloguing or describing 'daily living' that has come to be associated with a title like ours.

What does it mean to approach cultural production from the vantage point of everyday life? It means attempting to grasp the everyday without relegating it either to institutional codes and systems or to the private perceptions of a monadic subject. Between, for example, the traffic court and the angry driver who has received a moving violation, we would need to evoke a complex realm of social practice and to map out not merely a network of streets, but a conjunction of habit, desire, and accident.

When it is successful, everyday life analysis offers a new alternative to a subject/object opposition so basic to postwar continental thinking as to correspond to its two major intellectual movements: phenomenology and structuralism. By this we mean that everyday life is situated somewhere in the rift opened up between the subjective, phenomenological, sensory apparatus of the individual and reified institutions. Its starting point is neither the intentional subject dear to humanistic thinking nor the determining paradigms that bracket lived experience. Institutions, codes, and paradigms are not abstract constructs confronting us in some official 'out there'. Nor do we come to institutions alone. We live them in historically specific ways, and we live them — we must insist on this now, when it has become all the more difficult to do so — as collective or as virtually collective subjects.

To read everyday life, what Hegel called 'the prose of the world', is therefore to become engaged in an act of *poesis*. This means, for instance, that the everyday should not be assumed to be some quality inherent only in the great realist or mimetic narratives of the nineteenth and early twentieth centuries. Nor, as we suggested earlier, should it be located only in those specifically mimetic moments in a given text. It means, more importantly, that we understand *poesis* in the sense of a transformative or creative act. Everyday life harbors the texture of social change; to perceive it at all is to recognize the necessity of its conscious transformation.

Everyday life and 'national' culture

INTRODUCTION TO PART TWO

EVERYDAY LIFE necessarily poses questions to the idea of 'national' culture. Does national culture exist and, if so, does it exist at the level of the everyday? In some ways the everyday designates a site of heterogeneous particularity unsuited to being subsumed by the term 'national culture'. On the other hand contemporary everyday life seems to increasingly witness the effects of global forces. The material culture that constitutes the environment of everyday life (clothes, domestic appliances and such like) connect us to a network of transnational finance, and a global (yet also regional and national) proletariat (China, Korea and so on). But if the national is losing its centrality in relation to political economy, at the level of the cultural it still provides a powerful resource of images. And these images continually operate at the level of the everyday. Casting aside academic scepticism for the moment, what images come to mind when we imagine other national cultures? What jumble of sights, sounds and smells pop into consciousness (from the social pre-conscious) when we are asked to think of French-*ness*, or Japanese-*ness*, or Indian-*ness*, or American-*ness*? Do we not tend to locate these imaginary qualities at an everyday level of cuisine, manners, shops, work routines, and so on? And do not these sensory networks also inform a sense of 'our own' national culture?

Yet national culture has never been mono-cultural (think of the specificities of regional cultures) and for centuries national cultures have absorbed, rejected, adjusted to and been enlivened by a variety of cultures circulated through patterns of migration. What is imagined by 'British everyday culture'? And would this imaginary ensemble include or exclude the range of ethnic cultures that empirically constitute Britain? National culture is also contested by 'national' formations whose cultures clearly extend beyond the boundaries of nation-states (the Nation of Islam, for instance).

The 'national' is both a problem and an inevitable condition of everyday life. If we think about what impinges on the everyday, any list would necessarily need to include a number of *national* forms. Newspapers, radio, TV (although increasingly subject to global financial arrangements) continually privilege and promote the nation (national news, national culture, national everyday life). Governments persistently direct and examine everyday life as a national culture (as I write this a national census survey is being conducted about everyday life in the UK). Soap operas, novels, films, celebrity magazines, songs and so on tend to reflect and produce constructions of everyday national culture. How we relate to these, how we identify with these, how closely they match (or not) our experience of everyday life is a way of measuring these cultural significations as well as our everyday lives in relation to 'nation'.

Perhaps, then, so vague a concept as everyday life is ideally suited for the study of such an amorphous and problematic force as national culture.

Chapter 8

Leon Trotsky

HABIT AND CUSTOM [1923]

(**Source**: Trotsky, Leon (1973) *Problems of Everyday Life and Other Writings on Culture and Science*, New York: Monad Press, pp. 25–30)

Editor's introduction

It would be impossible to understand fully the importance of everyday life in social and cultural thought in the twentieth century without taking into consideration the Russian Revolution of 1917. Not only did this spell the start of an experimental moment in transforming everyday life at a national level, but also the success and failure (and, for many, the betrayal) of this experiment reverberates across the general social imagination in relation to the everyday. Leon Trotsky (1879–1940) can be seen as holding a pivotal position in regards to this moment of revolutionary reconfiguring of daily life. If the Soviet experiment is initially caught between an avant-gardist utopianism that would turn everyday life into a work of art, and a bureaucratic desire to organise the everydayness of revolutionary society from the centre, then Trotsky straddles both these tendencies. And it was his commitment to a Cultural Revolution that would *continually* attempt to liberate everyday life from all forms of oppression and alienation that can be seen as an implicit reason for his forced exile from the Soviet Union.

This essay was initially published on 11 July 1923 in *Pravda* (the official newspaper of the Communist Party of the Soviet Union) and along with some other essays on everyday life (also written for *Pravda*) was published in book form in 1924. Trotsky's emphasis on the everyday brings to the surface an incipient feminism, which might be the inevitable outcome of any serious attention to the everyday at this time. In the introduction to the Tatar language edition of the book, Trotsky wrote:

> The central task in the transformation of everyday life is the liberation of women, forced as they have been into the role of mere beasts of burden by the old conditions of the family, household, and economy.
>
> (Trotsky 1973: 79)

At the same time Trotsky recognised how little was actually known about everyday life:

> We must institute a library in which we must collect everything we possess
> relating to the customs of everyday life – classic works on the evolution of the
> family and popular writings on the history of custom – making an investigation
> into the different sides of our daily life.
>
> (Trotsky 1973: 70)

It is this insistence on a cultural politics located at the level of the everyday, alongside a recognition of everyday life's invisibility, that gives Trotsky's thought a continued pertinence for the study of everyday life. But it is also the negotiation between libertarianism and bureaucracy within the complex moment of the Soviet revolution that insists that Trotsky's writing on everyday life (as well as many other Soviet theorists and artists) must be seen within the historical moment of that fascinating and troubling social and national experiment. This is a historical moment whose short life ends in the name of Stalin, a name that signals another kind of attention to the everyday.

Further reading: Boym 1994; Fitzpatrick 2000; Mandel 1979; Matich 1996; Roberts 1998, 1999.

IN THE STUDY OF LIFE it is peculiarly manifest to what an extent individual man is the product of environment rather than its creator. Daily life, i.e., conditions and customs, are, more than economics, 'evolved behind men's backs', in the words of Marx. Conscious creativeness in the domain of custom and habit occupies but a negligible place in the history of man. Custom is accumulated from the elemental experience of men; it is transformed in the same elemental way under the pressure of technical progress or the occasional stimulus of revolutionary struggle. But in the main, it reflects more of the past of human society than of its present.

Our proletariat is not old and has no ancestry. It has emerged in the last ten years partly from the petty townspeople and chiefly from the peasantry. The life of our proletariat clearly reflects its social origin. We have only to recall *The Morals of Rasteryaev Street*, by Gleb Uspensky. What are the main characteristics of the Rasteryaevs, i.e., the Tula workmen of the last quarter of the last century? They are all townsmen or peasants who, having lost all hope of becoming independent men, formed a combination of the uneducated petty bourgeoisie and the destitute. Since then the proletariat has made a big stride, but more in politics than in life and morals. Life is conservative. In its primitive aspect, of course, Rasteryaev Street no longer exists. The brutal treatment accorded to apprentices, the servility practiced before employers, the vicious drunkenness, and the street hooliganism have vanished. But in the relations of husband and wife, parents and children, in the domestic life of the family, fenced off from the whole world, Rasteryaevism is still firmly implanted. We need years and decades of economic growth and culture to banish Rasteryaevism from its last refuge – individual and family life – recreating it from top to bottom in the spirit of collectivism.

Problems of family life were the subject of a particularly heated discussion at a conference of the Moscow propagandists, which we have already mentioned. In regard to this everyone had some grievance. Impressions, observations, and questions, especially, were numerous; but there was no answer to them, for the very questions remain semi-articulate, never reaching the press or being aired at meetings. The life of the ordinary workers and the life of the communists, and the line of contact between the two, provide such a big field for observation, deduction, and practical application!

Our literature does not help us in this respect. Art, by nature, is conservative; it is removed from life and is little able to catch events on the wing as they happen. *The Week*, by Libedinsky, excited a burst of enthusiasm among some of our comrades, an enthusiasm which appeared to me excessive, and dangerous for the young author.[1] In regard to its form, *The Week*, notwithstanding its marks of talent, has the characteristics of the work of a schoolboy. It is only by much persistent, detailed work that Libedinsky can become an artist. I should like to think that he will do so. However, this is not the aspect which interests us at the moment. *The Week* gave the impression of being something new and significant not because of its artistic achievements but because of the 'communist' section of life with which it dealt. But in this respect especially, the matter of the book is not profound. The 'gubkom' is presented to us with too much of the laboratory method; it has no deeper roots and is not organic. Hence, the whole of *The Week* becomes an episodic digression, a novel of revolutionary emigrants drawn from the life. It is, of course, interesting and instructive to depict the life of the 'gubkom' but the difficulty and significance come when the life of communist organization enters into the everyday life of the people. Here, a firm grip is required. The Communist Party at the present moment is the principal lever of every conscious forward movement. Hence, its unity with the masses of the people becomes the root of historic action, reaction, and resistance.

Communist theory is some dozen years in advance of our everyday Russian actuality – in some spheres perhaps even a century in advance. Were this not so, the Communist Party would be no great revolutionary power in history. Communist theory, by means of its realism and dialectical acuteness, finds the political methods for securing the influence of the party in any given situation. But the political idea is one thing, and the popular conception of morals is another. Politics change rapidly, but morals cling tenaciously to the past.

This explains many of the conflicts among the working class, where fresh knowledge struggles against tradition. These conflicts are the more severe in that they do not find their expression in the publicity of social life. Literature and the press do not speak of them. The new literary tendencies, anxious to keep pace with the revolution, do not concern themselves with the usages and customs based on the existing conception of morals, for they want to transform life, not describe it! But new morals cannot be produced out of nothing; they must be arrived at with the aid of elements already existing, but capable of development. It is therefore necessary to recognize what are these elements. This applies not only to the transformation of morals, but to every form of conscious human activity. It is therefore necessary first to know what already exists, and in what manner its change of form is proceeding, if we are to cooperate in the re-creation of morals.

We must first see what is really going on in the factory, among the workers, in the cooperative, the club, the school, the tavern, and the street. All this we have to understand; that is, we must recognize the remnants of the past and the seeds of the future. We must call upon our authors and journalists to work in this direction. They must describe life for us as it emerges from the tempest of revolution.

It is not hard to surmise, however, that appeals alone will not redirect the attentions of our writers. We need proper organization of this matter and proper leadership. The study and enlightenment of working class life must, in the first place, be made the foremost task of journalists – of those, at any rate, who possess eyes and ears. In an organized way we must put them on this work, instruct, correct, lead, and educate them thus to become revolutionary writers, who will write of everyday life. At the same time, we must broaden the angle of outlook of working class newspaper correspondents. Certainly almost any of them could produce more interesting and entertaining correspondence than we have nowadays. For this purpose, we must deliberately formulate questions, set proper tasks, stimulate discussion, and help to sustain it.

In order to reach a higher stage of culture, the working class – and above all its vanguard – must consciously study its life. To do this, it must know this life. Before the bourgeoisie came to power, it had fulfilled this task to a wide extent through its intellectuals. When the bourgeoisie was still an oppositional class, there were poets, painters, and writers already thinking for it.

In France, the eighteenth century, which has been named the century of enlightenment, was precisely the period in which the bourgeois philosophers were changing the conception of social and private morals, and were endeavoring to subordinate morals to the rule of reason. They occupied themselves with political questions, with the church, with the relations between man and woman, with education, etc. There is no doubt but that the mere fact of the discussion of these problems greatly contributed to the raising of the mental level of culture among the bourgeoisie. But all the efforts made by the eighteenth century philosophers towards subordinating social and private relations to the rule of reason were wrecked on one fact – the fact that the means of production were in private hands, and that this was the basis upon which society was to be built up according to the tenets of reason. For private property signifies free play to economic forces which are by no means controlled by reason. These economic conditions determine morals, and so long as the needs of the commodity market rule society, so long is it impossible to subordinate popular morals to reason. This explains the very slight practical results yielded by the ideas of the eighteenth century philosophers, despite the ingenuity and boldness of their conclusions.

In Germany, the period of enlightenment and criticism came about the middle of the last century. 'Young Germany', under the leadership of Heine and Boerne, placed itself at the head of the movement.[2] We here see the work of criticism accomplished by the left wing of the bourgeoisie, which declared war on the spirit of servility, on petty-bourgeois anti-enlightenment education, and on the prejudices of war, and which attempted to establish the rule of reason with even greater skepticism than its French predecessor. This movement amalgamated later with the petty-bourgeois revolution of 1848, which, far from transforming all human life, was not even capable of sweeping away the many little German dynasties.

In our backward Russia, the enlightenment and the criticism of the existing state of society did not reach any stage of importance until the second half of the nineteenth century. Chernyshevsky, Pisarev, and Dobrolyubov, educated in the Belinsky school, directed their criticism much more against the backwardness and reactionary Asiatic character of morals than against economic conditions.[3] They opposed the new realistic human being to the traditional type of man, the new human being who is determined to live according to reason, and who becomes a personality provided with the weapon of critical thought. This movement, connected with the so-called 'popular' evolutionists (Narodniks) had but slight cultural significance.[4] For if the French thinkers of the eighteenth century were only able to gain a slight influence over morals – these being ruled by the economic conditions and not by philosophy – and if the immediate cultural influence of the German critics of society was even less, the direct influence exercised by this Russian movement on popular morals was quite insignificant. The historical role played by these Russian thinkers, including the Narodniks, consisted in preparing for the formation of the party of the revolutionary proletariat.

It is only the seizure of power by the working class which creates the premises for a complete transformation of morals. Morals cannot be rationalized – that is, made congruous with the demands of reason – unless production is rationalized at the same time, for the roots of morals lie in production. Socialism aims at subordinating all production to human reason. But even the most advanced bourgeois thinkers have confined themselves to the ideas of rationalizing technique on the one hand (by the application of natural science, technology, chemistry, invention, machines), and politics on the other (by parliamentarism); but they have not sought to rationalize economics, which has remained the prey of blind competition. Thus the morals of bourgeois society remain dependent on a blind and non-rational element. When the working class takes power, it sets itself the task of subordinating the economic principles of social conditions to a control and to a conscious order. By this means, and only by this means, is there a possibility of consciously transforming morals.

The successes that we gain in this direction are dependent on our success in the sphere of economics. But even in our present economic situation we could introduce much more criticism, initiative, and reason into our morals than we actually do. This is one of the tasks of our time. It is of course obvious that the complete change of morals – the emancipation of woman from household slavery, the social education of children, the emancipation of marriage from all economic compulsion, etc. – will only be able to follow on a long period of development, and will come about in proportion to the extent to which the economic forces of socialism win the upper hand over the forces of capitalism.

The critical transformation of morals is necessary so that the conservative traditional forms of life may not continue to exist in spite of the possibilities for progress which are already offered us today by our sources of economic aid, or will at least be offered tomorrow. On the other hand, even the slightest success in the sphere of morals, by raising the cultural level of the working man and woman, enhance our capacity for rationalizing production, and promoting socialist accumulation. This again gives us the possibility of making fresh conquests in the sphere of morals. Thus a dialectical dependence exists between the two spheres. The economic conditions are the fundamental factor of history, but we, as a Communist Party and as a workers' state, can only influence economics with the aid of the working class, and to attain this we must work unceasingly to promote the technical and cultural capacity of the individual element of the working class. In the workers' state culture works for socialism and socialism again offers the possibility of creating a new culture for humanity, one which knows nothing of class difference.

Notes

1   *Yuri N. Libedinsky* (1898–1959) was a leader of the Russian Association of Proletarian Writers (RAPP). His novel *The Week* (1922) describes the crushing of a counterrevolutionary revolt among the peasantry. Libedinsky's works deal mostly with the lives of Communists during the revolution, civil war, and socialist construction.

   Gubkom is an abbreviation for *gubiernsky komitet*, or provincial committee. The committees were local party organizations in the provinces. – Translator.

2   '*Young Germany*' was a literary movement that began in the 1830s in Germany, strongly influenced by the mood of social unrest and the rise of industrialization.

   Heinrich Heine (1797–1856) was a German lyric poet and literary critic, and one of the best-known members of the 'Young Germany' movement.

   Ludwig Boerne (1786–1837), a leader of 'Young Germany', was a political writer and satirist. He published various journals in which he criticized German theater and German politics, and he emphasized social reforms and political freedom.

3   *Vissarion Belinsky* (1811–1848) was an influential literary critic whose support of socially critical writers affected the course of Russian literature. His writings are regarded by Marxists as an intellectual forerunner of socialist thought in Russia.

   Nikolai Chernyshevksy (1828–1889) was an author and critic whose novel *What Is To Be Done?* influenced the Russian populist movement.

   Dimitri Pisarev (1840–1868) was a literary critic concerned with family problems and with the ethical aspects of socio-economic reforms.

   Nikolai Dobrolyubov (1836–1861) was a journalist and critic and an early revolutionary activist.

4   *The Narodniks* (populists) were an organized movement of Russian intellectuals who conducted activities among the peasantry from 1876 to 1879, when they split into two groups. One was a terrorist group, which was crushed after the assassination of Czar Alexander in 1881. The other was led by Plekhanov, and split again, the Plekhanov group becoming Marxists while the right wing evolved into the Social Revolutionary Party.

Chapter 9

Raymond Williams

CULTURE IS ORDINARY [1958]

(**Source**: Williams, Raymond (1989a) *Resources of Hope: Culture, Democracy, Socialism*, London: Verso, pp. 3–14)

Editor's introduction

Raymond Williams (1921–1988) was a decisive influence on the formation of cultural studies. This early text, with its insistence that 'culture is ordinary, in every society and in every mind', marks out a preoccupation with *lived* culture that was to animate all of Williams's work. For Williams the word 'culture' meant both 'a whole way of life' (culture in the anthropological sense, synonymous with everyday life) and the forms of signification (novels, films, but also advertising and television) that circulate within a society. Thus the challenge for studying culture was to understand how these two meanings of culture coexist. In a society saturated by mass-circulated texts, any clear separation between the two notions of culture becomes impossible. Yet it is clearly a simplification to reduce the experience of culture to those meanings that are most visible (for instance those we find in magazines and on TV). Williams did not provide a solution to this problem; rather he continually strove to foreground the puzzling of culture as a problem. In this sense the idea of 'national culture' becomes an arena for thinking about the problem of ordinary culture within societies where local, national and global meanings circulate and collide.

Describing himself at times as a Welsh European, the correlations between 'nation' and 'culture' were a continual and problematic theme in Williams's writing. It is perhaps in his novels (the first significantly called *Border Country* (1960) – referring both to the region of Wales called the Borders and more metaphorically to the experience of living across local, national and global borders) that he articulates the most local (regional) sense of culture. Yet he also makes it clear that in modern society a sense of culture as a common resource of meaning seems to inevitably impact at the level of 'nation' even if that 'nation' is distinct from the nationalist images peddled by governments and media moguls. In an attempt to provide a form for articulating an experience of a common culture that resonates across both the amalgam of representations and the experience of living culture he coined the phrase 'structures of feeling'. Although a vague term the conjoining of 'structure' and 'feeling' (with all the seemingly irreconcilable differences that the two words suggest) offers a perspective from which to view anthropological culture saturated by a mass of representations. That 'structures of feeling' seem invariably to register a 'national' imaginary is of obvious importance for thinking about everyday life.

Further reading: Eldridge and Eldridge 1994; Hall 1993; Williams [1961] 1992.

T HE BUS STOP WAS OUTSIDE THE CATHEDRAL. I had been looking at the Mappa Mundi, with its rivers out of Paradise, and at the chained library, where a party of clergymen had got in easily, but where I had waited an hour and cajoled a verger before I even saw the chains. Now, across the street, a cinema advertised the *Six-Five Special* and a cartoon version of *Gulliver's Travels*. The bus arrived, with a driver and a conductress deeply absorbed in each other. We went out of the city, over the old bridge, and on through the orchards and the green meadows and the fields red under the plough. Ahead were the Black Mountains, and we climbed among them, watching the steep fields end at the grey walls, beyond which the bracken and heather and whin had not yet been driven back. To the east, along the ridge, stood the line of grey Norman castles; to the west, the fortress wall of the mountains. Then, as we still climbed, the rock changed under us. Here, now, was limestone, and the line of the early iron workings along the scarp. The farming valleys, with their scattered white houses, fell away behind. Ahead of us were the narrower valleys: the steel-rolling mill, the gasworks, the grey terraces, the pitheads. The bus stopped, and the driver and conductress got out, still absorbed. They had done this journey so often, and seen all its stages. It is a journey, in fact, that in one form or another we have all made.

I was born and grew up halfway along that bus journey. Where I lived is still a farming valley, though the road through it is being widened and straightened, to carry the heavy lorries to the north. Not far away, my grandfather, and so back through the generations, worked as a farm labourer until he was turned out of his cottage and, in his fifties, became a roadman. His sons went at thirteen or fourteen on to the farms, his daughters into service. My father, his third son, left the farm at fifteen to be a boy porter on the railway, and later became a signalman, working in a box in this valley until he died. I went up the road to the village school, where a curtain divided the two classes – Second to eight or nine, First to fourteen. At eleven I went to the local grammar school, and later to Cambridge.

Culture is ordinary: that is where we must start. To grow up in that country was to see the shape of a culture, and its modes of change. I could stand on the mountains and look north to the farms and the cathedral, or south to the smoke and the flare of the blast furnace making a second sunset. To grow up in that family was to see the shaping of minds: the learning of new skills, the shifting of relationships, the emergence of different language and ideas. My grandfather, a big hard labourer, wept while he spoke, finely and excitedly, at the parish meeting, of being turned out of his cottage. My father, not long before he died, spoke quietly and happily of when he had started a trade-union branch and a Labour Party group in the village, and, without bitterness, of the 'kept men' of the new politics. I speak a different idiom, but I think of these same things.

Culture is ordinary: that is the first fact. Every human society has its own shape, its own purposes, its own meanings. Every human society expresses these, in institutions, and in arts and learning. The making of a society is the finding of common meanings and directions, and its growth is an active debate and amendment under the pressures of experience, contact, and discovery, writing themselves into the land. The growing society is there, yet it is also made and remade in every individual mind. The making of a mind is, first, the slow learning of shapes, purposes, and meanings, so that work, observation and communication are possible. Then, second, but equal in importance, is the testing of these in experience, the making of new observations, comparisons, and meanings. A culture has two aspects: the known meanings and directions, which its members are trained to; the new observations and meanings, which are offered and tested. These are the ordinary processes of human societies and human minds, and we see through them the nature of a culture: that it is always both traditional and creative; that it is both the most ordinary common meanings and the finest individual meanings. We use the word culture in these two senses: to mean a whole way of life – the common meanings; to mean the arts and learning – the special processes of discovery and creative effort. Some writers reserve the word for one or other of these senses; I insist on both, and on the significance of their conjunction. The questions I ask about our culture are questions about our general and common purposes, yet also questions about deep personal meanings. Culture is ordinary, in every society and in every mind.

Now there are two senses of culture – two colours attached to it – that I know about but refuse to learn. The first I discovered at Cambridge, in a teashop. I was not, by the way, oppressed by Cambridge. I was not cast down by old buildings, for I had come from a country with twenty centuries of history written visibly into the earth: I liked walking through a Tudor court, but it did not make me feel raw. I was not amazed by the existence of a place of learning; I had always known the cathedral, and the bookcases I now sit to work at in Oxford are of the same design as those in the chained library. Nor was learning, in my family, some strange eccentricity; I was not, on a scholarship in Cambridge, a new kind of animal up a brand-new ladder. Learning was ordinary; we learned where we could. Always, from those scattered white houses, it had made sense to go out and become a scholar or a poet or a teacher. Yet few of us could be spared from the immediate work; a price had been set on this kind of learning, and it was more, much more, than we could individually pay. Now, when we could pay in common, it was a good, ordinary life.

I was not oppressed by the university, but the teashop, acting as if it were one of the older and more respectable departments, was a different matter. Here was culture, not in any sense I knew, but in a special sense: the outward and emphatically visible sign of a special kind of people, cultivated people. They were not, the great majority of them, particularly learned; they practised few arts; but they had it, and they showed you they had it. They are still there, I suppose, still showing it, though even they must be hearing rude noises from outside, from a few scholars and writers they call – how comforting a label is! – angry young men. As a matter of fact there is no need to be rude. It is simply that if that is culture, we don't want it; we have seen other people living.

But of course it is not culture, and those of my colleagues who, hating the teashop, make culture, on its account, a dirty word, are mistaken. If the people in the teashop go on insisting that culture is their trivial differences of behaviour, their trivial variations of speech habit, we cannot stop them, but we can ignore them. They are not that important, to take culture from where it belongs.

Yet, probably also disliking the teashop, there were writers I read then, who went into the same category in my mind. When I now read a book such as Clive Bell's *Civilisation*, I experience not so much disagreement as stupor. What kind of life can it be, I wonder, to produce this extraordinary fussiness, this extraordinary decision to call certain things culture and then separate them, as with a park wall, from ordinary people and ordinary work? At home we met and made music, listened to it, recited and listened to poems, valued fine language. I have heard better music and better poems since; there is the world to draw on. But I know, from the most ordinary experience, that the interest is there, the capacity is there. Of course, farther along that bus journey, the old social organization in which these things had their place has been broken. People have been driven and concentrated into new kinds of work, new kinds of relationship; work, by the way, which built the park walls, and the houses inside them, and which is now at last bringing, to the unanimous disgust of the teashop, clean and decent and furnished living to the people themselves. Culture is ordinary: through every change let us hold fast to that.

The other sense, or colour, that I refuse to learn, is very different. Only two English words rhyme with culture, and these, as it happens, are sepulture and vulture. We don't yet call museums or galleries or even universities culture-sepultures, but I hear a lot, lately, about culture-vultures (man must rhyme), and I hear also, in the same North Atlantic argot, of do-gooders and highbrows and superior prigs. Now I don't like the teashop, but I don't like this drinking-hole either. I know there are people who are humourless about the arts and learning, and I know there is a difference between goodness and sanctimony. But the growing implications of this spreading argot – the true cant of a new kind of rogue – I reject absolutely. For, honestly, how can anyone use a word like 'do-gooder' with this new, offbeat complacency? How can anyone wither himself to a state where he must use these new flip words for any attachment to learning or the arts? It is plain that what may have started as a feeling about hypocrisy, or about pretentiousness (in itself a two-edged word), is becoming a guilt-ridden tic at the mention of any serious standards whatever. And the word 'culture' has been heavily compromised by this conditioning: Goering reached for his gun; many reach for their chequebooks; a growing number, now, reach for the latest bit of argot.

'Good' has been drained of much of its meaning, in these circles, by the exclusion of its ethical content and emphasis on a purely technical standard; to do a good job is better than to be a do-gooder. But do we need reminding that any crook can, in his own terms, do a good job? The smooth reassurance of technical efficiency is no substitute for the whole positive human reference. Yet men who once made this reference, men who were or wanted to be writers or scholars, are now, with every appearance of satisfaction, advertising men, publicity boys, names in the strip newspapers. These men were given skills, given attachments, which are now in the service of the most brazen money-grabbing exploitation of the inexperience of ordinary people. And it is these men – this new, dangerous class – who have invented and disseminated the argot, in an attempt to influence ordinary people – who because they do real work have real standards in the fields they know – against real standards in the fields these men knew and have abandoned. The old cheapjack is still there in the market, with the country boys' half-crowns on his reputed packets of gold rings or watches. He thinks of his victims as a slow, ignorant crowd, but they live, and farm, while he coughs behind his portable stall. The new cheapjack is in offices with contemporary *décor*, using scraps of linguistics, psychology and sociology to influence what he thinks of as the mass mind. He too, however, will have to pick up and move on, and meanwhile we are not to be influenced by his argot; we can simply refuse to learn it. Culture is ordinary. An interest in learning or the arts is simple, pleasant and natural. A desire to know what is best, and to do what is good, is the whole positive nature of man. We are not to be scared from these things by noises. There are many versions of what is wrong with our culture. So far I have tried only to clear away the detritus which makes it difficult for us to think seriously about it at all. When I got to Cambridge I encountered two serious influences which have left a very deep impression on my mind. The first was Marxism, the second the teaching of Leavis. Through all subsequent disagreement I retain my respect for both.

The Marxists said many things, but those that mattered were three. First, they said that a culture must be finally interpreted in relation to its underlying system of production. I have argued this theoretically elsewhere – it is a more difficult idea than it looks – but I still accept its emphasis. Everything I had seen, growing up in that border country, had led me towards such an emphasis: a culture is a whole way of life, and the arts are part of a social organization which economic change clearly radically affects. I did not have to be taught dissatisfaction with the existing economic system, but the subsequent questions about our culture were, in these terms, vague. It was said that it was a class-dominated culture, deliberately restricting a common inheritance to a small class, while leaving the masses ignorant. The fact of restriction I accepted – it is still very obvious that only the *deserving* poor get much educational opportunity, and I was in no mood, as I walked about Cambridge, to feel glad that I had been thought deserving; I was no better and no worse than the people I came from. On the other hand, just because of this, I got angry at my friends' talk about the ignorant masses: one kind of Communist has always talked like this, and has got his answer, at Poznan and Budapest, as the imperialists, making the same assumption, were answered in India, in Indo-China, in Africa. There is an English bourgeois culture, with its powerful educational, literary and social institutions, in close contact with the actual centres of power. To say that most working people are excluded from these is self-evident, though the doors, under sustained pressure, are slowly opening. But to go on to say that working people are excluded from English culture is nonsense; they have their own growing institutions, and much of the strictly bourgeois culture they would in any case not want. A great part of the English way of life, and of its arts and learning, is not bourgeois in any discoverable sense. There are institutions, and common meanings, which are in no sense the sole product of the commercial middle class; and there are art and learning, a common English inheritance, produced by many kinds of men, including many who hated the very class and system which now take pride in consuming it. The bourgeoisie has given us much, including a narrow but real system of morality; that is at least better than its court predecessors. The leisure which the bourgeoisie attained has given us much of cultural value. But this is not to say that

contemporary culture is bourgeois culture: a mistake that everyone, from Conserva-
tives to Marxists, seems to make. There is a distinct working-class way of life, which I
for one value – not only because I was bred in it, for I now, in certain respects, live
differently. I think this way of life, with its emphases of neighbourhood, mutual
obligation, and common betterment, as expressed in the great working-class political
and industrial institutions, is in fact the best basis for any future English society. As for
the arts and learning, they are in a real sense a national inheritance, which is, or should
be, available to everyone. So when the Marxists say that we live in a dying culture, and
that the masses are ignorant, I have to ask them, as I asked them then, where on earth
they have lived. A dying culture, and ignorant masses, are not what I have known
and see.

What I had got from the Marxists then, so far, was a relationship between culture
and production, and the observation that education was restricted. The other things I
rejected, as I rejected also their third point, that since culture and production are
related, the advocacy of a different system of production is in some way a cultural
directive, indicating not only a way of life but new arts and learning. I did some writing
while I was, for eighteen months, a member of the Communist Party, and I found out
in trivial ways what other writers, here and in Europe, have found out more gravely:
the practical consequences of this kind of theoretical error. In this respect, I saw the
future, and it didn't work. The Marxist interpretation of culture can never be accepted
while it retains, as it need not retain, this directive element, this insistence that if you
honestly want socialism you must write, think, learn in certain prescribed ways. A
culture is common meanings, the product of a whole people, and offered individual
meanings, the product of a man's whole committed personal and social experience. It
is stupid and arrogant to suppose that any of these meanings can in any way be
prescribed; they are made by living, made and remade, in ways we cannot know in
advance. To try to jump the future, to pretend that in some way you *are* the future, is
strictly insane. Prediction is another matter, an offered meaning, but the only thing we
can say about culture in an England that has socialized its means of production is that
all the channels of expression and communication should be cleared and open, so that
the whole actual life, that we cannot know in advance, that we can know only in part
even while it is being lived, may be brought to consciousness and meaning.

Leavis has never liked Marxists, which is in one way a pity, for they know more
than he does about modern English society, and about its immediate history. He, on
the other hand, knows more than any Marxist I have met about the real relations
between art and experience. We have all learned from him in this, and we have also
learned his version of what is wrong with English culture. The diagnosis is radical, and
is rapidly becoming orthodox. There was an old, mainly agricultural England, with a
traditional culture of great value. This has been replaced by a modern, organized,
industrial state, whose characteristic institutions deliberately cheapen our natural
human responses, making art and literature into desperate survivors and witnesses,
while a new mechanized vulgarity sweeps into the centres of power. The only defence
is in education, which will at least keep certain things alive, and which will also, at
least in a minority, develop ways of thinking and feeling which are competent to
understand what is happening and to maintain the finest individual values. I need not
add how widespread this diagnosis has become, though little enough acknowledgement is still made to Leavis himself. For my own part, I was deeply impressed by it;

deeply enough for my ultimate rejection of it to be a personal crisis lasting several years.

For, obviously, it seemed to fit a good deal of my experience. It did not tell me that my father and grandfather were ignorant wage-slaves; it did not tell me that the smart, busy, commercial culture (which I had come to as a stranger, so much so that for years I had violent headaches whenever I passed through London and saw underground advertisements and evening newspapers) was the thing I had to catch up with. I even made a fool of myself, or was made to think so, when after a lecture in which the usual point was made that 'neighbour' now does not mean what it did to Shakespeare, I said – imagine! – that to me it did. (When my father was dying, this year, one man came in and dug his garden; another loaded and delivered a lorry of sleepers for firewood; another came and chopped the sleepers into blocks; another – I don't know who, it was never said – left a sack of potatoes at the back door; a woman came in and took away a basket of washing.) But even this was explicable; I came from a bit of the old society, but my future was Surbiton (it took me years to find Surbiton, and have a good look at it, but it's served a good many as a symbol – without having lived there I couldn't say whether rightly). So there I was, and it all seemed to fit.

Yet not all. Once I got away, and thought about it, it didn't really fit properly. For one thing I knew this: at home we were glad of the Industrial Revolution, and of its consequent social and political changes. True, we lived in a very beautiful farming valley, and the valleys beyond the limestone we could all see were ugly. But there was one gift that was overriding, one gift which at any price we would take, the gift of power that is everything to men who have worked with their hands. It was slow in coming to us, in all its effects, but steam power, the petrol engine, electricity, these and their host of products in commodities and services, we took as quickly as we could get them, and were glad. I have seen all these things being used, and I have seen the things they replaced. I will not listen with patience to any acid listing of them – you know the sneer you can get into plumbing, baby Austins, aspirin, contraceptives, canned food. But I say to these Pharisees: dirty water, an earth bucket, a four-mile walk each way to work, headaches, broken women, hunger and monotony of diet. The working people, in town and country alike, will not listen (and I support them) to any account of our society which supposes that these things are not progress: not just mechanical, external progress either, but a real service of life. Moreover, in the new conditions, there was more real freedom to dispose of our lives, more real personal grasp where it mattered, more real say. Any account of our culture which explicitly or implicitly denies the value of an industrial society is really irrelevant; not in a million years would you make us give up this power.

So then the social basis of the case was unacceptable, but could one, trying to be a writer, a scholar, a teacher, ignore the indictment of the new cultural vulgarity? For the plumbing and the tractors and the medicines could one ignore the strip newspapers, the multiplying cheapjacks, the raucous triviality? As a matter of priorities, yes, if necessary; but was the cheapening of response really a consequence of the cheapening of power? It looks like it, I know, but is this really as much as one can say? I believe the central problem of our society, in the coming half-century, is the use of our new resources to make a good common culture; the means to a good, abundant economy we already understand. I think the good common culture can be made, but before we can be serious about this, we must rid ourselves of a legacy from our most useful critics — a legacy of two false equations, one false analogy, and one false proposition.

The false proposition is easily disposed of. It is a fact that the new power brought ugliness: the coal brought dirt, the factory brought overcrowding, communications brought a mess of wires. But the proposition that ugliness is a price we pay, or refuse to pay, for economic power need no longer be true. New sources of power, new methods of production, improved systems of transport and communication can, quite practically, make England clean and pleasant again, and with much more power, not less. Any new ugliness is the product of stupidity, indifference, or simply incoordination; these things will be easier to deal with than when power was necessarily noisy, dirty, and disfiguring.

The false equations are more difficult. One is the equation between popular education and the new commercial culture: the latter proceeding inevitably from the former. Let the masses in, it is said, and this is what you inevitably get. Now the question is obviously difficult, but I can't accept this equation, for two reasons. The first is a matter of faith: I don't believe that the ordinary people in fact resemble the normal description of the masses, low and trivial in taste and habit. I put it another way: that there are in fact no masses, but only ways of seeing people as masses. With the coming of industrialism, much of the old social organization broke down and it became a matter of difficult personal experience that we were constantly seeing people we did not know, and it was tempting to mass them, as 'the others', in our minds. Again, people were physically massed, in the industrial towns, and a new class structure (the names of our social classes, and the word 'class' itself in this sense, date only from the Industrial Revolution) was practically imposed. The improvement in communications, in particular the development of new forms of multiple transmission of news and entertainment, created unbridgeable divisions between transmitter and audience, which again led to the audience being interpreted as an unknown mass. Masses became a new word for mob: the others, the unknown, the unwashed, the crowd beyond one. As a way of knowing other people, this formula is obviously ridiculous, but, in the new conditions, it seemed an effective formula — the only one possible. Certainly it was the formula that was used by those whose money gave them access to the new communication techniques; the lowness of taste and habit, which human beings assign very easily to other human beings, was assumed, as a bridge. The new culture was built on this formula, and if I reject the formula, if I insist that this lowness is not inherent in ordinary people, you can brush my insistence aside, but I shall go on holding to it. A different formula, I know from experience, gets a radically different response.

My second reason is historical: I deny, and can prove my denial, that popular education and commercial culture are cause and effect. I have shown elsewhere that the myth of 1870 — the Education Act which is said to have produced, as its children grew up, a new cheap and nasty press — is indeed myth. There was more than enough literacy, long before 1870, to support a cheap press, and in fact there were cheap and really bad newspapers selling in great quantities before the 1870 Act was heard of. The bad new commercial culture came out of the social chaos of industrialism, and out of the success, in this chaos, of the 'masses' formula, not out of popular education. Northcliffe did few worse things than start this myth, for while the connection between bad culture and the social chaos of industrialism is significant, the connection between it and popular education is vicious. The Northcliffe Revolution, by the way, was a radical change in the financial structure of the press, basing it on a new kind of revenue – the new mass advertising of the 1890s – rather than the making of a cheap popular press, in which he had been widely and successfully preceded. But I tire of making these points. Everyone prefers to believe Northcliffe. Yet does nobody, even a Royal Commission, read the most ordinarily accessible newspaper history? When people do read the history, the false equation between popular education and commercial culture will disappear for ever. Popular education came out of the other camp, and has had quite opposite effects.

The second false equation is this: that the observable badness of so much widely distributed popular culture is a true guide to the state of mind and feeling, the essential quality of living of its consumers. Too many good men have said this for me to treat it lightly, but I still, on evidence, can't accept it. It is easy to assemble, from print and cinema and television, a terrifying and fantastic congress of cheap feelings and moronic arguments. It is easy to go on from this and assume this deeply degrading version of the actual lives of our contemporaries. Yet do we find this confirmed, when we meet people? This is where 'masses' comes in again, of course: the people *we* meet aren't vulgar, but God, think of Bootle and Surbiton and Aston! I haven't lived in any of those places; have you? But a few weeks ago I was in a house with a commercial traveller, a lorry driver, a bricklayer, a shopgirl, a fitter, a signalman, a nylon operative, a domestic help (perhaps, dear, she is your very own treasure). I hate describing people like this, for in fact they were my family and family friends. Now they read, they watch, this work we are talking about; some of them quite critically, others with a good deal of pleasure. Very well, I read different things, watch different entertainments, and I am quite sure why they are better. But could I sit down in that house and make this equation we are offered? Not, you understand, that shame was stopping me; I've learned, thank you, how to behave. But talking to my family, to my friends, talking, as we were, about our own lives, about people, about feelings, could I in fact find this lack of quality we are discussing? I'll be honest – I looked; my training has done that for me. I can only say that I found as much natural fineness of feeling, as much quick discrimination, as much clear grasp of ideas within the range of experience as I have found anywhere. I don't altogether understand this, though I am not really surprised. Clearly there is something in the psychology of print and image that none of us has yet quite grasped. For the equation looks sensible, yet when you test it, in experience – and there's nowhere else you can test it – it's wrong. I can understand the protection of critical and intelligent reading: my father, for instance, a satisfied reader of the *Daily Herald*, got simply from reading the company reports a clear idea, based on names, of the rapid development of combine and interlocking ownership in British industry, which I had had made easy for me in two or three academic essays; and he had gone on to set these facts against the opinions in a number of articles in the paper on industrial ownership. That I understand; that is simply intelligence, however partly trained. But there is still this other surprising fact: that people whose quality of personal living is high are apparently satisfied by a low quality of printed feeling and opinion. Many of them still live, it is true, in a surprisingly enclosed personal world, much more so than mine, and some of their personal observations are the finer for it. Perhaps this is enough to explain it, but in any case, I submit, we need a new equation, to fit the observable facts.

Now the false analogy, that we must also reject. This is known, in discussions of culture, as a 'kind of Gresham's Law'. Just as bad money will drive out good, so bad culture will drive out good, and this, it is said, has in fact been happening. If you can't see, straight away, the defect of the analogy, your answer, equally effective, will have to be historical. For in fact, of course, it has not been happening. There is more, much more bad culture about; it is easier, now, to distribute it, and there is more leisure to receive it. But test this in any field you like, and see if this has been accompanied by a shrinking consumption of things we can all agree to be good. The editions of good literature are very much larger than they were; the listeners to good music are much more numerous than they were; the number of people who look at good visual art is larger than it has ever been. If bad newspapers drive out good newspapers, by a kind of Gresham's Law, why is it that, allowing for the rise in population, *The Times* sells nearly three times as many copies as in the days of its virtual monopoly of the press, in 1850? It is the law I am questioning, not the seriousness of the facts as a whole. Instead of a kind of Gresham's Law, keeping people awake at nights with the now orthodox putropian nightmare, let us put it another way, to fit the actual facts: we live in an expanding culture, and all the elements in this culture are themselves expanding. If we start from this, we can then ask real questions: about relative rates of expansion; about the social and economic problems raised by these; about the social and economic answers. I am working now on a book to follow my *Culture and Society*, trying to interpret, historically and theoretically, the nature and conditions of an expanding culture of our kind. I could not have begun this work if I had not learned from the Marxists and from Leavis; I cannot complete it unless I radically amend some of the ideas which they and others have left us.

Chapter 10

Karal Ann Marling

NIXON IN MOSCOW: THE KITCHEN DEBATE [1994]

(Source: Marling, Karal Ann (1994) *As Seen on TV: The Visual Culture of Everyday Life in the 1950s*, Cambridge, Mass. and London: Harvard University Press, pp. 243–50, 271–6)

Editor's introduction

Karal Ann Marling is a historian of popular visual and material culture. Her book *As Seen on TV: The Visual Culture of Everyday Life in the 1950s* is concerned with a variety of cultural practices: fashion, domestic appliances, cooking, cars and so on. While such material is in itself characteristic of the landscape of everyday life in a culture dominated by the commodity, Marling's focus emphasises the way that national culture acts as a context which saturates this material with meaning. By looking not simply at the practices and materials 'themselves', but at the way they were mediated by television, she attends to a national medium that in the postwar years can be seen as a central arena for the everyday. TV perhaps more than any other medium brings the world into the domestic sphere as everyday culture (the *daily* bombings, the *daily* suffering, the *daily* conquests and so on). And it brings the world into the home as national culture: after all national TV networks 'unite' cultures at the level of shared iconic and narrative material.

In this extract she gives an account of the way that the signs of US affluence were used for the articulation of cold war values. Alongside the more familiar 'heroic' narratives of two superpowers, battling for supremacy in the development of nuclear weapons and space travel, lies a more domestic, a more everyday story. The American Exhibition in Moscow in 1959 promoted an image of everyday life in the USA as streamlined, ultra-modern and luxurious. It did this by displaying (as trophies of success) dishwashers, Pepsi-Cola, cookers, fridges and fully automated kitchens. The 'American way of life' (or western capitalism more generally) was portrayed as fun, clean, technologically advanced and available to all (at least ideologically if not financially). These simulations of US domestic life are both everyday (they present the environment most insistently associated with the everyday) and non-everyday (obviously unused they are also designed to transcend the dreariness of everyday domesticity). For many Soviet commentators such a vision of life, with its emphasis on domestic gadgetry, was absurdly trivial. The image of Nikita Khrushchev and Richard Nixon meeting head to head across kitchen displays filled with the latest modern 'conveniences' distils a relationship between everyday life and national culture filled with bathos and ambiguity.

Further reading: Baxandall and Ewen 2000; Hine 1987; Silverstone 1996; Woodham 1997.

THE BATTLE BEGAN IN THE MORNING, with a sharp exchange on the subject of automatic washers in the kitchen of a typical, six-room, $14,000 ranch house put up by a Long Island builder of subdivisions and furnished by Macy's. It resumed in the evening, in a $250,000 RCA Whirlpool 'miracle' kitchen controlled by an electronic brain: at the push of a button, the dishwasher scurried to the dining table along an invisible track and a robot cleaner polished the floor. The combatants were two men lacking any prior association with household appliances, and the unlikely venue for their so-called Kitchen Debate was Sokolniki Park, in a leafy quarter of Moscow. But there, in July of 1959, at the height of the Cold War, the Soviet Premier and the Vice President of the United States locked horns over spin cycles, in-house intercom systems, and American domestic gadgetry in general. To Richard Nixon, the latest in kitchen consumerism stood for the basic tenets of the American way of life. Freedom. Freedom from drudgery for the housewife. And democracy, the opportunity to choose the very best model from the limitless assortment of colors, features, and prices the free market had to offer. To Nikita Khrushchev, the whole U.S. Exhibition was a display of wretched excess and bourgeois trivia. Where were the scientific displays, the American Sputniks? 'What is this?' asked the newspaper *Izvestia*. 'A national exhibit of a great country, or a branch department store?'[1]

Created under the provisions of a 1958 protocol agreement on the exchange of expositions of 'science, technology and culture', the $5 million American show had suffered from congressional parsimony. As a result, many details, including the golden geodesic dome by the visionary architect Buckminster Fuller through which Russian visitors (with hard-to-come-by one-ruble tickets) entered the grounds, were borrowed from successful American outings at international trade fairs. The Whirlpool kitchen (Figure 10.1), for example, had already appeared at a 1958 product show in Milan, while other planned attractions, like a fashion show presented as a series of vignettes from American life, had been tried out at the Brussels World's Fair of the same year. Model homes and supermarkets dramatized the benefits of mass production for the average American family. As such, they were always important Cold War propaganda devices, offering compelling, tangible evidence of the superiority of the economic system that so casually spewed forth labor-saving marvels, frozen dinners (steak and french fries), and tasteful living rooms furnished by *House Beautiful*. Although official government policy held that displays of consumer goods would inspire businesses in underdeveloped countries to produce items suitable for the vast American market and open new markets for American firms in nations still recovering from the ravages of World War II, these American showrooms also seem calculated to

Figure 10.1 The 'Mechanical Maid' scrubbed the floor and then put itself away in the RCA Whirlpool Miracle Kitchen at Moscow, 1959

arouse envy and discontent at a basic level of appetite, haptic pleasure, and sensory overload. And the Moscow Exhibition was even more dazzling than most.[2]

Inside the Fuller dome, a new IBM computer programmed to answer questions about American life was overshadowed by a series of seven giant TV screens that showed in living color and material specificity what printed words on a punchcard could never capture. One twelve-minute show, by the designers Charles and Ray Eames, traced the American workday in 2,000 flashing images. A second, by Hollywood director Billy Wilder, celebrated weekend leisure. Like a Hollywood movie, the America conjured up in Moscow's multiscreen TV autobiography was pictorial – not logical or spiritual or poetic. It was a look, a dream, something tantalizing to touch kept just beyond the reach of yearning fingers. Behind the dome and the enticing pictures, a glass pavilion with a pleated, fan-shaped roof held a modular 'jungle gym' or rack of metal with inset plastic panels in which more than 5,000 pots and pans, dishes, rolling pins, and small appliances were showcased like so many precious jewels: spectators could see the items from a special viewing balcony, but they remained just out of reach.[3]

Ironically, the Soviets themselves may have reinforced the impression that consumer products were forbidden fruit in the USSR by refusing to allow the distribution of free Coty lipsticks and, after long lines testified to public interest, by denying Russian women access to free makeovers at Helena Rubenstein's model beauty salon. When visitors did get close enough to touch, the result was pandemonium. In the opening days, they mistook the contents of the model supermarket for samples and nearly cleaned out the stock. They reached over the barriers and fingered the upholstery in the model home. Free glasses of Pepsi, dispensed from a kiosk between the glass pavilion and the model home, were consumed at a rate of 10,000 per hour for the forty-two-day duration of the show.[4]

There was a heart-lung machine in the dome, an art show in the pavilion, and a shed housing farm machinery adjacent to the restrooms and the exit, but the overall tenor of the U.S. Exhibition in Moscow was as effervescent as a Pepsi-Cola. The ultimate consumer frivolity, Pepsi had taken aim squarely at the housewife in the late 1940s and 50s. Pepsi was the take-home drink in the elegant new 'swirl' bottle. Less sugary, less substantial than the competition, it was the light drink, the one that guarded milady's slender, youthful image.[5] And image – specifically, an image of stylish domesticity, of exuberance and fizz – was the basis of the Moscow show.

The American home and the new iconographic center of that house, the kitchen, made up the core of the display, reinforced by the offerings of almost 800 manufacturers of sewing machines (a very popular demonstration), hi-fi sets, convenience foods, and lounge chairs. There were twenty-two cars, representing the latest 1959 models from all Detroit's leading automakers. There was a circular movie theater developed by Walt Disney. Under a cluster of plastic parasols planted in the park outside the buildings, the rituals of American family life, from the wedding and the honeymoon to the backyard barbecue and the country club dance, were enacted four times daily by fashion models in typical American outfits; in another outdoor enclosure were photographs and miniatures of typical American buildings, including churches, schools, and shopping centers. The Moscow Exhibition was 'an American Showcase', concluded one business journal.[6] It was also a shopping center on a grand, international scale. And what was for sale was nothing less than 'the American way of life'.

The items on display in Moscow – the houses, the groceries, the fancy cars, the pretty clothes – came from the everyday experience of individual Americans. They weren't abstractions or constructs. They were somebody's, everybody's, definition of the good life in the affluent 1950s. As such, they were the decade's most powerful icons, the things everybody thought about first when that lifestyle came under attack. A bizarre example of such 'contested' symbolism comes from a famous *Life* picture-essay on a Miami couple who spent their two-week honeymoon in a bomb shelter in August of 1959, less than a month after the Kitchen Debate in Moscow. Lured underground by a publicity-hungry builder, Mr. and Mrs. Minison did not go unprepared: their 'wedding gifts' included an impressive array of canned goods, brand-name cereals, cigarettes, and assorted doodads spread out on the lawn around them for the benefit of *Life*'s photographer.[7]

[. . .]

Nixon's meeting with Khrushchev in Sokolniki Park should have been a bland ceremonial affair; the Vice President had come to Moscow to do the same honors Comrade Kozlov had performed so amiably at the New York Coliseum. And Ike [President Eisenhower] pointedly reminded his second-in-command that he had no authority to negotiate with the Russians. What turned the encounter from a formality into an attention-grabbing debate was the Captive Nations Resolution. Passed by a Republican Congress every session since 1953, the legislation required the President to proclaim a week of prayer for people living under Communist tyranny. The document for 1959 was issued by the White House just as Nixon boarded his flight, and the coincidence enraged Khrushchev. With millions of Americans praying for the overthrow of his government, along came the U.S. Vice President, trying to stir up discontent with his TV sets and automatic washers! From their first meeting at the Kremlin, in which the Soviet leader used language that shocked the translators, it was clear that this was going to be no ordinary morning at the fair.[8]

Things began innocently enough in the Glass Pavilion, just before noon. The art show sparked no fireworks; Nixon adroitly guided the Premier past the greedy generals and downstairs, into the display of consumer products. For days the Soviet press had sniped at this particular portion of the exhibition, calling it unrepresentative of the life of the average American, and a 'traditional Moscow fair' had suddenly opened to sell comparable items, rarely seen in Russian stores. As the party passed RCA's mock television studio, an engineer called out an invitation. Would Khrushchev and Nixon like to see themselves on the new color monitors and try out a system for recording and replaying programs? With the tape rolling, a truculent Khrushchev resumed discussion of the Captive Nations issue, throwing his arms around a nearby worker and asking whether the man looked like a slave. Nixon tried to divert his attention to the TV sets. Khrushchev dismissed them with a flick of the wrist: 'In another seven years we will be on the same level as America. When we catch you up, in passing you by, we will wave to you,' he blustered, wiggling his fingers at the camera once more. How about color television? Nixon replied. The Soviets were ahead in rockets, but wasn't the United States in the lead in *this* technology? 'Nyet!' his adversary shot back, conceding nothing.[9]

The next stop was the Pepsi-Cola booth, where the emerging theme of competition was taken up again. Originally the State Department had suggested a nose-to-nose clash between Coca-Cola and Pepsi at the Moscow Exhibition to illustrate the free enterprise system at work, but Coke had declined to participate. Instead, Pepsi presented two versions of its product, one imported from the United States and the other made with Moscow water and, through Ambassador Llewellyn Thompson, begged the Vice President to nudge Khrushchev toward the kiosk. The company's new advertising slogan was 'Be Sociable, Have a Pepsi!' What better ad than a picture of America's foremost adversary (and the scourge of Coca-Cola, which the Party in Europe equated with capitalist decadence) acting sociable over a Pepsi made in the USSR? 'Don't worry,' Nixon is said to have told Pepsi's CEO. 'I'll bring him by.' It wasn't hard to arrange, as things turned out: the contest suited Khrushchev's bellicose mood to a tee. He expressed a predictable disdain for American Pepsi, but the Russian version, he growled, was 'very refreshing'. And he drank seven bottles for the company photographers before the clutch of journalists and officials tromped off toward the exit, just beyond the model home.[10]

Richard Nixon would later insist that the Kitchen Debate was all an accident, that the domestic setting, sure to rivet the attention of his American audience, had not been chosen for political effect. But it is worth noting that William Safire, a future Nixon speechwriter, was doing public relations for Macy's and the model house in Moscow and that photographer Elliot Erwitt was ready to shoot the exchange, moment by moment.[11] Erwitt recalls that Khrushchev was in high dudgeon by the time the entourage reached the viewing aisle that ran down the center of the

bifurcated 'Splitnik', as the Russians dubbed the three-bedroom house. He was spew-
ing earthy profanities in all directions and Nixon, sensing an opportunity, was grand-
standing for the press, citing facts and figures about home building. Suddenly, the Vice
President pulled up short at the kitchen area and leaned over the railing in front of an
automatic washer (Figure 10.2). 'I want to show you this kitchen,' he said. 'It is like
those of our houses in California.' 'We have such things,' Khrushchev shot back. But
anyone can afford a $14,000 house in the United States, Nixon continued – any
steelworker, for instance: 'This house costs about $100 a month to buy on a contract
running twenty-five to thirty years.' The house won't be standing then, the Premier
scoffed. In America, builders want to sell everybody new houses every few years: 'We
build firmly. We build for our children and grandchildren.'

'You Americans think that the Russian people will be astonished to see these
things,' he cried, in sheer frustration, gesturing toward the washer. 'We hope to show
our diversity and our right to choose,' Nixon retorted, on a note of triumph. 'We do
not want our decisions made at the top by one government official that all houses
should be the same. . . . [And] is it not far better to be talking about washing machines
than machines of war, like rockets? Isn't this the kind of competition you want? . . .
Let the people choose the kind of house, . . . the kind of ideas they want. We have
many different manufacturers and many different kinds of washing machines, so that
the housewives may have a choice.' 'Let's thank the housewife for letting us use her

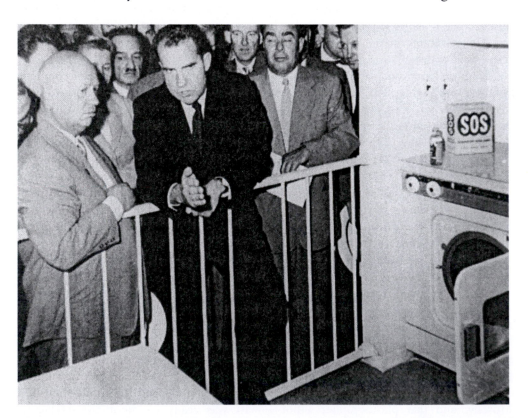

Figure 10.2 The famous Kitchen Debate, over an automatic washer: Khrushchev and
Nixon, Moscow, 1959, Associated Press

kitchen for our argument,' Khrushchev countered, bowing to the American guide, and shot out the door, ending the second phase of the confrontation.[12]

That evening, at the formal opening of the American Exhibition, Nixon took Khrushchev on another tour of the premises, and led him straight into a second kitchen, a futuristic display of household robots in the Glass Pavilion. 'In America, these are designed to make things easier for our women,' he noted sanctimoniously. 'Ha! These are mere gadgets!' huffed Khrushchev: 'Don't you have a machine that puts food into the mouth and pushes it down?' A product demonstrator pushed a button, sending a dishwasher careening toward him like some creature out of science fiction. 'This is not a rational approach. These are gadgets we will never adopt!' Khrushchev bellowed. Oblivious to his scorn, the uniformed guide in her pastel shirtwaist turned on a closed-circuit TV system designed to monitor activities in every corner of the house. Khrushchev's mood brightened visibly. 'This is probably always out of order,' he told Nixon, laughing. 'Da,' chortled the Vice President. And the Kitchen Debate ended on a note of bogus good humor with both sides in apparent agreement over the silliness of household gadgets.[13]

Notes

1   Stephen J. Whitfield, *The Culture of the Cold War* (Baltimore: Johns Hopkins University Press, 1991), 73; '"Made in U.S.A." – in Red Capital', *U.S. News and World Report*, Aug. 3, 1959, 38. Gereon Zimmerman and Bob Lerner, 'What the Russians Will See', *Look*, July 21, 1959, 52–54. *Izvestia* quoted in '"Ivan" Takes a Look at American Life', *U.S. News and World Report*, Aug. 10, 1959, 42.

2   'U.S. and U.S.S.R. Agree to Exchange Exhibitions in 1959', *Department of State Bulletin*, Jan. 26, 1958, 132–134. 'Architecture: Umbrella Man', *Newsweek*, July 13, 1959, 84. See, e.g., note on 1955 trade fairs in Paris and Milan, *Industrial Design*, Aug. 1955, 72–77. Arthur J. Pulos. *The American Design Adventure* (Cambridge, Mass.: MIT Press, 1990), 242–247.

3   'The Vice President in Russia: A Barnstorming Masterpiece', *Life*, Aug. 10, 1959, 34.

4   Milward W. Martin, *Twelve Full Ounces* (New York: Holt, Rinehart & Winston, 1962), 109.

5   Alvin Toffler, 'Coca-Cola vs. Pepsi-Cola: The Competition That Refreshes', *Fortune*, May 1961, 127.

6   '"Made in U.S.A." – in Red Capital', 39.

7   'Their Sheltered Honeymoon', *Life*, Aug. 10, 1959, 51.

8   Stephen E. Ambrose, *Nixon: The Education of a Politician* (New York: Simon & Schuster, 1987), 520–521. Richard M. Nixon, *Six Crises* (Garden City, N.Y.: Doubleday, 1962), 252.

9   For transcripts of the debate, see 'Better to See Once,' *Time*, Aug. 3, 1959, 12–14; 'Encounter', *Newsweek*, Aug. 3, 1959, 15–17; 'The Two Worlds: A Day-Long Debate', *New York Times*, July 25, 1959.

10   Herbert S. Parmet, *Richard Nixon and His America* (Boston: Little, Brown, 1990), 398–399. Martin, *Twelve Full Ounces*, 109–110.

11   J. C. Louis and Harvey Z. Yazijian, *The Cola Wars* (New York: Everest House, 1980), 93.

12   There is no complete sound recording of this portion of the event, and wording varies from account to account. My reconstruction depends on a variety of published stories; see note 9.

13   'That Famous Debate in Close-Up Pictures', *Life*, Aug. 3, 1959, 28.

Chapter 11

Kristin Ross

INTRODUCTION TO *FAST CARS, CLEAN BODIES* [1995]

(**Source**: Ross, Kristin (1995) *Fast Cars, Clean Bodies: Decolonization and the Reordering of French Culture*, Cambridge, Mass. and London: MIT Press, pp. 1–13)

Editor's introduction

Fast Cars, Clean Bodies: Decolonization and the Reordering of French Culture simultaneously investigates an intellectual culture fascinated by the everyday (Barthes, Baudrillard, Lefebvre and others) and a more general culture (adverts, movies, magazines) that is continually shaping and producing the everyday. In four chapters, Kristin Ross compiles what might be thought of (after Benjamin) as a range of thought-images for looking at French culture in the late 1950s and early 1960s. In a chapter called 'Hygiene and Modernization' (for instance) Ross describes adverts for newly available domestic technologies (washing machines, fridges and so on) and the rhetoric of hygiene that accompanied them. This rhetoric resonates with the same language that was being used to describe the French opposition to decolonisation in Algeria ('keeping the house in order'). Thus an everyday culture of commodities registers (in coded forms) the brutal torture of Algerians as they struggle for freedom from French control.

As clearly stated in the title of the book, national culture (French culture) is the topic of this study. But the emphasis on a national culture being reordered at a moment of decolonisation signals that we will need to qualify what is meant by 'national' here. With Lefebvre very much in mind, Ross articulates a national everyday that is the locus of a number of forces. On the one hand the period being described is one in which US culture penetrated French culture (and European culture more generally) through pop music, movies and so on. On the other hand decolonisation (particularly the liberation struggle of Algeria) impacts on French life (and, of course, on Algerian life) in a number of ways, such as returning 'white' French Algerians and the internalisation of colonial relations within French cities. 'Nation' here would have no meaning unless it is seen within both larger and smaller networks, yet it is of course 'nation' that is very much the issue for Algeria as it is for France. *Fast Cars, Clean Bodies* provides an approach to everyday life that foregrounds 'nation' while refusing to see the national as a discrete and stable formation. It also offers an example of the diverse range of materials that can make up an archive for studying the everyday.

Further reading: Fanon 1986; Kuisel 1993; Lefebvre 1991; Kristin Ross 1992.

I N CLAUDE CHABROL'S SECOND MOVIE, *Les Cousins* (1959), a young provincial boy called Charles arrives in Paris to study law, and shares an apartment with his cynical, worldly, 'Nietzschean' cousin, also a law student. While his debauched cousin pursues a frenetic social life, the country boy spends most of his time in his room writing fond, descriptive letters back to his mother in the village; tiring momentarily of this, he decides to read some Balzac. The bookstore owner is so pleased with his choice ('all the rest of them, they just want to read pornography and detective fiction') that he makes him a present of a copy of *Illusions perdues*.

Françoise Giroud, one of the key figures behind the proliferation of women's magazines in the 1950s in France and an important character in this book, recalls in her memoirs how she and the cofounder of *Elle* magazine, Hélène Lazareff, imagined the ideal reader of their new magazine as the first issue hit the stands. The reader envisioned by the staff at *Elle* was most likely young, between twenty-five and thirty-five, tired of wartime deprivation, in need of frivolity, and she lived in Angoulême. Why Angoulême? I don't remember, says Giroud. Perhaps because of Rastignac.[1]

In a series of articles that later came to be read as the manifesto of the French novel of the late 1950s, Alain Robbe-Grillet situates his own era and its realist mode of representation by comparing it with that of Balzac. Balzac's period was marked by 'the apogee of the individual', whereas today is the period of 'administrative numbers'. The objects that appear in Balzac's descriptions stagger under the weight of all that they are meant to signify; Robbe-Grillet's objects are present in and for themselves, unencumbered by human significance. Balzac, for Robbe-Grillet, represents 'the old myths of depth'; Robbe-Grillet proposes instead 'a flat and discontinuous universe where each thing refers only to itself.'[2]

Yet if Balzac and his mode of narrative representation provide Robbe-Grillet with the example of everything that the novels of the day should not now be, still Balzac's claim to have represented his own era accurately, realistically, and with authority goes unquestioned. In fact, Robbe-Grillet yearns to *be* the Balzac of his day, to follow his example and produce a new, modernized mode of realism suitable to representing the 'new man' and his era of numbers. The New Novel would be a Human Comedy without the humans.

The Balzac of his day, the Rastignac of her day, the Lucien de Rubempré of the present. In the late 1950s and early 1960s – the roughly ten-year period I examine in this book, the years after electricity but before electronics – Balzac provides a way for people to establish the particular hopes, anxieties, fears, and aspirations of their own era; he is a recurrent figure in an allegory by way of which the present appears as both a repetition and a difference, a means of continuity and a mark of rupture. Once more, as in the 1850s, the countryside is being depleted, and villagers flock to the new forms of employment, opportunities, and pleasures that can be found in the cities. But the newly arrived Parisians of the postwar era are likely to be provincial French women come to work as shopgirls as in Chabrol's *Les Bonnes femmes* (1960) or in Elsa Triolet's *Roses à crédit* (1959); village boys such as Charles who come to take an advanced degree at the moment when higher education is no longer the prerogative of a tiny elite; or Algerian immigrants seeking work in the car factories on the outskirts of Paris as in Claire Etcherelli's *Elise ou la vraie vie* (1966). Other realist characters have changed as well. The furtive calculations and the limited horizons of the Balzacian 'type' par excellence, the notary, are both repeated and surpassed by another kind of supreme calculator – one who by the very development of his discipline becomes an autonomous factor of the postwar acceleration: the engineer. 'And so beyond the engineer whose knowledge increases and whose machines perfect themselves and multiply, a manner of looking at things is forming, and soon a whole way of reasoning that marks our era.'[3] The stable old, propertied *honnête bourgeois* of Balzac's era reappears in a very different, streamlined, and fast-moving format: the forward-looking, hard-working *jeune cadre*. And yet in *Les Belles images* (1966) Simone de Beauvoir will uncover the strands of class interest that unite the two, reveal them to be the same man wearing different masks.

The essence of the recurring Balzac allegory in the decade I study in this book has to do with periodization. As formulated by Alain Touraine, it is an argument that presumes the epochal originality of Balzac's time in order to argue the same status for the present:

> At the dawning of French industrialization, Balzac was aware of the frenzy for money, the social upheaval, but 1848 had to arrive before all the problems surrounding industrial work and the proletariat could be seen in the light of day. Aren't we now, within the new society being organized before our eyes, existing in a moment comparable to the one in which Balzac wrote?[4]

Following Touraine's analogy, May '68 would be the new 1848, the confirming after-thought, the event that certified the massive social upheaval and land grab of the decade that proceeded it. With the largest strikes in French history, May '68 would bring all the problems and dissatisfactions surrounding the French lurch into modernization to the light of day. It was the event that marked the political end of that accelerated transition into Fordism: a protest against the Fordist hierarchies of the factories and the exaggerated statism that had controlled French modernization. (The economic confirmation of the end would come a few years later with the oil crisis and economic recession of the early 1970s.)

If I have stopped short of a consideration of the events of May '68 in this book, it is because I wanted to consider instead the event of French modernization in the decade that came before – to consider, that is, French modernization *as* an event. Modernization is, of course, not an event but a process, made up of slow- and fast-moving economic and social cycles. But in France the state-led modernization drive was extraordinarily concerted, and the desire for a new way of living after the war widespread. The unusual swiftness of French postwar modernization seemed to partake of the qualities of what Braudel has designated as the temporality of the event: it was headlong, dramatic, and breathless. The speed with which French society was transformed after the war from a rural, empire-oriented, Catholic country into a fully industrialized, decolonized, and urban one meant that the things modernization needed – educated middle managers, for instance, or affordable automobiles and other 'mature' consumer durables, or a set of social sciences that followed scientific, functionalist models, or a work force of ex-colonial laborers – burst onto a society that still cherished prewar outlooks with all of the force, excitement, disruption, and horror of the genuinely new.

It is this swiftness that fascinated me, and that I recall being made aware of when I first read Henri Lefebvre. Contrasting the French experience to the slow, steady, 'rational' modernization of American society that transpired throughout the twentieth century, Lefebvre evoked the almost cargo-cult-like, sudden descent of large appliances into war-torn French households and streets in the wake of the Marshall Plan. Before the war, it seemed, no one had a refrigerator; after the war, it seemed, everyone did. Fordist consumption, as Michel Aglietta points out (and as the organization of this book reflects) is governed by two commodities: 'the *standardized housing* that is the privileged site of individual consumption; and the *automobile* as the means of transport compatible with the separation of home and workplace.'[5] French people, peasants and intellectuals alike, tended to describe the changes in their lives in terms of the abrupt transformations in home and transport: the coming of objects – large-scale consumer durables, cars and refrigerators – into their streets and homes, into their workplaces and their *emplois du temps*. In the space of just ten years a rural woman might live the acquisition of electricity, running water, a stove, a refrigerator, a washing machine, a sense of interior space as distinct from exterior space, a car, a television, and the various liberations and oppressions associated with each. What were the effects of such a sudden series of changes? Where were these effects best registered, recorded? Who bore the costs? Modern social relations are of course always mediated by objects; but in the case of the French, this mediation seemed to have increased exponentially, abruptly, and over a very brief period of time. If I return throughout the book to the films of Jacques Tati, it is because they make palpable a daily life that increasingly appeared to unfold in a space where objects tended to dictate to people their gestures and movements – gestures that had not yet congealed into any degree of rote familiarity, and that for the most part had to be learned from watching American films. Was it a mark of the particular rapidity of French modernization that so much of the country's intellectual effort of the period – the earliest (and thus most materialist) works by Barthes and Baudrillard, for example, or that of the Situationists, Cornelius Castoriadis, Edgar Morin, or Maurice Blanchot in his review essays of Lefebvre – took the form of a theoretical reflection on 'everyday life'? Or that 'everyday life' is elevated to the status of a theoretical concept only at this particular conjuncture? Theoretical categories are not free-floating analytic devices, innocent of historical content. If they instead find their origins in forms of experience, then the transitory importance of critical categories like 'alienation' and 'everyday life', or the move to the forefront of the concept of 'reification' during these years, must then be another sign of the upheaval in social relations occasioned by the sudden, full-scale entry of capital into 'style of life', into lived, daily, almost imperceptible rhythms.[6] This is no less true for the dominant conceptual apparatus as well. A key ideological concept like 'communication', for example, began to refer in mid-century not only to the dawning of the new information technologies but to the ideal spatial arrangement of rooms in modern suburban homes; it was also the title of the leading journal of the day devoted to advances in structuralism. The word *communication* was everywhere – and yet the experience of communication itself, be it understood as spontaneous expression, reciprocity, or the contiguity necessary for reciprocity to exist, was precisely what was in the process of disappearing under the onslaught of merchandise and the new forms of media technologies. Merchandise (or exchange relations) is first of all the production of nonexchange between people; structuralism, the dominant intellectual movement of the period, fetishizes 'communication' at the very moment when various forms of direct, unmediated relations (*communicare*, Latin: to be in relation with) among people are waning or being decisively transformed.

Touraine's analogy then holds; his era is the dawning of a new economic and social era in France comparable to that of the beginnings of French industrialization in the 1830s and 1840s. Economists agree that the consolidation of a Fordist regime in France in the decade or so before 1968 – a period of 'growth without precedent of capitalism in France',[7] the peak decade, that is, of the thirty-year postwar economic boom – was an extraordinarily voluntarist and thus wrenching experience. It took place, for instance, at the cost of a relentless dismantling of earlier spatial arrangements, particularly in Paris where the city underwent demolitions and renovations equivalent in scale to those Haussman oversaw a hundred years earlier.[8] And it transpired in the decade that saw the stumbling and final collapse of the French Empire, from the decisive battle of Dien Bien Phu in the spring of 1954, to the first major Algerian uprisings a few months later, to the referendum on African independence in 1958, to the granting of that independence in 1960, all the way through to the Evian Accords that officially announced the hard-won independence of Algeria in May 1962.

Touraine makes no mention of the end of the empire in his characterization of the singularity of the age (nor does he mention the beginning of the empire in reference to Balzac's). His omission is characteristic of many such narratives of the period that tend, even today, to choose between the two stories, the story of French modernization and Americanization on the one hand, or the story of decolonization on the other.[9] I have tried instead throughout this book to hold the two stories in the tension of what I take to be their intricate relationship as it was lived then and as it continues into the present. The peculiar contradictions of France in that period can be seized only if they are seen as those of an exploiter/exploited country, dominator/dominated, exploiting colonial populations at the same time that it is dominated by, or more precisely, entering more and more into collaboration or fusion with, American capitalism. It is this particular tension, in fact, as I argue in the final section of the book, that makes the emergence of the character and social type of the *jeune cadre*, that high priest of Fordism, something of a national allegory for the modernizing France of the 1950s and 1960s. Midway between owner and worker, managing the proletariat but punching a time clock too, the *cadre*, like France itself, was a 'dominated agent of capitalist domination'.[10]

Thinking the two narratives together means taking seriously the catchphrase popularized by Lefebvre and the Situationists in the early 1960s: 'the colonization of everyday life'. In the case of France, in other words, it means considering the various ways in which the practice of colonialism outlived its history. With the waning of its empire, France turned to a form of interior colonialism; rational administrative techniques developed in the colonies were brought home and put to use side by side with new technological innovations such as advertising in reordering metropolitan, domestic society, the 'everyday life' of its citizens. Marxist theory had made considerable progress in refining theories of imperialism in the domain of international relations. Lefebvre now pushed that theory to apply the insights garnered from an international analysis to new objects: to the domain of interregional relations within France, for example, or the space of domesticity and practices of consumption. But it was above all the unevenness of the built environment of the city, its surroundings, and its social geography that came to crystallize, for Lefebvre, the contradictions of postwar life. For speculative capital, no longer drawn to foraging abroad, was increasingly directed toward investment in the built environment: Paris, the city itself, became the new site for a generalized exploitation of the daily life of its inhabitants through the management of space. At times the conversion from exterior to interior colonialism was facilitated by a literal transfer of personnel; thus, a city councilor involved in the Parisian renovation debates of the early 1960s remarked, 'France decolonized the Third World while colonizing Paris, appointing as head of the commission charged with making decisions about the capital functionaries who had made their careers in Black Africa or in Asia.'[11] But such literal transfers in personnel pale in importance when compared to the emergence, in those years, of what might be termed a *comprador* class serving the interests of the state: financiers, developers, speculators, and high administrative functionaries. Modernization brought into being a whole new range of middlemen and go-betweens, new social types that dominated and profited from the transformations wrought by the state. The *jeune cadre* elevated to an intermediate position in the corporate hierarchy, the housewife elevated to the role of technician or manager of the newly modern home – couldn't these social ascendancies, too, be seen in the light of a generalized 'compradorization' of the French middle class?

In the France of today the tendency to 'keep the two stories separate' has, I think, very serious social and political consequences, consequences that are being played out in the rise of the various neoracisms of the 1980s and 1990s that focus on the figure of the immigrant worker. Keeping the two stories apart is usually another name for forgetting one of the stories or for relegating it to a different time frame. This is in fact what has occurred. For, from this perspective (a prevalent one in France today), France's colonial history was nothing more than an 'exterior' experience that somehow came to an abrupt end, cleanly, in 1962.[12] France then careened forward to new frontiers, modern autoroutes, the EEC, and all-electric kitchens. Having decisively slammed shut the door to the Algerian episode, colonialism itself was made to seem like a dusty archaism, as though it had not transpired in the twentieth century and in the personal histories of many people living today, as though it played only a tiny role in France's national history, and no role at all in its modern identity. One of the arguments of this book is that the very logic of (racial) exclusion that would 'keep the two stories separate' is itself the outcome of the accelerated capitalist modernization the French state undertook in those years. The new contemporary racism centering on questions of immigration is, as the contemporary detective stories of Didier Daeninckx make clear, a racism that has its roots in the era of decolonization and modernization, in the inversion of movements of population between the old colonies and the old metropoles, in the conflict that crystallized in those days between the modern and the unmodern (or traditional) – the latter being directly referred to race and supposedly racial traits, such as laziness or filth. The immigration that haunts the collective fantasies of the French today is the old accomplice to the accelerated growth of French society in the 1950s and 1960s. Without the labor of its ex-colonial immigrants, France could not have successfully 'Americanized', nor competed in the post-war industrial contest. In the economic boom years, in other words, France made use of the colonies 'one last time' in order to resurrect and maintain its national superiority over them – a superiority made all the more urgent by the ex-colonies' own newly acquired nationhood.

If the colonies provided the labor, the fuel came from the West. Immediately after the war a particular fantasy was exported by the United States, along with the gadgets, techniques, and experts of American capitalism, to a Europe devastated by war: the fantasy of timeless, even, and limitless development. Capitalist modernization presents itself as timeless because it dissolves beginning and end, in the historical sense, into an ongoing, naturalized process, one whose uninterrupted rhythm is provided by a regular and unchanging social world devoid of class conflict. In this book I show how the arrival of the new consumer durables into French life – the repetitive, daily practices and new mediations they brought into being – helped create a break with the eventfulness of the past, or better, helped situate the temporality of the event itself as a thing of the past. I have also argued the complicity of much of the French intellectual production of the era – from structuralism to the Annales school of historiography – with that dissolution, because of the way in which these sciences eliminate from their horizon everything that might conceivably upset the processes of repetition, the way in which they have abandoned the event as a conceptual category. My own somewhat perverse consideration of French modernization as an event is an attempt to fly in the face of this still hegemonic practice. By historicizing France's transition into American-style mass culture, the prehistory of its postmodernism, I try to provide an experience of the historicity that theories of postmodernism, themselves rooted in the intellectual developments of the 1950s and 1960s and in the dissolution of the event and of diachronic agency, seek to efface.

But we must return now briefly to the most important promise made by modernization: its evenness. Modernization is even because it holds within itself a theory of spatial and temporal convergence: all societies will come to look like us, all will arrive eventually at the same stage or level, all the possibilities of the future are being lived now, at least for the West: there they are, arrayed before us, a changeless world functioning smoothly under the sign of technique. The process of development in the West has been completed; what comes now is already in existence: the confused syncretism of all styles, futures, and possibilities. Modernization promises a perfect reconciliation of past and future in an endless present, a world where all sedimentation of social experience has been leveled or smoothed away, where poverty has been reabsorbed, and, most important, a world where class conflict is a thing of the past, the stains of contradiction washed out in a superhuman hygienic effort, by new levels of abundance and equitable distribution.

And yet the French experience, in its highly concentrated, almost laboratory-like intensity, has the advantage of showing modernization to be instead a *means* of social, and particularly racial, differentiation; a differentiation that has its roots in the 1950s discourse on hygiene I examine in the second chapter of this book and take up again in the third. If the consolidation of a broad middle class more or less transpires during these years, it is also during these years that France distances itself from its (former) colonies, both within and without: this is the moment of the great cordoning off of the immigrants, their removal to the suburbs in a massive reworking of the social boundaries of Paris and the other large French cities. On the national level France retreats within the hexagon, withdraws from empire, retrenches within its borders at the same time that those boundaries are becoming newly permeable to a whirlwind of economic forces – forces far more destructive of some received notion of 'national culture' than any immigrant community could muster. The movement inward – a whole complex process that is in some ways the subject of each of my chapters and that Castoriadis, Morin, and Lefebvre all called 'privatization' – is a movement echoed on the level of everyday life by the withdrawal of the new middle classes to their newly comfortable domestic interiors, to the electric kitchens, to the enclosure of private automobiles, to the interior of a new vision of conjugality and an ideology of happiness built around the new unit of middle-class consumption, the couple, and to depoliticization as a response to the increase in bureaucratic control of daily life. Modernization requires the creation of such a privatized and depoliticized broad middle strata: a 'national middle class'; from this point on, national subjectivity begins to take the place of class. Now, in our own day, when the broad middle strata has become coterminous with the nation itself in France, more atavistic logics or principles of exclusion are coming to light. Class conflict, after all, implies some degree of negotiability; once modernization has run its course, then one is, quite simply, either French or not, modern or not: exclusion becomes racial or national in nature. If the ideology of modernization says convergence – all societies will look the same – what it in fact sustains and freezes into place is the very unevenness or inequality that it was supposed to overcome: they will never be like us, they will never catch up. In today's Paris that frozen temporal lag appears as a spatial configuration: the white, upper-class city *intra muros*, surrounded by islands of immigrant communities a long RER ride away.

Touraine's analogy falters when we look to find the writer who foresaw and undertook the monumental task of representing such a momentous transition. Despite his ambitions, Robbe-Grillet did not turn out to be the Balzac of his day. And Didier Daeninckx, who offers the most acute contemporary arguments that the conditions of the immediate present lie in the failures and events of the 1950s and 1960s, is a writer of today, not then. Perhaps the point is that no single writer could occupy the position of Balzac in a moment that was also characterized by the introduction of market research into book publishing, by the mass-marketing of paperback books, by the dawning of image culture, and by a profound crisis in the traditional novel that itself reflected the new fragmentation of social life. But Robbe-Grillet's novels and theoretical reflections, in particular, are themselves too imbued with the ideology of modernization to offer the necessary critical perspective; as Jacques Leenhardt's work has shown, the New Novel is part and parcel of that ideology, and of the whole contemporary movement whereby a naive or vulgar materialism comes to be substituted for dialectical materialism, and *mentalité* (or shared culture, shared values, or any of a number of prevalent designations of 'consensus' or averaging) takes the place of ideology. Like structuralism and the Annales school of historiography, the New Novel is complicitous with the workings of capitalist modernization, in part because of its avant-gardist refusal or dismantling of historical narrative.

For help in formulating a critical prehistory of postmodernism in France I have had to look elsewhere: to those artists and thinkers who historicized their era at the time and who gave full voice to the debates and controversies surrounding modernization. Novelists such as Christiane Rochefort, Simone de Beauvoir, and Georges Perec working in a realist mode; filmmakers from Jacques Tati to Jacques Demy; and those social theorists who turned their attention after the war to 'everyday life' performed the labor of accounting for the present – its disruptions and its social costs – that the historians, lost in a prolonged dream about the *longue durée* of feudalism, chose to avoid. If the single monumental realist author working to represent the totality of an era – a 'Balzac' – has been relegated to a definitive past, then it is still to the realist *mode* that we must look to find the narrative style best suited to portraying unevenness.[13] The realist mode attempts to come to terms with, or to give an historical account of, the fatigue and exhilaration of moments when people find themselves living two lives at once. As Raymond Williams has suggested, realism gives a shape to the experiences of those on the outer edges of modernization's scope, the ones caught just outside or the ones who have been left behind, the ones for whom abundance is accompanied by a degradation in their conditions of existence. Realism offers a voice to those who live in a different temporality, who follow a pace of life that is nonsynchronous with the dominant one. In the postwar period realist fiction and film offered a critique of official representations of a uniformly prosperous France, surging forward into American-style patterns of consumption and mass culture. It is in these works that we can still glimpse the 'democracy of consumption' for what it is: the newest form of bourgeois democracy, the alibi of a class society.

Notes

1   Françoise Giroud, *Leçons particulières* (Paris: Livres de poche, 1990), p. 123. Translations from the French are mine unless otherwise noted.

2   See Alain Robbe-Grillet, *Pour un nouveau roman* (Paris: Editions de Minuit, 1963), trans. Richard Howard as *For a New Novel* (New York: Grove, 1965).

3   Francis-Louis Closon, *Un homme nouveau: L'ingénieur économiste* (Paris: Presses universitaires françaises, 1961), pp. 13–14.

4   Alain Touraine, *La Société post-industrielle* (Paris: Editions Denoël, 1969), pp. 115–116.

5   Michel Aglietta, *Régulation et crises du capitalisme* (Paris: Calmann-Lévy, 1976), trans. David Fernbach as *A Theory of Capitalist Regulation: The U.S. Experience* (London: New Left Books, 1976), p. 159.

6   *Arguments*, an important neo-Marxist journal published between 1956 and 1962 for which Lefebvre, Morin, and Barthes, among others, wrote, published a translation of George Lukács's essay on reification in 1960.

7   André Gauron, *Histoire économique de la Vième république*, vol. 1 (Paris: Maspero, 1983), p. 6.

8   See Alain Lipietz, 'Governing the Economy in the Face of International Challenge: From National Developmentalism to National Crisis' in *Searching for the New France*, ed. James F. Hollifield and George Ross (New York: Routledge, 1991), pp. 17–42.

9   Richard Kuisel's *Seducing the French: The Dilemma of Americanization* (Berkeley: University of California Press, 1993) is a good example of a political/economic history that focuses entirely on the 'French economic miracle' and Americanization without any consideration of the end of empire.

10   The phrase is André Gorz's. See his *Critique de la division du travail* (Paris: Seuil, 1973).

11   Cited in Louis Chevalier, *L'Assassinat de Paris* (Paris: Calmann-Lévy, 1977), trans. David P. Jordan as *The Assassination of Paris* (Chicago: University of Chicago Press, 1994), p. 236.

12   See Etienne Balibar, 'L'avancée du racisme en France', in *Les Frontières de la démocratie* (Paris: La Découverte, 1992), pp. 19–98.

13   I have made this argument in the context of a reading of the detective fiction of Didier Daeninckx in 'Watching the Detectives', in *Postmodernism and the Rereading of Modernity*, ed. Francis Barker, Peter Hulme, and Margaret Iversen (Manchester: Manchester University Press, 1992), pp. 46–65.

Chapter 12

_____

Harry Harootunian

THE PROMISE OF 'MODERN LIFE' [2000]

(Source: Harootunian, Harry (2000b) *Overcome by Modernity: History, Culture, and Community in Interwar Japan*, Princeton, NJ and Oxford: Princeton University Press, pp. 95–101)

Editor's introduction

Harry Harootunian's book on Japanese culture in the 1920s and 1930s is partly a comparative study in everydayness and modernity. As he makes clear in this extract, an intense consideration of everydayness was common to philosophers and social thinkers in both Japan and Europe at this time. Yet whereas the everyday for most European thinkers offered a perspective from which to draw mostly negative conclusions about the impoverishing effects of capitalist modernisation, for Japanese thinkers it was the *potentiality* of the everyday that held most interest. To think of the everyday as a (potentially) radical transformation of social life relies on the ability to recognise the present as already undergoing the most extreme forms of transformation. But it also requires a context where the forms that such transformations are taking are as yet undecided (or at least appeared to be). It was precisely the revolutionary effects of modernisation that made the everyday a field of possibility for Japanese thinkers (whether this possibility included a rapprochement between tradition and modernisation or a more radical overhauling of daily life in the name of scientific rationality).

In his book *History's Disquiet: Modernity, Cultural Practice, and the Question of Everyday Life*, Harootunian (2000a) suggests that everyday life provides an arena which will allow both the particularity and commonality of a global (but also and always local) capitalist modernity to be registered. It is the common (and shockingly successful) explosion of commodity culture on a global scale in the twentieth century that allows connections to be made across various national cultures at the level of daily life. Yet it is also the particularism of how this impacted on specific national and regional contexts of everyday life (already 'thick' with traditions) that makes the cross-cultural study of modernity a study of uneven development.

Further reading: Harootunian 2000a; Mizuta 1993; Tobin 1992; Vlastos 1998.

AT THE SAME MOMENT that popular discourse exploded in new media like film, mass-circulating magazines, opinion journals, radio, and newspapers to figure and fantasize the new everydayness that was being installed in Japan's larger cities in the 1920s, thinkers, social researchers, and critics were busily involved in envisioning the experience of modernity and its constituent elements – speed, shock, sensation, and spectacle – through an optics that produced differing effects according to the angle of the lens through which experience was being refracted. These refractions distilled certain intensities in the experience of modern life and privileged others to present a vision of everyday life that was both enabling for the present and promising for a future as of yet unenvisaged. What is important about this activity is the way it centered the category of everyday life – its performativity in the present – as the informing principle of modern life. It made it both a condition of social research and critique and the occasion for looking to a new social and political imaginary in the future. Far from imagining everyday life as a source of negativity and mediocrity, as Martin Heidegger was already formulating in *Sein und Zeit* (1926), thinkers as diverse as Kon Wajirō and Tosaka Jun saw in the performance of the everyday an escape from a binding past that still managed to lay claim on the present and the full promise of modern life – including the hope for a better future.

We must, in any case, try to account for this overwhelming, almost over-determined, interest in and enthusiasm for everydayness in the 1920s and 1930s when, according to Kon, Europeans had not yet focused on this dimension of modern life. While this assessment was not entirely true and might easily be taken as an expression of self-aggrandizement employed to make Kon's own program (called 'modernology') of studying everyday life appear unique and original, it is, nonetheless, one of the interesting problems of Japan's modern history that so many thinkers were intensely concerned with the status of everydayness – a concern that often matched and even frequently exceeded European considerations. In Europe, concern for everyday life after World War I was dominated by the work of two thinkers, Georg Lukács and Heidegger, in the shadow of Max Weber's meditations on the identity of modern society. Lukács had powerfully formulated the way in which the commodity form mediated social relationships and the consequences of its effects for producing a 'reification of social life'. Heidegger had reduced *alltagslichkeit* to the mediocre world of the They (*das Man*) – the domain of complete negativity – and insisted on returning to the temporality of Being's 'authentic historicality'. Heidegger's conception of inauthenticity was thoroughly dehistoricized, as Lukács's understanding of reification was deeply embedded in a particular history of the capitalist present that marked, historically, its production. Even so, they were talking about the same kind of social formation. Among thinkers of the beleaguered Frankfurt School, there were attempts by Walter Benjamin and Siegfried Kracauer, especially, to imagine the role played by everyday life in mass society and advanced capitalism. But this intervention, which undoubtedly aimed at countering the negativity associated with everyday life, often shared Heidegger's dim estimate of the masses and its consequences for both culture and politics. Kracauer's brilliant essays on everyday life and his critique of the German white-collar class (*Die Angestellten*, 1930) went a long way to simply confirming the effects of commodification on the masses and its political and cultural consequences for producing spiritual 'homelessness', while only Benjamin seemed willing to envisage a new historical materialist program that could acknowledge the existence of alienation in the everyday brought on by commodification and routine yet at the same time see in it the 'mystery' of genuine possibility. If Marxism in general remained slow to respond to the category of experience in modern life, owing to the confidence invested in analyzing systems and structures, even Frankfurt Marxism shied away from everydayness in favor of an overwhelming concern that expressed a fear and distrust of the masses and the new culture industry. In short, their work reflected more conservative misgivings that had already been articulated by thinkers and writers during the decades of the twenties and thirties. During Italy's fascist regime, Antonio Gramsci worked out a conception of common sense and ordinary culture that closely resembled the everyday world and its difference from modernity. And in the Soviet Union, at the moment Trotsky was complaining how the daily life of workers had become commodified, constructivists like Boris Arvatov were trying to conceptualize a socialist everydayness that would make the consumer into a subject free from the commodity fetish by transforming objects into use-value.[1]

Japan perhaps came closer to the Soviet experience of seeing the everyday as the site for utopian aspiration. But this is not to say that there weren't Japanese who, following Heidegger's lead, sought to forget about the performative present altogether in favor of recalling an indeterminate past. Thinkers like Yanagita Kunio, Watsuji Tetsurō, and Kuki Shūzō tried mightily to offer what they believed to be a more enduring and less dangerous alternative to the new everydayness being lived and fantasized in the cities; they sought a theory of cultural reproduction that would check the production of the new culture based on things and consumption rather than custom and value. With their call to memory of a past age or in their move to poeticize a mode of existence, they appealed to cultural forms and practices that claimed for themselves an as yet unrealized sociotemporality outside of a temporal and temporalizing present. To offset a present that alone gave direction to history, they recalled a historical reason that already prefigured the whole history of the race from past to present and forged, therefore, an abstract and fictive continuity between then and now. The strength of this philosophically bankrupt archaism, as it was called by Tosaka Jun (and recently articulated in a critique by the contemporary Italian philosopher Gianni Vattimo that often resembles Tosaka's earlier view), is manifest in its capacity to persist down to the present, well after the historical crisis that produced it, and is still expressed in all of those attempts to show that no fundamental difference separates the Japanese of today from their Stone Age predecessors.

Yet, the Japanese, when contrasted to Europeans, seemed more enthusiastic about the promise offered by the new everydayness and thus willing to explore the possibility of newness for a life vastly different from the one most recently lived in the immediate past. New social constituencies and subject positions like the people (minshū), the masses (taishū), the modern boy (mobo), modern girl (mogarū), cafe waitress, bar maid, and so on, validated by recently introduced commodities people were encouraged to buy and use, called attention to a new kind of social life in Japan for the first time in its history, sometimes called modan raifu or simply seikatsu. What distinguished this conception of modern life was its materiality and its embeddedness in a culture of objects and their circulation. Its very materiality – its embeddedness in objects and their circulation – constituted the sign of a historicity of the present, its historical moment, the temporality of modernity. The question that thinkers tried to answer related to the givenness of the historical present and how it showed itself as present. But what the now of the present offered was little more than a minimal unity empowered to organize the experience of the everyday. That is to say, to speak of the present, as against merely the modern – the regime of the new – denoted the unification of a multiplicity of givens in a minimal unity of meaning. Moreover, it was a unity in time, marked by a kind of synthesis of apprehension, reproduction, and recognition, what Kantians called the 'synthetic unity of experience'. And this minimal unity of the present, however precarious, was increasingly seen by thinkers as the actual and unavoidable experience of everydayness which everywhere in the industrializing world – colonized and noncolonized – was identified with the distinctively modern, even though it sheltered a difference from the merely new.

When Tosaka proposed that everyday life provided the principles to organize both time and space, or Gonda Yasunosuke declared that people's pleasure derived from the experience of everydayness, or Kon Wajirō insisted on seeing daily life and its transactions in home and on the streets as the source of subjectivity, we are confronted with not the simple expression of enthusiasm for the newness of 'modern life' but with the conviction of what this new life had come to mean for Japanese living in a present they saw constantly opening up to a completed future. A partial explanation of this inordinate emphasis on everyday life, I believe, lies in the discovery of a personal and private world of experience available to large numbers of people for the first time in history now being installed in the 1920s and immediately juxtaposed to the public world of state and social system.

For many thinkers, the new culture of the people promised rationality and efficiency, not to mention accessibility and availability, what Hirabayashi Hatsunosuke celebrated as the scientific method in everyday life. Before, rationalization had been restricted to the state and public realm. In fact most thinkers could agree that rationalization in the register of everyday life called for a remodeling, what contemporaries called a 'reconstruction' (kaizō), of custom especially, and of those conditions of social life associated with shelter, clothing, and food. Without the rationalization of the 'means of life' (Kon's words) and 'life attitudes' linked to institutions implicated in everyday life, there could be no chance for the development of a democratic subject.[2] Modern custom announced rationality and the coming regime of rational expectations when people would be in a position to know what choices to make for themselves. (By end of the decade, Aono Suekichi was reporting how the Japanese white-collar class had exceeded its capacity to satisfy such rising expectations and was collapsing into psychological malaise.) The appearance of modern life was seen as rational, efficient, and even scientific, requiring at all times the steady flow and circulation of information and knowledge. It was for this reason that thinkers like Tosaka naively invested so much confidence in new modes of communication like journalism, newspapers, magazines, and reportage. The opening of the decade of the 1920s was greeted with optimistic calls for the establishment of 'cultural living' (bunka seikatsu) by enthusiasts like Morimoto Atsuyoshi, who quickly identified the modern with the prospect of 'rational, efficient living'. For Japanese this meant the possibility of rationalizing those segments of life that had remained outside of the modernizing process.[3] Everydayness was increasingly understood as that surplus left over from the public realm, the residue left behind by an official public domain of state and society that had no everyday, no place for its experience, no room in the officially sanctioned separation of public and private realms and its metonymical mode of relating. But if it was a product of a leftover that exceeded the boundaries of more formal categories like public and private (already marked off in the Meiji Civil Code), it was considered by many as a space in its own right, a spatial category – what Tosaka called 'everyday space' (*nichijō kūkan*) – that housed the new experience of living in the Now on the streets recorded by people like Kon Wajirō and Gonda Yasunosuke. The identity of this new space characterized by the experience of everyday life posed a challenge to both received social relationships and the tidy (and officially ideologized) organization of society into public and private (state and civil society) that delegated duties and determined conduct and behavior. For some, transforming the experience of everydayness to conform more closely to the requirements of rationality constituted the principal condition for remodeling society itself and altering the received political and social relationships in the name of science.

If the discourse on modernity was constituted in new media and necessarily overdetermined certain objects and images, social thinkers drew upon this vast inventory to imagine and figure a new reality they hoped would be lived and experienced more intensely, permeating all sectors of Japanese society. Although the new 'modern life' was identified principally with the large cities, few denied that it would become ubiquitous in the near future. This recognition of the power of everyday life to expand and reach every corner of the country explains why so many thinkers were committed to seeing it as the basis of a new social body; it also explains why so many turned away from the present to find lasting alternatives in the construction of fixed conceptions of community and culture. Yet the first impulse in the 1920s and early 1930s was to take stock of the experience and determine what it meant for society and its future. As a result, the 'experience' inscribed in the discourse on everyday life was inflected in such a way as to supply the raw material for producing a secondary revision capable of imaging the social totality. Thinkers and writers, usually progressives and Marxian, saw in the new configuration the occasion to evaluate its key imaginary dimensions such as custom, the people, and the masses; they saw it as the starting point for envisioning a new kind of human order that might yield the prospect of a better life. The idea of a better life retained the faith in rationality and science but in time developed a political purpose that took precedence and began to visualize new forms of political society. More often than not, this impulse exaggerated the crucial role to be played by science in the construction of a new social and political order for the masses. But what seemed to link a diversity of thinkers, writers, and social researchers in a common effort was the belief that what lay before them was still unfinished and incomplete, despite the worrisome effects of capitalism such as alienation, consumption, and commodification. In this regard they were convinced that they were responding to the demands of a historical conjuncture marked by the advent of new social imaginaries like the people and the masses, their lives, needs, and desires, and that in meeting the requirements of this conjuncture – submitting to its historical necessity – they were imagining how modernity might be completed. Above all else, they recognized the importance of new customs, new social relationships, new forms of work and leisure, and new patterns of consumption as the basis of both a proper social science founded on observation and critique, and a program of social construction.

What this program entailed was a confrontation with the phenomenological present and a recognition that the everydayness of *modan raifu* was, at its center, colonized by the commodity form and its effects. Both its capacity to conceal (and thus induce social forgetting), its enabling conditions of production, and its aptitude for interpellating consumers revealed its role in making the everyday the space of differing historical temporalizations. At the same time the everyday became the only place for producing anew the redemptive power associated with tradition in the time of modernity. If the commodity form produced the ever new in the ever same, thus 'atrophying experience', it would yield the necessary difference to transform the empty, homogenous time of the Now. It should be recalled that progressive thinkers like Tosaka and even Kon opposed the Now to the present, rather than past to present. The distinction derived from a prior phenomenological classification that differentiated the 'present' from the now of immediate experience, what Benjamin once described as the 'now of recognizability'. In this formulation, the present was seen as belonging to the order of history, whereas the now was the lived moment. Deciphering 'social hieroglyphics' for the social and historical character of the labor that produced them as objects that became commodities, while putting into question the very history they were made to have consumers forget, Japanese thinkers envisaged an everyday world filled with alienation brought on by routine yet still filled with possibility, the different in the same: the place of transformation. Social thinkers were thus left with the choice of finding a way to break through the commodity form that dominated modern life either to restore its forgotten history (Gonda), or to show how consumption was actually constitutive of a new subject capable of making choices for the first time (Kon), or to transform the daily objects in order to release a new aesthetic consciousness (Murayama), or to conceptualize it into a space that structured its temporality into accumulative layers that could only be disturbed by exploring the possibilities they offered at any given moment (Tosaka). This revolution came from *within* modernity, neither from the kind of repetition of custom or cultural stratigraphy envisaged by Yanagita Kunio and Watsuji Tetsurō, nor from an unrealized social and cultural form that the present had forgotten, as 'recalled' by Kuki Shūzō and Kobayashi Hideo. Whether it was the Marxist critic Hirabayashi Hatsunosuke calling for the establishment of a new mass culture or a 'culture of feminism', Tosaka Jun rethinking the relationship among custom, morality, and everyday life and finally defining everydayness as a spatial category that contained historical temporality comparable to the laws governing physical space, or Kon Wajirō, standing on Ginza street corners to put into practice a new discipline devoted to studying the modern (*kōgengaku*), this secondary revision upheld the claims of modernity as the product of a determinate history directed only by the present and a different temporality that would, according to stages of development, ultimately yield hitherto unimagined new forms of human existence and experience for Japan's masses. In this regard, the heady optimism manifest in the powers of the modern evoked – if not aped – the atmosphere of the carnivalesque. In this it recalled both M. M. Bakhtin's conception of how everyday life is capable of exploding into utopian aspiration, that is, the experience of Soviet Russia in the 1920s which produced this Bakhtinian inflection, and the enthusiasm for artistic and cultural experimentation that momentarily offered a glimpse of an unfulfilled future. In fact, Japanese in the 1920s were driven to see in the hard commodification of life the promise and design of an even more human order reached not by overcoming modernity (which in the late 1930s was nothing more than an escape route to a national fantasy) but being overcome by it, by bringing it to completion.

Notes

1   See Leo Trotsky, *Problems of Everyday Life* (New York: Monad Press, 1979). Gramsci, who was also concerned with defining the space of everydayness, showed keen interest in the concept of *byt* – one of the terms Trotsky and Boris Arvatov used to denote everyday life. This interest in everyday life was linked to a complementary concern for the phenomenon of 'Americanism', which appeared as a ubiquitous trope and elastic signifier throughout the industrializing world in the 1920s. See also Boris Arvatov, 'Everyday Life and the Culture of the Thing', trans. Christina Kiaer, *October* 81 (Summer 1997): 119–128. Bakhtin's theory of 'carnivelsque', worked out in the Soviet Union in the 1920s, can be read as an analogue of the commodity that objectifies social relationships but which still might yield a new possibility, or, put in another way, an image of everydayness constituted by hierarchical power and routine that is momentarily capable of exploding into its obverse. This obverse is, in fact, the difference of everydayness that remains hidden by modernity – capitalism as the reproduction of accumulation – but is ready to be actualized, as both Benjamin and Tosaka, in their own ways, recognized.

2   Shibata Shuji, *Seikatsu kenkyū josetsu* (Kyotoshi: Nakanishiya Shuppan, 1995), p. 11.

3   Terade Koji, *Seikatsu bunkaron e no shōtai* (Tokyo: Kyōbundo, 1994), pp. 92–93.

Chapter 13

Xiaobing Tang

THE ANXIETY OF EVERYDAY LIFE IN POST-REVOLUTIONARY CHINA [2000]

(**Source:** Tang, Xiaobing (2000) *Chinese Modern: The Heroic and the Quotidian*, Durham, NC and London: Duke University Press, pp. 277–90)

Editor's introduction

Xiaobing Tang's work on Chinese cultural forms in the twentieth century consistently fore-grounds everyday life as the arena in which competing approaches to social life are played out. Tang investigates Chinese modernity through a range of cultural texts (novels, plays, films and paintings) to uncover a general anxiety articulated at the level of everyday life. If anxiety is a general (global) experience for a modern secular and post-traditional daily life, how this anxiety gets *managed* can best be seen from the particular perspective of national (Chinese) culture.

For Tang the recent history of China witnesses two distinct responses to modern everyday life. At the height of China's Cultural Revolution, everyday life was something to be overcome by a heroic dedication to communal living. As China moved into a post-revolutionary period everyday life has been increasingly dominated by an emphasis on the details of domestic commodification, which seeks to ameliorate anxiety via a pana-cea of comfort and style. But if such orientations attempt to placate anxiety (a social existential anxiety to find meaning in the routines of everyday life) the cultural texts that Tang is concerned with evidence both the success and failure of such strategies. And here the texts of a national culture (specifically of course Chinese national culture) become important for their complex articulations of everyday life. In registering the symptoms of anxiety, as well as the practices that attempt to overcome it, cultural texts reveal the structural tenacity of anxiety. But cultural texts also provide articulations that make vivid the *form* that everyday life can take. If on the one hand the texts of the revolutionary period evidence a perspectival distance, the texts of the post-revolutionary period are marked by a proximity that articulate an incoherence at the level of the everyday. The everyday is either too far or too near; a correct distance in which the experiences of everyday life can be made intelligible seems to be, precisely, out of reach.

Further reading: Chow 1995; Dirlik and Zhang 2000; Lee 1999; Zhang 1996.

TO ALL APPEARANCES, everyday urban life as normalcy now seems success-fully instituted; for good reason, this is celebrated as a genuine cultural revolution in late twentieth-century China. Interestingly enough, this normalcy, which comes in the wake of a massive socialist experiment, can be readily theorized as well as rational-ized through Marxian terminology. It is not at all difficult, for instance, for the general social discourse to grasp that the market is the operating logic behind everyday urban life. The Janus face of the market, both a liberating 'angel' and a destructive 'devil', is very much accepted as a necessary reality principle. Thus, an article that appropriately appears in the 'Think Tank for the Coming Century' section in *Chinese Youth*, a popular magazine published by the League of Communist Youth, asserts:

> The market economy is an 'angel,' because it transforms the world into a colorful place; it is also a 'devil' because it puts existing values and social order in complete disarray. In the words of Karl Marx, this means a revolution in the realms of politics, consciousness, spirit, and morality.[1]

According to the article's author, the market economy will introduce a complete renewal of Chinese society in terms of its social organization. With the market as a leveling mechanism, the individual will be freed from total dependence on and control by the work unit, and the work unit in turn will itself be released from the rigid bureaucratic hierarchy. Another desirable consequence is that social life will be less politicized because society at large will become pluralized and politics will cease to provide the only meaningful content. Chinese society as a whole, concludes the author, is bidding farewell to a past in which politics dominated all details of everyday life. The new era of 'open and plural development', propelled by the market, will usher in a younger, more energetic, and more colorful society.[2]

As optimistic an assessment as that may be, the article nonetheless brings to our attention a central feature of twentieth-century Chinese revolutionary culture, and, at the same time, it sheds light on the making of contemporary urban culture. The author describes the social reality that the new market economy will help to dismantle as either the 'traditional socialist system' or simply the 'traditional system'. This traditional social organization valorizes communality, hierarchy, and ideological homogeneity, all of which contribute to an impoverishment of everyday life. This impoverishment takes the form of moralizing feelings, social relations, and quotidian routines; it is thus an impoverishment paradoxically sustained by an immense richness in political meanings and consequentialities. The ultimate injunction of this mode of social life is stated in a slogan popular during the radical 1960s: 'Make a revolution in the depths of your soul.'[3] With such an imperative for ethical politics, everyday life is not without its excitement or content; on the contrary, it is nothing but ritualized content, and it can be full of pious passion and longings. With ideology or political identity as its sole content or depth, everyday life is organized, rendered meaningful, and effectively reduced in form. This constitutes what Agnes Heller, following George Lukács, has described as an 'emergence' from everyday life through homogenization, more specifically a 'moral homogenization', the criteria of which are 'concentration on the given objective, subordination to it of everyday activities, even their partial or total suspension.'[4] Although Heller acknowledges that 'everyday life could not be reproduced without the heterogeneous human activities', she, as much as Lukács, emphasizes the process of homogenization as collective creation or re-creation for the 'objectivation' of human 'species-essentiality'.[5] Put differently, the heterogeneous forms of everyday life can be transcended or emerged from only when they are endowed with the content of homogenized social relations and pursuits.

A collective desire to resist the inertia of everyday life was an integral part of the grand socialist movement in modern China. Moreover, the same desire, which Agnes Heller characterizes as the 'necessity of philosophy' after religion, has been universally experienced in the age of modernity. After all, modernization arrives only when instrumental reason secures a desacralization of the human as well as the natural world and when a secular ordinary life is affirmed to be equally providential and indispensable to human identity. The humanist culture of modernity, according to Charles Taylor, affirms the full human life 'in terms of labour and production, on one hand, and marriage and family life on the other'.[6] Against such massive democratization or cultural leveling, various modernisms, conservative or radical, arise in protest and 'in the search for sources which can restore depth, richness, and meaning to life'.[7] The modernist aspiration of writers like T. S. Eliot or D. H. Lawrence, observes Taylor, 'is usually made more urgent by the sense that our modern fragmented, instrumentalist society has narrowed and impoverished our lives.'[8] To emerge from this secularized everyday life, to transform *the ordinary life* into *the good life*, therefore, is as much a modernist desire as a critique of modernity. This antimodern and yet modernist rejection of everyday life seems to be a deeply embedded impulse of the revolutionary culture in modern China, which often expresses itself in the Maoist utopian longing for a full and complete life. The success of such a politics of utopia, however, can perhaps be measured only in its failure, in its negation by late twentieth-century consumerism and mass culture, which, I wish to argue, in fact helps to retroactively release the utopian potency of a revolutionary tradition. 'In terms of political positions and ideologies,' as Fredric Jameson comments on the failed radical traditions in literature and culture,

> all the radical positions of the past are flawed, precisely because they failed. . . . What they achieved, however, was something rather different from achieved positivity; they demonstrated, for their own time and culture, the *impossibility* of imagining Utopia.[9]

To demonstrate that a deep utopian impulse of the Chinese revolutionary culture is to overcome ordinary everyday life would be a complex process, and it probably could be achieved only negatively, namely, through an examination of *signifying absences*. The four general developments that Charles Taylor believes to have contributed to the culture of modernity, for example, could be a useful point of departure in a cultural studies approach: the new valuation of commerce, the rise of the novel, the changing understanding of marriage and the family, and the new importance of sentiment.[10] We would likely find in the revolutionary tradition a systematic suppression or reorientation of these activities that would have helped to affirm and define a secular everyday life. A persisting paradox here is that the fuller life envisioned by Maoist social engineering reflects both an essentially agrarian imagination and a fascination with modern industrial power, both an egalitarian commitment to social harmony and an almost aristocratic refusal of the mundane and the physical.

From such a vision of the good life, which valorizes completeness and transcendence, is derived an aesthetics of scale rather than of detail, for immediacy and particularity would only swamp any effort to overcome the daily routine. This in part explains why artwork from the revolutionary period is dominantly perspectival and panoramic.[11] In *New Look of a Village* (1974) (Figure 13.1), a representative Huxian (Huhsien) County peasant painting from the heyday of the socialist revolution, we see the way that a politicized public space has endowed labor with global significance. The continuity of spatial structure neatly defers gratification and yet keeps in perspective the consummating *promesse de bonheur* (promise of happiness). In a similar spirit, *The Whole Family Studies the Communiqué* (1974) (Figure 13.2) presents the extended family as a political unit and projects a domestic interior that is open and public, simple but productive, and ultimately centered on the communal as well as spiritual act of reading. In these stylized images of happiness, the political economy of the sign forcefully distributes the socialist ideals of equality, use value, self-reliance, and homogenized social relations. It is by no accident, moreover, that these socialist realist representations of rural life were acclaimed as emblematic of 'the socialist new culture' at the time.[12] As mentioned, the ruralization policies, or the 'development without urbanization' model, of the 1960s and 1970s could be seen as a collective effort to ensure an organic and connected life that threatens to unravel in the urban landscape. These Huxian County peasant paintings, which enjoyed considerable popularity and official sponsorship in the mid-1970s, best capture an age for which *la sociabilité villageoise* (village harmony) was the norm and the ideal form of life.[13]

In fact, we have to understand this particular art form, together with many other signifying practices from that period (such as the 'revolutionary model theater', public squares, and massive parades), as constituting a revolutionary mass culture. It is a mass culture that emphasizes content over form, use value over exchange value, participatory communal action over heterogeneous everyday life. Hence, such a mass culture is profoundly romantic in its form and utopian in its vision; it is necessarily didactic rather than entertaining, production-oriented rather than consumption-oriented. The historical relevance of this specific mass culture, especially its utopian vision, however, may become all the more recognizable and even compelling only when it is negated as a hegemonic, practiced social order. Only in absentia does this revolutionary mass culture reveal itself to have been a heroic effort to overcome a deep anxiety over everyday life, often at the cost of impoverishing it. When everyday life is affirmed and accepted as the new hegemony, when commodification arrives to put a price tag on human relations and even on private sentiments, participatory communal action may offer itself as an oppositional discourse and expose a vacuity underlying the myriad of commodity forms. The persistent nostalgia for Mao and his era in late twentieth-century China is a good sign of the collective anxiety that the market economy has given rise to.[14] But it cannot be concluded that this postrevolutionary culture is

Figure 13.1 Peasant painting, *New Look of a Village*, 1974. From *Peasant Paintings from Huhsien County* (Peking: Foreign Language Press, 1974)

without its consolation or even its utopian appeal. In fact, a direct function of the rising consumerism is to contain and dissolve the anxiety of everyday life, to translate collective concerns into consumer desires, by which means even the revolutionary past may be made profitable.

Thus, the transitional quality of late twentieth-century Chinese culture can be observed as two related social discourses: an anxious affirmation of ordinary life and a

Figure 13.2 Peasant painting, *The Whole Family Studies the Communiqué*, 1974. From *Peasant Paintings from Huhsien County* (Peking: Foreign Language Press, 1974)

continuous negotiation with the utopian impulse to reject everyday life. This transition, part of the long revolution toward modernity, is readily observable as the tension between the city and the country. As has been pointed out, urbanization has certainly shifted the focus of the social imaginary, but the country still refuses to disappear, and frequently it flashes back, so to speak, to throw an unsettling light on the urban landscape. While an apparently amorphous urban everyday life becomes the norm and an alienating institution, rustic simplicity and authenticity seem to possess a greater peculiar attraction. In this light, just as there can be a revolutionary mass culture, so there is bound to be another mass culture that observes the logic of the reproduction of everyday life. Whereas the revolutionary mass culture needs to project a life that is wholesome but abstract, the new urban culture has to present a secular existence that, routine though it may be, is full of concrete expectations and fulfillments.

At this juncture it is useful to examine some contemporary literary works in order to appreciate the emergent and contested urban consciousness, with the aim of determining whether the works in question belong to mass culture or high literature. A good case in point is the 1993 novella *Shenghuo wuzui* (*Life Is Not a Crime*) by a young writer, He Dun. This story, a loosely organized first-person narrative about a young man's various efforts to make money on his own in the inland city of Changsha, may be paradigmatic of the narratable experience of a whole genuinely postrevolutionary generation of urban youth. The world in which the young man finds himself is one of entrepreneurial adventure, prostitution, violence, organized crime, commodities, and quick money. As in his other novella, *Wo bu xiangshi* (*I Don't Care*), He Dun hurriedly narrates in a factual, indifferent tone of understanding, but with no compassion, moments and sensations in the hero's busy, directionless life. The series of events is barely coherent, and its multiplicity seems to be the only narratable content of the young man's experience. The story begins with a brief ritual of initiation, a moment at which the hero, He Fu, then an impoverished high school teacher, is invited to enter the symbolic space of the narrative – a domestic space pointedly exhibiting its contemporaneity through an ostentatious display of objects, commodities, and details. One afternoon in May, He Fu and his wife, Zhu Li, decide to pay a visit to an old friend of his, who now runs a department store and self-consciously belongs to the new managerial class.

> When I, having made love with Zhu Li around noon, walked into Qu Gang's apartment and saw how luxuriously furnished it was, I felt reasonably calm. Qu Gang owned an apartment with four rooms, one of them used as the living room. The surrounding walls were decorated with pink enameled tiles, a chandelier hung from the ceiling, and the floor was covered with inlaid parquet. There was a nicely crafted, snow-white composite dresser, on which stood an imposing 28″ Toshiba color TV. Next to it was a video machine; further down stood an American-made Sherwood stereo system. After my wife and I had settled down in the elegant sheepskin sofa, my wife said: 'Your sofa is so comfortable to sit in.' 'Imported from Italy,' Qu Gang replied, throwing over to me a '555' cigarette. 'Cost me about ten grand. It better be comfortable to sit in.' 'That much money?' Zhu Li felt the sofa. 'That was too expensive.' Qu Gang smirked without comment, 'Do you guys want coffee or tea?'[15]

This initial moment is pivotal to the story in that it introduces desire, or, more exactly, it gives concrete, physical shape and expression to a desire for self-transformation. The material world becomes a prominent index not so much of vulgarity as of an enviable spiritual resilience. The same moment also offers a redefinition of everyday life, of domestic existence as graspable through various tangible forms – in this case, expensive consumer goods. This stuffed showroom will not be entered again, but it provides meaning and image to the space in which He Fu, the aspiring consumer/entrepreneur, wishes to participate. (At this point, however, he feels embarrassed to even talk about money because he has to save every penny in order to purchase a color TV.)

Before rushing ahead to condemn this unabashed consumerism, we need to realize that it probably has its origin in a not-so-distant past when consumption was maximally suppressed from the reproduction of everyday life. Almost directly, this commodity fetishism comes as a rebellion against, or an overcompensation for, the utopian life depicted in an artwork such as *The Whole Family Studies the Communiqué*. In the wake of such a clearly defined and community-oriented form of life, in which spiritual elevation was the predominant need, there is a striking lack of perspective in He Dun's story about the bestirring life in late twentieth-century Changsha. The narrator, moreover, consistently refuses to impose moral judgment or even indicate indignation. As the story rapidly unfolds, the day-to-day events, frustrations, and expectations that befall him and fellow city dwellers keep his attention riveted, and the city in which he moves never emerges as a totalizable spatiality. Only toward the very end of the story do we find a pause and a moment of doubt. And this occurs when another old friend, like a specter from the unspeakable past, returns to question He Fu's increasingly complacent daily life. Very tellingly, this friend is an artist who lives in the distant frontier of Xinjiang and finds himself not welcomed while visiting Hunan, his place of birth. In the story, the artist serves to pose a fundamental question about value, which He Fu, with a lot of sarcasm, dismisses as metaphysical and pointless. But when the artist friend leaves in disappointment early the next morning, the hero feels the warm flow of an old friendship and becomes guilt-stricken. Then rain starts pouring down outside:

> Several times I made up my mind to go out, but lacked the courage to walk in a thunderstorm. I gazed at the heavy rain that would possibly never stop and said to myself: 'This world really makes people suffer.' As soon as I said this, it dawned on me that all those things – about which I had been too excited to fall asleep normally in the past few months, and which could be described as forming a beautiful blueprint – had all of a sudden turned into a pile of broken tiles.[16]

This is where the narrative ends, and we leave the hero with the pouring rain, pondering over the transcendental meaning of the world.

Despite a final, reflective moment like this one (perhaps an 'epiphany'?), *Life Is Not a Crime* resolutely subscribes to the urban space it depicts. It is a paradigmatic narrative of the city because it is motivated by a fascination with the apparently infinite possibilities of form that a city now allows. This 'guilt-free life' is a fragmented but concrete existence, the moral content of which is realized in action rather than in contemplation. The fact that the idealistic artist appears unexpectedly, only at the end of the story, calls our attention to a spectrality about his being. Perhaps he is a residual modernist bent on revealing the incompleteness of life in modernity. Even though this artist figure disappears altogether from He Dun's later work, his fleeting presence here reveals a fundamental lack. His lonely departure also suggests that the pursuit of a full life is now a personal commitment and has to be conducted at the margin, far away from the crowded urban landscape.

If what He Dun chooses to depict is the heterogeneous 'stuff' of everyday urban life, the satisfaction of which is frequently achieved through objects and commodities, then Wang Anyi, an established and prolific contemporary writer, presents an intriguing examination of urban sensibility and emotional life. What I have in mind is her novella *Xianggang de qing yu ai* (*Love and Sentiment in Hong Kong*), a piece of writing that bears an uncanny resemblance to Zhang Ailing's (Eileen Chang's) story from roughly fifty years earlier, *Qingcheng zhi lian* (*Love in a Fallen City*). Critically acclaimed for having a strong 'future look', Wang Anyi's contemporary story tells of an affair in Hong Kong between an aging but wealthy Chinese-American businessman and his crass and practical mistress, who is an immigrant from Shanghai and now desperately wants to go to the United States. The tale begins as yet another affair based on an exchange of favors, and it ends with the woman heading for Australia several years later, leaving behind an older Lao Wei, who, in her absence, finds himself more than ever attached to the city of Hong Kong. In an associational and even nostalgic style, Wang Anyi patiently explores all aspects of the question of 'how the bustling and prosperous metropolis participates in the emotional life of people.'[17] The story is equally a rich and complex narrative about Hong Kong, the spectacular city that may strike one at first as a 'great encounter, a miraculous coming together',[18] but eventually reveals its many depths and dimensions over time. For the protagonists in the story, Hong Kong is a city of both past and future, a transit stopover that nonetheless indiscriminately shelters homeless souls and even nurtures attachment and love. The fact that Lao Wei and his mistress, Fengjia, are no longer young and are perhaps much too practical also indicates a mature approach to the city, what Raymond Williams calls the perspective of 'an adult experience'.[19] For the author of the story, too, Hong Kong, as a completely urbanized space, presents an enormous field of multiple new possibilities and expectations, a whole new civilization that stands in need of comprehending, representing, and probably evaluating.[20]

Yet, just as in *Life Is Not a Crime*, the narrative of *Love and Sentiment in Hong Kong* is a careful withholding of moral judgment or criticism. Instead, it continuously marvels at the protean shape possessed by the contemporary city and the endless variations – in lived space as well as in the human heart – that the city constantly provokes. With deliberate slowness, the narrative moves us through a series of spatial structures that are emphatically urban: courteous service but impersonal hotel rooms, private and yet uniform apartments in a twenty-story building, and new but empty homes waiting to be furnished with a personal touch. It assembles into a colorful picture such activities as shopping, dining, riding the double-decker bus, pursuing domestic pleasures, and engaging in small talk on the phone. In the eyes of the narrator, Hong Kong is no less than the city of all cities. Just as every detail of leisurely urban life offers instant satisfaction and is savored with deliberate pleasure, so every moment is charged with ambiguities and open to interpretation. For instance, taking a double-decker bus to go home, Lao Wei and Fengjia look out to enjoy the busy street scenes, in particular those apartment windows seemingly within arm's reach. 'These windows reveal the most sincere, most practical ways of sustaining life; these are ways that will remain unchanged forever, as permanently as rivers flowing and the sun and the moon revolving. They belong in the same category as the sky and the ocean beyond the lights in Hong Kong, as the rocks standing in the sea water. They are the solid foundation of the marvelous spectacle of Hong Kong. Here you find the most ordinary life, as ordinary as the intriguing spectacle of Hong Kong can be.'[21] Against this backdrop of heterogeneous coexistence, human experience is described as anything but uneventful. Here, the narrator is greatly fascinated by the new modality that Hong Kong promises to human sensibility.

> In such a hot and humid evening, you never know how many stories are strolling along the streets, pausing and moving hesitantly. Some of them just have a beginning, some of them are coming to an end, and some others are right in the middle. This is why evenings in Hong Kong are full of turns and suspense. These are the least quiet and peaceful evenings, with numerous comedies and tragedies unfolding at the same time . . . [The drama of Hong Kong] offers you excitement that cannot be total, and despair that will never be complete. *It promises you a last ray of hope when everything turns out to be a disappointment; it also adds a broken piece when you finally possess everything.* Yet no matter what, the story of Hong Kong will never come to

an end. There will always be instruments playing in the theater of Hong
Kong, and there will never be a dying out of the lights in Hong Kong.
(Emphasis added)[22]

These observations by themselves may not be profound or original, and some of them
already have been made – for instance, in Zhang Ailing's stories about Hong Kong and
Shanghai in the 1940s[23] – but in the context of contemporary Chinese social discourse,
the Hong Kong that Wang Anyi narrates here is undoubtedly a purposeful metaphor
for a cultural choice. As a geographical embodiment of the social imaginary, Hong
Kong indeed stands as a city of the future. It offers itself as an ideal instance of the
heterotopian urban life that the Chinese postrevolutionary culture seems anxious to
understand and eventually to acquire.

Most noticeably, therefore, the broken but concrete life stories that Wang Anyi
tells us here are hardly affected by either collective consciousness or political aspirations. There is barely any reference to recent history. However, this does not necessarily mean that there is no shared vision of the future. The peculiarity of Hong Kong,
as portrayed in Wang Anyi's narrative, is that it is completely postindustrial and
urbanized. This is perhaps where the writer sees the relevance of Hong Kong as a
paradigmatic space for an approaching future. On the one hand, the city of Hong Kong
appears to be an enormous postmodern shopping mall, where everything is for sale
and all anxieties can be shopped away; on the other hand, the city is full of human
drama because, ceaselessly, 'it throws an inclusive party by inviting all kinds of loneliness, and arranges a grand reunion by bringing together all moments of solitude.'[24]
The story of Lao Wei and Fengjia and their use and understanding of each other should
ultimately be read as a defense of the richness of a mundane urban life. In her novella,
Wang Anyi anticipates a major cultural transformation in contemporary China as
much as He Dun does in his fragmented stories about the city of Changsha. Both
writers grasp the city as central to a postrevolutionary reality, and, in doing so, they
make representable an age in which the emergent hegemony is no longer Ideology or
Collectivity, but rather everyday life. Also in this sense, they blend mass cultural and
high literature and directly participate in the making of a new urban culture, the
historical function of which is to help absorb the shock of urbanization and ultimately
to legitimate modernity.

Notes

1   Xu Weixin, 'Shichang jingji jiang shi Zhongguo shehui quanmian gengxin' (The market economy
    will completely renew Chinese society), *Chinese Youth* (August 1993): 22.
2   Ibid., 22–23. Xu's conclusion concurs with Gordon White's well-documented analysis that the
    spread of market relations has effectively 'created the basis of, and context for, new forms of
    sociopolitical participation and organization, to varying degrees independent of and/or in oppos-
    ition to the Party/state.' See White, *Riding the Tiger: The Politics of Economic Reform in Post-Mao
    China* (Stanford, Calif.: Stanford University Press, 1993), 217.
3   In Chinese, the slogan usually goes 'Linghun shenchu nao geming.'
4   Agnes Heller, *Everyday Life*, trans. G. L. Campbell (London: Routledge & Kegan Paul, 1984), 87.
5   See ibid., 56–59.
6   Charles Taylor, 'Part III: The Affirmation of Ordinary Life', in *Sources of the Self: The Making of the
    Modern Identity* (Cambridge, Mass.: Harvard University Press, 1989), 213.

7   Ibid., 495.

8   Ibid., 490.

9   Fredric Jameson, 'Immanence and Nominalism in Postmodern Theoretical Discourse', in *Post-modernism, Or, the Cultural Logic of Late Capitalism* (Durham, N.C.: Duke University Press, 1991), 208–09. See also in the same volume Jameson's discussion of artist Robert Gober's work in 'Utopianism After the End of Utopia', 154–80. My line of reading here is deeply indebted to Jameson's 'Marxian positive hermeneutic', even though I may be simplifying some of his ideas.

10   See Taylor, *Sources of the Self*, 285–302.

11   Ellen Johnston Laing, in her *The Winking Owl: Art in the People's Republic of China* (Berkeley: University of California Press, 1988), traces the political history of art during the radical 1960s. '[Other] landscapes done during this period,' she observes, 'are also vast panoramic vistas, and their subjects are usually, if not the already established themes based on revolutionary history, then clearly delineated motifs of socialist triumphs in public projects: bridges, busy ports, dams, reforestation' (78).

12   In the foreword to the English edition of *Peasant Paintings from Huhsien County* (Peking: Foreign Languages Press, 1974), the government compilers laud the peasant artists as 'masters of the socialist new culture'. Moreover, 'they have set a pattern for developing fine arts as a spare-time activity in rural areas and become a model for professional artists.'

13   The phrase *la sociabilité villageoise* is from historian Jean-Pierre Gutton's book *La Sociabilité villageoise dans l'ancienne France: solidarités et voisinages du XIIe au XVIIIe siècle* (Paris: Hachette, 1979).

14   Sociologist Wang Yanzhong also points out that 'Mao Zedong fever' reflects a popular longing for the charismatic leader in an age of growing institutionalization. See Zhang Zhanbing and Song Yifu, *Zhongguo: Mao Zedong re* (China: Mao Zedong fever) (Taiyuan: Beiyue wenyi, 1991), 275–76, 280–81. One of the good things about this popular sentiment, according to the authors of the book, is that it will call attention to issues such as inflation, social security, justice, and a communal spirit (284–85).

15   *Shenghuo wuzui* (*Life Is Not a Crime*), in *Shouhuo* (Harvest), no. 99 (1993): 25; *Wo bu xiangshi* (*I don't Care*), in *Shanghai wenxue* (*Shanghai Literature*), no. 192 (September 1993): 4–41.

16   He Dun, *Life Is Not a Crime*, 53.

17   See the 'Editor's Words' section at the front of *Shanghai Literature*, no. 191 (August 1993), in which Wang's story appears.

18   Wang Anyi, *Xianggang de qing he ai* (*Love and Sentiment in Hong Kong*), in *Shanghai Literature*, no. 191 (August 1993): 4.

19   At the beginning of his *The Country and the City* (New York: Oxford University Press, 1973), Williams writes in a personal tone: 'I have felt also the chaos of the metro and the traffic jam; the monotony of the ranks of houses; the aching press of strange crowds. But this is not an experience at all, not an adult experience, until it has come to include also the dynamic movement, in these centres of settled and often magnificent achievement' (5).

20   This is not to say that the city has not appeared in Wang Anyi's work until this moment. Based in Shanghai, Wang Anyi is probably one of the very few contemporary Chinese writers who take the city as a serious subject of their writings. In a short essay, 'Nanren he nüren, nüren he chengshi' (Men and women, women and the city), written in 1986, she already theorized on the freedom and opportunity that the city may present to women. For her, the city represented a welcome break with the agrarian tradition in which only men could have excelled. See Wang Anyi, *Huangshan zhi lian* (*Love on a Barren Mountain*) (Hong Kong: South China Press, 1988), 243–48.

21   Wang, *Love and Sentiment in Hong Kong*, 10.

22   Ibid., 15.

23   For an insightful analysis of the sense of 'incompleteness' and modernity in Zhang Ailing's fiction, see Meng Yue, 'Zhongguo wenxue "xiandai xing" yu Zhang Ailing' (The modernity of Chinese literature and Zhang Ailing), *Jintian* (Today), no. 3 (1992): 176–92.

24   Wang, *Love and Sentiment in Hong Kong*, 15.

PART THREE

Ethnography near and far

INTRODUCTION TO PART THREE

TRADITIONALLY ANTHROPOLOGY (or its older cognate ethnology) has been the academic arena most attentive to everyday life. In its modern form anthropology has privileged the practice of ethnography (the empirical registering of ways of life) as the form most suited to the understanding of culture as an everyday experience. Ethnography has also been an essential tool in a number of other academic arenas, most notably sociology and cultural studies. Indeed it might be that the study of ethnography (as a range of practices that vary across and within disciplines) allows for a metatheoretical assessment of the social sciences in general. For instance the critique of anthropology as a perspective that necessarily implies that everyday life is what 'other' people are submerged in (while refusing to scrutinise its own everyday existence) could similarly be levelled at sociologies of working class life, or studies of subcultures. And, as interestingly, the way that anthropology has been problematised by, and has reflected on, cross-cultural encounters would make for a relevant perspective for examining empirical work in sociology or cultural studies.

Recent ethnographic works in the humanities, specifically in the field of filmmaking and art making (see Chapters 19, 20 and 21), have witnessed a use of ethnography not so determined by a rhetoric of science (a rhetoric that has tended to underwrite traditional approaches to ethnography in the social sciences). This has coincided with an investigation of ethnography in the social sciences as necessarily a literary production (its dominant form is writing) and open to the kinds of critical scrutiny traditionally reserved for novels and such like. The work of James Clifford and George E. Marcus, particularly in their edited collection *Writing Culture: The Poetics and Politics of Ethnography* (Clifford and Marcus 1986), offers a vivid example of this work. Alongside this has been the recovery of a number of projects that had been seen to exist on the margins of academic work and that problematically crossed the divide between art and science (for instance the work of Mass-Observation – see Chapter 15).

If the practice of ethnography is going to grant academic access to the everyday, then it will need to internalise the vigorous critiques that have been made of its practice while generating new and inventive ways of operating (so as not to be simply stymied by critique). The extracts in Part Three provide examples of both the problems and potentials of ethnography. They all implicitly pose ethnography as a *question* of practice. How should the everyday life of others be studied? Should anthropology in the West scrutinise its own everyday rituals and practices rather than the everyday life of its (presumed) exotic other? Can ethnography be a practice that does not render the voices of its informants subservient to the interpretative performance of the ethnographer? How can the 'politics and poetics of ethnography' be reinvented for the future?

Chapter 14

Bronislaw Malinowski

PROPER CONDITIONS FOR ETHNOGRAPHIC WORK [1922]

(Source: Malinowski, Bronislaw (1984) *Argonauts of the Western Pacific*, Prospect Heights, Ill.: Waveland Press, pp. 6–8, 11–13)

Editor's introduction

Malinowski (1884–1942) was born in Poland but for most of his academic career was associated with the London School of Economics. Between 1914 and 1918 he conducted his first sustained ethnographic research in the Trobriand Islands, an archipelago to the north-east of Papua New Guinea. This complex of cultures and communities was central to nearly all of Malinowski's anthropological writing. While many of Malinowski's innovations might now seem like conventional common sense (while others register an obvious ideological paternalism) they need to be seen within the deeply racist context of western colonialism. To give up the 'comfortable position in the long chair on the veranda of the missionary compound, Government station or planter's bungalow' (Malinowski quoted in Stocking 1996) for a tent pitched in the 'tribal' village was a radical break from ethnological orthodoxy. To insist, as Malinowski does, that an anthropologist might find it necessary to spend considerable time in the field and should learn the native language was part of a movement that revolutionised a science that had all too often relied on hearsay. In this extract from his book *Argonauts of the Western Pacific*, Malinowski proposes an ethnographic approach that requires participation in the everyday life of the culture being studied (so as to understand it from the 'native's point of view') while maintaining an observational distance (the anthropologist's point of view). Participant observation, such as this implies, became the dominant approach to ethnography throughout most of the twentieth century.

When Malinowski's Trobriand diaries were posthumously published in 1967, it became clear that such transcultural activity was much more easily espoused than practised. What the diaries revealed was not simply a 'man of his time' who in his private journals evidenced a disturbing mix of fear and fascination towards 'natives' (a dominant characteristic of transcultural *colonial* encounters); the diaries also revealed a profound epistemological problem. The question of how one culture can know another had of course been part of anthropological inquiry, but the evident trauma that Malinowski experienced in attempting to immerse himself in Trobriand culture, and the dangers that he felt he was exposing himself to in doing so, framed these questions in a new light. If Malinowski promoted a serious consideration of the everyday life of other cultures, he also showed how his own everyday life culture was a 'deep structure' that could not be simply shrugged off during fieldwork.

It is also worth noting that for Malinowski the anthropologist's task was to find the 'permanent and fixed' regularities of a culture. That these were to be located at the level of everyday life is of course a crucial and contested idea in the study of everyday life.

Further reading: Clifford 1988; Kuper 1996; Malinowski 1967; Stocking 1996.

PROPER CONDITIONS FOR ETHNOGRAPHIC WORK. These consist mainly in cutting oneself off from the company of other white men, and remaining in as close contact with the natives as possible, which really can only be achieved by camping right in their villages. It is very nice to have a base in a white man's compound for the stores, and to know there is a refuge there in times of sickness and surfeit of native. But it must be far enough away not to become a permanent milieu in which you live and from which you emerge at fixed hours only to 'do the village'. It should not even be near enough to fly to at any moment for recreation. For the native is not the natural companion for a white man, and after you have been working with him for several hours, seeing how he does his gardens, or letting him tell you items of folk-lore, or discussing his customs, you will naturally hanker after the company of your own kind. But if you are alone in a village beyond reach of this, you go for a solitary walk for an hour or so, return again and then quite naturally seek out the natives' society, this time as a relief from loneliness, just as you would any other companionship. And by means of this natural intercourse, you learn to know him, and you become familiar with his customs and beliefs far better than when he is a paid, and often bored, informant.

There is all the difference between a sporadic plunging into the company of natives, and being really in contact with them. What does this latter mean? On the Ethnographer's side, it means that his life in the village, which at first is a strange, sometimes unpleasant, sometimes intensely interesting adventure, soon adopts quite a natural course very much in harmony with his surroundings.

Soon after I had established myself in Omarakana (Trobriand Islands), I began to take part, in a way, in the village life, to look forward to the important or festive events, to take personal interest in the gossip and the developments of the small village occurrences; to wake up every morning to a day, presenting itself to me more or less as it does to the native. I would get out from under my mosquito net, to find around me the village life beginning to stir, or the people well advanced in their working day according to the hour and also to the season, for they get up and begin their labours early or late, as work presses. As I went on my morning walk through the village, I could see intimate details of family life, of toilet, cooking, taking of meals; I could see the arrangements for the day's work, people starting on their errands, or groups of men and women busy at some manufacturing tasks. Quarrels, jokes, family scenes, events usually trivial, sometimes dramatic but always significant, formed the atmosphere of my daily life, as well as of theirs. It must be remembered that as the natives saw me constantly every day, they ceased to be interested or alarmed, or made self-conscious by my presence, and I ceased to be a disturbing element in the tribal life which I was to study, altering it by my very approach, as always happens with a new-comer to every savage community. In fact, as they knew that I would thrust my nose into everything, even where a well-mannered native would not dream of intruding, they finished by regarding me as part and parcel of their life, a necessary evil or nuisance, mitigated by donations of tobacco.

Later on in the day, whatever happened was within easy reach, and there was no possibility of its escaping my notice. Alarms about the sorcerer's approach in the evening, one or two big, really important quarrels and rifts within the community, cases of illness, attempted cures and deaths, magical rites which had to be performed, all these I had not to pursue, fearful of missing them, but they took place under my very eyes, at my own doorstep, so to speak. And it must be emphasised whenever anything dramatic or important occurs it is essential to investigate it at the very moment of happening, because the natives cannot but talk about it, are too excited to be reticent, and too interested to be mentally lazy in supplying details. Also, over and over again, I committed breaches of etiquette, which the natives, familiar enough with me, were not slow in pointing out. I had to learn how to behave, and to a certain extent, I acquired 'the feeling' for native good and bad manners. With this, and with the capacity of enjoying their company and sharing some of their games and amusements, I began to feel that I was indeed in touch with the natives, and this is certainly the preliminary condition of being able to carry on successful field work.

[. . .]

Having settled this very general rule, let us descend to more detailed consideration of method. The Ethnographer has in the field, according to what has just been said, the duty before him of drawing up all the rules and regularities of tribal life; all that is permanent and fixed; of giving an anatomy of their culture, of depicting the constitution of their society. But these things, though crystallised and set, are nowhere *formulated*. There is no written or explicitly expressed code of laws, and their whole tribal tradition, the whole structure of their society, are embodied in the most elusive of all materials; the human being. But not even in human mind or memory are these laws to be found definitely formulated. The natives obey the forces and commands of the tribal code, but they do not comprehend them; exactly as they obey their instincts and their impulses, but could not lay down a single law of psychology. The regularities in native institutions are an automatic result of the interaction of the mental forces of tradition, and of the material conditions of environment. Exactly as a humble member of any modern institution, whether it be the state, or the church, or the army, is *of* it and *in* it, but has no vision of the resulting integral action of the whole, still less could furnish any account of its organisation, so it would be futile to attempt questioning a native in abstract, sociological terms. The difference is that, in our society, every institution has its intelligent members, its historians, and its archives and documents, whereas in a native society there are none of these. After this is realised an expedient has to be found to overcome this difficulty. This expedient for an Ethnographer consists in collecting concrete data of evidence, and drawing the general inferences for himself. This seems obvious on the face of it, but was not found out or at least practised in Ethnography till field work was taken up by men of science. Moreover, in giving it practical effect, it is neither easy to devise the concrete applications of this method, nor to carry them out systematically and consistently.

Though we cannot ask a native about abstract, general rules, we can always enquire how a given case would be treated. Thus for instance, in asking how they would treat crime, or punish it, it would be vain to put to a native a sweeping question such as, 'How do you treat and punish a criminal?' for even words could not be found to express it in native, or in pidgin. But an imaginary case, or still better, a real occurrence, will stimulate a native to express his opinion and to supply plentiful information. A real case indeed will start the natives on a wave of discussion, evoke expressions of indignation, show them taking sides – all of which talk will probably contain a wealth of definite views, of moral censures, as well as reveal the social mechanism set in motion by the crime committed. From there, it will be easy to lead them on to speak of other similar cases, to remember other actual occurrences or to discuss them in all their implications and aspects. From this material, which ought to cover the widest possible range of facts, the inference is obtained by simple induction. The *scientific* treatment differs from that of good common sense, first in that a student will extend the completeness and minuteness of survey much further and in a pedantically systematic and methodical manner; and secondly, in that the scientifically trained mind, will push the inquiry along really relevant lines, and towards aims possessing real importance. Indeed, the object of scientific training is to provide the empirical investigator with a *mental chart*, in accordance with which he can take his bearings and lay his course.

Chapter 15

Mass-Observation

TWO LETTERS AND 'THEY SPEAK FOR THEMSELVES' [1936–7]

(**Sources**: Madge, Charles (1937a) 'Anthropology at Home', *The New Statesman and Nation*, 2 January, p. 12; Harrisson, Tom, Jennings, Humphrey and Madge, Charles (1937) 'Anthropology at Home', *The New Statesman and Nation*, 30 January, p. 155; Madge, Charles and Jennings, Humphrey (1937) 'They Speak for Themselves: Mass Observation and Social Narrative', *Life and Letters*, 17, pp. 37–42)

Editor's introduction

The two letters reproduced here mark the emergence of the Mass-Observation project. This project, which was to 'collect a mass of data based upon practical observation, on the everyday life of all types of people', was initially formulated by Charles Madge (a poet and journalist), Tom Harrisson (an anthropologist and ornithologist) and Humphrey Jennings (a filmmaker and painter). Based primarily on an expansion of ethnographic techniques to study the everyday life of Britain, it (at least initially) suggested a radical reconfiguring of ethnographic practices. In certain ways the assumption that a 'civilised' culture like Britain in the 1930s could be approached using the same language of ritual and belief that guided anthropologists in their discussion of 'uncivilised' cultures, challenged any assumed 'natural' superiority of western culture. As Tom Harrisson observed, an English boarding school (a bastion of upper-class protocols) evidences an excess of ritualistic and (unusually bizarre) hierarchical behaviour (Harrisson 1942: 152).

Mass-Observation's methodology also challenged anthropological practices. For Mass-Observation one of the main goals was to allow people's everyday experience to circulate within the culture, and to thereby provide a challenge to the way that 'the people' were continually invoked in the national and local press (and the ideological motivation that accompanied it). (Incidentally it was through Mass-Observation that one of the very few challenges to Appeasement was articulated in Britain at the time.) Less concerned with interpreting the material that was being observed (often diaristic self-observation), Mass-Observation was interested in letting people 'speak for themselves'. In ethnographic terms

Mass-Observation dislodged some of the interpretative authority of the anthropologist to allow 'native informants' to become their own ethnographers.

While it is impossible to precisely clarify the intentions or outcomes of the Mass-Observation project (too many different kinds of projects being undertaken, too many people involved), it offers a fascinating moment in the history of anthropology at home. Continually weaving between a truly surreal anthropology at home, and the more banal and often oppressive practices of market research and governmental census, Mass-Observation sticks out as an awkward moment in the study of everyday culture.

Further reading: Calder and Sheridan 1985; Highmore 2002; Jeffrey 1978; Pickering and Chaney 1986.

S IR, – M R. GEOFFREY PYKE suggested in your columns the other week that the constitutional crisis had begun to produce material for an anthropology of our own people.

Some days before the precipitation of the crisis, a group was formed for precisely this purpose. English anthropology, however, hitherto identified with 'folk-lore', has to deal with elements so repressed that only what is admitted to be a first-class upheaval brings them to the surface. Such was the threatened marriage of the new 'Father-of-the-people' to Mrs. Ernest Simpson. Fieldwork, i.e., the collection of evidence of mass wish-situations, has otherwise to proceed in a far more roundabout way than the anthropologist has been accustomed to in Africa or Australia. Clues to these situations may turn up in the popular phenomenon of the 'coincidence'. In fact it is probable that in the ultra-repressed condition of our society they can only material-ise in this form, so mysterious in appearance. But the 'mystery' is part of the mechan-ism of repression. It can be reduced scientifically into the constituent terms of the hidden wish, and referred back to the accepted principles of anthropology. These principles and those of psycho-analysis, and the sciences dealing with the behaviour of man, have been applied by the group to the Crystal Palace-Abdication symbolic situation.[1]

The real observers in this case were the millions of people who were, for once, irretrievably involved in the public events. Only mass observations can create mass science. The group for whom I write is engaged in establishing observation points on as widely extended a front as can at present be organised. We invite the co-operation of voluntary observers, and will provide detailed information to anyone who wants to take part. CHARLES MADGE 6 Grotes Buildings, Blackheath, S.E.3.

SIR, – Man is the last subject of scientific investigation. A century ago Darwin focused the camera of thought on to man as a sort of animal whose behaviour and history would be explained by science. In 1847, Marx formulated a scientific study of eco-nomic man. In 1865, Tylor defined the new science of anthropology which was to be applied to the 'primitive' and the 'savage'. In 1893, Freud and Breuer published their first paper on hysteria; they began to drag into daylight the unconscious elements in individual 'civilised' man. But neither anthropology nor psychology has yet become more than an instrument in the hands of any individual, which he applies (according to his individuality) to primitives and abnormals.

By 1936 chaos was such that the latent elements were crystallised into a new compound. As so often happens, an idea was being worked out in many separate brains. A letter in THE NEW STATESMAN AND NATION from Geoffrey Pyke, arising out of the Simpson crisis, explicitly mentioned the need for an 'anthropology of our own people'. A fortnight later a letter called attention to a group centred in London for the purpose of developing a science of Mass Observation, and this group effected contact with other individuals and with a group working in industrial Lancashire, which had so far concentrated on field work rather than formulation of theory. These interests are now united in the first, necessarily tentative, efforts of Mass Observation.

Mass Observation develops out of anthropology, psychology, and the sciences which study man – but it plans to work with a mass of observers. Already we have fifty observers at work on two sample problems. We are further working out a complete plan of campaign, which will be possible when we have not fifty but 5,000 observers. The following are a few examples of problems that will arise:

> Behaviour of people at war memorials.
> Shouts and gestures of motorists.
> The aspidistra cult.
> Anthropology of football pools.
> Bathroom behaviour.
> Beards, armpits, eyebrows.
> Anti-semitism.
> Distribution, diffusion and significance of the dirty joke.
> Funerals and undertakers.
> Female taboos about eating.
> The private lives of midwives.

In these examples the anthropological angle is obvious, and the description is primarily of physical behaviour. Other inquiries involve mental phenomena which are unconscious or repressed, so that they can only be traced through mass-fantasy and symbolism as developed and exploited, for example, in the daily press. The outbreak of parturition-images in the press last October may have been seasonal, or may have been caused by some public stimulus: continuous watch on the shifting popular images can only be kept by a multitude of watchers. The observers will also provide the points from which can be plotted weather-maps of public feeling in a crisis.

The subject demands the minimum of prejudice, bias and assumption; the maximum of objectivity. It does not presuppose that there are any inexplicable things. Since it aims at collecting data before interpreting them, it must be allowed to doubt and re-examine the completeness of every existing idea about 'humanity', while it cannot afford to neglect any of them.

Equally, all human types can and must assist in this work. The artist and the scientist, each compelled by historical necessity out of their artificial exclusiveness, are at last joining forces and turning back towards the mass from which they had detached themselves.

It does not set out in quest of truth or facts for their own sake, or for the sake of an intellectual minority, but aims at exposing them in simple terms to all observers, so that their environment may be understood, and thus constantly transformed.

Whatever the political methods called upon to effect the transformation, the knowledge of what has to be transformed is indispensable. The foisting on the mass of ideals or ideas developed by men apart from it, irrespective of its capacities, causes mass misery, intellectual despair and an international shambles.

We hope shortly to produce a pamphlet outlining a programme of action. We welcome criticism and co-operation.

TOM HARRISSON
HUMPHREY JENNINGS
CHARLES MADGE.

They speak for themselves

Mass Observation and social narrative

[*The reports which are written for Mass Observation come largely from people whose lives are spent in a world whose behaviour, language, and viewpoint are far removed from academic science and literature. Sociologists and realistic novelists – including proletarian novelists – find it difficult if not impossible to describe the texture of this world. After reading hundreds of Mass Observation reports, we find that they tend to cover just those aspects of life which the others miss. Why is this? Because, we suggest, in these reports people are speaking in a language natural to them – their spelling, punctuation, etc., are their OWN – in spite of a uniform State education. This is hardly a 'well of English undefiled' since into it continually flow more or less muddy streams from press, radio, advertising, film, and 'literature'. But in actual social usage, all the jungle of words grow up together in Darwinian conflict until they establish their own ecology and functions. Contrast this functional value with the use of words by sensitive, stylist writers. Each phrase is paralysed by fear of cliché. Yet each phrase must have a class or family resemblance to one of the known accents of literature. In reaction against this paralysis, there is a general wish among writers to be UNLIKE the intellectual, LIKE the masses. Much 'proletarian fiction' is a product of this wish. But it is not enough for such fiction to be ABOUT proletarians, if they in their turn become a romantic fiction, nor even for it to be BY proletarians, if it is used by them as a means of escaping out of the proletariat.*

Mass Observation is among other things giving working-class and middle class people a chance to speak for themselves, about themselves. How little they are affected by the paralysis of language, even in their first attempts, may be judged from the extracts from Mass Observation reports which follow.]

C. M. and H. J.

From report on self

The last child of six, I was an accidental conception, there being six years between my sister and I. My mother spoilt me as a child, father ignored me. Our family had just settled down to civil life after many years of travelling. My brothers and sisters all left home whilst I was still young. Father's intolerance and cussedness was the cause, as I learned later, and still later I learned the cause of his cussedness – cancer. No one suspected his disease which killed him after an unpleasant illness.

As a child from the age of nine I was an enthusiastic choirboy, once leading a strike of my colleagues for an injustice done to our organist and choirmaster. At the age of 7 or 8 I remember being the boy who was told off to look after other small boys whose bowels had suddenly lost their power of retention.

At the elementary school I won a scholarship giving me a grant and five years free training at a secondary school. Here my work was moderate. I enjoyed singing, speaking French, geometry, and the annual play for the school concert. I was soundly drubbed by the English master for criticising the literary style of the Bible adversely, and I gave mother the excuse that I wanted to be an actor to explain why I wasn't doing much prep.

Throughout my school life my home life was a separate entity, school and home neither met nor mixed. Neither helped the other. At 16 I left school failing to matriculate and got a job by my own efforts with —— by whom I am still employed.

When in the choir I made the acquaintance of a homosexual padre. A great chap in many ways he started a serious train of thought about religion and life. I hadn't thought much before but with the passage of my 'teens I began to read more and more, took an extra-mural course in psychology and woke up to a new adult world of thought and feeling.

At work I was industrious but not specially able. My industry gained me notice and in 1929 I was able to specialize in mechanical accounting.

Although I had had a girl friend when I began working the office attractions were much more impressive than local ladies. I contracted a strong affection, by telephone originally, with an operator and we became very friendly. Eventually as too serious-minded young people do we settled down to save our money to be married. I left home for convenience and cheapness. The scheme worked well but slowly till the summer of 1932 when a gradually worsening situation came to a climax. I flew off the handle, left my woman, went with a younger and very lovely girl, took a room on the other side of London and began quite voluntarily to blue my savings.

The new and lovely lady was daughter to a most curious household in a near-slum. Mother a slattern, father unknown, home dirty – but the girl a marvel of level-headedness and the saner virtues, to say nothing of her beauty. In March 1933 I was moved to —— (North of England) and the new romance became more difficult. We even tried an elopement on August Bank Holiday 1933 but were frustrated by crazed and half-drunk parents. We gave up in good grace and decided to go our several ways.

In —— lodgings I soon grew tired of bad cooking and in July 1934 I married my old love. We are thoroughly happy and live a normal married life.

From report on environment

Live in a street practicaly closed in, the backs of one row of houses face our back, and the fronts of another row of houses face our front, across the bottom there is a Methodist Sunday School & at the top an open Meadow, across the Meadow is the public maternity Hospital, we live about $\frac{3}{4}$ of a mile out of town which is mostly up hill, plenty of open country around. all hilly. Where I work is in the railway coal yard, very dreary & dull, it is situated in the lowest part of the town, as I look out my office window to my left I see coal waggons, beyond them on the hill side a row of rather dirty looking houses, and beyond them a hill side of green fields very drab and steep, with a pylon for electric top and bottom. In front the railway arcade more waggons, the fruit shed, a mill, and two mill chimbney's to the right. the railway weigh bridge the yard gates the bottom of the main street which I can see about half, with a hotel at the bottom, shops, a garage & a cinema as it goes up to a left turn. at my back there is some spare ground on which traveling fairs stay – a few dirty shops with the passenger station which I cannot see to the back.

The life of the district where I live is practicaly all home life, with the exeption of a few shops. The life of the district where I work, is all industry. I am surrounded by the station, Mills, Engineering Shops, and a few smaller industries.

From report on a normal day

This morning I started work with a new firm, specialists in oil, petrol & water pumps in my usual capacity as centre-lathe turner, I awoke early, washed and pulled on my greasy coveralls, I felt pleasantly excited & a 'lets get at it' feeling at the same time, I wanted to see the type & class of work so I could form an estimate of my chances of success & steady employment with my new employers, checked my tool-bag over, admired the intricatices and splendid workmanship of some U.S.A. caliper guages I possess, I like the very best in tools and save till I can buy just what I want, my tools are a hobby with me, had my breakfast & watched the clock more than usual, left for work twice as early as I usually do as I was carrying $\frac{1}{2}$cwt of tools and riding a bike and intended riding slow and sure, arrived, put my bike away, introduced myself to my immediate work-neighbours & indulged in a little 'pumping' (hours, overtime, tools in stores, temperament of foreman, 'Easy' or 'hell driver', quality of tool-steel supplied etc) had a look over my machine, checked over the positions of gear, surfacing, traversing, lead, self-act, back-gear handles for any unfamiliar reactions, all well, no snags, orthodox-built machine, smaller class of work than my last job, pleased to find good stock of various cutting-tools in cupboard, save me making them just touch them on the grinder to conform with my personal ideas of design, a gong whirs throughout the shop, 'we're off!' report to the foreman, come back with him to the machine, he compliments me on having my tools laid out etc. 'cleared for action eh?' I grin and think 'seems O.K., we'll get along alright!' he fetches a blue-print, details the job, how he wants this, how that, is puzzled himself over one detail, walks off and whispers to another turner, smiles, comes back and rattles off the details in a more athurative manner than before, 'Well, got it? watertight? O.K.?' 'Yes, all O.K.' 'Right! go to it' and off he goes, settle down to the job, no trouble, finish it off & give it a close check-over & supalative finish as I know I'm being carefully watched at the first few jobs I do to see if I know my job (efficient) after that I can work with the minimum of supervision, I become 'alright' 'O.K.' my fellow workers are also covertly watching and my degree of skill puts me in a certain strata, a subtle business, in the 'social' life of the shop, a inefficient worker, however strong a personality he may have, is never quite accepted & respected in a machine-shop 'He knows his job' is the guinea stamp, many a man who is aborred in his private life, finds respect and homage at his craft, & vice-versa, – 11 p.m report to the foreman, he examines the job Ive completed, eyes screwed, his face clears & I know alls well before he speaks, another blue-print a brass nozzle, 'right?' 'right!' I like turning brass, the keen tools rip into it like butter, I start whistling, as I get closer to the finished nozzle, I whistle in spasms, then when I come to the final 1/1000" accuracy of size required I stop and concentrate, mind & eye completly on the job, suddenly my attention is distracted, I feel something, look up, look around, everyone is apparently working away, but there is a indefinable slowing up, a reaction known to all machine-men the note of even the motors & purring belts seems changed, I *know* its close on knocking off time I ask, 'near time, chum?' 'about 5 to go, mate' thought so! uncoil a blower (compressed air tube) and clear the swarf (metal cuttings) from my lathe, collect my tools & put them in my case, notice on wall says 'We are all honest in this shop, there is no necessity to lock up your tools' signed by the manager, very pious I think, I bet he doesn't forget to lock his office up, the majority of people *are* honest but – mans a weak vessel, so I lock up, Ive lost more than one favourite tool in the district, gong whirs, wash my hands, first in oil, then soap and water, hear a Northern voice in the wash place, ask him where he's from 'Manchester, where you?' 'Liverpool' little discussion how long we've been down here, how we like it, no place like home! part mutual expressions of good-will, 'If you want to know anything – Im here' 'Right' clannishness I suppose, Ive made a immediate pal because we are both from Lancs, I help him he'll help me, get my bike, 12.5, outside its a grand day, hot but breezy, cars glisten as they shoot by, lots of brown necks & faces, sight of cool bathers in the Social Centre make me ride harder to get to the digs for a real old scrub & change, look at my watch, the King & Queen pass through ——— today at 3.45 advertised time, $3\frac{1}{2}$ hrs yet, bag of time, see a old pal 'Hi there, pal' skim round the last corner. buy a paper & cigarettes, pound of apples next door, down the road, feel good, new job, gorgeous day, money in my pocket, day & a half of leisure in front, wheel my bike down the garden, the dog rushes out & snarls then makes peculiar snuffling noises of apology, light up the bath geyser, take my overalls off, sit on a chair in my room and eat apples while I wait for hot water, –

From another report on a normal day
(*By a Housewife*)

1.5   Eldest boy in to dinner. Quite forgot he'd to go back to work at 2 o/c. Rush some fried fish on to table & bread & jam for his 'afters'. Tell him he can have pudding for tea. He says 'O.K.' Good job he's good tempered. Gives me his wages 10/-. How thoughtful of his employer to give it him at dinner time! Many would not.

1.45   Having fried chips we all sit down to meal Rhubarb from garden for pudding with vanilla sauce Normans chum turns up from Biggin Hill – cheery little chap – says he didn't have dinner, just something to eat. Give him egg & chips – & pudding.

2.20   Clear away. Sid (my husband) washes up. I tidy dining room. Hectic scramble to wash twins. Mr. H ——— looks in scullery window whilst I do this. He's done for the day & going home. Teases twins & self unmercifully. Tell him to come in & be paid. Does so. Finished Joy, she does look nice in the frock her grandma made. Do Micky. he hates washing & says so in no uncertain voice. Thank goodness Norman's done himself.

3.10   See Mother passing scullery window. She gets in door & twins rush at her.

How smart she is for all her 71 yrs. Feel very conscious of own grubby frock & untidy hair – Take her round downstairs. She likes it & says so. Deplores bad state of decoration & the general neglect left by last tenant. I tell her it will all come right in time. She says the view is beautiful & so it is – Vastly pleased to see what is left of the Old Crystal Palace. Make her China tea.

4.0   Wash & change. Feel better. Send children out for biscuits for tea. No time to make scones I planned. Get tea. All jabbering. Much of 'do you remembers' series – Always the same when Mother, Sid, & I get together. Himself goes to Bromley. Clear up tea. Mother washes up. Joy helping much to her delight. Mother asks for mending & gets a pile of it. What a picture of serenity she is sitting on the old couch – Her busy fingers flying to and fro with the needle.

7.0   Put Normans chum on bus for home. Put twins to bed.

8.0   Fly along to little general shop for last minute shopping. Meet him coming back from Bromley on bike. Looks very fit & strong in his second best tweed & sports shirt. We walk round garden.

9.30   Mother goes up to bed, & Norman too – She likes upstairs as much as down.

10.0   Go along with Sid to Local to 'have one' Feel I've need of same desperately. His beer & my wine both tepid. Go along to next pub at top of hill. Beer & wine better. Enjoy walk home. Jim in from cycle ride round. Get supper. Good cheese – & Beetroots Mother brought. Fix Jim up with blankets on couch. Go up to bed. All quiet. Hear Jim lock Shed up.

11.15   Shout at Jim to put gas out – Gosh I'm tired – He's put gas out now.

Note

1   Charles Madge is referring to two recent events; the fire that consumed Joseph Paxton's Crystal Palace (on the night of November 30 and December 1, 1936) and the abdication of and King Edward VIII (publicly announced December 10, 1936) [ed.].

Chapter 16

Edgar Morin

THE MULTIDIMENSIONAL METHOD [1967]

(Source: Morin, Edgar (1971a) *Plodémet: Report from a French Village*, translated by A. M. Sheridan-Smith, London: Allen Lane, pp. 254–63)

Editor's introduction

Edgar Morin's diverse career (philosopher of science, sociologist, film semiotician and so on) continually seems to evade the epithet 'fashionable' (or so it would seem from an Anglophone perspective). In relation to everyday life it is his work in the 1960s that seems most important. In 1960/1 he directed a film with the ethnographic filmmaker Jean Rouch titled *Chronique d'un été*, which has come to be seen as a landmark moment in documentary film. It also offers a useful introduction to Morin's ethnographic concerns in the 1960s. Shot in Paris it evidences intense self-reflexivity (we continually see the two directors discussing how to make the film); a combination of various ethnographic approaches (situational observation, direct questioning, psychodrama, etc.); and an anthropological approach to modern French life.

This chapter is the methodological appendix to *Plodémet*; Morin's sociological attempt to grasp modernity as it registers in a relatively 'traditional' region in France. While *Plodémet* is in some senses a more conventional work than *Chronique* it shares many of the same concerns. In this chapter Morin suggestively lays down a number of proposals for a cultural sociology, yet rather than suggest a set of methodological paradigms, Morin encourages the breaking of various traditional sociologic rules. His endorsement of a more literary approach to sociological description (or 'phenomenographic observation' as Morin puts it) still remains pertinent even though the authors mentioned suggest a classic realist approach (how might a Duras-like approach to sociology operate, for instance?). Likewise the decision to focus on 'extreme cases' continues to challenge sociological protocols that in the name of science might privilege means and averages. Yet it is the *encouragement* to intervene *actively* in the field (even if critics of ethnography warn us that intervention is an unavoidable outcome) that most radically challenges conventions of thought in the social sciences. For Morin ethnographic sociology offers the potential for a praxis that can alter the field of study. This reconfiguring of ethnography offers a profound challenge for the study of everyday life, suggesting as it does the possibility of a cultural politics practised within the field of inquiry.

Further reading: Kofman 1996; Loizos 1993; MacDougall 1998; Morin 1971b; Rigby 1991.

T HE PRINCIPLE OF THE METHOD employed in Plodémet is to encourage the flow of concrete data, to capture human realities on various levels, to bring out and reveal the features of the terrain, to begin with the sociological individual, which is a commune, to recognize the original features of the double nature, unique and microcosmic, of the phenomenon studied.

Interpretation and research cannot be separated in time. The corpus of hypotheses cannot be established once and for all, but must be capable of development and modification as the inquiry develops, and in turn modify the course of the inquiry and even the techniques of investigation. In short, it is a question of finding rigor, not in rigidity but in a strategy of permanent adaptation.

This means that the standard method used in inquiries is not only inadequate but distorting. It seeks verification by means of a questionnaire addressed to a sample of the population.

The instrument of verification, the questionnaire, is as insensitive to the various concrete features of a local society as it is to sociological multidimensionality. Above all, the standard inquiry reduces the true research to the preinquiry phase when hypotheses are formulated, methods worked out, and a sample of the population picked. From then on, the inquiry refuses any retraction, correction, or innovation. The phase of collecting the questionnaires is an intellectually passive one. Thought comes back into its own only later.

We therefore abandoned initial programming and the use of a questionnaire, though we did not preclude the possibility of using one as a final check.

We retained the use of the sampling method, as a population of 3,700 is too large for a direct house-to-house study. We built up the sample in the course of the inquiry in such a way as to respect the special problems of the terrain.

The means of investigation

An investigation must encourage the flow of concrete data, and therefore it must be flexible enough to include on-the-spot documentation (descriptions of actual events, tape-recorded discussions, conversation with a minimum of direction).

It must capture the various dimensions of the phenomenon studied and make use of different approaches.

It must be capable of correction and verification in the development of an interpretation. The variety of approaches allows a confrontation and concentration of means on points of verification.

We made particular use of the following:

1   Phenomenographic observation (which is related to methods in use in ethnography but neglected by standard sociology).
2   The interview.
3   Participation in group activities (social praxis).

Phenomenographic observation

The investigation should be applied as much to the various centers of social life as to the individual household. It should be complemented by other methods of investigation, but remain autonomous. Ideally, it should cover the totality of the objective, including the observer in the act of observing.

It should try to be both panoramic (capturing the whole of the visual field) and analytic (distinguishing each element in the visual field).

The visual sense is so atrophied among sociologists who depend on the questionnaire and the tape recorder, or conversely on unsupported speculation, that they must learn to observe facts, gestures, dress, objects, landscapes, houses, lanes. We believe in the need for a Balzac-like and Stendhal-like approach in sociology.

The Balzac-like approach is encyclopedic description; the Stendhal-like, that of the 'significant detail'. To these should be added a sense of the sociological snapshot.

As the terrain becomes intelligible, the mass of accumulated documentation becomes a breeding ground in which data are transformed into signs, and in which the detail becomes less and less incidental and more and more rewarding.

The qualities needed in observation are those needed in the inquiry as a whole: an interest equally sustained in general ideas, concrete realities, and men and women in their uniqueness. The purely professional attitude, on the other hand, atrophies perception; a monomaniacal interest in a single idea distorts that idea; indifference to human beings is blindness; indifference to ideas blinds one to the proliferation of signs of which the phenomenal world is composed; an inadequate capacity to interpret leads to an inadequate capacity to perceive, and vice versa.

Each worker recorded his observations in a personal diary, which was not an accumulation of notes but a narrative that led of itself to the recall of a series of unconsciously recorded facts. The diary, complemented by subjective accounts of impressions and feelings, provides the external eye – which may be the second sight of the observer himself – with material that can assist in the elucidation of the observer-phenomenon relationship. This subject-object relationship is the key to any effort at objectification in research.

The interview

The interview was used throughout the inquiry, and it was for this purpose that we built up a population sample based on the usual categories.

The choice of interviewees was made (1) by chance (and throughout the inquiry we left room for chance); (2) by scanning diverse areas (Menez-Ru, Kéravrez, Bravez, Kerminou); and (3) by systematic selection.

In the case of villages, groups, and individuals, the criterion of choice was not average representativeness, as in the method of quotas or random selection, but maximum significance. We looked for extreme cases that would allow the formation of typological poles of opposition (young-old, modernist-traditionalist, bourgeois-rustic). We looked for subjects that were experiencing the crucial conflicts most closely (in Plodémet, these conflicts are linked to the development of modernity which constitutes the main theme of our study); for social leaders (union and party activists, initiators, and not only Lazarsfeld's 'leaders of opinion'); for deviants, passive or rebellious; and, of course, for key persons occupying socially strategic positions, and those at the center of multiple communications.

According to opportunity and circumstances, we made use of the pseudoconversation, the limited interview (asking a limited number of open questions that could be used in all fields), and the interview in depth.

The function of the interview in depth is to reveal the personality, basic needs, and view of life of the interviewee. Our great problem was to direct the interview toward areas of non-directivity. We tried to confine our own role to that of initiating rather than directing the conversation, letting ourselves be guided by intuition rather than by preconceived rules. In fact, patience and sympathy, not technique and skill, were the determining factors of success.

The interview succeeded from the moment the speech of the interviewee was freed of inhibition and embarrassment and became communication.

It was usually after one to two hours that the struggle between inhibition and exhibition was resolved to the advantage of the extravert forces.[1]

It appeared to us that the interviewee was fully satisfied with having talked to us only when he could himself ask questions, either to get to know his observer or to learn something from a 'scientist'. On our side, we felt embarrassed at making the interview a captive operation. The fact of having an interviewee who disliked letting himself be manipulated and an interviewer who disliked manipulating drove us to introduce dialogue as the final stage of the interview.

The interview, regarded as drudgery by sociologists and market researchers, was for us one of the essential means of communication. These 'dives', with tape recorder as oxygen tank and microphone as harpoon, led us to the secret dimension of lives that seemed two-dimensional at first sight.

Groups and praxis

What we have retained from Marxism (which we assimilated and integrated in an anthroposociology) makes us attentive to the social praxis, to the reality and action of social groups. Action not only reveals realities that rarely reach the level of verbal expression and consciousness, but it is also the dynamic reality of social life.

Through the methods of investigation outlined above, we were able to get hold of groups in an indirect way only, but when possible we did so directly through professional, political, ideological, religious, and other bodies. We tried to discover the conflicts and tensions they aroused in action: in the case of the youth club, internal class conflicts, tensions with adults, difficulties in relations with teachers, the municipality, the clergy.

Within the social praxis, on-the-spot events or on-the-spot reactions to external events provided us with spontaneous social tests. Land redistribution (1961–1966), for example, was regarded as a great multipurpose test of peasant life and consciousness in Plodémet.

In addition to observation, we also provoked test situations, like the showing of the film *The Wild Ones* to the teen-agers, or the plan for a holidays committee, which we proposed to different social groups. As observers of group behavior, we were sometimes led to intervene as purveyors of information and even as advisers. Our experience with the provoked tests and the youth committee brought us to the conclusion that intervention should be a necessary method of research. We used the basic idea of interventionist psychosociology, that of action-research, but without confining ourselves to the precepts of any particular school. Our principles of intervention were the following:

1   The maieutic principle. We were led to intervene when we thought we detected a situation pregnant with change or innovation.
2   The nondirective principle. Our intervention had to be catalytic. It could initiate movement, but not fix its norms and program. It could help, but not orient.
3   The principle of primitive experimentation (test situations or paraexperimental situations).
4   The principle of psychosociological 'Socratism'. The intervention must lead those involved to reflect on their principal problems.
5   The principle of utility, common to both research workers and their subjects.

We caught only a glimpse of the possibilities and difficulties of intervention-research. *The difficulties*: The experience of the youth club, however moderate its disturbing effect on the commune may appear to have been, presented us with a problem in responsibility and prudence.

The possibilities: One envisaged the formation of 'general sociological states' in which the various groups of Plodémet society would be led to formulate and compare their aspirations and needs.

Intervention needs a policy that goes beyond the framework of immediate utility for the group under study. A norm should be conceived that should not necessarily be the reduction of tensions and conformity to the general norm.

Subjectivity and objectivity

Our method seeks to envelop the phenomenon (observation), to recognize the forces within it (praxis), to provoke it at strategic points (intervention), to penetrate it by individual contact (interview), to question action, speech, and things.

Each of these methods poses the fundamental methodological problem: the relationship between the research worker and the subject.

It is not merely a subject-object relationship. The 'object' of the inquiry is both object and subject, and one cannot escape the intersubjective character of all relations between men.

We believe that the optimal relationship requires, on the one hand, detachment and objectivity in relation to the object as object, and on the other, participation and sympathy in relation to the object as subject. As this object and subject are one, our approach must be a dual one.

In most of our methods a lack of sympathy would be a grave obstacle to communication. We wanted to stimulate reciprocal sympathy by using the technique of drinking together and eating together. Drinking together is necessary everywhere, and especially so in Plodémet. The *buvette* is a forum, a center of comradeship. In Bigoudennie, a man who drinks well is accepted as a naturalized Breton. Eating together is an occasion of warmth. Unfortunately, I was not able to carry my efforts in this direction far enough. On the one hand, my digestion still suffers the effects of such previous research into human communication, and on the other, financial disbursers appear not to realize that expenses for entertainment are a sociological investment.

Apart from these friendly encounters, our immersion in the life of Plodémet by virtue of our extended residence there (adoption of customs and sometimes participation in work) was also a subjective immersion. Our sympathy with the future development of Plodémet not only made us wish to assist the development, it also made us in a sense naturalized citizens of Plodémet.

The scientifically indispensable dissociation between observation and participation is an intellectual divorce which does not exclude effective participation. Yet participation requires a sustained and permanent effort of distancing and objectification. The researcher must constantly elucidate what he feels and reflect on his experience. He cannot escape his internal duality. Moreover, this duality must be apparent to the subject-object of the inquiry. The fact that he carries a tape recorder with him wherever he goes designates him in his objective capacity as a 'scientist', while daily contact shows him to be a human being like everyone else. In fact, he must be both practitioner and friend. He must be like everyone else and also the possessor of special knowledge like the priest and the doctor. The art of the sociological inquiry is to experience this dual personality internally and express it externally, to dialectically enrich participation and objectification. We do not claim to have succeeded; we do claim that it is necessary to attempt to do so.

In one sense, the subject remains an inaccessible object: this is reflected on the part of the research worker in a cynical desire to know. This is why we must counterbalance this cynicism with a device to obtain the flow of everything that is in the nature of a confidence, or exchange. Exchange is our key value, although it does not settle our problem of dual responsibility to knowledge and to those whom we are studying.

The research workers

Standard inquiries take elaborate technical precautions about obtaining their data, forgetting that this also depends on who is obtaining them. We paid more attention to the personal qualities of the workers we recruited than to their technical qualifications. The multidimensional method requires a curiosity open to all dimensions of the human phenomenon, and the full use of varied aptitudes. Each worker is versatile in that he must practice observation, interview, and group action, and be a specialist in whatever sector suits him best.

We had to struggle against too great a need for mental security on the part of the younger workers who expected schemata and programs drawn up in advance, work that might be boring but easy to separate from the rest of one's life, or an assurance at the outset of the validity of the method of analysis and of the theoretical value of our final conclusions. They were disturbed by the freedom of initiative they were given. The open attention to facts struck them as 'impressionistic'; the open attention to ideas, as 'experimental'. They failed to see that these impressions and experiments, as well as errors of intelligence, must be used, criticized, and integrated, not rejected. They understood the method only when they began to feel personally involved in the work.

Curiously enough, the resistance to the full expression of sociological aptitudes among young research workers is a result of their sociological vocation, serving as a religious conversion rather than an elucidation of consciousness. In such cases, devotion to objectivity is too closely linked to the repression of a guilty subjectivity. Mathematical order and ambitious intellectual structures exorcise the disorder of the world and internal disorders. Their mistrust of their subjectivity leads them to mistrust their professional gifts.

Development of the inquiry

The research developed in successive stages, which we called 'campaigns'. In 1965, there were six campaigns, separated by periods of methodological elaboration or correction, examination of collected data, criticism of the methods used, re-examination of hypotheses, and the drawing up of strategy for the next campaign – the sectors and populations to be studied and the problem to elucidate.

Within each campaign, the day-to-day orientation and regulation of our work was assured by our presence and participation in the field, by meetings of the research team, and by the intercommunication of the inquiry diaries, including my own.

By means of innumerable day-to-day confrontations, an overall control was established whereby norms could be laid down, dissipation of effort avoided, and errors corrected. Control and progressive focalization gradually reduced the element of error in the inquiry (but the principle of the open door to the unexpected was maintained to the end).

Thus the constant effort to elucidate a social personality is one designed to isolate the subject's uniqueness and understand its metabolism, and to see it as well as a microcosm of the social macrocosm.

Is it paradoxical to affirm that the more particular a study should be, the more general it should be?

Without a general constitutive model that is both complex and articulated, one does little more than carry out a census that would be inadequately catalogued in any case by schemata based ultimately on private ideological commonplaces and the journalistic ideas of the specialists themselves.

The constitutive model is that of French society, but it is not a strictly national model; it is the French variant of a Western model, and more widely still, of a technological, industrial, capitalist, urban, bourgeois, wage-earning, statist, consumptionist civilization whose fundamental dimensions must be articulated, rather than largely excluded in the manner of single-dimensional minds.

In order to articulate our constitutive model, we had to historicize our study of

Plodémet. We had to study the past (and here previous historical research was most valuable), and above all, at the level of our own research we postulated space in relation to time. We wished to situate the data we collected in relation to evolution.

This led us to elaborate a multidimensional battery of indicators of modernity in relation to a tradition; to use as much as possible the oppositions of generations as indices of transformation; and finally, to use the heterogeneities of the terrain as temporal landmarks. Thus Menez-Ru, a backward village, and Kerminou, a highly advanced hamlet, helped us to chart a whole process. Inequality of development is the spatiotemporal notion that enabled us to transmute space into time and to integrate change into space.

In concentrating our work on the elucidation of the personality of Plodémet, we remained at the crossroads of space and time; we tried to encapsulate this tiny society within its own future and its relation to the general future.

Finally, the question 'What is Plodémet?' implied the question 'What is the modern world?' It was this dual and inevitable question that we tried to press as far as possible.

Note

1   We had the good fortune to be studying an open, good-natured, curious population, which helped us to gain access to the need for communication that exists in most human beings. Communication was helped by having the interview take place in the home of the interviewee, in the presence of two or three research workers; the participants were able in this way to help each other get over their nervousness. The tape recorder is both the 'spy' that sets up inhibition and the microphone that arouses the desire to communicate and gives the interviewee a stronger sense of personal existence. The art of the interview is to overcome inhibitions and to appeal to the interviewee's need to communicate. We have examined some of these problems in 'L'Interview dans les sciences sociales et la radio-télévision', Communications, 7, 1966, pp. 59–73.

Chapter 17

Pierre Bourdieu

THE KABYLE HOUSE OR THE WORLD REVERSED [1970]

(Source: Bourdieu, Pierre (1992) 'The Kabyle House or the World Reversed' in *The Logic of Practice*, translated by Richard Nice, Cambridge: Polity Press, pp. 271–83)

Editor's introduction

Pierre Bourdieu has coined a number of terms that have passed into common currency within the study of society and culture. Terms such as 'habitus' and 'cultural and symbolic capital' have been applied to all sorts of everyday cultural activity: everything from the culture of professional institutions to the domestic collection of objects. So it might seem slightly perverse to offer a piece of writing that only just touches some of the concerns for which he would later become famous. There is another reason for choosing this particular text: it is a classic example of a 'structuralist' approach to the everyday — in this case Kabyle housing in Algeria. Bourdieu's analysis of this domestic example of Berber culture (first published in 1970) shows the productivity of a structuralist perspective on everyday life. The divisions between different areas of the house and between the house and the world outside are made to resonate with distinctions between male and female culture.

But it also demonstrates some of the limitations of structuralism. The productivity of structuralist attention to the everyday can be seen to depend on the stability of the culture being studied. After all, here we are presented with a culture that seems to epitomise the traditional. Yet the conditions under which Bourdieu began his Algerian research were far from stable: Bourdieu came to Algeria as the conscripted soldier for an army that was struggling to maintain colonial relations in a country engaged in a fierce war for independence. Perhaps, then, Berber culture offered a 'still point' in a country actively pursuing revolutionary change. The limitations of a structuralist approach become evident when we imagine it trying to attend to everyday life in the Arab quarters of Algiers at this time. There, everyday life meant having to adapt to a violence that reorganised both time and space (curfews, road checks, no-go areas) and continually invaded the domestic world of the casbah (army searches, arrests, bombings).

At the time Bourdieu also wrote about other aspects of Algerian culture that explicitly addressed the colonial situation, and he has also spoken about how his army experience was a moment of political awakening, which perhaps also entailed an eventual dissatisfaction with certain forms of structuralism. The point here however is to note the extent to which structuralism *both* productively registers the symbolic orchestration of everyday life *and* necessarily relies on a 'conservative' understanding of everyday cultures. More recently Bourdieu has directed a three-year research project into the everyday world of 'social suffering' in France. The publication *The Weight of the World*, written by a team of sociologists, maps an everyday world plagued by racism, unemployment and a declining infrastructure. It is a world that is continually changing and where daily life is often a matter of surviving against all the odds.

Further reading: Bourdieu *et al.* 1999; Fowler 2000; Richard Jenkins 1992; Robbins 1999.

T HE INTERIOR OF THE KABYLE HOUSE is rectangular in shape and divided into two parts, at a point two-thirds of the way along its length, by a small openwork wall half as high as the house (Figure 17.1).[1] The larger of the two parts, some fifty centimetres higher and covered with a layer of black clay and cowdung which the women polish, is reserved for human use. The smaller part, paved with

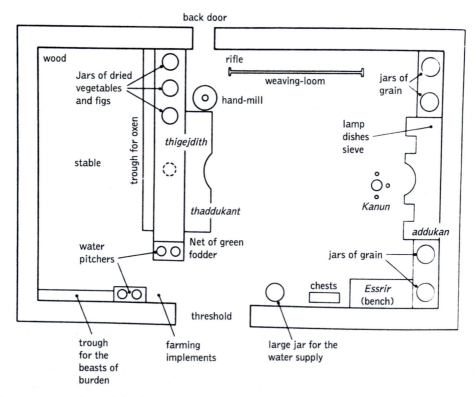

Figure 17.1 Plan of the house

flagstones, is occupied by the animals. A door with two wings gives access to both rooms. On top of the dividing wall are kept, at one end, the small earthenware jars or esparto-grass baskets used to store the provisions kept for immediate consumption, such as figs, flour and leguminous plants, and at the other end, near the door, the water jars. Above the stable is a loft where, next to all kinds of tools and implements, quantities of hay and straw to be used as animal fodder are piled up. It is here that the women and children usually sleep, especially in winter. Against the gable wall, known as the wall (or more precisely the 'side') of the upper part or of the *kanun*, stands a brickwork construction, in the recesses and holes of which the kitchen utensils (the ladle, the cooking pot, the dish used to cook wheatcake – *aghrum* – and other earthenware objects blackened by the fire) are kept, and at each end of which are placed large jars filled with grain. In front of this construction is the fireplace, a circular hollow three or four centimeters deep at its centre, around which, arranged in a triangle, are three large stones to hold the cooking utensils.[2]

In front of the wall opposite the door, generally referred to by the same name as the outside wall that is seen from the rear courtyard (*tasga*),[3] or else called the weaving-loom wall or the 'facing' wall (one faces it on entering), stands the weaving loom. The opposite wall, where the door is, is called the wall of darkness, or the wall of sleep, of the maiden, or of the tomb (it is also said 'the maiden is the dusk', or 'the maiden is the wall of darkness', or 'when a boy is born, the walls of light rejoice, when a dead man leaves the walls of darkness weep': Bassagna and Sayad 1974). A bench wide enough for a mat to be spread out on it is set against this wall. This is the place set aside for the festal sheep or small calf, sometimes for the wood or the water pitcher. Clothes, mats and blankets are hung, in the daytime, on a peg or a wooden crossbar next to the wall of darkness, or else they are put under the dividing bench. Thus, the *kanun* wall is opposed to the stable as the high to the low (*adaynin*, stable, comes from the root *ada*, the bottom), and the loom wall is opposed to the door wall as the light to the dark. One might be tempted to give a purely technical explanation of these oppositions, since the loom wall, facing the door, which itself faces east, is the most brightly lit and the stable is indeed at a lower level than the rest (the house usually being built at right angles to the contour lines, to facilitate the drainage of animal waste and dirty water). However, a number of indices suggest that these oppositions are the centre of a cluster of parallel oppositions, the necessity of which never stems directly from technical imperatives and functional requirements.

The dark, nocturnal, lower part of the house, the place for things that are damp, green or raw – jars of water placed on the benches on either side of the stable entrance or next to the wall of darkness, wood, green fodder – and also the place for natural beings – oxen and cows, donkeys and mules – natural activities – sleep, sexual intercourse, childbirth, and also death – is opposed to the light-filled, noble, upper part. This is the place for human beings and especially the guest, for fire and things made with fire, such as the lamp, kitchen utensils, the rifle – the attribute of the male point of honour (*nif*) which protects female honour (*h'urma*) – and the loom, the symbol of all protection. It is also the site of the two specifically cultural activities performed within the house: weaving and cooking. In fact, the meaning objectified in things or parts of space is fully yielded only through practices structured according to the same schemes that are organized in relation to them (and vice versa). An honoured guest is invited to sit in front of the loom (the verb *qabel*, to honour, also means to face up to someone and to face the east). When a man has been badly received, he will say: 'He made me sit beside his wall of darkness, as in a grave.' The wall of darkness is also called the invalid's wall, and the phrase 'to keep to the wall' means to be ill and, by extension, idle; a sick person's bed is in fact placed next to this wall, especially in winter. The connection between the dark part of the house and death is also shown in the fact that the washing of the dead takes place at the entrance to the stable. The homology between sleep and death is explicitly stated in the precept that on going to bed one should first lie for a moment on one's right side and then on one's left, because the first position is that of the dead in the tomb. The funeral chants represent the grave, 'the house underground', as an inverted house (white/dark, up/down, adorned with paintings/roughly dug out), sometimes exploiting a homonymy associated with analogy in shape, as in a chant sung at wakes, quoted by Genevois (1955: 27): 'I found people digging a tomb, With their pickaxes they carved out the walls, They were making benches (thiddukanin), with mortar below the mud.' Thaddukant (plural thiddukanin) is the name of the bench set against the dividing wall, opposite the gable wall (addukan) and also of the bank of earth on which a man's head rests in the grave (the slight hollow in which a woman's head is laid is called thakwath, as are the small recesses in the walls of the house, in which women keep small objects). It is traditionally said that the loft, which is made entirely of wood, is supported by the stable as the corpse is carried by the bearers; thaârichth designates both the loft and the stretcher used to transport the dead.[4] It is clear why a guest cannot, without offence, be invited to sleep in the loft, which is opposed to the loom wall in the same way as is the wall of the tomb.

It is also in front of the loom wall, facing the door, in full daylight, that the young bride is made to sit, as if to be shown off, like the decorated plates that hang there. When one knows that a baby girl's umbilical cord is buried behind the loom and that, to protect a maiden's virginity, she is made to step through the warp, from the side facing the door to the side next to the loom wall, then the function of magical protection attributed to the loom becomes clear.[5] Indeed, from the standpoint of her male kin, the girl's whole life is in a sense summed up in the successive positions she successively occupies vis-à-vis the loom, the symbol of male protection. Before marriage she is placed behind the loom, in its shadow, under its protection, just as she is kept under the protection of her father and brothers; on her wedding day she is seated in front of the loom, with her back to it, with the light upon her, and thereafter she will sit weaving, with her back to the wall of light, behind the loom.

The low, dark part of the house is also opposed to the upper part as the female to the male. Not only does the division of labour between the sexes (based on the same principle of division as the organization of space) give the woman responsibility for most of the objects belonging to the dark part of the house, the carrying of water, wood, manure, for instance; but the opposition between the upper part and the lower part reproduces, within the internal space of the house, the opposition between the inside and the outside, between female space – the house and its garden – and male space.

> The opposition between the part reserved for receiving guests and the more intimate part (an opposition also found in the nomad's tent, which is divided by a curtain into two parts, one open to guests, the other reserved

for the women) is expressed in ritual forecasts such as the following. When a cat, a beneficent animal, enters the house with a feather or a thread of white wool in its fur, if it goes towards the hearth, this portends the arrival of guests, who will be given a meal with meat; if it goes towards the stable, this means that a cow will be bought, if this occurs in spring, or an ox if it is the ploughing season. The cat, an accidental intruder which is chased away, is only there as a bearer of symbols that performs practically the movement of entering. The feather is implicitly treated as equivalent to the wool, probably because these substances are seen as bearers of a beneficent quality, whiteness. The opposition between the hearth and the stable, which structures the whole sequence – that is, that between the noble part where meat, the food *par excellence* for guests, is roasted, and where guests are received, and the lower part, reserved for the livestock – only has to be combined with the opposition between two seasons – autumn, the time of collective sacrifice, the ox and ploughing, and spring, the time of milk – to yield the ox and the cow.

The lower part of the house is the place of the most intimate secret within the world of intimacy, that is, the place of all that pertains to sexuality and procreation. More or less empty during the daytime, when all the (exclusively female) activity in the house is centred on the fireplace, the dark part is full at night, full of human beings and also full of animals, since the oxen and cows, unlike the mules and donkeys, never spend the night outdoors; and it is never fuller than in the wet season, when the men sleep indoors and the oxen and cows are fed in the stable. The relationship that links the fertility of humans and the fields with the dark part of the house, a privileged instance of the relation of equivalence between fertility and the dark, the full (or the process of swelling) and the damp, is here established directly. Whereas the grain intended for consumption is kept in large earthenware jars next to the wall of the upper part, on either side of the fireplace, the grain kept for sowing is stored in the dark part of the house, either in sheepskins or in wooden chests placed at the foot of the wall of darkness, sometimes under the conjugal bed; or else in chests placed under the bench against the dividing wall (Servier 1962: 229, 253).[6] When one knows that birth is always the rebirth of an ancestor, it can be understood how the dark part of the house can simultaneously and without contradiction be the place of death and of procreation.

At the centre of the dividing wall, between 'the house of the humans' and 'the house of the animals', stands the main pillar, supporting the 'master beam' and the whole framework of the house. The master beam (*asalas alemmas*, a masculine term) which extends the protection of the male part of the house to the female part, is explicitly identified with the master of the house, whereas the main pillar, a forked tree trunk (*thigejdith*, a feminine term), on which it rests, is identified with the wife (according to Maunier the Beni Khellili call it *Masâuda*, a feminine first name meaning 'the happy one'), and their interlocking symbolizes sexual union – represented in the wall paintings, in the form of the union of the beam and the pillar, by two superimposed forked shapes (Devulder 1951).

Around the main beam, the symbol of male potency, there is coiled another symbol of the fertilizing power of man and also of resurrection: the snake, the 'guardian' of the house. The snake is sometimes represented (in the Collo region, for example) on the earthenware jars made by the women and containing the seed-corn. It is also said to descend sometimes into the house, into the lap of a sterile woman, calling her 'mother'. At Darma, a sterile woman ties her girdle to the central beam (Maunier 1930); the foreskin and the reed that has been used for circumcision are hung from the same beam; if the beam is heard to crack, those present hasten to say 'may it be for the good', because this portends the death of the head of the family. When a son is born, the wish is made that 'he may be the master beam of the house', and when he has completed the ritual fast for the first time, he takes his first meal on the roof, that is, on the central beam (in order, so it is said, that he may be able to carry beams). A number of riddles and sayings explicitly identify woman with the central pillar. A young bride is told: 'May God make you the pillar firmly planted in the middle of the house.' Another riddle says: 'She stands upright but she has no feet.' This fork open upwards is female nature, fertile, or rather, capable of being fertilized.

Thus this symbolic summary of the house, the union of *asalas* and *thigejdith*, which extends its fertilizing protection over all human marriage, is, like ploughing, a marriage of heaven and earth. 'Woman is the foundations, man the master beam', says another proverb. *Asalas*, defined in another proverb as 'born in the earth and buried in the sky' (Genevois 1963), fertilizes *thigejdith*, which is rooted in the soil and open towards the sky.

Thus, the house is organized in accordance with a set of homologous oppositions – high : low :: light : dark :: day : night :: male : female :: *nif* : *h'urma* :: fertilizing : able to be fertilized. But the same oppositions also exist between the house as a whole and the rest of the universe. Considered in relation to the male world of public life and farming work, the house, the universe of women, is *h'aram*, that is to say, both sacred and illicit for any man who is not part of it (hence the expression used in swearing an oath: 'May my wife (or, my house) become illicit (*h'aram*) to me if . . . '). A distant relative (or a close one, but through women, such as the wife's brother) who is brought into the house for the first time will give the mistress of the house a sum of money that is called 'the sight' (*thizri*). As the place of the sacred of the left hand, *h'urma*, with which all the properties associated with the dark part of the house are bound up, it is placed in the safekeeping of the male point of honour (*nif*) just as the dark part of the house is placed under the protection of the master beam. Every violation of the sacred space therefore takes on the social meaning of sacrilege. Thus, theft from an inhabited house is treated in customary law as a heinous act – an outrage upon the *h'urma* of the house and an offence against the *nif* of the head of the family.

The woman can be said to be confined to the house only so long as it is also pointed out that the man is kept out of it, at least in the daytime. A man's place is outside, in the fields or in the assembly; boys are taught this at a very early age. Hence this formula, which the women repeat, meaning by it that men are unaware of much that goes in the house: 'O man, poor wretch, out in fields all day like a donkey put out to pasture!' As soon as the sun has risen, in summer a man must be out in the fields or at the assembly; in winter, if he is not in the fields, he must be at the assembly or on the benches set in the shelter of the pentroof over the door to the courtyard. Even at night, at least in the dry season, the men and the boys, as soon as they are circumcised, sleep outside the house, either near the haystacks, on the threshing floor, beside the shackled mule and donkey, or on the fig-drying floor, or in the fields, or more rarely in the assembly house, *thajmaâth*.[7] A man who spends too much time at home in the daytime is suspect or ridiculous; he is a 'house man', who 'broods at home like a hen in its nest'. A self-respecting man must offer himself to be seen, be constantly in the eyes of others, confront them, face up to them: he is the man among men (*argaz yer irgazen*). Relations among men are established outdoors: 'Friends are outdoor friends, not *kanun* friends.'

It is understandable that all biological activities, sleeping, eating, procreating, should be banished from the external universe ('The hen does not lay in the market') and confined to the house, the sanctuary of privacy and the secrets of nature, the world of woman, who is assigned to the management of nature and excluded from public life. In contrast to man's work, which is performed outdoors, woman's work is essentially obscure and hidden ('God conceals it'): 'Inside the house, woman is always on the move, she bustles like a fly in the whey; outside the house, nothing of her work is seen.' Two very similar sayings define woman's estate as that of one who can know no other abode than the tomb: 'Your house is your tomb'; 'Woman has but two dwellings, the house and the tomb.'

Thus, the opposition between the women's house and the men's assembly, private life and public life, the full light of day and the secrecy of night, corresponds exactly to the opposition between the dark, nocturnal, lower part of the house and the noble, brightly lit, upper part.[8] The opposition between the external world and the house only takes on its full significance when it is seen that one of the terms of this relation, that is, the house, is itself divided in accordance with the same principles that oppose it to the other term. So it is both true and false to say that the external world is opposed to the house as the male to the female, day to night, fire to water, etc., since the second term in each of these oppositions splits, each time, into itself and its opposite.

The house, a microcosm organized by the same oppositions and homologies that order the whole universe, stands in a relation of homology to the rest of the universe. But, from another standpoint, the world of the house, taken as a whole, stands in a relation of opposition to the rest of the world, an opposition whose principles are none other than those that organize both the internal space of the house and the rest of the world and, more generally, all areas of existence. Thus, the opposition between the world of female life and the city of men is based on the same principles as the two systems of oppositions which it opposes to one another. The application to opposing areas of the same *principium divisionis* that establishes their opposition ensures economy and a surplus of consistency, without involving confusion between those areas. The structure $a : b :: b_1 : b_2$ is doubtless one of the simplest and most powerful that a mythico-ritual system could use, since it cannot counterpose without simultaneously uniting, and is capable of integrating an infinite number of data into a single order by the endlessly repeated application of the same principle of division. Each of the two parts of the house (and, by the same token, each of the objects that are put there and each of the activities carried on there) is, in a sense, qualified at two degrees, that is, first as female (nocturnal, dark) in so far as it belongs to the universe of the house, and secondly as male or female in so far as it belongs to one or other of the divisions of that universe. Thus, for example, when the proverb says 'Man is the lamp of the outside, woman is the light of the inside', this must be taken to mean that man is the true light, the light of day, and woman the light of darkness, a dark light; and we know in other ways that woman is to the moon as man is the sun. Similarly, by her work on wool, woman produces the beneficent protection of weaving, whose whiteness symbolizes happiness ('white' days are happy days, and a number of marriage rites, such as the sprinkling of milk, seek to make the bride 'white'). The loom, the instrument *par excellence* of female activity, *raised* facing the east like a man and like the plough, is at the same time the east of the internal space and has a male value as a symbol of protection. Again, the hearth, the navel of the house (which is itself identified with the belly of a mother), where the embers smoulder with a secret, hidden, female fire, is the domain of the woman of the house, who is invested with total authority in all matters concerning cooking and the management of the food stores.[9] She takes her meals by the fireside, whereas the man, turned towards the outside, eats in the middle of the room or in the courtyard. However, in all the rites in which they play a part, the fireplace and the stones surrounding it derive their magical power, whether to give protection from the evil eye or from illness, or to bring fine weather, from the fact that they belong to the order of fire, the dry, and the heat of the sun.[10] The house itself is endowed with twofold significance. Though opposed to the public world as nature to culture, it is also, from another standpoint, culture; it is said of the jackal, the incarnation of wild nature, that he builds no house.

The house, and by extension, the village, the 'full country' (*laâmara* or *thamurth iâamaran*), the precinct peopled by men, are opposed in one respect to the fields empty of men which are called *lahkla*: empty, sterile space. Thus the inhabitants of Taddert-el-Djeddid believed that those who build their houses outside the village boundary run the risk of their family dying out (Maunier 1930). The same belief is found elsewhere and the only exceptions made are for the garden, even when remote from the house, the orchard, or the fig-dryer, all of which are places that are in some way linked to the village and fertility. But the opposition does not exclude the homology between the fertility of humans and the fertility of the field, each of which is the product of the union of the male principle and the female principle, solar fire and the wetness of the earth. This homology in fact underlies most of the rites intended to ensure the fertility of human beings and the earth, whether the rites of cooking, which are closely dependent on the oppositions that structure the farming year and are therefore tied to the rhythms of the farming calendar; the rites of renewing the fireplace and its stones (*iniyen*), which mark the passage from the wet season to the dry season, or the beginning of the calendar year; and, more generally, all the rites performed within the microcosm of the house. Whenever the women play a part in the specifically agrarian rites, it is again the homology between agricultural fertility and human fertility, the form *par excellence* of all fertility, that underlies their ritual actions and endows them with their magical potency. A considerable number of rites that take place within the house are only apparently domestic rites, since they aim simultaneously to ensure the fertility of the fields and the fertility of the house, which are inextricably linked. For, in order for the field to be full, the house must be full, and woman contributes to the prosperity of the field by dedicating herself, *inter alia*, to accumulating, economizing and conserving the goods that man has produced and to fixing, as it were, within the house all the goodness that can enter it. 'Man is the conduit, woman the basin'; one supplies, the other holds and keeps. Man is 'the hook on which the baskets are hung'; like the beetle, the spider and the bee, he is the provider. It is women who say: 'Handle your riches like a log on the fire. There is today, there is tomorrow, there is the grave; God forgives those who have saved, not those who have eaten.' And again: 'A thrifty woman is worth more than a yoke of oxen ploughing.' Just as 'the full country' is opposed to 'empty space', so 'the fullness of the house' (*laâmmara ukham*), that is to say, usually, the 'old woman' who saves and accumulates, is opposed to 'the emptiness of the house' (*lakhla ukham*), usually the daughter-in-law. In summer, the door of the house must remain open all day long so that the fertilizing light of the sun can enter, and with it prosperity. A closed door means dearth and sterility; sitting on the threshold, and so blocking it, means closing the passage to happiness and prosperity. To wish someone prosperity, the Kabyles say 'May your door remain open' or 'May your house be like a mosque'. A rich and generous man is one of whom it is said: 'His house is a mosque, it is open to all, rich and poor alike, it is made of wheatcake and couscous, it is full' (*thaâmmar* – applied to a woman, *âammar* means to be a good, thrifty housewife). Generosity is a sign of prosperity which guarantees prosperity.

Most of the technical and ritual actions that fall to women are oriented by the objective intention of making the house, like *thigejdith* opening its fork to *asalas alemmas*, the receptacle of the prosperity that comes to it from without, the womb which, like the earth, receives the seed the male has put into it; and, conversely, the intention of thwarting all the centrifugal forces that threaten to dispossess the house of the goods entrusted to it.

> For example, it is forbidden to give anyone a light from the fire on the day a child or a calf is born, and also on the first day of ploughing;[11] when the threshing has been done, nothing must leave the house and the woman retrieves all the objects that she has lent; the milk produced in the three days following calving must not leave the house; the bride must not cross the threshold before the seventh day after her wedding; a woman who has given birth must not leave the house before the fortieth day; the baby must not go out before the Aïd Seghir; the hand-mill must never be loaned and must not be left empty for fear of bringing famine upon the house; woven cloth must not be taken out before it is finished; sweeping, an act of expulsion, is, like giving embers to make a fire, forbidden during the first four days of ploughing; when someone has died, the removal of the corpse is 'facilitated' so that prosperity does not leave with it;[12] the first 'goings-out', the cow's, for example, four days after calving, or the newborn calf's, are marked by sacrifices.

'Emptiness' can result from an act of expulsion. It can also find its way in with certain objects, such as the plough, which must not enter the house between two days' ploughing, or the ploughman's shoes (*arkasen*), which are associated with *lakhla*, empty, sterile space (like the solitary spendthrift, called *ikhla*); or certain people may bring it in, such as old women, because they are bearers of sterility (*lakhla*) and have caused many houses to be sold or to be visited by thieves. Conversely, a number of ritual acts aim to ensure the 'filling' of the house, such as those that consist of casting the remains of a marriage lamp (whose shape represents sexual union and which plays a part in most fertility rites) into the foundations, after first sacrificing an animal; or of making the bride sit on a leather bag full of grain, on first entering the house. Every first entry into the house is a threat to the fullness of the world inside, a threat which the threshold rites, at once propitiatory and prophylactic, must ward off. A new yoke of oxen is met by the mistress of the house, 'the fullness of the house', who places on the threshold the sheepskins on which the hand-mill stands at other times and which receives the flour. Most of the rites intended to bring fertility to the stable and, therefore, to the house ('a house without a cow is an empty house') tend to give magical reinforcement to the structural relationship between milk, the colour blue-green (azegzaw, which is also the raw, thizegzawth), grass, springtime – the childhood of the natural world – and human childhood. At the spring equinox, on the 'return of azal', the young shepherd, who has twofold affinities with the growth of the fields and the cattle on account of his age and his task, gathers a bouquet to be hung from the lintel of the door, made up of 'all that the wind shakes in the countryside' (Rahmani 1936). A little bag of herbs, containing cumin, benjamin and indigo, is buried at the threshold of the stable, with the words: 'O blue-green (azegzaw), keep the butter from waning!' Freshly picked plants are hung on the butter-churn, and the receptacles used for the milk are rubbed with them.

Above all, the young bride's entry is fraught with consequences for the fertility and plenitude of the house. While she is seated on the mule that has brought her from her father's house, she is presented with water, grains of wheat, figs, nuts, cooked eggs, or fritters, all of which (whatever the local variants) are things associated with the fertility of women and the land. She throws them towards the house, thus ensuring that she is preceded by the fertility and plenitude she must bring there herself. She crosses the threshold carried on the back of one of the bridegroom's kinsmen or sometimes (Maunier 1930) on the back of a Negro, who interposes himself to inter-cept the malignant forces, concentrated on the threshold, which might affect her fertility. A woman must never sit on the threshold holding her child; and a child or a bride, who, like all beings that are in a liminal position, are especially vulnerable, must not cross it too often. Thus woman, through whom fertility comes to the house, makes her own contribution to the fertility of the fields. Consigned to the world of the inside, she also acts on the outside by ensuring fullness for the inside and, in her role as guardian of the threshold, by supervising those unequal exchanges which only the logic of magic can conceive, through which each part of the universe expects to receive from the other nothing but fullness while giving it only emptiness.[13]

But one or the other of the two systems of oppositions that define the house, either in its internal organization or in its relationship with the external world, is brought to the forefront depending on whether the house is considered from the male or the female point of view. Whereas for the man the house is not so much a place he goes into as a place he comes out of, the woman is bound to give opposite importance and meaning to these two movements and to the different definitions of the house they imply, since, for her, movement outwards consists above all in acts of expulsion, while inward movement is her specific concern. The significance of outward movement is most clearly demonstrated by the rite performed by a mother, seven days after giving birth, 'in order that her son may be valorous': striding across the threshold, she sets her right foot upon the carding comb and simulates a fight with the first boy she meets. Going out is the essentially male movement, which leads towards other men and also towards the dangers and trials that must be confronted with the determination of a man who, in matters of honour, is as prickly as the spikes of the carding comb.[14] A self-respecting man must leave the house at daybreak. Hence the importance of the things encountered, which are a portent for the whole day, so that in the event of an undesirable encounter (a blacksmith, a woman carrying an empty leather bag, shouts or a quarrel, a deformed being), it is best to go back and 'remake one's morning' or one's 'going out'.

It is now clear why it is so important which way the house faces. The front of the main house, the one which shelters the head of the family and which contains a stable, almost always faces east, and the main door – as opposed to the low, narrow door, reserved for women, which leads to the garden – is commonly called the east door (*thabburth thacherqith*), or the street door, the upper door, or the great door.[15] The aspect of the villages and the lower position of the stable mean that the upper part of the house, with the fireplace, is in the north, the stable in the south and the loom wall in the west. It follows from this that the movement by which one enters the house is oriented east–west, in opposition to the movement effected when coming out, in accordance with the orientation *par excellence*, towards the east, that is, towards the high, the bright, the good and the prosperous. The ploughman turns his oxen to face the east when he harnesses and unharnesses them, and he starts his ploughing from west to east; the harvesters work eastwards, and the sacrificial ox is slain facing east. Countless actions are performed in accordance with this cardinal orientation; they include all portentous acts, that is, all those involving the fertility and prosperity of the group.[16]

If we now go back to the internal organization of the house, we can see that its orientation is exactly the reverse of that of external space, as if it had been obtained by a half-rotation on the axis of the front wall or the threshold. The loom wall, which a man entering the house immediately faces on crossing the threshold, and which is lit directly by the morning sun, is the daylight of the inside (just as woman is the lamp of the inside), that is, the east of the inside, symmetrical to the macrocosmic east from which it draws its borrowed light. The dark, inside face of the front wall represents the west of the house, the place of sleep, which one leaves behind as one moves towards the *kanun*; the door corresponds symbolically to the 'door of the year', the opening of the wet season and the farming year. Likewise, the two gable walls, the stable wall and the fireplace wall, receive two opposing meanings depending on which of their sides is being considered: to the external north corresponds the south (and summer) of the inside, that is, the part of the house in front of and to the right of a person who enters facing the loom; to the external south corresponds the internal north (and winter), that is, the stable, which is behind and to the left of someone going from the door towards the fire. The division of the house into a dark part (the west and north sides) and a bright part (east and south) corresponds to the division of the year into a wet season and a dry season (Figure 17.2). In short, to each external face of the wall (*essur*) corresponds a region of the internal space (called *tharkunt*, meaning, roughly, a side) which has a symmetrical but opposite meaning in the system of internal oppositions. Each of the two spaces can thus be derived from the other by means of half-rotation on the axis of the threshold. The importance and symbolic value of the threshold within the system cannot be fully understood unless it is seen that it owes its function as a magical boundary to the fact that it is the site of a meeting of contraries as well as of a

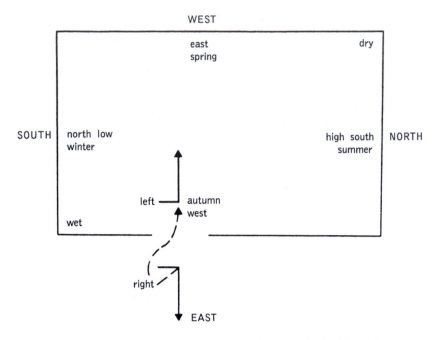

Figure 17.2 The dual spatial orientation of the house (the bold angles represent the positions of the subject's body)

logical inversion and that, as the necessary meeting-point and crossing-point between the two spaces, defined in terms of socially qualified body movements,[17] it is the place where the world is reversed.[18]

Thus, each of the two universes has its own east, and the two movements most charged with magical significance and consequences – movement from the threshold to the hearth, which should bring fullness and is performed or ritually controlled by woman, and movement from the threshold to the outside world, which, by virtue of its inaugural value, contains all that the future will bring, especially the future of farming work – can each be performed in accordance with the beneficent orientation, that is, from west to east.[19] The dual orientation of the space of the house means that one is able both to go in and to go out on the right foot (in both senses), with all the magical benefit attached to this observance, without any break in the relationship linking the right-hand side to the high, the bright and the good. The half-rotation of space around the threshold thus ensures, so to speak, the maximization of magical profit, since both centripetal movement and centrifugal movement are performed in a space so organized that one enters it facing the light and also comes out of it facing the light.[20]

These two symmetrical and opposite spaces are not interchangeable but hierarchized. The orientation of the house is primordially defined from outside, from the standpoint of men and, as it were, by men and for men, as the place men come out of. ('Men look at things from outdoors, women look at things from indoors'; 'A house prospers through woman; its outside is beautiful through man.') The house is a world within a world, but one that always remains subordinate, because, even when it displays all the properties and relationships that define the archetypal world, it remains an inverted reflexion, a world in reverse. 'Man is the lamp of the outside, woman the lamp of the inside.' The apparent symmetry must not mislead us: the lamp of day is apparently defined in relation to the lamp of night. In fact the nocturnal light, the female male, remains subordinate to the diurnal light, the lamp of day, that is, the light of the sun. 'Man trusts in God, woman looks to man for everything.' 'Woman', it is also said, 'is twisted like a sickle'; and so even the straightest of these warped natures is never more than straightened up. Once married, woman too finds her east, within the house of man, but her east is only the inversion of a west: for 'the maiden is the west'. The supremacy given to movement outwards, in which man affirms his manliness by turning his back on the house in order to face other men, is merely a form of the categorical refusal of nature, the inevitable origin of man's movement away from nature.

Notes

1   This text is a slightly modified version of an article first published in 1970 (Bourdieu 1970). Although the principles of subsequent analyses are already present in it (as is shown by the attention given to the movements and displacements of the body), this interpretation of the space inside the Kabyle house remains within the limits of structuralist thought. I have none the less chosen to reproduce it here, as an appendix, because of the status of the house as an inverted microcosm: the reduced image of the world that if offers could serve as an introduction to the more complete and more complex analyses elsewhere in this book. As well as providing add-itional evidence to support them, it gives an idea of the objectivist reconstruction of the system of relationships that was a necessary stage in moving to the final interpretation, which itself sometimes seems close to intuitionist apprehension.

2   Even the most precise and methodical descriptions of the Berber house (Laoust 1912: 12–15; 1920, 50–53; Maunier 1930: 120–77; Genevois 1955) present, in their very meticulousness, systematic lacunae which had to be made good by direct inquiry.

3   With this one exception, the walls are given different names, according to whether they are considered from the inside or the outside. The outside is plastered over with a trowel by the men, whereas the inside is whitewashed and hand-decorated by the women. This opposition between the two points of view is, as will be seen, a fundamental one.

4   The transporting of beams, which are identified with the master of the house, is also called *thaârichth*, like the loft and like the stretcher used to carry a corpse or a wounded animal which will be slain far from the house. It gives rise to a social ceremony the meaning of which is exactly similar to that of burial. By virtue of its imperative character, the ceremonial form it assumes and the extent of the group that it mobilizes, this collective task (*thiwizi*) has no equivalent other than burial. As much merit (*h'assana*) accrues from taking part in the carrying of the beams, an act of piety always performed without remuneration, as from taking part in the collective activities connected with funerals (digging the grave, extracting or transporting the stone slabs, helping to bear the coffin or attending the burial).

5   Among the Arabs, to perform the magic rite intended to render women unfit for sexual relations, the betrothed girl is made to step through the slackened warp on the loom, from the outside inwards, that is, from the middle of the room towards the wall before which the weavers sit and work. The same operation, performed in the opposite direction, undoes the charm (Marçais and Guiga 1925: 395).

6   House building, which always takes place when a son is married and which symbolizes the birth of a new family, is forbidden in May, as is marriage (Maunier 1930).

7   The duality of rhythm linked to the division between the dry season and the wet season is manifested, *inter alia*, in the domestic order. Thus in summer the opposition between the lower part and the higher part of the house takes the form of the opposition between the house proper, where the women and children retire to bed and where the stores are kept, and the courtyard

where hearth and hand-mill are set up, meals are eaten, and feasts and ceremonies take place.

8   The opposition between the house and the assembly (*thajmaâth*) is seen clearly in the different designs of the two buildings. Whereas the house is entered by the door in its front wall, the assembly building is designed as a long covered passage, completely open at the two gables, which one can walk right through.

9   The blacksmith is the man who, like women, spends his days indoors, beside the fire.

10 The hearth is the site of a number of rites and the object of taboos that make it the opposite of the dark part of the house. For example, it is forbidden to touch the ashes during the night, to spit into the fireplace, to spill water or to weep tears there (Maunier 1930). Likewise, those rites that aim to bring about a change in the weather and are based on an inversion, make use of the opposition between the wet part and the dry part of the house. Thus, to change the weather from wet to dry, a wool-packing comb (an object made with fire and associated with weaving) and a glowing ember are left on the threshold overnight; conversely, to change from dry to wet weather, the wool-packing and carding combs are sprinkled with water on the threshold during the night.

11 Conversely, the bringing of new fireplace stones into the house, on inaugural dates, is a filling-up, an input of goodness and prosperity. The divinations performed at such times are therefore concerned with prosperity and fertility. If a cockchafer grub is found under one of the stones, there will be a birth in the course of the year; a green plant means a good harvest; ants, a bigger flock; a woodlouse, more cattle.

12 The bereaved are told, to console them, 'He will leave you *baraka*', if an adult has died, or '*Baraka* has not gone out of the house', in the case of a baby. The corpse is placed near the door with the head turned towards the outside. Water is heated on the stable side and the washing of the corpse is done near the stable; the embers and ashes of this fire are scattered outside the house; the board used in washing the corpse is left in front of the door for three days.

13 Various objects are hung over the door. Their common feature is that they manifest the dual function of the threshold, a selective barrier which must keep out emptiness and evil while letting in fullness and goodness.

14 A newborn girl is wrapped in the softness of a silk scarf; a boy is swathed in the dry, rough bindings that are used to tie sheaves.

15 It goes without saying that the opposite arrangement (as in a mirror image of the ground-plan of the house) is possible, though rare. It is explicitly said that all that comes from the west brings misfortune, and a door facing that way can only receive darkness and sterility. In fact, if the inversion of the 'ideal' ground-plan is rare, this is firstly because when secondary houses are set at right angles around the courtyard, they are often simply lodging rooms, without kitchen or cowshed, and the courtyard is often closed off, on the side opposite the front of the main house, by the back of a neighbouring house, which itself faces east.

16 The two *s'uffs*, political and martial factions which were mobilized as soon as any incident occurred (and which were related in variable ways to the kinship-based social units, ranging from superimposition to complete separation), were named *s'uff* of the upper part (*ufella*) and *s'uff* of the lower part (*buadda*), or *s'uff* of the right (*ayafus*) and *s'uff* of the left (*azelmadh*), or *s'uff* of the east (*acherqui*) and *s'uff* of the west (*aghurbi*). The last pair of terms was less common but was kept to designate the two sides in ritual games (from which the traditional battles between the two *s'uffs* derived their logic); it still survives nowadays in the language of children's games.

17 In some regions of Kabylia, two people in a liminal situation – the young bride, and a boy circumcised at the time of the same celebration – must cross paths on the same threshold.

18 This explains why the threshold is directly or indirectly associated with the rites intended to bring about a reversal of the course of events by carrying out a reversal of the basic oppositions: the rites to obtain rain or fine weather, for instance, or those performed at the turning-points of the year (e.g. the night before *en-nayer*, the first day of the solar year, when charms are buried at the threshold).

19 The correspondence between the four corners of the house and the four cardinal points is expressed clearly in some propitiatory rites observed in the Aures. When the fireplace is renewed, on new year's day, the Chaouia woman cooks some fritters, breaks the first one cooked into four pieces, and throws them towards the four corners of the house. She does the same thing with the ritual dish prepared on the first day of spring (Gaudry 1929: 58–9).

20   To show that this is probably an instance of a very general form of magical thought, one further, very similar, example will suffice. The Arabs of the Maghreb considered it a good sign, Ben Cheneb (1905–7: 312) relates, for a horse to have its front right foot white and its rear left foot white. The master of such a horse cannot fail to be happy, since he mounts towards white and dismounts towards white (Arab horsemen mount on the right and dismount on the left).

References

Bassagana, R. and Sayad, A. (1974) *Habitat traditionnel et structures familiales en Kabylie*. Algiers: Mémoires du CRAPE.

Ben Cheneb, M. (1905–7) *Proverbes arabes d'Alger et du Maghreb*. Paris: Leroux.

Bourdieu, P. (1970) La maison kabyle ou le monde renversé, in J. Pouillon and P. Maranda (eds) *Echanges et communications: Mélanges offerts à Claude Lévi-Strauss à l'occasion de son 60ᵉ anniversaire*. Paris/The Hague: Mouton.

Devulder, M. (1951) Peintures murales et pratiques magiques dans la tribu des Ouadhias, *Revue africaine*, 95.

Gaudry, M. (1929) *La Femme chaouia de l'Aurès: Etudes de sociologie berbère*. Paris: Geuthner.

Genevois, H. (1955) L'habitation kabyle. Fichier de documentation berbère (published at Fort National), no. 49.

Genevois, H. (1963) Trois cent cinquante énigmes kabyles. Fichier de documentation berbère (published at Fort National).

Laoust, E. (1912) *Etudes sur le dialecte berbère du Chenoua*. Paris: Leroux.

Marcais, W. and Guiga, A. (1925) *Textes arabes de Takrouna*. Paris: Leroux.

Maunier, R. (1930) *Mélanges de sociologie nord-africaine*. Paris: Alcan.

Rahmani, S. (1936) Rites relatifs à la vache et au lait, in 2ᵉ Congrés de la Fédération des sociétés savantes de l'Afrique du Nord (Tlemcen, 1936), Algiers, 791–809.

Servier, J. (1962) *Les Portes de l'année*. Paris: Laffont.

Chapter 18

Georges Perec

APPROACHES TO WHAT? [1973]

(Source: Perec, Georges (1997) *Species of Spaces and Other Pieces*, translated by John Sturrock, Harmondsworth: Penguin, pp. 205–7)

Editor's introduction

This short chapter by the novelist Georges Perec (1936–1982) was first published in *Cause Commune* in 1973 before it became part of his collection *L'Infra-ordinaire*. The term 'infra-ordinary' designates an everydayness that requires a kind of quixotic or excessive attention. Perec uses neologisms like 'infra-ordinary' and 'endotic' to describe an everyday that is neither ordinary nor extraordinary, neither banal nor exotic. The everyday that Perec is interested in is not simply the everyday of the surrealists (that 'sense of the marvellous suffusing everyday existence' that Louis Aragon wrote about: Aragon [1926] 1987: 24). In many ways it should be seen as a kind of surreal 'take' on the social sciences. Perec's everyday requires a ruthless systematic attention that, while it can be read as simply eccentric, suggests the possibility of an anthropology that has yet to differentiate between the significant and the insignificant. Perec's task then is to foreground what is continually missed when traditional notions of significance are applied. For instance in 'An Attempt to Exhaust a Place in Paris' he begins by cataloguing what exists in the street (the shops, cafés and so on) only to suggest that these are already too significant. Instead he writes that he intends to 'describe what remains: that which we generally don't notice, which doesn't call attention to itself, which is of no importance; what happens when nothing happens, what passes when nothing passes, except time, people, cars, and clouds' (Perec quoted in Adair 1993: 104). Given the quasi-sociological slant of this approach it may be of more than anecdotal interest that Perec was for a while friendly with Henri Lefebvre and that Lefebvre helped the impoverished Perec get a job doing market research.

Perec's literary affiliation was to a literary group called Oulipo (*Ouvroir de littérature potentielle* – Workshop for Potential Literature), a group originally founded by Raymond Queneau and François Le Lionnais. While the kind of austere self-imposed strictures that these writers placed on themselves might seem a world away from the everyday (for instance writing a novel without the letter 'e' in it), much of Oulipo work has an evident everyday quality about it. Certainly Perec's most famous novel *Life: A User's Manual* (1978) can be seen as a novelistic version of the 'infra-ordinary' as it weaves together the everyday minutiae of a host of lives that are never reducible to such a vacuous epithet as 'ordinary'.

Further reading: Adair 1993; Bellos 1999; Highmore 2000b; Mathews and Brotchie 1998; Perec 1987.

WHAT SPEAKS TO US, seemingly, is always the big event, the untoward, the extra-ordinary: the front-page splash, the banner headlines. Railway trains only begin to exist when they are derailed, and the more passengers that are killed, the more the trains exist. Aeroplanes achieve existence only when they are hijacked. The one and only destiny of motor-cars is to drive into plane trees. Fifty-two weekends a year, fifty-two casualty lists: so many dead and all the better for the news media if the figures keep on going up! Behind the event there has to be a scandal, a fissure, a danger, as if life reveals itself only by way of the spectacular, as if what speaks, what is significant, is always abnormal: natural cataclysms or historical upheavals, social unrest, political scandals.

In our haste to measure the historic, significant and revelatory, let's not leave aside the essential: the truly intolerable, the truly inadmissible. What is scandalous isn't the pit explosion, it's working in coalmines. 'Social problems' aren't 'a matter of concern' when there's a strike, they are intolerable twenty-four hours out of twenty-four, three hundred and sixty-five days a year.

Tidal waves, volcanic eruptions, tower-blocks that collapse, forest fires, tunnels that cave in, the Drugstore des Champs-Elysées burns down. Awful! Terrible! Monstrous! Scandalous! But where's the scandal? The true scandal? Has the newspaper told us anything except: not to worry, as you can see life exists, with its ups and its downs, things happen, as you can see.

The daily papers talk of everything except the daily. The papers annoy me, they teach me nothing. What they recount doesn't concern me, doesn't ask me questions and doesn't answer the questions I ask or would like to ask.

What's really going on, what we're experiencing, the rest, all the rest, where is it? How should we take account of, question, describe what happens every day and recurs every day: the banal, the quotidian, the obvious, the common, the ordinary, the infra-ordinary, the background noise, the habitual?

To question the habitual. But that's just it, we're habituated to it. We don't question it, it doesn't question us, it doesn't seem to pose a problem, we live it without thinking, as if it carried within it neither questions nor answers, as if it weren't the bearer of any information. This is no longer even conditioning, it's anaesthesia. We sleep through our lives in a dreamless sleep. But where is our life? Where is our body? Where is our space?

How are we to speak of these 'common things', how to track them down rather, flush them out, wrest them from the dross in which they remain mired, how to give them a meaning, a tongue, to let them, finally, speak of what is, of what we are.

What's needed perhaps is finally to found our own anthropology, one that will speak about us, will look in ourselves for what for so long we've been pillaging from others. Not the exotic any more, but the endotic.

To question what seems so much a matter of course that we've forgotten its origins. To rediscover something of the astonishment that Jules Verne or his readers may have felt faced with an apparatus capable of reproducing and transporting sounds. For that astonishment existed, along with thousands of others, and it's they which have moulded us.

What we need to question is bricks, concrete, glass, our table manners, our utensils, our tools, the way we spend our time, our rhythms. To question that which seems to have ceased forever to astonish us. We live, true, we breathe, true; we walk, we open doors, we go down staircases, we sit at a table in order to eat, we lie down on a bed in order to sleep. How? Where? When? Why?

Describe your street. Describe another street. Compare.

Make an inventory of your pockets, of your bag. Ask yourself about the provenance, the use, what will become of each of the objects you take out.

Question your tea spoons.

What is there under your wallpaper?

How many movements does it take to dial a phone number? Why?

Why don't you find cigarettes in grocery stores? Why not?

It matters little to me that these questions should be fragmentary, barely indicative of a method, at most of a project. It matters a lot to me that they should seem trivial and futile: that's exactly what makes them just as essential, if not more so, as all the other questions by which we've tried in vain to lay hold on our truth.

Chapter 19

Mary Kelly

DOCUMENTATION VI: PRE-WRITING ALPHABET, EXERQUE AND DIARY [1977–8]

(**Source**: Mary Kelly (1983) *Post-Partum Document*, London: Routledge & Kegan Paul, pp. 170–84)

Editor's introduction

During the years 1973 and 1978 the artist Mary Kelly produced the various sections that make up the *Post-Partum Document*. Kelly's work is an extensive documentation of her relationship with her child as it changes from birth to the moment the child can write his name. Using a variety of materials (typed-on baby vests, the infamous 'dirty nappies', plaster casts, butterflies, slate, and so on) and a variety of 'languages' (biological, diaristic, psychoanalytic, conversational) the everyday life of mother and child is spread across a range of registers.

While the work as a whole resembles some of the visual strategies of conceptual art, any straightforward categorising of the artwork as conceptual is frustrated by the nature of the material documented (rather than the dominant 'cool' of most conceptual work Kelly offers us an arena of passionate intensity). The work also refuses the dominant forms for representing a mother and her child (there is no 'image' here of a mother and child). In many ways Kelly's work operates as a feminist intervention in the patriarchal world of art, opening up space for the representation of women's culture and desire. As she writes in the introduction to the book version of the *Post-Partum Document*, the work 'parodies a familiar type of display in so far as it allows my archaeology of everyday life to slip unannounced into the great hall and ask impertinent questions of its keepers' (Kelly 1983: xvi). But this 'archaeology of everyday life' is rendered into objects that materially resonate in a way that is only hinted at in reproduction.

Within the context of this *Reader*, however, it might also operate as a classic instance of 'blurred genres'. So while it intervenes in the genre of art (on a variety of levels – not least in terms of its sustained intellectual inquiry) it could also be seen as intervening in other genres – psychology, child development, ethnography, etc. Indeed, as a form of self-ethnography it can be seen to overcome many of the difficulties of that genre (the difficulty of being both 'native informant' and 'interpretative observer') by inventively weaving together so many different discursive genres. So much so that no voice seems to speak from the place of authority.

Since *Post-Partum Document,* Kelly has continued producing substantial long-term projects (a form seemingly closer to social science research than art) and continued insistently to smuggle in the everyday (an everyday that is always scarred by the psychical management of the self) to the bastions of high art.

Further reading: Iversen *et al.* 1997; Kelly 1983, 1986; Molesworth 2000.

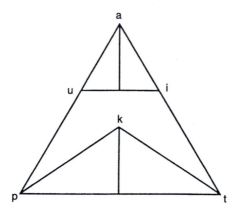

THE FORMATIVE PHASE in which the child began to read and write was documented over a period of 18 months from January 1977 to April 1978. During this time (age 3.5–4.8) he started to identify certain letter shapes and map out a system of markings related to the traditional alphabet. Notations were made on his observations following 'ABC sessions' (i.e., reading from favourite alphabet books as part of the bed-time story repertoire), and the documentation was concluded when he began to write his own name. At the same time he entered infants' school, an event which was equally significant for the mother because the learning process, once assumed to be a 'private' discourse, was then clearly seen to be determined by an institutional context.

The documentation is inscribed on slates and set out in chronological order. Each inscription is divided into three registers (analogous to the Rosetta Stone) with the child's 'hieroglyphic' letter-shapes (pre-writing alphabet) in the upper portion; the mother's print-script commentary (exerque) in the middle section and her type-script narrative (diary) in the lower part.

Alphabet

The letter shapes deciphered in these inscriptions do not constitute a logical alphabet (there are 15 figures beginning with x and ending in B rather than 26 from A to Z); but they do demonstrate the child's propensity to develop a system of graphic representation.

Pre-writing succeeds a mode of purposeful scribbling which already includes diagrammatic markings such as crosses and circles. At this moment the significant difference is that the child's expressed intention in making these marks is *writing*. The x, called 'a cross', ref. 3.501x constitutes a kind of universal grapheme class. It is virtually the functional equivalent of all letters, as the commentary indicates, 'he substitutes different letter names for the same mark'; as yet, the child does not recognise the distinctive features which are necessary to distinguish one letter or grapheme class from another. In ref. 6.6020, the distinctive feature of o, curvedness, displays an optimal contrast with the straight lines (ascenders) of x. o is generally associated with anything round, but at the same time it designates a more specific letter category than x in so far as when he writes o, he calls it 'a round **and an o**'. The development of a graphemic system follows from this initial opposition of marks, but it is ultimately dependent upon filling in the gaps between x and o. The first split occurs on the side of curvedness between the closedness of o and the openness of e, ref. 3.6030. At this point an extensive number of variations or graphs are included in the grapheme class e but together with x and o, they comprise a triangle defining the distinctive features closedness-openness on the horizontal axis and straightness-curvedness on the vertical axis:

x

o   e

In turn, straightness is differentiated by symmetry, x, versus asymmetry, r. The grapheme r, called 'a hook', ref. 3.704r, also introduces curvedness into this category and by an extension of the 'hook' produces n and m. Next the ascender 1 is marked by the addition of a feature-i which he calls 'a dot and an i', ref. 3.805i, and c, significantly unnamed, ref. 3.806c, is marked by the addition of ascenders and descenders – b,d,p,q, 'a round and a straight', ref. 3.908p, thus combining the distinctive features of both axes of the triangle.

Then capital letter configurations arise from combinations, additions or subtractions of ascenders; first placing an emphasis on the distinctive feature straightness as in E, F, 'a straight one and another straight one', ref. 3.909E, and later introducing curvedness as in R, ref. 4.113R. This is followed by the letters K and B, ref. 4.414K–4.515B, which are constructed with the specific intention of writing his own name. By this time the child's discrimination of distinctive features is adequate enough to categorise most letters of the alphabet and designate them by a spoken name. In addition, he recognises that letters such as E and e constitute alternatives for a single grapheme class and that although they have no distinctive features in common, they are equated when identifying a letter category in reading. The concept of reading also implies directionality; as evidenced in ref. 4.515K, the child's name is insistently printed from left to right, and significantly, previous inversions and reversals of letters such as ə q ɔ are corrected in this process. As a result his letters effectively represent the minimal contrasts necessary to distinguish a word in writing and at this moment his 'writing' articulates the letter as a material locus, a visual configuration, a concept and a category name.

Exerque

The commentary and quotations set out below the child's inscription, identify the letter as material support of a concrete discourse. Within this space emphasis is placed on the intersubjective relations between mother and child in the act of reading and writing. Thus the gaps, omissions and inversions of the prewriting alphabet are crucial for the mother in deciphering the child's text. His incipient agraphia – the provocative ə, ref. 3.603e, the unspoken ɔ, ref. 3.806c, the overstated Ɛ, ref. 4.012 H, in so far as it is symptomatic of a resistance to the repression of Oedipal sexuality, implicates the mother and gives a place to her phantasies as well as those of the child. In this sense the intertextuality of alphabet and exerque efface the distinction between an object-letter and a subject who deciphers it. The hieroglyphic residue of the child's letter-shapes – the ideographic x, ref. 3.501x, the pictographic i, ref. 3.805i, the phonographic s, ref. 3.1111s – undermine a notion of the alphabet as absolute representation, i.e., as a system of arbitrary signs purged of all figurative regressions.

On the one hand, the repression, condensation and displacement of graphemic signifiers in the child's text, suggest a writing anterior to speech, an insistence of the letter in the discourse of the unconscious which is resistant to signification as such. And on the other hand, the graphic rhetoric of children's books referred to in the mother's annotations to the child's script, such as A is for apple, B is for balloon, C is for cake, etc., implies a certain coagulation of the signified, underlining the logocentric bias of the system of language to which the letter ultimately subscribes; a system that privileges naming and the proper name and that pronounces the beginning of writing with the child's inscription of his father's name.

Diary

The diary narrative inserts the intersubjective discourse of the letter into a complex of institutional practices and systems of representation which produce the social subordination of the mother. First, there is the representation of a specific socio-economic category. The diary events surrounding the child's entry into infants' school 'take place' in an urban, industrial, multi-racial, working-class area of the inner city often designated as disadvantaged or 'deprived', ref. 3.806c. In sociological rhetoric, 'disadvantage' is constituted by a signifying chain of percentages concerning one-parent families, working mothers, low income, poor housing, inadequate transport, overcrowded schools, accidents, disease, pollution, illiteracy and crime. The place the mother occupies as an effect of the signifying chain is inevitably that of failure or at best a victim of circumstance; but the position she takes up in the process of representing this place to herself is by no means fixed as one of resignation; in ref. 3.704r, it is resistance, in ref. 3.908p, denial, in ref. 3.1111s, disassociation. Ultimately, it is not the mother's hopes, aspirations and ambitions for her child that are lacking, but the possibility of their realisation which is circumscribed by the economic constraints, social practices and political effects of separation from the means of production, possession and 'advantage'.

Second, there is the construction of the agency of the mother/housewife. In this position the mother is assigned certain responsibilities, moral attributes and legal statuses by the education authority. For instance in ref. 4.414K, the form of address employed by the headmistress, i.e., 'Mrs', at once confirms the parent's legal status as wife and her moral attribute as mother, implying the child's 'legitimacy'. It is to this agent/addressee that the school sends all memoranda concerning the dates of term, of holidays, the requirements for school outings, bazaars and benefits, the cost of school dinners, the rules and regulations concerning absenteeism, tardiness, fires, floods, the lending of library books, and the lending of a helping hand, such as supervising the playgroup, ref. 3.501x.

In addition the local health authority, in collaboration with the school, administer a medical service which consists primarily of monitoring the child's health (illnesses, immunisation, physical growth, mental progress and general social adjustment), and which designates the mother as guarantor of his well-being. This process of surveillance is epitomised by the yearly check-up, ref. 3.909E, and the mother's attendance is 'strongly advised'. Unavoidably the child's symptom is read as a sign of her capacity/incapacity to fulfill the agency of the mother/housewife at the level of the attributes deemed essential to that agency such as common sense, practicality and discipline mediated by an intimate, 'natural' bond with the child. However, the mother never sufficiently corresponds to the agency this institutional discourse defines and that is demonstrated by the father's participation in the realisation (also always partial) of those capacities, for instance when the mother is working, ref. 4.113R. Nor does the father ever conform to the agency of the father/husband fulfilling the function of breadwinner or possessing a 'natural' aptitude for authority, etc. On the one hand, there is often conflict between the husband and the wife over responsibility for the child, ref. 4.414K, but on the other hand there is unmitigated deference shown by both parents towards the assumed authority of the headmistress/ teacher in matters concerning childcare, ref. 3.807m. Thus the mother's secondary social status is not necessarily a result of the subordination of women by men, but rather it is an effect of the position occupied as the agent of childcare within the legal, moral, medical and pedagogic discourses of the educational institution. But there is a difference for the mother with respect to that position because these discourses also assign a place to the child which radically displaces her representation of him as a part of herself. Consequently, the school becomes the site of a struggle for 'possession' of the child; it is a struggle the mother always loses and it is this sense of 'loss' which produces a specific form of subordination for the woman in her capacity as the mother/housewife.

(age 3.5) X IS FOR X. He calls it "a cross". He substitutes different letter names for the same marks. It seems to mean writing in general. X is arbitrary but not indifferent. X is the body—repressed, represented, enjoyed. X IS FOR ALLIGATORS X-ING X3. X IS FOR A XENURUS HAVING A X-RAY. GOOD NIGHT LITTLE X. XENOPHON XERXES XEPHOSURA. GOOD NIGHT LITTLE X.

January 25, 1977: Parents(ip, mothers) are required to help supervise children at the playgroup once a fortnight. How I dread it. I dont really want to know what he's like at school. I'll only worry about it if he doesn't get along with the supervisors or the other children. Today, I noticed they blamed one boy constantly for starting trouble and I felt sorry for him. Two little girls(twins) seemed to need special attention but the supervisors usually became impatient with them, no wonder, there were just too many children. Another little girl (barely 3 yrs. old) was trying to write her name. I was amazed. I told her how clever she was and made quite a fuss over her. Kelly watched very intently and that evening he asked Pauline to show him how to write.

3501X

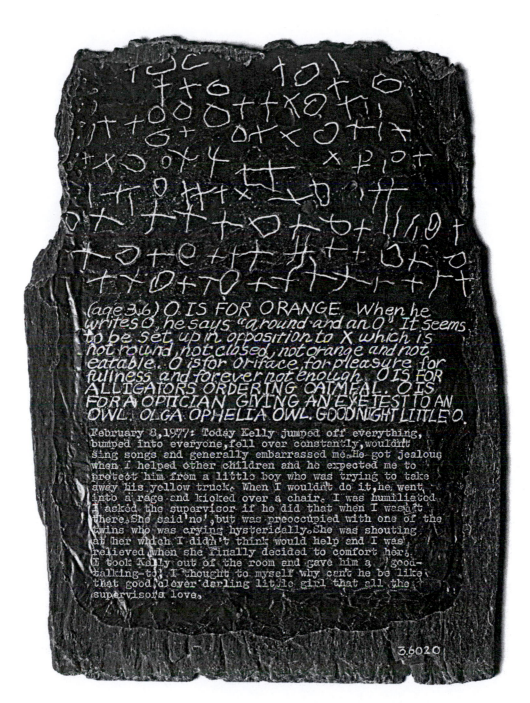

(age 3.6) O IS FOR ORANGE. When he writes O, he says "a round and an O". It seems to be set up in opposition to X which is not round, not closed, not orange and not eatable. O is for Oriface, for pleasure for fullness and forever not enough. O IS FOR ALLIGATORS ORDERING OATMEAL. O IS FOR A OPTICIAN GIVING AN EYE TEST TO AN OWL. OLGA OPHELIA OWL. GOODNIGHT LITTLE O.

February 8, 1977: Today Kelly jumped off everything, bumped into everyone, fell over constantly, wouldn't sing songs and generally embarrassed me. He got jealous when I helped other children and he expected me to protect him from a little boy who was trying to take away his yellow truck. When I wouldn't do it, he went into a rage and kicked over a chair. I was humiliated. I asked the supervisor if he did that when I wasn't there. She said 'no', but was preoccupied with one of the twins who was crying hysterically. She was shouting at her which I didn't think would help and I was relieved when she finally decided to comfort her. I took Kelly out of the room and gave him a good-talking-to. I thought to myself why can't he be like that good, clever darling little girl that all the supervisors love.

3.6020

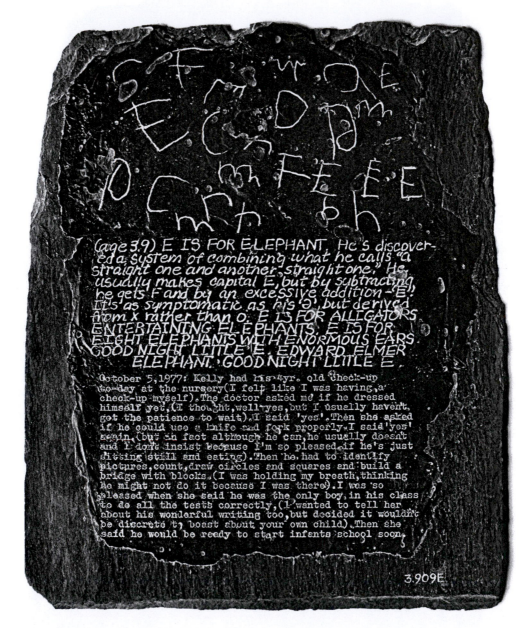

(age 3.9) E IS FOR ELEPHANT. He's discovered a system of combining what he calls "a
straight one and another straight one." He
usually makes capital E, but by subtracting
he gets F and by an excessive addition — E!
It's as symptomatic as his ∂, but derived
from x rather than o. E IS FOR ALLIGATORS
ENTERTAINING ELEPHANTS. E IS FOR
EIGHT ELEPHANTS WITH ENORMOUS EARS.
GOOD NIGHT LITTLE E. EDWARD ELMER
ELEPHANT. GOOD NIGHT LITTLE E.

October 5, 1977: Kelly had his 4 yr. old check-up
to-day at the nursery (I felt like I was having a
check-up myself). The doctor asked me if he dressed
himself yet, (I thought, well yes, but I usually haven't
got the patience to wait). I said 'yes'. Then she asked
if he could use a knife and fork properly. I said 'yes'
again, (but in fact although he can, he usually doesn't
and I don't insist because I'm so pleased if he's just
sitting still and eating). Then he had to identify
pictures, count, draw circles and squares and build a
bridge with blocks. (I was holding my breath, thinking
he might not do it because I was there). I was so
pleased when she said he was the only boy, in his class
to do all the tests correctly, (I wanted to tell her
about his wonderful writing too, but decided it wouldn't
be discrete to boast about your own child). Then she
said he would be ready to start infants school soon.

3.909E

(age 4.1) R IS FOR RABBIT. This R is derived from P and H rather than r. It extends his system of constructing capital letters from "straight ones." P plus a straight makes R and minus a curve gives the H he uses in attempting to write his first name. R IS FOR ALLIGATORS RIDING REINDEER. R IS FOR A ROMAN RHINOCEROS ON ROLLER-SKATES GOOD NIGHT LITTLE R. RICHARD ROBINSON RABBIT. GOOD NIGHT LITTLE R.

March 7, 1978. It looks like the school near the estate is not the best but the 'least problematic', all things considered. They've recently sent us a letter offering Kelly a place after Easter, and a friend of mine who is a teacher says it would be a definite advantage for him to start at 4½. Besides, he seems interested in learning, he knows most of the letters of the alphabet and he can write his own name quite well (he says his name is Kelly Barrie, his dad's name is Ray Barrie and his mum's is just Mary). Also, he would only get bored if he stayed at nursery much longer and the newer school can't take him yet. Then there is the overdetermining factor which is that Ray wants him to start school because he needs the free time. Since I'm teaching 3 sometimes 4 days a week and he's the one looking after him, I'm really not in a position to object. I still feel like a complete failure resorting to sending him there. I was so sure I could find an infants school as nice as the nursery. I can't believe it. Maybe I just didn't try hard enough.

4113R

(age 3,8) I IS FOR INK. He calls it "a dot and an i". Sometimes he points to his eye but seems to know it's a pun. He's fascinated by it. Little 'i'-the object watched by I -the subject. T IS FOR ALLIGATORS IMITATING IN-DIANS. I IS FOR AN IBEX IN AN INDIAN OUTFIT CHASING INSECTS ABSCONDING WITH AN ICE CREAM CONE. GOOD NIGHT LITTLE I. IGOR ILLYCH IGUANA. GOOD NIGHT LITTLE I. GOOD NIGHT.

April, 1977: Today I was told about the 'gang of six' (troublesome boys) of which Kelly is apparently one. The superviser said they were 'very loud' but tried to assure me that he wasn't any worse than the others. I was wishing that I wouldn't have to witness it, but at the same time, I wanted to get to the bottom of things'. In fact, almost all of the boys ran about the hall incessantly shouting and imitating batman, spider-man, bionic man, and an assortment of 'monsters' and 'badies'. Most of the girls, sat at the tables playing with puzzles and lego. Obviously, the supervisors including myself, didn't encourage them to do anything else, we were so relieved that at least some of the children were sitting down. We occasionally tried to get the boys to do 'something constructive' but they do it for about 2 mins. and then rush off again. It seems to be more difficult to handle boys, but then the teachers are always women, I've never seen a father at the playgroup or a man on the staff of any nursery I've visited.

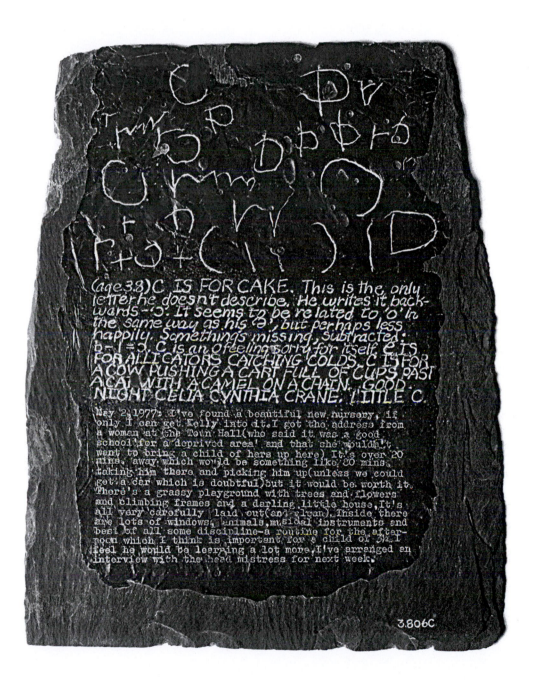

(age 3.8) C IS FOR CAKE. This is the only letter he doesn't describe. He writes it backwards – 'Ɔ'. It seems to be related to 'o' in the same way as his 'Ꝺ', but perhaps less happily. Somethings missing, subtracted: b – 1 = Ɔ. C is an ofeeling sorry for itself e IS FOR ALLIGATORS CATCHING COLDS. C IS FOR A COW PUSHING A CART FULL OF CUPS PAST A CAT WITH A CAMEL ON A CHAIN. GOOD NIGHT CELIA CYNTHIA CRANE. LITTLE C.

May 2, 1977: I've found a beautiful new nursery, if only I can get Kelly into it. I got the address from a woman at the Town Hall (who said it was a good school for a deprived area' and that she wouldn't want to bring a child of hers up here) It's over 20 mins. away which would be something like 80 mins. taking him there and picking him up (unless we could get a car which is doubtful) but it would be worth it. There's a grassy playground with trees and flowers and climbing frames and a darling little house. It's all very carefully laid out (and clean). Inside there are lots of windows, animals, musical instruments and best of all some discipline—a routine for the afternoon which I think is important for a child of 3½. I feel he would be learning a lot more. I've arranged an interview with the head mistress for next week.

3.806C

(age 3.3) M IS FOR MICE. He seems to have arrived at m by extending the hook on r. He calls it "an up and a down". He turns m upside down to get w, subtracts to make n, and turns it upside-down again to get u. M IS FOR ALLIGATORS MAKING MACARONI. M IS FOR A MOUSE MENDING A MACHINE WHILE A MONKEY RIDES A MOTERCYCLE. GOOD NIGHT LITTLE MARCO MCMILLAN MONKEY

May 10, 1977: I went for the interview at the new nursery to-day. I felt more nervous about this event than being interviewed for a job myself. I had to bring Kelly along. I dressed him in his navyblue coat. He looked very neat and I tried to make myself look 'respectable' too, putting on a long coat to cover most of my jeans. I was afraid Kelly would leap all over the head-mistress' office and ruin our chances but miraculously he didn't. He was very quiet and well behaved and I was terribly proud of him. I think she took note of the fact that I was a teacher (of course I didn't say part-time and definitely not that I was an artist). I said I wanted him there for educational reasons. She sounded convinced and encouraged me by saying she'd write a letter very soon.

(age 3.9) P IS FOR POSTMAN. He recognises all the combinations of what he calls "a straight and a round". 0 + l = p, d, b and sometimes backwards a.— "b". He often turns p upside down expecting to get b and seeing q instead — a mirror image. It seems to mark a turning point. He can identify most of the letters in his abc book. P IS FOR ALLIGATORS PUSHING PEOPLE, P IS FOR A PANDA PLAYING ON A POGO-STICK. GOOD NIGHT LITTLE P. PERRY PONSONBY PENGUIN. GOOD NIGHT.

May 19, 1977: The letter arrived to-day and they've accepted Kelly at the new nursery. I feel like a 'good mother' because I made an effort and actually changed his situation for the better. I didn't think it would be possible to find such a lovely place here. When I told the health visitor where Kelly was going to go to school she said to him "your mummy looks after you very well, doesn't she?" It struck me then how unfair it was to assume that some children were in 'bad' schools because their parents didn't care. On the contrary, all the mothers I've met at the playgroup talk about nothing else. Danny's mother rushed up to me on the street to say she'd found a super infants school and that 'they didn't use i.t.a. either' (I didn't even know what that meant). Ronnie's mother takes him to school in Swiss Cottage on her way to work every morning and Cloe's mother has moved back to her mother's, taking Cloe with her.

3.908P

(age 3,6) e IS FOR ELEPHANT. He calls it the "curvy one" and pronounces it—"eeh". He often forgets it and sometimes writes it upside down—"ə". When he sees an e a present or a breast, he says, "What's that?" Something at once lost, forgotten, remembered and hoped for. "ə" as in "me." E IS FOR ALLIGATORS ENTERTAINING ELEPHANTS. E IS FOR AN EAGLE ON AN ELEPHANT IN AN EGG AND SPOON RACE. GOOD NIGHT EDWARD ELMER ELEPHANT. GOOD NIGHT LITTLE E.

February 22, 1977: I noticed the general conditions more than the children this time, like the rubbish outside the building and the dust inside. When I washed the cups the rag looked so grey I couldn't bring myself to use it. But I suppose they do the best they can, it isn't their own space, its only rented during the day from a boys club. There's no playground and the children have to stay indoors. All but about 20 mins of the 2 hrs. is 'unstructured' and seems to get out of hand, I'm afraid they'll get hurt. I can't stand the bad grammar after about an hour of it - I can't believe I could be so uptight and pretentious. I feel inadequate myself because I cant offer Kelly more. I wish he could go to a good school, but it's hopeless in this area. I went to the Social Services Dept. and self-righteously demanded the names and addresses of proper nursery schools. They just smiled and refused, saying it would be of no use since all of them had at least a 2 yr. waiting list.

3.603e

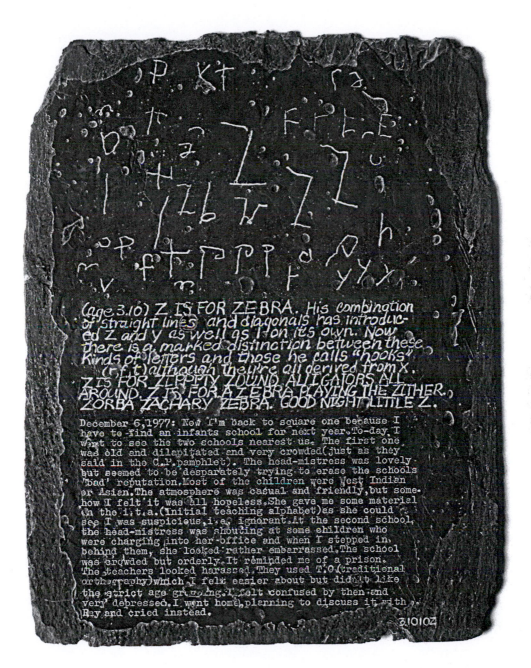

(age 3.10) Z IS FOR ZEBRA. His combination
of straight lines and diagonals has introduced Z and Y as well as I on its own. Now
there is a marked distinction between these
kinds of letters and those he calls "hooks"
(F, f, r) although they're all derived from X.
Z IS FOR ZIPPITY ZOUND, ALLIGATORS ALL
AROUND. Z IS FOR A ZEBRA PLAYING THE ZITHER.
ZORBA ZACHARY ZEBRA. GOOD NIGHT LITTLE Z.

December 6,1977: Now I'm back to square one because I
have to find an infants school for next year.To-day I
went to see the two schools nearest us. The first one
was old and dilapidated and very crowded(just as they
said in the C.P. pamphlet). The head-mistress was lovely
but seemed to be desparately trying to erase the schools
'bad' reputation.Most of the children were West Indian
or Asian.The atmosphere was casual and friendly,but somehow I felt it was all hopeless.She gave me some material
th the i.t.a.(Initial teaching alphabet)as she could
see I was suspicious,i.e. ignorant.At the second school,
the head-mistress was shouting at some children who
were charging into her office and when I stepped in,
behind them, she looked rather embarrassed.The school
was crowded but orderly.It reminded me of a prison.
The teachers looked harassed.They used T.O(traditional
orthography)which I felt easier about but didn't like
the strict age grouping.I felt confused by then and
very depressed.I went home,planning to discuss it with
Ray and cried instead.

3.10102

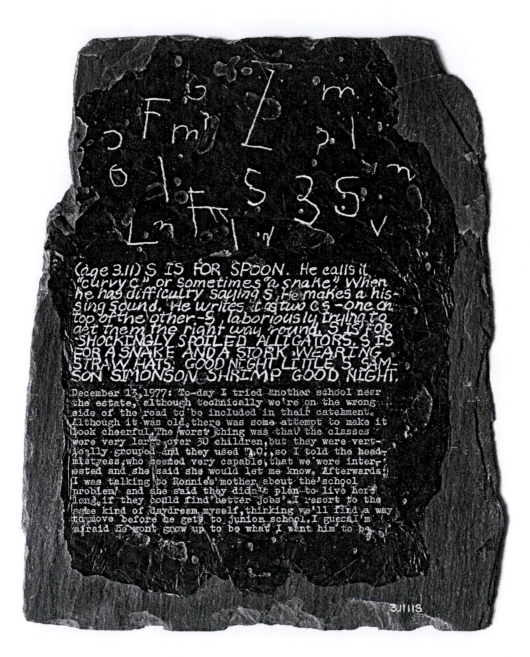

(age 3.11) S IS FOR SPOON. He calls it "curvy c" or sometimes "a snake." When he has difficulty saying S He makes a hissing sound. He writes it as two c's -one on top of the other -S, laboriously trying to get them the right way 'round. S IS FOR SHOCKINGLY SPOILED ALLIGATORS. S IS FOR A SNAKE AND A STORK WEARING STRAW HATS. GOOD NIGHT LITTLE S. SAMSON SIMONSON SHRIMP GOOD NIGHT.

December 13, 1977: To-day I tried another school near the estate, although technically we're on the wrong side of the road to be included in their catchment. Although it was old, there was some attempt to make it look cheerful. The worst thing was that the classes were very large over 30 children, but they were vertically grouped and they used I.T.A., so I told the headmistress, who seemed very capable, that we were interested and she said she would let me know. Afterwards, I was talking to Ronnie's mother about the school problem, and she said they didn't plan to live here long if they could find better jobs. I resort to the same kind of daydream myself, thinking we'll find a way to move before he gets to junior school. I guess I'm afraid he wont grow up to be what I want him to be.

(age 40) H IS FOR HOUSE. H seems to have the function of 'blocks' – building letter shapes. He says he's "doing his work" and intently fills up the page from right to left or left to right, including all his little para praxes – backwards 'e' upsidedown 'b', and excessive 'E'. H IS FOR ALLIGATORS HAVING HEADACHES. H IS FOR A HAMSTER AND A HEDGEHOG FLYING A HELICOPTER OVER A HOUSE AND A HUT ON A HILL. HILARY HAGGERTY HEDGEHOG. GOOD NIGHT.

February 17, 1978. The head-mistress at the nursery (whom I'm very anxious to please) dropped some fairly strong hints about looking in another area for an infants school. So I decided to go and see one near there. It was another 20mins. from the nursery making about 40mins. in all from home and there's no direct public transport. But I did feel more at ease there. It was a new building, less crowded, with more equipment and even a special music teacher-a man! (which is important for Kelly who already has very fixed ideas about what men and boys do and women and girls don't do) The head-master said he could give a place but not before next autumn. The possibility of getting him there everyday, without a car seems like pure fantasy-I almost wish I hadn't seen it.

4012H

(age 3.7) r IS FOR RABBIT. He calls r 'a hook' —
an open curve. IT'S prompted variations
like b — a closed curve. r is to 'x' as 'e' is to 'o',
a recognition of difference, and at the same
time a kind of refusal — a part-object. R IS
FOR ALLIGATORS RIDING REINDEER. R IS
FOR A RABBIT AND A RACOON PULLING A
RHINOCEROS ON A ROPE WHILE THREE
RAT ROBBERS AND A ROBOT ROCK ON
IN THE RAIN. GOOD NIGHT LITTLE R.
RICHARD ROBINSON RABBIT. GOOD NIGHT.

March 21, 1977: This time, I felt quite relaxed. Kelly
didn't demand any 'special attention' and in fact none
of the children need so much help now. He's always anxious to go to the play group and I'm really pleased
he's getting along so well. I don't even seem to notice
what I once thought were such 'shocking conditions'
but I'm still wondering what to do about school next
year. I also met Cloe's mother who had recently moved
to Hackney and who was concerned about the schools
and the poor conditions generally in the borough, she,
insisted that it was due to improve but it would take
a long time and meanwhile, if you persevered you could
get your child into a better school in another area.
She's the first woman I've talked to at the playgroup
who seems like she might try to change things but I
thought, well, I won't bring up 'politics' to-day, maybe
next time.

3.70 4 r

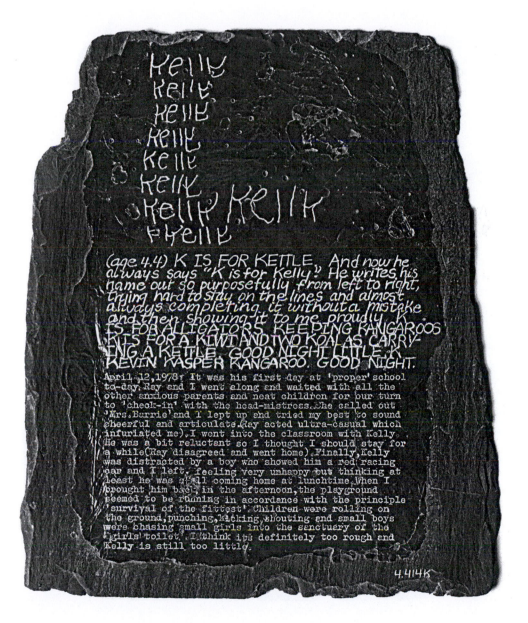

(age 4.4) K IS FOR KETTLE. And now he always says "K is for Kelly." He writes his name out so purposefully from left to right, trying hard to stay on the lines and almost always completing it without a mistake and then showing it to me proudly. K IS FOR ALLIGATORS KEEPING KANGAROOS. K IS FOR A KIWI AND TWO KOALAS CARRYING A KETTLE. GOOD NIGHT LITTLE K. KEVIN KASPER KANGAROO. GOOD NIGHT.

April 12,1978. It was his first day at 'proper' school to-day. Ray and I went along and waited with all the other anxious parents and neat children for our turn to 'check-in' with the head-mistress. She called out 'Mrs. Barrie' and I lept up and tried my best to sound cheerful and articulate.(Ray acted ultra-casual which infuriated me). I went into the classroom with Kelly. He was a bit reluctant so I thought I should stay for a while(Ray disagreed and went home). Finally, Kelly was distracted by a boy who showed him a red racing car and I left, feeling very unhappy but thinking at least he was still coming home at lunchtime. When I brought him back in the afternoon, the playground seemed to be running in accordance with the principle 'survival of the fittest'. Children were rolling on the ground, punching, kicking, shouting and small boys were chasing small girls into the sanctuary of the 'girls' toilet'. I think its definitely too rough and Kelly is still too little.

4.414K

Kelly
Kelly Bapi

Ki
Kelly Brrie
Kelly
Barrie

(age 4.5) B IS FOR BALLOON. This is the
first letter he has constructed with the
express purpose of writing a specific word-
his surname. He draws 'P and carefully
adds Ɔ. Learning to write 'Barrie' has also
sorted out his 'backwards 'b' and the upside down 'Ɔ. B IS FOR ALLIGATORS
BURSTING BALLOONS. B IS FOR BEARS PLAY-
ING BAGPIPES IN A BAND GOOD NIGHT LIT-
TLE B. BERTRAM BULLFINCH BASSET HOUND

April 19, 1978. Now Kelly is at school all day. Ray
insisted that he was ready to stay for school dinners.
He said Kelly was quite happy and I had to admit it
did seem to be true so far. When he comes home I try
to ask him what he does at school, what he has for
lunch, but he's usually not very informative he's in
such a hurry to change his clothes and go out to play
with Ronnie. They've become very good friends. Once he
said he didn't think he needed a mummy and daddy
because he and Ronnie could live together and look
after themselves. He brought home some flash cards
which seem to take the place of our 'a.b.c.' sessions
and he keeps a little notebook at school which I can
go and look at from time to time. Things have definitely
changed, and so quickly. When I told Rosalind that
he'd started infant's school she said "well, your're a
real mother now".

4515B

Experimentum mentis VI
On the insistence of the letter

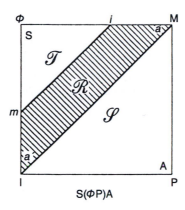

S(ΦP)A

Pre-writing emerges as post-script to the Oedipus complex and as preface to the moment of latency. In so far as the child's sexual researches are repressed by the Law and the Father, they are sublimated in the body of the letter; *but it is the mother who first censors the look, who wipes the slate clean with her silence and prepares the site of inscription. For the mother, the child's text is a fetish object; it desires her. The polymorphous perversity of the letter explores the body beyond the limit of the look. The breast (e), the hook (r), the lack (c), the eye (i), the snake (s); forbidden anatomies, incestuous morphologies; the child's alphabet is an anagram of the maternal body. For the child the grapheme-as-body-in-the-position-of-the-signifier plays with difference, not the difference of the founding moment of castration, the ultimatum of being or having, but rather a re-play of differences and separations already sanctioned in the structuring and dissolution of the Oedipus complex. A cross (x), a round (o), an up and a down (n, m), a straight and a round (p, b, d, q); pairs of graphemic oppositions designate the symbolic function of presence and absence in a double movement of memory and forgetting. Faeces, mark, imprint, utterance; a residue of corporality subtends the letter and overflows the text. The gift unfolds the child's desire to-be-what-she-wants-him-to-be; but the letter constructs the cannot-be of his autonomy and instigates the unexpected pleasure of deferment.*

With the inscription of his proper name, the child is instituted as the author of his text. Each purposeful stroke disfigures the anagram, dismembers the body. The mother is dispossessed of the phallic attributes of the pre-Oedipal instance, but only as if re-tracing a vague figure of repletion on a distant screen. Fading, forgetting; she cannot remember although 'it seems like only yesterday'. This wound to her narcissism is now a caricature: a tearful bliss, a simulated ecstasy, a veritable stigmata in the Name-of-the-Father. With the child's insistent repetition of the Name, he appropriates the status of the Father, the dead Father, the absent Father, the pre-condition of the 'word'. The incestuous meaning of the letter is ciphered by the paternal metaphor. But at the same time this introduces the possibility of 'truth', the truth of the mother; that is, the fiction of the 'real mother', not the Madonna, but the Pietá, dispelling imputations of guilt with patience, self-sacrifice, long-suffering and resignation. Resignation punctuated with protests: 'he is too little . . . he is too young . . . they are too rough . . . it is too far'. In phantasy, the mother endures an endless series of threats to the child's well-being; sickness, accident, death. Her castration fears take the form of losing her loved objects, primarily her children; but underlying this is the fear of losing love, that is, the fear of being unable to reconstitute her narcissistic aim, of being unable to see herself as infinitely good and unconditionally loved. Ultimately, it is the fear of her mother's death and of her own death as the imaginary stake in the representation of that loss. This negation is constituted by a recognition of unbearable dependence; but it is also an affirmation of life since the child's independence is implicated in the renunciation he imposes on her desire.

The effects of repressing Oedipal pleasure for both the mother and the child are evaded through sublimation, that is, through their mutual inscription in an order of extra-familial discourse and social practice. But the very movement towards a non-parental ideal that prompts the child's creative initiatives or indiscretions and constructs the representation of his social place, returns the mother to the site of the family, to the parental ideal of her own mother and to the representation of maternal femininity. Such a circuitous passage is problematic; being the phallus, she cannot have it; not having it, she cannot represent herself as subject of desire. She finds it difficult to assume responsibility for her pleasure without guilt; to provoke her sexual partner, to slight her child. Fearing failure, she is distracted from the projects which interest her most. There is a reprieve; another child, the fullness of the dyad, the sweetness of that imaginary encapsulation which reduces the 'outside world' to absurdity. But there is also the inevitable moment of separation reiterating a lack *always already inscribed and impossible to efface. She asks herself 'What will I do? . . . when he starts school . . . when he grows up . . . when he leaves home . . . when he leaves me . . . '. This moment signifies more than separation; it articulates a rupture, a rent, a gap and a confrontation — a confrontation not only because of the way in which her desire, as desire of the child, to-be-what-she-wants-him-to-be, is produced within a field of social and economic constraints; but also because of the way in which the dialectic of desire, the movement of subject and object with its insistence on bisexuality, continually transgresses the system of representation in which it is founded. The construction of femininity as essentially natural and maternal is never finally fixed but forever unsettled in the process of articulating her difference, her loss. And it is precisely at such moments, that it is possible to desire to speak and to dare to change.*

(WHAT WILL I DO?)

s

Chapter 20

Jean-Luc Godard and Anne-Marie Miéville

FRANCE/TOUR/DETOUR/TWO/CHILDREN (EPISODE ONE) [1978]

(**Source**: Godard, Jean-Luc and Miéville, Anne-Marie (1982) 'France/Tour/Detour/Two/Children', *Camera Obscura* 8–9–10, pp. 61–72)

Editor's introduction

At the start of the 1970s the well-known filmmaker Jean-Luc Godard suffered a nearly fatal motorcycle accident in Paris. While recuperating he moved to Switzerland where he set up Sonimage (a production company) with Anne-Marie Miéville. If Godard's early 'new wave' films were often concerned with the gestures and practices of everyday life, his work with Miéville established a discursive form where everyday life became the insistent context within which to raise questions about the (social) nature of images and sound.

In their twelve-part television series (*France/Tour/Detour/Two/Children*), Godard and Miéville investigate the everyday life of two French children as they go about their daily routines (getting ready for bed, going to school and so on). In Godard and Miéville's refusal to condescend to a normative idea of childhood, the interviewer (Godard) questions the children in what might be considered a relentlessly adult way and there is no doubt that Camille (the interviewee) is at times uncomfortable with this. In doing this the programme foregrounds the uneasy relationship between interviewer and interviewee in ways that are usually hidden (though not of course absent) in mainstream television documentaries. If these interviews are uncomfortable, this partly reflects the unease that is so much part of a child's everyday life and so insistently erased in representations of childhood.

Unrecoverable from the script below is the movement of the video image. Godard and Miéville continually slow-down the image (sometimes bringing it to a stuttering stop) as if the image is in a permanent state of hesitation. In some respects this continual slow-motion corresponds with Walter Benjamin's call for an ethnographic cinema based on slow-motion that might reveal an 'optical unconscious' in the gestures and habits of everyday life (Benjamin 1982b: 239). It maybe entirely incidental, but on leaving school in 1948 Godard studied ethnology at the Sorbonne. *France/Tour/Detour/Two/Children* is an ethnography of aspects of everyday life that are buried deep beneath layers of sentiment. At the same time it provides a vantage-point from which the everyday life of adults (or 'monsters' as they are called in the series) is vividly 'made strange'.

Further reading: Bellour 1992; MacCabe 1980; Penley 1982; Silverman and Farocki 1998; Sterritt 1998.

Title: Loosely inspired by G. Bruno's work:
Le Tour de la France par Deux Enfants

(Camille *holding boom mike*; Armand *looking through camera. Studio noises and music*)

Title: FRANCE/TOUR/DETOUR/DEUX/ENFANTS

Julien Clerc (*sings*):
   Folk like us are sometimes happy –
   When we're sad the sky clouds over . . .
   Our moods veer with the winds –
   Vary with the times.
   You can change the name of the place you live –
   Change the way it looks . . .

Title: FIRST MOVEMENT

(Camille *getting ready for bed, at times in slow motion*)
Mother: Is your satchel ready?
Camille: Yes!
Mother: And your drawing things, darling?
Camille: It's not today, it's tomorrow.
Mother: Is it? OK . . . but be quick if you don't mind . . .
What are you doing, Camille?
Camille: I'm taking off my tights.
Mother: Hurry up . . . please.
Camille: OK.
Narrator (*male*): Preparing one's body for the night. Discovering a secret, and then covering it again. The beginning of a story, or the story of a beginning. Slowing down. Decomposing.

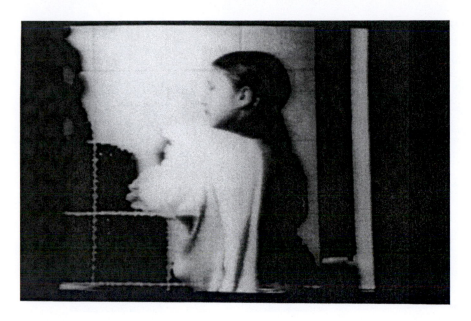

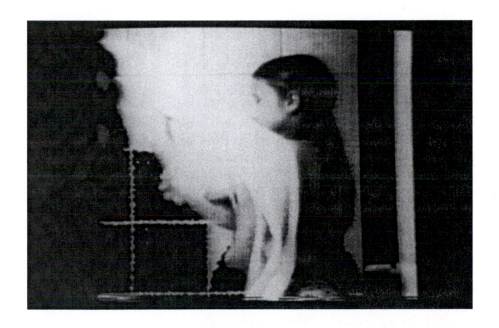

Title: DARK

(*Shot of an owl*)

Title: DARK CHEMISTRY

(*Shots of freeway at night. Music and street noises*)
Narrator (*male*): The monsters go home, with as little delay as possible, like atoms. They travel across the landscape they have laid waste . . . the lifework of the tourists. Laying waste a countryside. Devastating. It's a vast undertaking. Solitary. The wolves switch on their parking lights. The diamond. A solitaire. Still like atoms. Lit up. A dark lunacy. An industrial disaster. The dawn of the age of steel.

Title: TRUTH

(Camille *sitting on her bed; faint sounds of another child talking off-screen throughout*)
Camille: . . . to try to know . . . I don't know
Interviewer: This is your room? . . . This room's yours?
(Jean-Luc Godard's *voice throughout*)
Camille: And my brother's.
Interviewer: Yours and your brother's?
Camille: Yes.
Interviewer: And you pay a lot to live here?
Camille: No . . . it's mommy who pays.
Interviewer: OK, so we were saying we were . . . what time of day is it now?
Camille: Evening.

Interviewer: Evening. And you're all by yourself on your bed.
Camille: I'm all by myself on my bed, but there's someone else in the room.
Interviewer: Well yes, there's me.
Narrator (*male*): So there he is; and he's telling himself that one of these days . . . one of these days, he'll have to make a beginning with the night; and that tonight, to get the job done, he'll have to make a beginning here. Perhaps after all, that's as far as he's got. So with her or another – what's the difference? Everything has its price. And I suddenly realize that to approach someone sometimes needs an awful lot of courage.
Interviewer: Are you a brave girl?
Camille: It depends what about.
Interviewer: For instance, what frightens you? . . . There are things that frighten you?
Camille: Well . . . I don't really know.
Interviewer: Space – do you know what that is?
Camille: Yes.
Interviewer: And time – do you know what that is too?
Camille: Yes.
Interviewer: But what about the night? Do you think it's space or time?
Camille: Both.
Interviewer: But not more one than the other? Or not?
Camille: . . . I don't know.
Interviewer: And silence . . . which do you like best, silence or noise?

Title: TRUTH

Camille: Noise.
Interviewer: And silence, does it worry you if there's silence? If someone looks at you in silence?
Camille: . . . No.
Interviewer: Do you think silence belongs more to the day or to the night?
Camille: More to the night.
Interviewer: More to the night?
Narrator (*male*): He's still there, facing her, and the night is breaking. As she neglected to tell him earlier, at the beginning of the program, she didn't want to show her bottom; he didn't make a point of it, so that now he can only see part of her shoulder and a mass of thick blond hair . . .
Interviewer: . . . you remember last time, when we were talking about existing . . .
Camille: Yes . . .
Interviewer: And about existence?
Camille: Yes.
Interviewer: Have you thought about it any more?
Camille: No.
Interviewer: No? Are you still sure you have an existence?
Camille: Yes.
Interviewer: And one . . . not several.
Camille: No.
Interviewer: You're quite sure?

Camille: Yes.

Interviewer: And apart from you, there are other things which have an existence?

Camille: My bed – that exists.

Interviewer: How do you know?

Camille: Because I can see it.

Interviewer: Suppose you were blind?

Camille: Well, I'd touch it so I'd know it exists.

Interviewer: And if you had no senses?

Camille: I don't know.

Interviewer: Because you can see and touch, and hear as well.

Camille: Yes, because if someone sat down, there might be a creak.

Interviewer: Yes. Last time we were talking about when you undress, or just now when you were undressing . . . There are times when you can see yourself in the mirror?

Camille: Yes.

Interviewer: And who was it you saw?

Camille: My reflection.

Interviewer: Your reflection?

Camille: Yes.

Interviewer: And your reflection – is that you or someone else?

Camille: It's me.

Interviewer: And this 'me' you can see – has that got an existence too?

Camille: No, because it's me that's looking at myself in the glass.

Interviewer: Yes, but the reflection, has that an existence too?

Camille: Yes.

Interviewer: So it's as if you had two existences?

Camille: Maybe.

Interviewer: And just now you said you had only one, and the reflection had no existence . . . and that you weren't double.

Camille: Well I do know I'm not double.

Interviewer: You're not double?

Camille: No.

Interviewer: Even so, the other one's exactly like you.

Camille: Yes.

Interviewer: And when there's two of the same thing, doesn't one call them 'double'?

Camille: Yes but . . . if there wasn't a mirror, I wouldn't be double.

Interviewer: No . . . but there is one.

Camille: Yes . . . but I'm not double, all the same.

Interviewer: But sometimes there's no need of a mirror . . . your mother, for instance, can't see you at the moment . . .

Camille: No . . .

Interviewer: But she knows you exist?

Camille: Yes.

Interviewer: And that's because she's got – why is it? – It's because she's got a picture of you in her mind; it's like a mirror – isn't it? . . . No?

Camille: No.

Interviewer: So for your mother, at the moment, you don't exist?

Camille: Yes I do, but not in a mirror.

Interviewer: No, it's not in a mirror, but all the same, it is an existence.

Camille: Yes . . .

Interviewer: So you really are double. You're both here and maybe with your mother as well . . . and perhaps you're with me and with lots of other people too. So you may be much more than double – triple perhaps . . .

Camille: Yes but when anyone sees me I'm just one person.

Interviewer: Do you think one should call it a picture of you or a picture that belongs to you . . . what you . . . when you see yourself in the glass or when you see a photograph of yourself?

Camille: It's my picture – it's . . .

Interviewer: But would you say it's a picture of you – or a picture that belongs to you?

Camille: A picture that belongs to me.

Interviewer: And would you say it's a picture *with* you as well? You wouldn't use the word 'with'?

Camille: No.

Interviewer: So you think a picture of you hasn't an existence in relation to you? You have one but not your picture?

Camille: Yes, but when I look at myself in the glass, the image that's in the glass is not someone who exists.

Interviewer: It's not someone who exists?

Camille: Yes it is . . . but in the glass . . .

Interviewer: In the glass it doesn't exist?

Camille: No.

Interviewer: But all those people, for instance, who are going to . . . who can see you right now on television . . . they're going to see the picture of a little girl. Do you think they'll believe that this picture of a little girl is a real little girl, or that it's a little girl who doesn't have an existence?

Camille: A real one.

Interviewer: A real one? And yet they won't see the real you, they'll just see a picture.

Camille: Yes . . .

Interviewer: So this picture has an existence. Because you agree that when they see your picture, they'll say it's a real little girl, and though they won't be able to touch you, they'll think it's a real little girl.

Camille: Yes . . .

Interviewer: But a picture is really an object, all the same, a bit like a bed or something . . .

Title: TRUTH

Narrator (*male*): She's hardly moving, numbed by her day's work. And he goes on looking at her. I don't believe he wants to get an image of her – whatever one might think – or a sound. He's simply sending out a signal and waiting to see what happens when the signal reaches her. Often it reaches her and conveys nothing.

Interviewer: Was it you who painted your bedroom walls white?

Camille: No.

Interviewer: It makes the room very light. And do you do the housework? It all looks very clean.

Camille: No – it's the – the concierge.

Interviewer: You don't even make your bed?

Camille: Yes, sometimes.

Interviewer: Sometimes. And when the sheets get dirty, do you do the laundry?

Camille: No.

Interviewer: Never?

Camille: No.

Interviewer: Well, who does do it?

Camille: Either mommy or the – the concierge, when she comes to do the cleaning.

Interviewer: Is your mother well paid for the work she does?

Camille: No.

Interviewer: But cleaning the house – that's work, don't you think?

Camille: Yes.

Interviewer: And don't you think one should get paid for working?

Camille: Yes.

Interviewer: Then why doesn't your mother get paid?

Camille: Because no one could pay her.

Interviewer: No one could pay her?

Camille: No.

Interviewer: Why? Because it would cost too much?

Camille: No because . . . I don't earn any money so I couldn't pay her.

Interviewer: But doesn't your father pay her?

Camille: No.

Interviewer: But you're sure she doesn't get paid?

Camille: Yes.

Interviewer: How do you know she doesn't get paid? Perhaps she's paid without your knowing.

Camille: I should be surprised if she was.

Interviewer: You'd be surprised? Perhaps there's someone who pays her – I don't know – you've heard of the state?

Camille: Yes.

Interviewer: The government, it's the . . . If you're talking about the state, would you say 'Mrs. State' or 'Mrs. Government' or would you say 'Mr. Government' or 'Mr. State'?

Camille: Mr.

Interviewer: Mr. Well then this Mr., don't you think he might be paying your mother. Perhaps not with money, with something instead of money. Sometimes you can pay with words.

Camille: I don't know.

Interviewer: With the words . . . you see I think it might be with words like 'thank you.' Mr. State says to your mother: Well Madam, you're a very good mother and you love your little girl, so you have to wash her socks and her undies, and so I say to you 'Thank you.' And your mother finds . . . thinks she's been paid, don't you think?

Camille: She couldn't be paid like that.

Interviewer: No, but she'll think that the 'thank you' is as good as money, that she

doesn't need to be paid . . . that she's doing a favor.
Camille: I don't know.
Interviewer: You don't know?
Camille: I've never asked her.
Interviewer: What about you, have you got any money?
Camille: Yes.
Interviewer: How much have you got?
Camille: I get two francs a week.
Interviewer: Two francs a week . . . I've been thinking: when you said you existed –
when you say you exist – in your opinion, is it something that's as clear, for instance,
as your room? When you think of your existence, is it something clear, something
light?
Camille: Yes.
Interviewer: And in a minute when you go to sleep, the lights in here will be put out.
Camille: Yes.
Interviewer: And when the lights are out, it'll be dark?
Camille: Yes.
Interviewer: And do you think you'll still exist, when it's dark?
Camille: Yes.
Interviewer: But once the lights are out, will your existence be something clear or
something dark? . . . Will it stay light or will it get dark?
Camille: It will be light because it'll be clear that I exist; but it will be dark because it
will be night and no one will be able to see me.
Interviewer: But even at night, it'll be clear to you that you exist.
Camille: Yes.
Interviewer: Are there things – can you give me any examples of things in your life
that you don't see clearly?
Camille: There's the night.
Interviewer: But the night belongs to everyone. Something that belongs to you, that
you don't see clearly, and something that you do see clearly.
Camille: Going to school.
Interviewer: Going to school – that's something you can see clearly? Well then . . .
Camille: Eating.
Interviewer: Eating . . . But I'm thinking about school . . . Yes?
Camille: Daytime.
Interviewer: In that case you could say light as well!
Camille: Yes.
Interviewer: OK but to continue, let's say school . . . I don't know . . . but I have the
feeling that when you put out the light soon to go to sleep, you yourself – your body –
once it's dark, is rather like a school where they've left all the lights on, as if they'd
closed the shutters but it's still light inside. You have a kind of feeling that your body
is . . .
Camille: Yes . . .
Interviewer: . . . is like a house where they've left all the lights on.
Camille: Yes.
Interviewer: And what sort of house? a school or . . . because you say you can see a
school clearly.

Camille: Yes . . . maybe a school.

Interviewer: And when you . . . you shut your eyes when you go to sleep?

Camille: Yes.

Interviewer: And when you shut them, that makes it dark too – it's hard to see. Shut your eyes now for a second. Now is it the same darkness when you close your eyes as the darkness that comes when you put the light out, do you think – or is it a different darkness?

Title: TELEVISION

Narrator (*female*): I dream sometimes of the kind of society in which people, meeting a television reporter, would question him. They would go into details. It would take time . . . they would dare to take time and the reporter would answer quickly, I mean without delay. Because in this society, television would already have done its home-work. Instead of questioning the workers, they would have worked on the questions, as they say. So – to come back to the point – the little girl, to whom no one says hello, except when her mother says goodbye, this little girl wouldn't take up too much time – any more than she does now.

(*Blank screen*)

Title: TELEVISION

Interviewer: Even when it's all quite dark, your existence is still clear?
Camille: Yes, because mommy knows I exist, even when I'm asleep.
Interviewer: And you can still see . . .

Title: STORY[1]

Narrator (*male*): Thank you, Robert Linard. And I think . . . I think it's time for a story. Not *her* story, not a story coming from her. But her coming from a story. And both. But both before. Her before and the story after. The story before and her after. Or superimposed. The story of . . .

Title: IL ETAIT UNE FOIS[2]

. . . not the story of 'Once upon a time there was a little girl,' but the story of . . . 'Il-y-avait une fois.'

Title: ELLE ETAIT UNE FOIS[3]

– 'il' not 'elle' – so perhaps the story of 'elle-y-avait une fois.' It's more the story – a story of a beginning.

Title: STORY (with HISTOIRE
gradually changing to TOI = YOU)

Narrator (*male*): Generally, to follow a story, you mustn't lose the thread. But where does this thread have its beginning? For instance, how can one tell, before one speaks of it, that the future exists, that it will still be clear even when the lights are put out – to the right and to the left. How did Camille know that it would still be clear even if everything was switched off?

Title: YOU

(*Shot of a pregnant woman. Music.*)
Narrator: The truth. It is unable to visualize tomorrow but it can remember yesterday. Once this memory is inside, it can be projected outwards; and because it is projected outwards, it becomes a picture. A picture, the trace of what will come after. No one can see what will come after, but we can see the shape it had before – and in that, there's darkness. But let this be the trace of two and not of one. The memory of two peoples' desire. Before and after. Father and mother. A sickly desire to be more than one. And inevitably fatal . . . An *other* who comes to announce our death.
(*Music*)

Title: TELEVISION

Narrator (*female*): I find your story a bit obscure, Albert.
Narrator (*male*): Yes, but you see earlier on, she couldn't think of any examples for obscurity.
Narrator (*female*): Yes, that's true. Only examples for clarity, like the school.
Narrator (*male*): OK. The story you've just seen – that was an example of obscurity; and I don't understand how it could be so clear . . . In fact, it wasn't a story, I quite agree, but the story of this story – even the prehistory of this prehistory. All right we're stopping. We must sleep.
Narrator (*female*): Why 'must'?
Narrator (*male*): That's another story.

Translated by Tom Milne and Gilbert Adair

Notes

1   HISTOIRE can mean HISTORY or STORY.
2   An untranslatable pun involving the use of genders in the phrase 'Il était une fois' = 'once upon a time.'
3   As note 2.

Chapter 21

Trinh T. Minh-Ha

REASSEMBLAGE [1983]

(**Source:** Trinh T. Minh-ha (1992) 'Reassemblage (Film Script)' in *Framer Framed*, New York and London: Routledge, pp. 95–105)

Editor's introduction

Trinh T. Minh-ha works across a number of different cultural forms: music, poetry, anthropology, feminist and postcolonial theory, and filmmaking. This chapter is the script of her 1982 film *Reassemblage*. Shot in Senegal and picturing the dwellings and everyday life of the Sereer people, *Reassemblage* might seem to directly connect with a tradition of ethnographic filmmaking. Yet the soundtrack provides no sustained description of village life or of the ethnographer's attempts to understand Sereer culture. Instead the soundtrack voices a number of fragmentary thoughts that, like pebbles dropped in a pool, send out ripples that disturb the reflective surface of the film. Questions about the meaning of 'development', the relationships between observer and observed, the naked female body as sign, and the nature of western aid in Africa, work to render the job of ethnography deeply problematic. Perhaps then *Reassemblage* might be thought of as a poetic evocation of the dilemma facing the ethnographic imagination. But rather than launch a rationalist critique of western anthropology, Trinh counterpoints the everydayness of the observed, and the everydayness of the observer, in a way that suggests the possibility of a different kind of ethnography. The way these 'everyday worlds' clash, or the way they simply 'miss' each other is the subject of the film. For Trinh, it would seem, any attempt at the writing or picturing of a culture impacts within a world system of intricate and powerful forces that are impossible to register in a realist mode. Given the impossibility of speaking objectively about another culture, the challenge is to find new ways of speaking that can register the complexity of cultural relations without opting for the relatively safe position of simply critiquing anthropology.

As in Chapter 20, what is missing from the static presentation of this project is its sense of movement and time. *Reassemblage* is filmed and edited in a way that might seem to mirror the fragmentary nature of the soundtrack. Jerky panning and emphatic editing continually make vivid the materiality of observation. Cross-cutting between different viewpoints and interrupting the naturalistic conventions of documentary filmmaking, the film renders everyday culture as a complex assemblage that cannot be either holistically assembled or critically disassembled but can be only provisionally and inventively reassembled.

Further reading: Nichols 1994; Russell 1999; Trinh 1992, 1999.

Sketch of sound track

Music: Joola

Scarcely twenty years were enough to make two billion people define themselves as underdeveloped

I do not intend to speak about
Just speak near by

The Casamance
Sun and palms
The part of Senegal where tourist settlements flourish

A film about what? my friends ask.
A film about Senegal; but what in Senegal?

In Enampor
Andre Manga says his name is listed in the tourist information book.
Above the entry of his house is a hand-written sign which says
'Three hundred and fifty francs'
A flat anthropological fact

In numerous tales
Woman is depicted as the one who possessed the fire
Only she knew how to make fire
She kept it in diverse places
At the end of the stick she used to dig the ground with for example
In her nails or in her fingers

Reality is delicate
My irreality and imagination are otherwise dull

The habit of imposing a meaning to every single sign

She kept it in diverse places
At the end of the stick she used to dig the ground with for example
First create needs, then, help

Sitting underneath the thatched roof which projects well beyond the front wall of his newly built house, a Peace-Corps Volunteer nods at several villagers who stop by to chat with him. While they stoop down beside him and start talking, he smiles blankly, a pair of headphones over his ears and a Walkman Sony cassette player in his lap

'I teach the women how to grow vegetables in their yard; this will allow them to have an income' he says and hesitates before he concludes: 'I am not always successful, but it's the first time this has been introduced into the village.'

The first time this has been introduced into the village

Woman is depicted as the one who possessed the fire. Only she knew how to make fire

What can we expect from ethnology?

Voices: Sereer language; excerpts of conversation and voice of Djumalog, femme savante *of the village of Boucoum*

The land of the Sereer people

Women pounding: sound of pestle against mortar and laughter

The land of the Manding and the Peul peoples

A film about what? my friends ask.
A film about Senegal, but what in Senegal?

I feel less and less the need to express myself
Is that something else I've lost?
Something else I've lost?

Voices: same conversation in Sereer language

Filming in Africa means for many of us
Colorful images, naked breast women, exotic dances and fearful rites.
The unusual

First create needs, then, help
Ethnologists handle the camera the way they handle words
Recuperated collected preserved
The Bamun the Bassari the Bobo
What are *your* people called again? an ethnologist asks a fellow of his

In numerous tales

Diversification at all costs
Oral traditions thus gain the rank of written heritage

Fire place and woman's face
The pot is known as a universal symbol for the Mother the Grand-Mother
the Goddess

Nudity does not reveal
The hidden
It is its absence

A man attending a slide show on Africa turns to his wife and says with guilt in his voice: 'I have seen some pornography tonight'

Documentary because reality is organized into an explanation of itself

Every single detail is to be recorded. The man on the screen smiles at us while the necklace he wears, the design of the cloth he puts on, the stool he sits on are objectively commented upon

It has no eye it records   *Cicada sound*

'A fine layer of dust covers us from head to toe. When the sandstorm comes,' says a child, 'we lay on our mat with our mother's headscarf on our face and wait until it goes away'

The omnipresent eye. Scratching my hair or washing my face become a very special act

Watching her through the lens. I look at her becoming me becoming mine

Entering into the only reality of signs where I myself am a sign

Music: Bassari. Repeated hootings of a woman; drum beats; men's chanting.

The land of the Bassari and the Peul peoples

Early in the morning. A man is sitting with his little girl on his lap next to the circular stone hut built after the model of a Bassari house. A catholic white sister comes up to him and blurts out: 'it's only 7 am. Your little girl is not that sick. How many times have I told you our dispensary is closed on Sunday? Come back on Monday'

An ethnologist and his wife gynecologist come back for two weeks to the village where they have done research in the past. He defines himself as a person who stays long, long enough, in a village to study the culture of an ethnic group. Time, know-ledge, and security. 'If you haven't stayed long enough in a place, you are not an ethnologist' he says
    Late in the evening, a circle of men gathers in front of the house where the ethnologist and his wife gynecologist stay
    One of the villagers is telling a story, another is playing music on his improvised lute, the ethnologist is sleeping next to his switched-on cassette recorder

He thinks he excludes personal values. He tries or believes so but how can he be a Fulani? That's objectivity

Along the Senegal River, the land of the Sarakhole and the Peul peoples

(*Sound used in this section: women's pounding; cicada sound; hooting of Bassari woman*)

> I come with the idea that I would seize the unusual by catching the person unawares. There are better ways to steal I guess. With the other's consent. After seeing me laboring with the camera, women invite me to their place and ask me to film them

> The habit of imposing
> Every single sign

For many of us the best way to be neutral and objective is to copy reality meticulously

Speak about
Kabout

The eternal commentary that escorts images

Stressing the observer's objectivity
Circles round the object of curiosity
Different views from different angles
The a, b, c . . . of photography

Creativity and objectivity seem to run into conflict. The eager observer collects samples and has no time to reflect upon the media used

> Scarcely twenty years were enough to make two billion people define themselves as underdeveloped

> What I see is life looking at me

> I am looking through a circle in a circle of looks

115° Farenheit. I put on a hat while laughter bursts out behind me. I haven't seen any woman wearing a hat

Children, women and men come up to me claiming for gifts
>   A van drives in the dust road, greeted by another boisterous wave of children.
>   'Gift, gift' they all yell while the car stops under the shade of a tree.
>   A group of tourists step out and immediately start distributing cheap candies

Just speak near by

A woman comments on polygamy: 'it's good for men . . . not for us. We accept it owing to the force of circumstances. What about you? Do you have a husband all for yourself?'

Same passage of Joola music as in the beginning of the film

PART FOUR

Reclamation work

INTRODUCTION TO PART FOUR

RECLAMATION HERE IS A DUAL ACTIVITY. On the one hand it suggests that the everyday is what often gets suppressed in presentations of the past and the present (presentations that have tended towards concentrating on exceptional events and people). As such it points to historiographic and ethnographic work that requires the everyday to be reclaimed and reconstructed. For the historian this might mean scouring the available archives for everyday material. Yet some 'everydays' might not just be hard to find: the 'condescension of history' has clearly cast much of social life into oblivion. And in the place of this absence it has actively constructed something to take its place. How, for instance, would we reclaim the everyday lives of nineteenth-century servants? If they did not keep diaries or write letters, are their lives simply irretrievable? Yet the lives of servants, children, labourers, vagabonds and others do exist in archival form, only for the most part that archiving was done in the interests of bosses, government agencies, educational institutions and so forth. So reading the archive is never simply a matter of transferring snippets of knowledge into understandable stories, but of reading the archive against the grain (so to speak), against the interests of those that orchestrated them.

But alongside the intellectual work of recovering aspects of everyday life that are in danger of becoming erased from historical memory, reclamation also suggests a transformatory practice (and politics) that works to bring the everyday to the foreground of social life so as to reorientate its practices. Here reclamation has often meant the active participation in practices that oppose the status quo. For those seeking a revolution of everyday life (a complete transformation of the very basis of our social life) the everyday needs to be understood for the express purpose of changing it. Here reclamation ranges from recovering forms of pleasure and creativity that have become colonised by commodification to rescuing contemporary radical practices from a conformism that seeks to overcome them.

One aspect of reclamation work that might seem particularly central to the study of everyday life is the reclamation of complexity and contradiction from accounts that might all too easily sideline such troublesome material. The awkward actualities to be found in the everyday, the uneasy ambivalence that makes it difficult to either condemn or condone, might seem to characterise the landscape of the everyday.

Chapter 22

Henri Lefebvre

WORK AND LEISURE IN EVERYDAY LIFE [1958]

(**Source**: Lefebvre, Henri (1991) *Critique of Everyday Life*, translated by John Moore, London: Verso, pp. 29–42)

Editor's introduction

Henri Lefebvre (1901–1991) spent most of his life insisting that the everyday was a critical arena within capitalist culture. His book *Critique of Everyday Life, Volume One: Introduction* was initially published in 1947 and was followed in subsequent decades by a number of other 'critiques of everyday life'. When Volume One was reissued in 1958 he added a Foreword that was nearly as long as the original book. One of the reasons for this continued rearticulation of the project was due to the attempt to grasp contemporary everyday life as a complex totality. In this sense Lefebvre was always chasing a dynamic actuality that continually out distanced attempts to capture it, both philosophically and empirically.

At the heart of Lefebvre's writing is a dialectical approach based in Marxism. Even when Lefebvre's assessment of modern everyday life is at its bleakest, the everyday always evidences the potential for transformation. In this sense Lefebvre was never seduced by utopian thought, or at least only to the point where it was understood that any seeds for an emancipatory future had to be found in the material actuality of the present. In this extract from the 1958 Foreword, he shows how a dialectic approach to everyday life can reveal the extent of alienation and commodification within the everyday, without relinquishing the task of mapping areas of contestation. Thus Lefebvre's project is both a diagnosis of modern everyday life and a reclamation of its critical potential. For Lefebvre the business of 'critique' is not simply to provide an analytic perspective for assessing contemporary everyday life, it must always include the recovery of critical practices (or potential critical practices) to be found within everyday life itself.

Lefebvre's final work pursued the theme of everyday life by approaching it as a time-space that could be open to 'rhythmanalysis'. Though this suggestive idea remains underdeveloped it is clear that potentially it would be an approach to society that would be attentive to the variety of rhythms at work at any time and in any space. By registering the various rhythms that are active in daily life (from the blood flow and the nervous system to the circulatory rhythms of international capital) Lefebvre once again perceives the everyday as the critical totality of social life.

Further reading: Gardiner 2000; Highmore 2002; Jay 1984; Lefebvre 1984, 1995; Poster 1976; Shields 1999.

THROUGHOUT HISTORY, criticism of everyday life has been carried on in a number of ways: by philosophy and contemplation, dream and art, violent political or warlike action. By flight and escape.

These criticisms have a common element: they were the work of particularly gifted, lucid and active *individuals* (the philosopher, the poet, etc.). However, this individual lucidity or activeness concealed an appearance or an illusion, and therefore a hidden, deeper reality. In truth their work belonged to a time and a class whose ideas were thus raised above the everyday onto the level of the exceptional and the dominant. Hence the criticism of everyday life was in fact *a criticism of other classes*, and for the most part found its expression in contempt for productive labour; at best it criticized the life of the dominant class in the name of a transcendental philosophy or dogma, which nevertheless still belonged to that class. This is how we must understand the criticism of the 'world' and the 'mundane' carried out from the Middle Ages until the era – the bourgeois eighteenth century – when the 'mundane' element burst forth into art and philosophy.

In our era, one of the most recent forms which criticism of everyday life has taken is criticism of the *real* by the *surreal*. By abandoning the everyday in order to find the marvellous and the surprising (at one and the same time immanent in the real and transcending it), Surrealism rendered triviality unbearable.[1] This was a good thing, but it had a negative side: transcendental contempt for the real, for *work* for example (the long-inevitable rift between Surrealists and Marxists took place during a memorable meeting of the Association of Writers and Revolutionary Artists (AEAR) over the Soviet film *Road to Life*).[2]

And yet, be he an author or not, the man of our times carries out in his own way, spontaneously, the critique of *his* everyday life. And this critique of the everyday plays an integral part in the everyday: it is achieved in and by *leisure activities*.

The relation between leisure and the everyday is not a simple one: the two words are at one and the same time united and contradictory (therefore their relation is dialectical). It cannot be reduced to the simple relation in time between 'Sunday' and 'weekdays', represented as external and merely different. Leisure – to accept the concept uncritically for the moment – cannot be separated from work. After his work is over, when resting or relaxing or occupying himself in his own particular way, a man is still the same man. Every day, at the same time, the worker leaves the factory, the office worker leaves the office. Every week Saturdays and Sundays are given over to leisure as regularly as day-to-day work. We must therefore imagine a 'work–leisure' unity, for this unity exists, and everyone tries to programme the amount of time at his disposal according to what his work is – and what it is not. Sociology should therefore study the way the life of workers as such, their place in the division of labour and in the social system, is 'reflected' in leisure activities, or at least in what they demand of leisure.

Historically, *in real individuality* and its development, the 'work–leisure' relation has always presented itself in a contradictory way.

Until the advent of bourgeois society, individuality, or rather personality[3] could only really develop outside productive labour. In Antiquity, in the Middle Ages, and even during the period when bourgeois social relations still retained aspects of the social relations bequeathed by feudalism – in the seventeenth century of the *honnête homme* – the man who was able to develop himself never worked.

However, whether they were aristocrats, clerks still tied to feudalism, or bourgeois *honnêtes hommes*, such men only *appeared* to remain outside the social division of labour and social practice. In reality they were prisoners of the separation of manual and intellectual work. Moreover, directly or not, consciously or not, they had a social function, if only on the ideological level. Leonardo da Vinci was an engineer as well as an artist. Rabelais was a doctor and then a writer, at once an encyclopedic brain and an epic novelist. Montaigne worked in local government. And Descartes was an army officer before becoming a scholar . . . In so far as the man of those times was *genuinely* separated from social practice and devoted to leisure alone – to laziness – he was doomed both in a personal sense and from the point of view of class.

Another element must be considered which makes the question even more complicated. In those eras, in those modes of production, productive labour was merged with everyday life: consider the lives of peasants and craftsmen, for example. What distinguishes peasant life so profoundly from the life of industrial workers, even today, is precisely this inherence of productive activity in their life in its entirety. The workplace is all around the house; work is not separate from the everyday life of the family. Formerly the imperatives of the peasant community (the village) regulated not only the way work and domestic life were organized, but festivals as well. Thus up to a point a way of living which strictly speaking did not belong to any one individual, but more to a group of men committed to the ties – and limits – of their community or guild, could be developed.

With bourgeois society these various elements and their relations were overturned: in one sense they became differentiated, separate, in another they came to constitute a unified whole. Bourgeois society reasserted the value of labour, above all during the period of its ascendancy; but at the historical moment when the relation between labour and the concrete development of individuality was emerging, labour took on an increasingly fragmented character. At the same time the individual, more and more involved in complex social relations, became isolated and inward-looking. Individual consciousness split into two (into the private consciousness and the social or public consciousness); it also became atomized (individualism, specialization, separation between differing spheres of activity, etc.). Thus at the same time a distinction was made between man 'as man' on the one hand and the working man on the other (more clearly among the bourgeoisie, of course, than among the proletariat). Family life became separate from productive activity. And so did leisure.

As a result there is a certain obscurity in the very concept of *everyday life*. Where is it to be found? In work or in leisure? In family life and in moments 'lived' outside of culture? Initially the answer seems obvious. Everyday life involves all three elements, all three aspects. It is their unity and their totality, and it determines the concrete individual. And yet this answer is not entirely satisfactory. Where does the living contact between the concrete individual man and other human beings operate? In fragmented labour? In family life? In leisure? Where is it acted out in the most concrete way? Are there several modes of contact? Can they be schematized as representational models? Or must they be reduced to fixed behaviour patterns? Are they contradictory or complementary? How do they relate? What is the decisive essential sector? Where are we to situate the poverty and wealth of this everyday life which we know to be both infinitely rich (potentially at least) and infinitely poor, bare, alienated; which we know we must reveal to itself and transform so that its richness can become actualized and developed in a renewed culture? . . .

The discreteness of the elements of the everyday (work – family and 'private' life – leisure activities) implies an alienation; and perhaps at the same time a differentiation – certain fruitful contradictions. In any event, like all ensembles (or totalities), it must be studied in terms of the interrelation of its elements.

The social history of leisure shows that during the course of a development in which its various stages may have overlapped or contradicted each other, it has been transformed in fact as well as in theory,[4] and new needs have come into being.

At first, leisure gives rise to an undifferentiated global activity which is difficult to distinguish from other aspects of the everyday (family strolls on Sunday, walking).

On a higher level, leisure involves passive attitudes. Someone sitting in front of a cinema screen offers an example and a common model of this passivity, the potentially 'alienating' nature of which is immediately apparent. It is particularly easy to exploit these attitudes commercially.[5] Finally, on the highest level of all, leisure produces active attitudes, very specialized personal occupations, linked to techniques and consequently involving a technical element independent of any professional specialization (photography, for example). This is a cultivated or cultural leisure.

This brief examination immediately reveals the contradictory character of leisure, both in terms of itself and in relation to the everyday. Leisure embraces opposing possibilities and orientations, of which some tend to impoverish through passivity while others are more enriching. Some are undifferentiated (although they may still be worthwhile on a certain level), others very much the reverse. And while some involve escape into a vacuum, others rediscover 'nature', an immediate, sensory life, through what is sometimes a highly developed technical expertise (organized sports or amateur films, for example).

Therefore, with its fragmentation of labour, modern industrial civilization creates both a *general need for leisure* and differentiated *concrete needs* within that general framework.

Leisure is a remarkable example of a new social need with a *spontaneous* character which social organization, by offering it various means of satisfaction, has directed, sharpened, shifted and modified. In response to such new needs, our civilization creates techniques which nevertheless have an 'extra-technical' meaning and character. It produces 'leisure machines' (radio, television, etc.). It creates new types of play which transform the old ones, sometimes conflicting with other activities, sometimes overlapping (in the camping holiday, work and leisure are barely distinguishable, and everyday life in its entirety becomes play). Concrete social needs are determined in a way which increasingly differentiates them according to age, sex and group. They also fall spontaneously into the categories of individual needs and collective needs (for example, the distinction between individual sports and team sports).

There is no doubt that today – in capitalist, bourgeois *society*, which has its own way of manipulating the needs arising from a specific level of *civilization* – the most striking imperative as far as the needs of leisure among the masses are concerned is that it must produce a *break*. Leisure must break with the everyday (or at least appear to do so) and not only as far as work is concerned, but also for day-to-day family life. Thus there is an increasing emphasis on leisure characterized as distraction: rather than bringing any new worries, obligations, or necessities, leisure should offer liberation from worry and necessity. Liberation and pleasure – such are the essential character-istics of leisure, according to the parties concerned.[6] There is no more of a sense of genuine 'leisure' about a family get-together than there is about gardening or doing odd jobs around the house. So those involved tend to reject ambiguous forms of leisure which might resemble work or entail some kind of obligation. The cultural aspect strikes them as being irrelevant (which is not to say that *it really is so*). They mistrust anything which might appear to be educational and are more concerned with those aspects of leisure which might offer *distraction, entertainment* and *repose*, and which *might compensate* for the difficulties of everyday life. If we are to believe the subjective opinions revealed by surveys, this is as true for workers (proletarians) as it is for the other social classes.

It is thus not the work of art, in so far as it has a role to play in everyday life (the picture or the reproduction hanging in the bedroom), that is liable to constitute an element of leisure. Nor armchair reading, unless it provides thrills or escapism (travel books, stories about exploration, or crime novels), or relaxation (picture books, strip cartoons, or 'readers' digests' – evoking nothing so much as predigested food). The constitutive elements of leisure are more likely to be images and films. And images and films which are (or at least appear to be) as far away from *real life* as possible.

The first obvious thing that the so-called 'modern' man around us expects of leisure is that it should stop him from being tired and tense, from being anxious, worried and preoccupied. To use a term which is now very widely used by the public at large, he craves relaxation. There is a veritable ideology, and a technicity, and a technocracy of relaxation (which is obtained by a variety of procedures, some passive, ridding life of its content, creating a vacuum – others active, exerting control over actions and muscles). Thus the so-called 'modern' man expects to find something in leisure which his work and his family or 'private' life do not provide. Where is his happiness to be found? He hardly knows, and does not even ask himself. In this way a 'world of leisure' tends to come into being entirely outside of the everyday realm, and so purely artificial that it borders on the ideal. But how can this pure artificiality be created without permanent reference to ordinary life, without the constantly renewed contrast that will embody this reference?

There are plenty of examples in the past of art aiming to embellish everyday life by skilfully transposing it: presenting it in a flattering light, imposing a style on it while acknowledging its real achievements – Flemish and Dutch painting, for example. What is new today in bourgeois society is that a complete break has become impera-tive (a fact that constitutes a serious obstacle for any attempt at realism in art).

Consequently the art of obtaining this break is now a specific and eagerly exploited commercial technique. Clever images of the *everyday* are supplied *on a day-to-day basis*, images that can make the ugly beautiful, the empty full, the sordid elevated – and the hideous 'fascinating'. These images so skilfully and so persuasively exploit the demands and dissatisfactions which every 'modern' man carries within himself that it is indeed very difficult to resist being seduced and fascinated by them, except by becoming rigidly puritanical, and, in rejecting 'sensationalism', rejecting 'the present' and life itself.

The sudden eruption of sexuality in the domain of the image – and more generally in leisure – calls for an investigation in its own right. Our era has witnessed the demise of a certain number of ridiculous taboos – which before becoming ridiculous were very serious indeed – which had imposed a ban on sexual matters, on clothes that externalized sexual characteristics, on bodies, on nudity. And yet it still produces a shock whenever this ban is transgressed, as though it were still in force. Images with a (more or less explicit) erotic meaning, or simply the display of a woman's body, are violently attractive. The excessive use of such images in advertising has not yet exhausted the effect they have on us, and we may conclude that they correspond to something profound. Displays of sexuality and nudity break with everyday life, and provide the sense of a break which people look for in leisure: reading, shows, etc.[7] On posters, in shop windows, on the covers of magazines, in films, everywhere there are unclothed women. It is a kind of escapism which from certain angles is more like a generalized neurosis: this sexuality is depressing, this eroticism is weary and wearying, mechanical. There is nothing really sensual in this unbridled sexuality, and that is probably its most profound characteristic. From this point of view, we will not criticize eroticism for being immoral, or immodest, or corrupting to children, etc. We leave that to other people. What we will criticize 'modern' eroticism for is its lack of genuine sensuality, a sensuality which implies beauty or charm, passion or modesty, power over the object of desire, and fulfilment. With 'modern' eroticism we step outside of the everyday, without actually leaving it: it shocks, it seems brutal, and yet this effect is superficial, pure appearance, leading us back towards the secret of the everyday – dissatisfaction.

Chaplin gave us a *genuine reverse image* of modern times: its image seen through a living man, through his sufferings, his tribulations, his victories. We are now entering the vast domain of the *illusory reverse image*. What we find is a false world: firstly because it is not a world, and because it presents itself as true, and because it mimics real life closely in order to replace the real by its opposite; by replacing real unhappiness by fictions of happiness, for example – by offering a fiction in response to the real need for happiness – and so on. This is the 'world' of most films, most of the press, the theatre, the music hall: of a large sector of leisure activities.

How strange the split between the real world and its reverse image is. For in the end it is not strange at all, but a false strangeness, a cheap-and-nasty, all-pervasive mystery.[8]

Of course, the fictional and mystifying 'world' of leisure is not limited to the exploitation of sex, sentimentality and crime. Sport too will have to be scrutinized.

Sport has developed by presenting itself as the culture of the body, of individual energy and team spirit: as a school for health. What have these lofty ambitions achieved? A vast social organization (commercialized or not) and a great and often magnificently spectacular *mise en scène* devoted to competitiveness. The vocabulary is not without its humour. People who go to the races and bet on their favourite horse are known officially as 'sportsmen'. Every football club has its 'supporters'[9] and a supporter can be someone who has never kicked a ball in his life. He goes to the match in his car, or by bus or the metro. He participates in the action and plays sport via an intermediary. He quivers with enthusiasm, he fidgets frenetically, but he never moves from his seat. A curious kind of 'alienation'. Sport is an activity which is apparently incompatible with illusion, and yet in fact it confronts us with a reverse image, a compensation for everyday life.

So the analysis of the relation between the needs of leisure and the other areas which globally make up everyday life presents many difficult problems. It is not sufficient simply to describe the facts. To obtain an analysis of content, we need a conceptual apparatus to supplement description. In particular the philosophical concept of alienation is essential. In a sense it has been introduced from outside, but placed in the context of sociology it becomes scientific and allows the sociology of everyday life to become a science as well as a critique.

Georges Friedmann[10] has undertaken a long and very richly documented investigation into human labour in which he has attempted to pose the problem of the relations between leisure and work.

In substance, this work (*Où va le travail humain*) identifies leisure with freedom and work with necessity. Every day the sum total of techniques is transforming the conditions of existence. 'Every instant of life is more and more penetrated by them' and the *technical environment* surrounding man is becoming more substantial by the day.[11] The notion of a technical environment generalizes the relation between man and machine and extends it to everyday life. However, the sciences of man, whose right to examine mechanization and its effects cannot be contested,[12] themselves modify the technical environment. They do this by an intellectual, moral and social reassertion of the value of labour which 'tightens the link of interest between the worker and society, by strengthening the incentives which justify his work, even if it is fragmented, and integrate him within a collectivity'.[13] The human problem is therefore a dual one: on the one hand how to organize labour rationally, and on the other how to organize leisure rationally – especially 'compensatory leisure', in which the workers can express their personality.[14] It would seem therefore that freedom in and through work comes principally from the intervention of psychotechnical or sociological theoreticians, in a word from an intervention of the 'sciences of man applied to industrial labour',[15] which assures freedom 'in so far as it exists in this domain' – which according to Friedmann is not very far. For the technical environment is following its destiny. It characterizes not only capitalist society,[16] but also industrial civilization as a whole.

Only the domain of leisure escapes the technical environment, escapes necessity, in other words, escapes depersonalization. In our leisure activities we are already beyond techniques. We achieve a leap from necessity into freedom, from the enslavement of the individual into whatever will permit his self-development.

Georges Friedmann has had the indisputable merit of posing problems and posing them in a wide-ranging way. He takes Marx's arguments about the worker alienated by a labour which is itself alienated and renders them concrete in terms of the era we live in. (For Marx, however, the alienation of the worker by fragmented labour and machines is only one aspect of a larger – a total – alienation which as such is inherent in capitalist society and in man's exploitation of man.)

It is certain that the development of the productive forces (in other words of techniques) has consequences within the *social relations* structurally linked to these techniques. Many Marxists have shut themselves away in a class subjectivism; their understanding of the social relations of production (in capitalist regimes) is restricted to and blinkered by the notion of class struggle. They have thus neglected to study the relations of production in so far as they are linked with the development of the productive forces. And this despite what Lenin had to say on the subject. Analysing monopoly capitalism, he demonstrated that 'underlying this interlocking . . . its very base, are the changing social relations of production . . . it becomes evident that we have socialisation of production . . . that private economic and private property relations constitute a shell which no longer fits its contents'.[17] By starting from an abstract notion of the class struggle, some Marxists have neglected not only to study the recent modifications of capitalism as such, but also the 'socialization of production', and the new contents of specifically capitalist relations. Such a study could perhaps have modified the notion of class struggle, leading to the discovery of new forms of struggle.

These questions have been put by 'industrial sociology'. Has it resolved them accurately and completely? That is another matter. The undisputed fact is that since Marx's analyses, and since Lenin's, the productive forces have developed, and this economic fact cannot but have had consequences on the level of social phenomena.

Rather than resolving all the problems, Marx's statements about labour and its relation with leisure inaugurated an area of research. He predicted that work would become man's foremost need. The formula is only superficially clear. Objectively, for society, for the social man, for the 'collective worker', work has always been the foremost need. Does Marx mean that the *individual* man will transform this objective need into an essentially subjective one? So that by and in this work he will eliminate alienation? No doubt, but the formula is difficult to accept in relation to 'modern' fragmented labour. Moreover, if we put ourselves at the vanguard of technique and the modern productive forces, and consider the implications of automation, then we will need to interpret it afresh. For automation and transfer-machines tend to differentiate labour by splitting it into very highly skilled work and work for which no skill at all is required.

We may certainly affirm that work is the foundation of personal development within social practice. It links the individual with the other workers (on the shop floor, in the social class, in the social system) and also with knowledge; it is through work that the multi-technical education which controls the sum total of the productive processes and social practice is made possible, and necessary. And yet the fulfilment of these possibilities presents considerable difficulties. And under no circumstances can the 'bitty' character of labour be seen as conducive to the development of personality: whatever its social and political context, it is 'alienating'.

Elsewhere Marx wrote that 'this always remains a realm of necessity. *The true realm of freedom, the development of human powers as an end in itself, begins beyond it, though it can only flourish with this realm of necessity as its basis.* The reduction of the working day is the basic prerequisite.'[18] Therefore, according to Marx, the development of the need for leisure and the needs of leisure is deeply significant. Recent French sociology, and

Georges Friedmann, have been right to bring this to the fore. But once that has been said, ought we to accept unreservedly the notion of leisure as the breakthrough of freedom into necessity? Or as a leap from necessity into freedom? As Marx said (and as Hegel said before him), necessity does not disappear in freedom, and freedom relies upon necessity. We cannot conceive of them as external to one other, except relatively. The notion of free leisure is valid up to a certain point. Beyond that point it is inadequate. If we push it too far we run the risk of forgetting that there can be *alienation in leisure just as in work* (and alienation precisely in so far as the worker is trying to 'disalienate' himself!).

Thus the dialectical analysis of leisure and its relation with work (an analysis which is an integral part of the critique of everyday life) would seem in some ways to complement the investigations of both the 'industrial sociologists' and the 'sociologists of leisure'.

Within the framework of bourgeois society (and the capitalist regime) work is lived and undergone by the worker as an alien and oppressive power. Not only do the technical division and the social division of labour overlap and impose themselves on him without his knowing the reasons why, but also he knows that he is not working for himself, either directly or indirectly. Moreover the fragmented character of individual labour is in fact interdependent with the increasingly complete socialization of productive labour. Fragmentation and socialization are the dialectically contradictory aspects of the labour process wherever the productive forces are highly developed. Fragmented labour can only be meaningful and productive within global or total labour. Thus for the worker a dual need develops in respect of his own labour.

On the one hand, the worker aspires to a *knowledge* of the system in which he plays an integral part: a firm, and also a global society. And this is already a means of not submitting, a freeing himself from imposed constraints, of mastering necessity. In capitalist firms this confused but real aspiration is answered in a mystifying way by 'human relations' and 'public relations'.[19] Marxists who have criticized these recent, originally American, institutions have made the mistake of merely seeing the ideology they embody, and of ignoring the fact that they correspond to a real *social need*, born precisely from the socialization of labour. They have disregarded this socialization of labour, imagining that it happens only in socialist regimes, whereas it is in fact also a function of the development of the productive forces. They have not understood that in socialism knowledge satisfies a need which under capitalism is answered by an ideology. Reciprocally, the mistake of the non-Marxist industrial sociologists has been that they have not always shown that these innovations (human relations, etc.) were responding to needs purely in order to harness them, twist them, deflect them from their meaning, by reducing them to the dimensions of the firm and to cooperation with the employers.

Moreover, the worker craves a sharp break with his work, a compensation. He looks for this in leisure seen as entertainment or distraction.

In this way leisure appears as the non-everyday in the everyday.

We cannot step beyond the everyday. The marvellous can only continue to exist in fiction and the illusions that people share. There is no escape. And yet we wish to have the illusion of escape as near to hand as possible. An illusion not entirely illusory, but constituting a 'world' both apparent and real (the reality of appearances and the apparently real) quite different from the everyday world yet as open-ended and as closely dovetailed into the everyday as possible. So we work to earn our leisure, and leisure has only one meaning: to get away from work. A vicious circle.

Thus is established a complex of activities and passivities, of forms of sociability and communication which the sociologist can study. Although he cannot describe or analyse them without criticizing them as being (partially) illusory, he must neverthe-less start from the fact that they contain within themselves their own spontaneous critique of the everyday. They *are* that critique in so far as they are *other* than everyday life, and yet they are *in everyday life*, they are *alienation*. They can thus hold a real content, correspond to a real need, yet still retain an illusory form and a deceptive appearance.

Thus leisure and work and 'private life' make up a dialectical system, a global structure. Through this global structure we can reconstruct a historically real picture of man and the human at a certain step in their development: at a certain stage of alienation and disalienation.

Examples? Some are to be found in the present volume. Others will be analysed in the next. Let us list them briefly:

> *The café*: generally an extra-familial and extra-professional meeting place, where people come together on the basis of personal affinities (in principle and at least apparently), because they have the same street or the same neighbourhood in common rather than the same profession or class (although there do exist cafés where the clients are predominantly of the same class or profession). It is a place where the regulars can find a certain luxury, if only on the surface; where they can speak *freely* (about politics, women, etc.), and where if what is said may be superficial, the freedom to say it is fiercely defended; *where they play*.

> *The funfair*: a people's event whose survival and indeed industrialization have occasioned much astonishment. The noise and the deafening music supply the required break. Here we enter a humble, restless microcosm, extraordinary and vulgar. And apparently cheap. Only things which might remind us of work excluded from this microcosm. In it we find know-ledge (the aquarium, anatomical displays), eroticism (naked dancers), travel, wonders, departures, sport, etc.

> *Radio and, even more so, television*, the sudden violent intrusion of the whole world into family and 'private' life, 'presentified' in a way which directly captures the immediate moment, which offers truth and participation, or at least appears to do so . . .

Here again we come up against certain characteristics specific to cultural or cultivated leisure. These forms of leisure have functions which are both new and traditional (comparable with reading books, listening to songs and poems, or perhaps dancing as it used to be). Their content is not only entertainment and relaxation, but also knowledge. They do not exclude productive activities – specialized techniques – but they control them. Sometimes it is a matter of techniques which have been rendered obsolete by production and which have become or are in the process of becoming sports (sailing, for example). Finally, as we have already mentioned, the ultimate characteristic of such cultivated leisure activities is that they lead us back towards the feeling of presence, towards nature and the life of the senses (or, as the experts would say, towards an audio-visual milieu revitalized by modern techniques).

Of all the leisure activities concrete sociology should scrutinize, there is one which nowadays seems particularly remarkable.

Everyone knows that for more than a century the French school of painting has enjoyed world-wide renown. But do enough people realize that in France painting is becoming a mass art? That France – for reasons which as yet remain obscure – is becoming a nation of painters? 'Sunday painters', people who spend their leisure time painting, exist in their tens and perhaps hundreds of thousands. Innumerable local or corporate 'art exhibitions' are held. Thus, at a very high cultural level, leisure transcends technical activity to become art. On this level it seems to be using a certain means of expression in order to re-establish a hold on life in its entirety. In this context leisure involves an original search – whether clumsy or skilful is unimportant – for a style of living. And perhaps for an art of living, for a kind of happiness.

To sum up, work, leisure, family life and private life make up a whole which we can call a 'global structure' or 'totality' on condition that we emphasize its historical, shifting, transitory nature. If we consider the critique of everyday life as an aspect of a concrete sociology we can envisage a vast enquiry which will look at professional life, family life and leisure activities in terms of their many-sided interactions. Our particular concern will be to extract what is living, new, positive – the worthwhile needs and fulfilments – from the negative elements: the alienations.

Notes

1   Autocritique: in the text below, first published in 1947, the reader will find a partially unjust assessment of Surrealism. The author was carried away by his polemic, and consequently his point of view was one-sided. The errors of Surrealism as a doctrine (pseudo-philosophical, with a pseudo-dialectic of the real and the dream, the physical and the image, the everyday and the marvellous) notwithstanding, it did express some of the aspirations of its time. As a doctrine, Surrealism ended up with some particular forms of alienation: with the *image-thing*, magic and the occult, semi-morbid states of mind. However, its scorn for the prosaic bourgeois world, its radical rebellion, did mean something. And the hypothesis that only the *excessive* image can come to grips with the profundity of the real world – a hypothesis which one can identify just as much with Picasso, Eluard and Tzara as with André Breton – needs to be taken seriously.

2   (*Trans.*) Made in 1931, Nikolai Ekk's celebrated film was about the rehabilitation of a group of juvenile delinquents in Russia.

3   Reserving the term *individuality* stricto sensu for forms of consciousness and activity which emerged in the eighteenth century.

4   Definition of leisure given by Joffre Dumazedier: 'An occupation to which the worker can devote himself of his own free will, outside of professional, familial and social needs and obligations, in order to relax, to be entertained or to become more cultivated' (Symposium on Leisure at the Centre d'études sociologiques, 10.1.54). Cf. also the article by the same author in the *Encyclopédie française* on 'la Civilisation quotidienne'.

5   Such exploitation was examined during a study week at Marly, from 28 March 1955 to 3 April 1955 (Publications du centre d'Education populaire de Marly [roneo]). (*Trans.*: This study week dealt specifically with the problems of youth activities with special concern for leisure and cultural activities. Lefebvre's own contribution was a paper on the women's press. His interest in this area in the 1950s is touched upon in this Foreword, but left undeveloped. The paper itself,

though short, is much more explicit, and presents a model and a method for cultural analysis which seems well ahead of its time.)

6   Replies to various surveys, notably those carried out by Joffre Dumazedier and his team.

7   Psycho-physiologically the sexual image abruptly 'refreshes' the unconditioned stimulus which is already linked to a number of conditional stimuli and inserted in 'stereotypes'. It links it to a new signal (for example the trademark on a poster). That these images are effective presupposes both conditioning (triviality) and the inadequacy of this conditioning, the absence of social fixation and human determination by 'instinct'. It presupposes the hidden demands imposed by the shift from habitual but unstable and uncontrolled conditioning to a new type of conditioning: i.e. dissatisfaction.

8   Genuine strangeness (a *valid* aesthetic category) can be seen in Melville, Gogol or Kafka. It must be properly distinguished from a strange (and mystifying) *tone* used to speak about trivial things in a trivial way. The reverse image can also produce valid literary procedures (*In Camera*, a dark, brilliant, *definitive* little play, and Jean-Paul Sartre's best). The case of the children's press is different from the 'case' of the romantic press and crime fiction. They have a common element: the break with – and transport out of – normality. However, the children's press and children's literature have their own set of themes. Less structured than, and differently structured to, the world of the adult, the child's world does not require the same kind of reverse image. In fact there is no world of the child. The child lives in society, and in his eyes the adult world is what is strange and marvellous – or odious. *Simply being a child makes him already a critic of adult everyday life*, but it is in this everyday life that he must search for his future and disentangle his own potential. In the works which are most successful from this point of view, a familiar animal (a dog, a duck, a mouse) supports a reverse image in which the trivial changes into fantasy and the fantastic, with an element of explicit criticism.

9   (*Trans.*) 'Sportsmen' and 'supporters' are in English in the original.

10   (*Trans.*) An independent Marxist sociologist who specialized in the world of work and leisure. Lefebvre and he were fellow students at the Sorbonne, but after Friedmann left the PCF in 1939, their relationship became increasingly acrimonious.

11   Georges Friedmann, *Où va le travail humain*, Gallimard, Paris 1950, p. 22.

12   Ibid., p. 242.

13   Ibid., p. 244.

14   Ibid., pp. 336–64.

15   Ibid., p. 268.

16   Ibid., p. 370.

17   Lenin, 'The Highest Stage of Capitalism', in *Selected Works*, vol. 1, Progress Publishers, Moscow 1967, p. 776.

18   Marx, *Capital*, vol. 3, trans. D. Fernbach, Penguin, Harmondsworth 1981, p. 959.

19   (*Trans.*) In English in the original.

Chapter 23

Guy Debord

PERSPECTIVES FOR CONSCIOUS
ALTERATIONS IN EVERYDAY LIFE [1961]

(**Source**: Knabb, Ken (ed.) (1981) *Situationist International Anthology*, Berkeley, Calif.: Bureau of Public Secrets, pp. 68–75)

Editor's introduction

Guy Debord (1933–1994) was the animating spirit of various radical cultural movements, most famously the Situationist International (SI). For a while (and prior to an acrimonious split) Debord and the SI actively joined forces with Henri Lefebvre (Chapter 22) and the context for this text is a conference organised by Lefebvre for the Group for Research on Everyday Life. Situationist practice can perhaps best be thought of as searching out the loose threads in the fabric of spectacular society (a society in love with its own image of itself) so as to pull that fabric apart. Or to put it differently, Situationists attempted to make the alienation of modern everyday life evident by intensifying the condition of alienation to the point where it would become inescapable. In a minor way then the performance of this text was itself part of a Situationist practice. Refusing the false authenticity of speaking 'in person', Debord relayed his paper via a tape recorder and suggested that the appearance of 'free' dialogue at academic conferences was itself an illusion. The 'poverty' of daily life, for Debord, includes aspects of all social practices (even of those practices traditionally thought of as privileged) and was built around the scarcity of creative time. The trouble was that this poverty became unnoticeable in a society where routine and habit naturalised the most oppressive forms of tedium. The task for the revolutionary would be to render such daily life 'unnatural' by experimentally altering the forms of its practice.

Debord's most famous text is undoubtedly *The Society of the Spectacle* (first published in France in 1967). In it he details the totalising effects advanced capitalism produces, most notably the mirage of 'satisfaction' and 'freedom' that overlays the impoverishment of daily life. For Debord these effects were most noticeable in relation to the 'culture industries' (Hollywood, for instance) who had managed to colonise everyday life with their dream-works. It is clearly with this in mind that Debord made a number of film critiques (including a film of *The Society of the Spectacle* [1973]) that collages together Debord's astringent critique of the spectacle with some of the spectacle's most strident images.

Further reading: Debord 1983; Gardiner 2000; Jappe 1999; Plant 1992; Sadler 1998; Wollen 1993.

T̲O̲ ̲S̲T̲U̲D̲Y̲ ̲E̲V̲E̲R̲Y̲D̲A̲Y̲ ̲L̲I̲F̲E̲ would be a completely absurd undertaking, unable even to grasp anything of its object, if this study was not explicitly for the purpose of transforming everyday life.[1]

The lecture, the exposition of certain intellectual considerations to an audience, being an extremely commonplace form of human relations in a rather large sector of society, itself forms a part of the everyday life that must be criticized.

Sociologists, for example, are only too inclined to remove from everyday life things that happen to them every day, and to transfer them to separate and supposedly superior spheres. In this way habit in all its forms – beginning with the habit of handling a few *professional* concepts (concepts produced by the division of labor) – masks reality behind privileged conventions.

It is thus desirable to demonstrate, by a slight alteration of the usual procedures, that everyday life is right here. These words are being communicated by way of a tape recorder, not, of course, in order to illustrate the integration of technology into this everyday life on the margin of the technological world, but in order to seize the simplest opportunity to break with the appearance of pseudocollaboration, of artificial dialogue, established between the lecturer 'in person' and his spectators. This slight discomforting break with accustomed routine could serve to bring directly into the field of questioning of everyday life (a questioning otherwise completely abstract) the conference itself, as well as any number of other forms of using time or objects, forms that are considered 'normal' and not even noticed, and which ultimately condition us. With such a detail, as with everyday life as a whole, alteration is always the necessary and sufficient condition for experimentally bringing into clear view the object of our study, which would otherwise remain uncertain – an object which is itself less to be studied than to be altered.

I have just said that the reality of an observable entity designated by the term 'everyday life' stands a good chance of remaining hypothetical for many people. Indeed, the most striking feature of the present 'Group for Research on Everyday Life' is obviously not the fact that it has not yet discovered anything, but the fact that the very existence of everyday life has been disputed from its very inception, and increasingly so with each new session of this conference. Most of the talks we have heard so far have been by people who are not at all convinced that everyday life exists, since they haven't encountered it anywhere. A group for research on everyday life with this attitude is comparable in every way to an expedition in search of the Yeti, which might similarly come to the conclusion that its quarry was merely a popular hoax.

To be sure, everyone agrees that certain gestures repeated every day, such as opening doors or filling glasses, are quite real; but these gestures are at such a trivial level of reality that it is rightly objected that they are not of sufficient interest to justify a new specialized branch of sociological research. A number of sociologists seem disinclined to recognize any aspects of everyday life beyond these trivialities. They thus accept the definition of it proposed by Henri Lefebvre – 'whatever remains after one has eliminated all specialized activities' – but draw a different conclusion: that every-day life is nothing. The majority of sociologists – and we know how much they are in their element in specialized activities, in which they generally have the blindest faith! – recognize specialized activities everywhere and everyday life nowhere. Everyday life is always elsewhere. Among others. In any case, in the nonsociologistic classes of the population. Someone said here that it would be interesting to study the workers as guinea pigs who have probably been infected with this virus of everyday life because they, having no access to specialized activities, have *only* everyday life to live. This condescending manner of investigating the common people in search of an exotic primitivism of everyday life – and above all this ingenuously avowed self-satisfaction, this naive pride in participating in a culture whose glaring bankruptcy no one can dream of denying, this radical inability to understand the world that produces this culture – all this never ceases to astonish.

There is in this an evident will to hide behind a development of thought based on the separation of artificial, fragmentary domains so as to reject the useless, vulgar and disturbing concept of 'everyday life.' Such a concept covers an uncatalogued and unclassified residue of reality, a residue some people are averse to confronting because it at the same time represents the standpoint of the totality; it would imply the necessity of an integral political judgment. Certain intellectuals seem to flatter them-selves with an illusory personal participation in the dominant sector of society through their possession of one or more cultural specializations; these specializations, however, have placed them in the best position to realize that the whole of this dominant culture is manifestly moth-eaten. But whatever one's opinion of the coherence of this culture or of the interest of one or another of its fragments, the particular alienation it has imposed on these intellectuals is to make them think, from their position in the heaven of the sociologists, that they are quite outside the everyday life of the common people, or to give them an exaggerated idea of their rank on the scale of human powers, as if their lives, too, were not *impoverished*.

Specialized activities certainly exist; they are even, in a given period, put to a certain general use which should be recognized in a demystified manner. Everyday life is not everything – although its osmosis with specialized activities is such that in a sense we are never outside of everyday life. But to use a facile spatial image, we still have to place everyday life at the center of everything. Every project begins from it and every realization returns to it to acquire its real significance. Everyday life is the measure of all things: of the fulfillment or rather the nonfulfillment of human relations; of the use of lived time; of artistic experimentation; of revolutionary politics.

It is not enough to recall that the old stereotypical image of the detached scientific observer is fallacious in any case. It must be stressed that disinterested observation is even less possible here than anywhere else. What makes for the difficulty of even recognizing a terrain of everyday life is not only the fact that it has already become the ostensible meeting ground of an empirical sociology and a conceptual elaboration, but also the fact that it presently happens to be the stake in any revolutionary renewal of culture and politics.

To fail to criticize everyday life today means accepting the prolongation of the present thoroughly rotten forms of culture and politics, forms whose extreme crisis is expressed in increasingly widespread political apathy and neoilliteracy, especially in the most modern countries. On the other hand, a radical critique in acts of prevailing everyday life could lead to a supersession of culture and politics in the traditional sense, that is, to a higher level of intervention in life.

'But,' you may ask, 'how does it happen that the importance of this everyday life, which according to you is the only real life, is so completely and directly underrated by people who, after all, have no direct interest in doing so – many of whom are even far from being opposed to some kind of renewal of the revolutionary movement?'

I think this happens because everyday life is organized within the limits of a scandalous poverty, and above all because there is nothing accidental about this poverty of everyday life: it is a poverty that is constantly imposed by the coercion and violence of a society divided into classes, a poverty historically organized in line with the evolving requirements of exploitation.

The use of everyday life, in the sense of a consumption of lived time, is governed by the reign of scarcity: scarcity of free time and scarcity of possible uses of this free time.

Just as the accelerated history of our time is the history of accumulation and industrialization, so the backwardness and conservative tendency of everyday life are products of the laws and interests that have presided over this industrialization. Everyday life has until now resisted the historical. This represents first of all a *verdict against the historical* insofar as it has been the heritage and project of an exploitative society.

The extreme poverty of conscious organization and creativity in everyday life expresses the fundamental necessity for unconsciousness and mystification in an exploiting society, in a society of alienation.

Henri Lefebvre has extended the idea of uneven development so as to characterize everyday life as a lagging sector, out of joint with the historical but not completely cut off from it. I think that one could go so far as to term this level of everyday life a colonized sector. We know that underdevelopment and colonization are interrelated on the level of global economy. Everything suggests that the same thing applies at the level of socioeconomic structure, at the level of praxis.

Everyday life, policed and mystified by every means, is a sort of reservation for good natives who keep modern society running without understanding it – this society with its rapid growth of technological powers and the forced expansion of its market. History – the transformation of reality – cannot presently be used in everyday life because the people of everyday life are the product of a history over which they have no control. It is of course they themselves who make this history, but not freely.

Modern society is viewed through specialized fragments that are virtually incommunicable; and so everyday life, where all questions are liable to be posed in a unitary manner, is naturally the domain of ignorance.

Through its industrial production this society has emptied the gestures of work of all meaning. And no model of human behavior has retained any real relevance in everyday life.

This society tends to atomize people into isolated consumers, to prohibit communication. Everyday life is thus private life, the realm of separation and spectacle.

It is thus also the sphere of the specialists' resignation and failure. It is there, for example, that one of the rare individuals capable of understanding the latest scientific conception of the universe will make a fool of himself by earnestly pondering Alain Robbe-Grillet's aesthetic theories or by sending petitions to the President of the Republic in the hope of convincing him to change his policies. It is the sphere of disarmament, of the avowal of the incapability of living.

Thus the underdevelopment of everyday life cannot be characterized solely by its relative inability to put technology to use. This trait is an important, but only partial, consequence of the everyday alienation as a whole, which could be defined as the inability to invent a technique for the liberation of everyday experience.

In fact many techniques do more or less markedly alter certain aspects of everyday life: the domestic arts, as has already been mentioned here, but also the telephone, television, the recording of music on long-playing records, mass air travel, etc. These elements arise anarchically, by chance, without anyone having foreseen their interrelations or consequences. But on the whole this introduction of technology into everyday life – ultimately taking place within the framework of modern bureaucratized capitalism – certainly tends rather to reduce people's independence and creativity. The new prefabricated cities clearly exemplify the totalitarian tendency of modern capitalism's organization of life: the isolated inhabitants (generally isolated within the framework of the family cell) see their lives reduced to the pure triviality of the repetitive combined with the obligatory absorption of an equally repetitive spectacle.

One can thus conclude that if people censor the question of their own everyday life, it is both because they are aware of its unbearable misery and because sooner or later they sense – whether they admit it or not – that all the real possibilities, all the desires that have been frustrated by the functioning of social life, were focused there, and not at all in the specialized activities or distractions. That is, awareness of the profound richness and energy abandoned in everyday life is inseparable from awareness of the poverty of the dominant organization of this life. Only the perceptible existence of this untapped richness leads to the contrasting definition of everyday life as poverty and as prison; and then, in the same movement, to the negation of the problem.

In these conditions, repressing the political question posed by the poverty of everyday life means repressing the depth of the demands bearing on the possible richness of this life – demands that can lead to nothing less than a reinvention of revolution. Of course an evasion of politics at this level is in no way incompatible with being active in the Parti Socialiste Unifié, for example, or with reading *Humanité* with confidence.

Everything effectively depends on the level at which this problem is posed: How is our life? How are we satisfied with it? Dissatisfied? Without for a moment letting ourselves be intimidated by the various advertisements designed to persuade us that we can be happy because of the existence of God or Colgate toothpaste or the CNRS.

It seems to me that this phrase 'critique of everyday life' could and should also be understood in this reverse sense: as everyday life's sovereign critique of everything that is external or irrelevant to itself.

The question of the use of technological means, in everyday life and elsewhere, is a political question (and out of all the possible technical means, those that are implemented are in reality selected in accordance with the goal of maintaining one class's domination). When one envisions a future such as that presented in science fiction, in which interstellar adventures coexist with a terrestrial everyday life kept in the same old material indigence and archaic morality, this implies precisely that there is still a class of specialized rulers maintaining the proletarian masses of the factories and offices in their service; and that the interstellar adventures are nothing but the particular enterprise chosen by those rulers, the way they have found to develop their irrational economy, the pinnacle of specialized activity.

Someone posed the question, 'What is private life deprived of?' Quite simply of life itself, which is cruelly absent. People are as deprived as possible of communication and of self-realization. Deprived of the opportunity to personally make their own history. Hypotheses responding positively to this question on the nature of the privation can thus only be expressed in the form of projects of enrichment; the project of a different style of life; or in fact simply the project of a style of life . . . Or, if we regard everyday life as the frontier between the dominated and the undominated sectors of life, and thus as the terrain of risk and uncertainty, it would be necessary to replace the present ghetto with a constantly moving frontier; to work ceaselessly toward the organization of new chances.

The question of intensity of experience is posed today – with the use of drugs, for example – in the only terms in which the society of alienation is capable of posing any question: namely, in terms of false recognition of a falsified project, in terms of fixation and attachment. It should also be noted how much the image of love elaborated and propagated in this society has in common with drugs. A passion is first of all presented as a denial of all other passions; then it is frustrated and finally reappears only in the compensations of the reigning spectacle. La Rochefoucauld observed, 'What often prevents us from abandoning ourselves to a single vice is that we have several.' This is a very constructive observation if we ignore its moralist presuppositions and put it back on its feet as the basis of a program for the realization of human capacities.

All these questions are of present significance because our time is visibly dominated by the emergence of the project borne by the working class – the abolition of every class society and the inauguration of human history – and thus also dominated by the fierce resistance to this project and by the distortions and failures it has encountered until now.

The present crisis of everyday life takes its place among the new forms of the crisis of capitalism, forms that remain unnoticed by those who cling to the classical calculation of the date of the next cyclical crisis of the economy.

The disappearance in developed capitalism of all the old values, of all the frames of reference of past communication; and the impossibility of replacing them by any others before having rationally dominated, within everyday life and everywhere else, the new industrial forces that escape us more and more – these facts produce not only the virtually official dissatisfaction of our time, a dissatisfaction particularly acute among young people, but also the self-negating tendency of art. Artistic activity had always been alone in conveying the clandestine problems of everyday life, albeit in a veiled, deformed, partially illusory manner. Evidence of a destruction of all artistic expression now exists before our eyes: modern art.

If we consider the whole extent of the crisis of contemporary society, I don't think it is possible still to regard leisure activities as a negation of the everyday. It has been recognized here that it is necessary to 'study wasted time.' But let us look at the recent evolution of this idea of wasted time. For classical capitalism, wasted time was time that was not devoted to production, accumulation, saving. The secular morality taught in bourgeois schools has instilled this rule of life. But it so happens that by an unexpected turn of events modern capitalism needs to increase consumption, to 'raise the standard of living' (if we bear in mind that this expression is completely meaningless). Since at the same time production conditions, compartmentalized and clocked to the extreme, have become indefensible, the new morality already being conveyed in advertising, propaganda and all the forms of the dominant spectacle now frankly admits that wasted time is the time spent at work, which latter is only justified by the hierarchized scale of earnings that enable one to buy rest, consumption, entertainments – a daily passivity manufactured and controlled by capitalism.

If we now consider the artificiality of the consumer needs prefabricated and ceaselessly stimulated by modern industry – if we recognize the emptiness of leisure activities and the impossibility of rest – we can pose the question more realistically: What would *not* be wasted time? The development of a society of abundance should lead to an abundance of *what*?

This can obviously serve as a touchstone in many regards. When, for example, in one of those papers where the flabby thinking of 'leftist intellectuals' is displayed – I am referring to *France-Observateur* – one reads a title like 'The Little Car Out To Conquer Socialism' heading an article that explains that nowadays the Russians are beginning to pursue an American-style private consumption of goods, beginning naturally with cars, one cannot help thinking that one need not have assimilated all of Hegel and Marx to realize that a socialism that gives way in the face of an invasion of the market by small cars is in no way the socialism for which the workers movement fought. The bureaucratic rulers of Russia must be opposed not on the level of their tactics or their dogmatism, but fundamentally, on the fact that the meaning of people's lives has not really changed. And this is not some obscure fatality of an everyday life doomed to remain reactionary. It is a fatality imposed on everyday life from the outside by the reactionary sphere of specialized rulers, regardless of the label under which they plan and regulate poverty in all its aspects.

The present depoliticization of many former leftist militants, their withdrawal from one type of alienation to plunge into another, that of private life, represents not so much a return to privacy, a flight from 'historical responsibility', but rather a withdrawal from the specialized political sector that is always manipulated by others – a sector where the only responsibility they ever took was that of leaving all responsibility to uncontrolled leaders; and where the communist project was betrayed and frustrated. Just as one cannot simplistically oppose private life to public life without asking: what private life? what public life? (for private life contains the factors of its negation and supersession, just as collective revolutionary action harbored the factors of its degeneration), so it would be a mistake to assess the alienation of individuals in revolutionary politics when it is really a matter of the alienation of revolutionary politics itself. It is right to dialectize the problem of alienation, to draw attention to the constantly recurring possibilities of alienation arising within the very struggle against alienation; but we should stress that this applies to the highest level of research (to the philosophy of alienation as a whole, for example) and not to the level of Stalinism, the explanation of which is unfortunately more gross.

Capitalist civilization has not yet been superseded anywhere, but it continues to produce its own enemies everywhere. The next rise of the revolutionary movement, radicalized by the lessons of past defeats and with a program enriched in proportion to the practical powers of modern society (powers already constituting the potential material basis that was lacking in the so-called utopian currents of socialism) – this next attempt at a total contestation of capitalism will know how to invent and propose a different use of everyday life, and will immediately base itself on new everyday practices, on new types of human relationships (being no longer unaware that any conserving, within the revolutionary movement, of the relations prevailing in the existing society imperceptibly leads to a reconstitution of one or another variant of this society).

Just as the bourgeoisie, in its ascending phase, had to ruthlessly liquidate everything that transcended earthly life (heaven, eternity), so the revolutionary proletariat – which can never, without ceasing to be revolutionary, recognize itself in any past or any models – will have to renounce everything that transcends everyday life. Or rather, everything that claims to transcend it: the spectacle, the 'historical' act or pronouncement, the 'greatness' of leaders, the mystery of specializations, the 'immortality' of art and its importance outside of life. In other words, it must renounce all the by-products of eternity that have survived as weapons of the world of the rulers.

The revolution in everyday life, breaking its present resistance to the historical (and to every kind of change), will create the conditions in which the *present dominates the past* and the creative aspects of life always predominate over the repetitive. We must therefore expect that the side of everyday life expressed by the concepts of ambiguity – misunderstanding, compromise or misuse – will decline considerably in importance in favor of their opposites: conscious choice and gamble.

The present artistic calling in question of language – appearing at the same time as that metalanguage of machines which is nothing other than the bureaucratized language of the bureaucracy in power – will then be superseded by higher forms of communication. The present notion of a decipherable social text will lead to new methods of writing this social text, in the direction my situationist comrades are presently seeking with unitary urbanism and some preliminary ventures in experimental behavior. The central production of an entirely reconverted industrial work will be the organization of new configurations of everyday life, the free creation of events.

The critique and perpetual re-creation of the totality of everyday life, before being carried out naturally by all people, must be undertaken in the present conditions of oppression, in order to destroy these conditions.

An avant-garde cultural movement, even one with revolutionary sympathies, cannot accomplish this. Neither can a revolutionary party on the traditional model, even if it accords a large place to criticism of culture (understanding by that term the entirety of artistic and conceptual means through which a society explains itself to itself and shows itself goals of life). This culture and this politics are worn out and it is not without reason that most people take no interest in them. The revolutionary transformation of everyday life, which is not reserved for some vague future but is placed immediately before us by the development of capitalism and its unbearable demands – the alternative being the reinforcement of the modern slavery – this transformation will mark the end of all unilateral artistic expression stocked in the form of commodities, at the same time as the end of all specialized politics.

This is going to be the task of a new type of revolutionary organization from its inception.

Note

1   A tape recording of this talk was presented 17 May 1961 at a conference of the Group for Research on Everyday Life convened by Henri Lefebvre in the Center of Sociological Studies of the CNRS.

Chapter 24

Jacques Rancière

PREFACE TO *PROLETARIAN NIGHTS* [1981]

(**Source**: Rancière, Jacques (1982) 'Proletarian Nights' translated by Noel Parker, *Radical Philosophy* 31, pp. 11–13. Also published as the preface to Rancière, Jacques (1989) *The Nights of Labor: The Worker's Dream in Nineteenth Century France*, translated by John Drury, Philadelphia, Pa: Temple University Press, pp. vii–xii)

Editor's introduction

In the middle of the 1960s Jacques Rancière was primarily associated with the structural Marxism of Louis Althusser and was an active participant in his rereading of *Capital*. Yet in those fiercely political times it was not long before Rancière and many other activist students sought to distance themselves from Althusser. In retrospect Rancière's frustration with Althusser's brand of Marxism is probably most succinctly registered in the language of the militant students (which included Rancière) of May 1968, particularly the anti-structuralist slogan 'structures don't take to the street'.

In 1975 Rancière and a small group of similarly minded philosophers and historians published the first issue of their journal *Les Révoltes Logiques*. The journal was dedicated to resuscitating archives of working-class writing as an attempt to chart proletarian dreams and proletarian desires. If political philosophy abstracted a working class identity from a generalised idea of proletarian daily life (from the 'dignity of labour' to the relentless of alienation) Rancière and others worked to ground the study of class in the details of specific daily lives. What would it mean to reclaim those nightly hours when, after a day of work, worker poets and bohemians set to write and drink the night away and to fill it with their dreams? What would it offer the history of revolutionary struggle to find people not simply demanding better working conditions or ownership of the factories but something more fundamental: a different everyday life?

To take seriously such demands (and May 1968 reverberated with such fundamental desires) would mean rethinking a politics of class based on some essential structural division between proletarian and bourgeois. It would also mean attending to the 'voice of the proletariat' as multifarious and as an active agent of desire (rather than as passively reflecting 'its' historical condition). In some ways Rancière's position has some curious similarities with Michel de Certeau's (Chapter 6) in that both authors take 'belief' as a concrete element of history and as a complex activity within class struggles.

Further reading: Althusser and Balibar [1968] 1979; Rancière 1989, 1994; Rattansi 1989; Rifkin and Thomas 1988.

THERE IS NOTHING METAPHORICAL in this title *Proletarian Nights*. The point is not to revive memories of the sufferings of factory slaves, of the squalor of workers' hovels or the misery of bodies sapped by unbridled exploitation. All that will only be present via the views and the words, the dreams and the nightmares of the characters of this book.

Who are they? A few dozen, a few hundred workers who were twenty years old around 1830 and who then resolved, each for himself, to tolerate the intolerable no longer. It was not so much the poverty, the low wages, the comfortless dwellings, or the ever-present threat of hunger. More fundamentally, it was anguish at the daily theft of their time as they worked wood or stone, sewed clothing or stitched shoes; and all for nothing but the indefinite maintenance of the forces both of servitude and of domination. It was the humiliating absurdity of having to beg day after day for work which frittered their lives away. And it was the weight of others too; the ones in work, with the petty vanity of fairground muscle-men or the obsequiousness of conscientious workers; those outside waiting for a place you would be glad to hand over; and finally those who drove by, casting a disdainful glance from their open carriages over all that blighted humanity.

To have done with all that, to know why it had still not been brought to an end, to change their lives. . . . Overturning the world begins at an hour when ordinary workers ought to be enjoying the peaceful slumber of those whose trade calls for no thought whatever. For example, at precisely eight o'clock on that night of October 1839, a meeting is called at the house of Martin Rose, the tailor, to found a working man's newspaper. Vincard, the maker of measures, who writes songs for the singing club at the local bar, has invited Gauny, the carpenter, who gives expression to his more taciturn temperament in vengeful couplets. Ponty, another poet, who clears cesspools, will certainly not be there: Bohemian that he is, he has chosen to work at night. But the carpenter will be able to tell him the outcome in one of those letters he copies out around midnight, after several drafts, letters describing their blundered childhoods and their wasted lives, plebeian passions and those other existences beyond death – which may be beginning at that very moment. He writes those letters out, in an effort to delay to the very last minute that sleep which will restore the powers of the servile machine.

The main subject of this book is those nights wrested from the normal sequence of work and sleep. They were imperceptible, one might almost say inoffensive breaks in the ordinary course of things, where already the impossible was being prepared, dreamt and seen: the suspension of that ancient hierarchy which subordinates those dedicated to labour to those endowed with the privilege of thought. They were nights of study and intoxication, and days of labour prolonged to hear the word of the apostles or the lectures given by teachers of the people, to learn, to dream, to talk or to write. They are Sunday mornings begun early so as to leave for the country together and take the dawn by surprise. Some will do well out of these follies. They will finish up as entrepreneurs or senators for life – and not necessarily traitors for all that. Others will die of them: by suicide because their aspirations are impossible; by the lethargy which follows crushed revolutions; by that phthisis which strikes exiles in the northern fogs; by the plagues of Egypt, where they went seeking the Woman-Messiah; or by the malaria of Texas where they went to build Icaria. Most will spend the rest of their lives in that anonymity which occasionally throws up in the name of a worker poet, a strike-leader, the organiser of an ephemeral association, or the editor of a paper that is here today and gone tomorrow.

The historian will ask what they represent. What are they by comparison with the anonymous mass of factory workers or even the activists in the labour movement? What do their lines of poetry or even the prose in their 'workers' papers' amount to compared with the multitude of day-to-day practices, of acts of oppression and resistance, or of complaints and struggles at the workplace and on the streets? This is a question of method, which tries to link cunning with 'straightforwardness' by identifying the statistical requirements of science with political principles which proclaim that only the masses make history and enjoin those that speak in their name to represent them faithfully.

But perhaps the masses who are invoked have already given their answer. Why do the striking Parisian tailors of 1833 and 1840 want their leader to be André Troncin, who divides his time between student cafés and the study of the great thinkers? Why will painters in 1848 ask the bizarre café-owner Confais to draft them a constitution, when he normally bores them stiff with his talk of Fourieresque harmonies and phrenological experiments? Why did hatters engaged in struggle seek out a one-time seminarist called Philippe Monnier, whose sister has gone to play the Free Woman in Egypt and whose brother-in-law died in pursuit of his American utopia? Certainly those men, whose sermons on the dignity of working people and on evangelical devotion the masses normally avoid, do not represent their daily labours or their daily anger.

But it is precisely because those men are *other*. That is why they go to see them the day they have something they want to *represent*, something they want to show to the bourgeoisie (bosses, politicians, judges). It is not simply that those men can talk better. It is that what had to be represented before the bourgeoisie was something deeper than salaries, working hours or the thousand irritations of wage-labour. What has to be represented is what those mad nights and their spokesmen already make clear: that proletarians have to be treated *as if* they have a right to more than one life. If the protests of the workplace are to have a voice, if worker emancipation is to possess a human face, if workers are to exist as subjects of a collective discourse which gives meaning to their multifarious assemblies and combats, those representatives must already have made themselves *other* in a double, hopeless rejection, refusing both to *live* like workers and to *talk* like the bourgeoisie.

This is the history of isolated utterances, and of an impossible act of self-identification at the very root of those great discourses in which the voice of the proletariat as a whole can be heard. It is a story of semblances and simulacra which lovers of the masses have tirelessly tried to cover up – either by fixing a snap-shot in sepia of the young working class Movement on the eve of its nuptials with proletarian

Theory, or by splashing onto those shadows the colours of everyday life and of the popular mind. Solemn admiration for the unknown soldiers of the proletarian army has come to be mixed with tender-hearted curiosity about their anonymous lives and a nostalgic passion for the practised movements of the craftsman or the vigour of popular songs and festivals. These different forms of homage unite to show that people like that are the more to be admired the more they adhere strictly to their collective identity, and that they become suspect, indeed, the moment they want to live as anything other than legions and legionaries, when they demand that individual wanderlust which is the monopoly of 'petty-bourgeois' egoism or the illusion of the 'ideologist'.

The history of these proletarian nights is explicitly intended to prompt an examination of that jealous concern for the purity of the masses, the plebeians or the proletariat. Why has the philosophy of intelligentsia or activists always needed to blame some evil third party (petty bourgeoisie, ideologist or master thinker) for the shadows and obscurities that get in the way of the harmonious relationship between their own self-consciousness and the self-identity of their 'popular' objects of study? Was not this evil third party contrived to spirit away another more fearsome threat: that of seeing the thinkers of the night invade the territory of Philosophy. It is as if we were pretending to take seriously the old fantasy which underlies Plato's denunciation of the sophists, the fear of philosophy being devastated by the 'many whose natures are imperfect and whose souls are cramped and maimed by their meannesses, as their bodies are by their trades and crafts'.[1] Unless the issue of dignity lies in another quarter. Unless, that is, we need to exaggerate the positivity of the masses as active subject so as to throw into relief a confrontation with the ideologist which enables intellectuals to accord to their philosophy a dignity independent of their occupational status alone.

These questions are not meant to put anyone in the dock. But they explain why I make no apologies for sacrificing the majesty of the masses and the positivity of their practices to the discourses and the illusions of a few dozen 'non-representative' individuals. In the labyrinth of their real and imaginary travels, I simply wanted to follow the thread of two guiding questions: What paradoxical route led these deserters, who wanted to tear themselves free from the constraints of proletarian existence, to come to forge the image and the discourse of working class identity? And what new forms of false construction affect that paradox when the discourse of workers infatuated with the night of the intellectuals meets the discourse of intellectuals infatuated with the glorious working days of the masses? That is a question we should ask ourselves. But it is a question immediately experienced within the contradictory relations between the proletariat of the night and the prophets of the new world — Saint-Simonians, Icarians or whatever. For, if it is indeed the word of 'bourgeois' apostles which creates or deepens a crack in their daily round of work through which some workers are drawn into the twists and turns of another life, the problems begin when the preachers want to change those twists and turns into the true, straight road that leads to the dawn of New Labour. They want to cast their disciples in their identity as good soldiers of the great militant army and as prototypes of the worker of the future. Surely, the Saint-Simonian workers, blissfully listening to these words of love, lose even more of that tough workers' identity that the calling of New Industry requires. And, looking at the matter from the other direction, surely the Icarian proletariat will be able to rediscover that identity only by discrediting the fatherly teachings of their leader.

Perhaps these are so many missed opportunities, dead-ends of a utopian education, where edifying Theory will not long delude itself that it can see the path to self-emancipation beaten out for any proletariat that is instructed in Science. The tortuous arguments of *L'Atelier*, the first great newspaper 'made by the workers themselves', suggest in advance what the agents detailed to spy on the workers' associations which emerged from this twisting path were to discover with surprise: that once he is master of the instruments and the products of his labour, the worker cannot manage to convince himself that he is working 'in his own interest'.

Nonetheless, we should not be too quick to rejoice at recognising the vanity of the path to emancipation in this paradox. We may discover that obstinate initial question with even greater force: What precisely is it that the worker can pursue *in his own interest*? What exactly is at work in the strange attempt to rebuild the world around a centre that the inhabitants only want to escape? And is not *something else* to be gained on these roads that lead nowhere, in these efforts to sustain a fundamental rejection of the order of things, beyond all the constraints of working-class existence? No one will find much to strengthen the grounds of his disillusionment or his bitterness in the paths of these workers who, back in July 1830, swore that nothing would be the same again, or in the contradictions of their relations with the intellectuals who aligned themselves with the masses. The moral of this tale is quite the reverse of the one people like to draw from the wisdom of the masses. It is to some extent the lesson of the impossible, that of the rejection of the established order even in the face of the extinction of Utopia. If, for once, we let the thoughts of those who are not 'destined' to think unfold before us, we may come to recognise that the relationship between the order of the world and the desires of those subjected to it presents more complexity than is grasped by the discourses of the intelligentsia. Perhaps we shall gain a certain modesty in deploying grand words and expressing grand sentiments. Who knows?

In any case, those who venture into this labyrinth must be honestly forewarned that no answers will be supplied.

Translated by Noel Parker[2]

Notes

1   Plato, *The Republic*, trans. Jowett, VI. 495.
2   With acknowledgement for help and suggestions from Pete Dews, Jonathan Ree, Mike Short-land, Carolyn Sumberg.

Chapter 25

Stuart Hall

RECONSTRUCTION WORK: IMAGES OF POSTWAR BLACK SETTLEMENT [1984]

(Source: Hall, Stuart (1984) 'Reconstruction Work: Images of Post War Black Settlement', *Ten-8*, 16: 2–9)

Editor's introduction

Stuart Hall has been active in cultural studies from its start (he was the second director of the Centre for Contemporary Cultural Studies at the University of Birmingham from 1969 to 1979) and is perhaps now the most influential spokesperson for the discipline. He has increasingly focused his work on issues of cultural identity and difference, specifically addressing questions of ethnicity, 'race' and racism. His work on ethnicity and identity has always combined everyday materials (personal reminiscences, empirical observations about the everyday lives of black British youth, 'domestic' photography and such like) with historical, political and theoretical investigations.

A central issue faced in this chapter is how to *recover* and *rescue* the experiences of postwar black British immigrants from accounts that would represent them as either a problem (for 'British culture') or simply as victims of racism. For Hall what needs recovering is the agency and liminality (the in-between-ness) in the transition from one culture to another, where colonial relations and class-based propriety saturate both cultures. In reading the traces of experience in these journalistic and High Street photographs, Hall shows how larger social meanings can be found in the details of everyday life. Clothes, gestures, posture all have a story to tell, and the story is one of attitudes, aspirations and apprehensions. For Hall these photographs are part of an archive of a history of migration and they need to be attended to with knowledge of their pictorial conventions and the social uses that they were put to. Interestingly it is the ability of photography to fabricate (and fabulate) an image which might most productively bear the traces of everyday life. The conventions of High Street photography (the limited range of props and backdrops) make everyday life vivid precisely through its exclusion (unlike the non-professional family album, here we know everyday life is elsewhere). Yet in fabricating images that register personal and social desires they articulate an aspect of everyday life that for the most part remains hidden.

Further reading: Hall 1993, 1995, 1996; Hirsch 1997; Kuhn 1995; G. Turner 1992.

THE HISTORY OF BLACK SETTLEMENT IN BRITAIN in the post-war years is only just beginning to be written. One of the essential preconditions of such an account is the collection, preservation and interpretation of 'documents', public and private, formal and informal, as well as the oral testimonies of those who actually went through the experience in the early days. The past cannot speak, except through its 'archive'.

When such histories do come to be written, the photographic evidence is likely to play an extremely important role in their construction. One hopes that by then the historians will have gained some experience in 'how to read' it. This contribution examines some of the difficulties inherent in reconstructing those histories from existing photographic texts, which are themselves extremely diverse.

There is no such unitary thing as 'photography'. Photography is a convenient way of referencing the diversity of practices, institutions and historical conjunctures in which the photographic text is produced, circulated and deployed. Many of the photographs relevant to the history of post-war migration will already have made a public appearance in the field of representation (in the press, magazines, etc.) – and are therefore already inscribed or 'placed' by that earlier positioning. Their meanings will already have been inflected by the discourses of photographic studio, high-street shop, news-photo agency, book publishing, newspaper or magazine, colour supplement or gallery. The vast majority will already have been organised within certain systems of classification which transfer to them the supplementary imprint of their own generic meanings, etc.: family portrait, news shot, agency scrapbook, photo exposé, etc. Each practice, each placing, each discourse thus slides another layer of meaning across the frame . . .

It is difficult, if not by now impossible, to recapture the earlier meanings of these photographs. In any event, the search for their 'essential Truth' – an original, founding moment of meaning – is an illusion. The photographs are essentially multiaccentual in meaning. No such previously natural moment of true meaning, untouched by the codes and social relations of production and reading, and transcending historical time, exists.

The exercise in interpretation thus calls for considerable caution, historical judgement – in essence, a politics of reading. The evidence which the photographic text may be assumed to represent is already overendowed, overdetermined by other, further, often contradictory meanings, which arise within the intertextuality of all photographic representation as a social practice. It is unclear which constitutes the greater danger: the confusions caused by the relays of meanings in which the photographs are already overinscribed; or the riot of deconstructions to which they are certain to be exposed, not least from some of the new orthodoxies of the 'cultural left', caught as they sometimes are in the spirals of the post-Marxist, post-structuralist, post-modernist deluge. Black historians, especially, handling these explosive little 'documents', will have to steer their way through the increasingly narrow passage which separates the old Scylla of 'documentary realism as Truth' from the new Charybdis of a too-simplistic 'avant-gardism'.

Take, for example, the news agency photographs of the arrival of black people from the Caribbean on the boat-trains (Figure 25.1). These shots were taken at the big London rail-stations, where the steamers spewed out their human cargo at the end of their long journeys – Kingston via Southampton, Avonmouth-Bristol and Liverpool docks; then by steam-train through the English rural and urban-industrial heartland, to Paddington, Victoria and Waterloo. Here are the crowded stations; people sitting on their luggage or standing about, hands clasped, waiting: waiting to be met, or to recognise a friend or an unexpected relative or even just for an acknowledgement from a friendly face amongst the crowds with their bulging suitcases and straw baskets. Men, women and children, already battened down against the freezing weather by the ubiquitous wearing of hats. People 'dressed up to the nines', formally, for 'travelling' and even more for 'arrival'. Wearing that expectant look – facing the camera, open and outward, into something they cannot yet see . . . the new life.

These people are in the liminal – the in-between – state: in suspended animation. This, for better or worse – their faces seem to say – is the dead end of one thing and the uncertain beginning of another. It is a scene of transition which occurred any day of the week in the immigration 'high season' throughout the 1950s and early 1960s, until the barriers closed. Trickling out from these focal points into the grey light of Paddington, Notting Hill, Brixton, Handsworth, Moss Side . . . A graphic record. But what do these pictures mean? Can they fix and prescribe their own reading, decipherment? What do we make of these images *now*?

Figure 25.1 Victoria Station, London, 1956, Hulton-Deutsch Collection

For one thing, they contradict our expectations. Why are the men and women so formally got up? Why does everybody wear a hat? Why are they carrying their clothes in straw baskets? Why do they look so respectable? Where are the street fighters, the rude boys, the Rastas, the reggae? How are we to read what these photographs most powerfully construct: a certain form of innocence?

Innocence is a dangerous, ambiguous, ambivalent construction for black people. White discourses so often represent us as simpletons, simple-minded primitives, smiling country people, not quite keeping up in the fast lanes of the advanced world. It is a reading to be refused. These are not country bumpkins, or indigent cousins 'from the Tropics', or primitives just swinging down from the coconut trees, or anybody's *Smile Orange* folks. These people have just survived the longest, hardest journey in their lives: the journey to another identity. They are people 'in transition' to a new state of mind and body: migranthood. They are probably from a city, like Kingston, as big and swinging in its poverty and style as any small colonial capital. They have torn themselves up by their roots, saved up what for them (considering the annual average wage) is a colossal sum, paid it over to a steamship company travelling incognito under some assumed Panamanian flag. Half the family is left behind and nobody knows when or whether they will ever be united again. These men and women have just burnt their boats in the determination to carve out a better life.

All this may be 'beyond the frame'; but it registers inside the frame – precisely as a kind of 'innocence'. This is another way of referring to that moment of 'waiting' just before you step off the end of the earth into . . . into Britain, the ingrained, embattled nature of whose racism you do not yet know (that is, of which you are still, in a way, 'innocent') because it hasn't yet hit you hard between the eyes . . . A liminal movement, caught between two worlds, hesitating on the brink.

We can find this trace of innocence too, if you know where to look, elsewhere inside the frame. The people are 'dressed up' because they are on the longest one-way journey of their lives, literally and figuratively. Jamaicans travelled as they went to church, or visited their relatives – in their 'Sunday best'; the best thing you had in your wardrobe, for special occasions. The suits and dresses are the clothes of someone who is determined to make a mark, make a favourable impression. The formality is a signifier for self-respect. These are not the victims of migration, like the Jews and East Europeans photographed by Thomas Hine arriving at Ellis Island in New York. These folks are in good spirits. They mean to survive. The angle of the hats is universally jaunty, cocky. Already, there is *style*. 'Face the music, darling, and let's make a move.'

There is a similar problem of interpretation about the vast, uncatalogued collection of formal 'high-street' photo-portraits which are certain to be brought to light by a systematic search, crumbling away in files or shoved under the beds in boxes. For example, the young woman with the gloves and handbag, holding up or being held up by the basket of artificial flowers (Figure 25.2). (There is a wonderful re-presentation of the same idea in the self-portrait by the black painter Sonia Bryce, of herself, surmounted by her parents and sisters, entitled *She Ain't Holding Them Up, She's Holding On (Some English Rose)*.) The well-dressed young man held together by the clip-on fountain pen is talking on a phone which is not connected to anything, but sits incongruously on top of a mock-Greek column, straight from the disused basement of the British Museum (Figure 25.3). Or: nurse, in formal head-dress – smiling? Not smiling? Would anyone dream of posing for a picture like that now?

Figure 25.2 Studio portrait, Birmingham, 1961

Yet despite these ambiguities and disavowals of meaning, these high-street portraits also contain a sort of alternative history of black people in Britain — alternative
to the documentary or the 'social problem' traditions, their codes and meanings,
which now construct the dominant reading of that history (and to which we will come
in a moment). Every photograph is a structure of 'presences' (what is represented, in a

Figure 25.3 Studio portrait, Birmingham, 1961

definite way) and 'absences' (what is unsaid, or unsayable, against which what is there 'represents'). We will have to struggle to bring out what these formal portraits, so powerfully inscribed by the practices of the high-street photographer, so much under subjection to the codes of late-Edwardian portraiture, have to 'say' – as well as their silences.

They signify a certain democratisation of representation. They are poor-person's 'portraits'. The camera did, for the poor, what painting could not do. The formality and sense of occasion of these photographs are inscribed in the ways in which the figures are formally posed, frozen, in the way they have been suspended in formal space and time. They are certainly not 'at home'. They are not at work either. In fact, they are not represented as being *in* any human or social environment. They exist only in and for studio time, studio space. They are the bearers of the professional, small-time photographer's aspiration to 'art'. They have been transferred directly under his rules of construction. They exist for him. (I use the male pronoun advisedly, since overwhelmingly – but not exclusively – these professional photographers were, until recently, men.) You can see what has been 'constructed out' by the very positive functions of the composition only by contrast with, say, the same figures, but this time 'caught' *in* time, *in* place – for example, a photo of a roadsweeper at work.

And yet, before we think we have a complete grasp of these archaic representations, it is worth recalling that these formal portraits were also, in their own time, 'documentary'. They documented where people were at a certain stage of life, and how they imagined themselves, how they became 'persons' to themselves and to others, through the ways in which they were represented. The photos were what you sent home as 'evidence' that you had arrived safely, landed on your feet, were getting somewhere, surviving, doing all right. It would therefore be wrong to read these portraits as exclusively the result of the imposition of the codes of formal (white) portrait photography on an alien (black) subject, for that simplification would be precisely to collude, however unconsciously, with the construction of West Indians as objects, always 'outside time', outside history. The photographed subjects also had a real investment in these representations. In fact, Edwardian portraiture and the formal photograph – icons in the domestic gallery of memories – were as common in my childhood in poor but respectable homes in Kingston as they were in Kingston upon Thames. The round centre-table in my grandmother's living-room in a tiny country village in Old Harbour in rural Jamaica was crammed with them; one formal pose (my grandfather, resplendent in his gold watch-chain and three-piece suit) jostling for a place behind another (my wistful fading great-grandmother, grey hair in a bun, with a Victorian tortoiseshell comb resolutely stuck through it).

Our family history was constructed through these representations. The codes of respectability and of respect were every bit as powerful, and as complex, amongst black people in post-Victorian colonial Jamaica as they were in post-Victorian colonising Britain. Slavery, colonisation and colonialism locked us all – them (you) and us (them) – into a common but unequal, uneven, history, into the same symbolic and representational frames. Afro-Caribbean culture is precisely the result of the contradictory ways these symbolic histories were irrevocably bound together. Those who doubt the complexities of positioning which this history of uneven development contains should read C.L.R. James, the English-speaking Caribbean's most outstanding Marxist historian and intellectual, on the subject of cricket in *Beyond a*

Boundary – and think again. Jamaicans may have been placed in the subordinate position by the codes of the formal family portrait, but they were never *outside* those codes.

This is one aspect of the history of black migration that is going to be all too tempting to forget or disavow, since it does not fit easily with current expectations. It does not fit with either 'Jamaica', the Black Nation, or 'Jamaica', the sign of the Tropical-Exotic. That is why I am pleased this informal evidence exists. Its ambiguities *resist* simplification and disrupt our reading. That is also why I admire the corrective provided by Val Wilmer's photographs of 'everyday Jamaican life' in Britain in the 1960s – and why I refuse to be absolutist either about the fact that she is a white photographer photographing blacks or about the so-called 'documentary-realist tradition' in which her images are often constructed. I find an astonishing plenitude in the constructed complexities of some of those photographs: the pastor and his wife at his front gate; the church-going family – everyone (again) in a hat, including the babe in arms. These images are part of the frequently unrecorded, unrecognised, unspoken history of everyday life and practice in the black communities in Britain. The cultural historian who sets out to interpret this record without an understanding of the complex position which religion has played in the life of the black communities in the Black Diaspora will undoubtedly see something, but will not have learnt to read the cultural signposts and multiaccented traces which history has left behind – traces, as Gramsci says, 'without an inventory'.

And yet, of course – to repeat an earlier point – what 'signifies' is not the photographic text in isolation but the text, caught in the network of the chains of signification which overprint it, its inscription into the currency of other discourses, its intertextuality. The photograph of boat-loads of West Indians at the Customs actually appeared, already in place with others, in a *Picture Post* article of 1956. It was part of a very distinctive way of constructing its subject: black migrants as a *problem*: 'Thirty Thousand Colour Problems'. Three thousand, the article tells us, is the rate of arrivals per month. Thirty thousand are expected in 1956. And every last one of them 'a problem'. The written text anchors – as the preferred, the *dominant*, meaning – one of the many potential meanings which the multireferentiality of the photographic texts supports. This is how a problem is produced within representation. Black people come in such large numbers. Surprisingly, they all want to work and to live in homes. They don't understand how to dress for the uncertainties of the English climate. They don't have an accurate picture of life 'over here'. The problem they pose for 'us' is universal, ubiquitous. It is overdetermined from every conceivable direction. It is outside the norm, beyond the pale. It is – they are – the Other.

I have written elsewhere about the particular strengths and weaknesses of *Picture Post*'s social documentary style of 'realism'. In many ways, the critique of social documentary is strengthened and reinforced by the discourses of social exposure which are in play in this example. *Picture Post* turned an observant, socially enquiring eye on many corners of English life and society, before and after the war, which were excluded or invisible to the media of social communication. It became part of a significant ideological formation – what I once called the 'eye' or 'gaze' of social democracy.

This way of looking at England was capable of representing hitherto invisible social issues; but, characteristically, it always constructed them as *social problems*. It represented the subjects of its 'look' as the intensely interesting, intensely human, intensely ordinary, objects of forces they could not control or comprehend. It summoned up a concern which made powerful claims on our humanism; but it could not penetrate more deeply because it had no language for social contradiction, no way of breaking the surfaces of 'naturalism' in which the problem presented itself, or of 'speaking' the oppositional forces out of which radical social transformation might be generated. I have argued that both the strengths and the limitations of this particular 'way of seeing' were bound up with its actual codes and practices of representation: the observing eye, the external, objective character of reality, the documenter in a position of knowledge, the confinement of meaning to the rich surface of things: its particular variant of what I have called (for I believe it to be articulated as a political formation as well as an ideological and discursive field) 'social democratic realism'.

This 'look', inscribed through a particular set of codes and discourses, is all too plainly to be seen again in some of the 'best' documentary photojournalism about 'the problem of blacks' in the early decades of migration. How much this is the product of the practices of representation, how little the outcome of 'natural', inevitable, or in any simple way 'true' ways of seeing and believing is shown, I think, by an intriguing paradox. In the issue of *Picture Post* for 30 October 1954, 'the problem' is constructed as the black presence. However, in the news-photo of the first major race riots – Notting Hill, 1958 – which shows young people charging through the streets of North Kensington in ways which might be thought to be part of 'the problem', there is not a black face to be seen. Absences sometimes speak louder than words.

However, it must also be said that the current critical orthodoxy has somewhat trivialised the argument about documentary realism by assimilating all 'realisms' (which one ought to be at pains to discriminate and differentiate) into one great, essential so-called 'realist discourse'. This, in turn, has been assimilated, not as a negotiation of the dominant discursive codes (which *Picture Post* clearly was) but as a mere repetition of the *[sic]* dominant code, *tout court*; and this in turn, via a Foucaul-dean descant, has been identified, without qualification, with the univocal, scrutinising 'gaze' or the surveillance of the populace by the ruling class. Of course, all regimes of representation are inscribed in the 'play' between power and knowledge, and Foucault's work is wonderfully insightful on this score. But the kind of account outlined above is built on a sliding series of reductions, of an astonishing – and in the end unacceptable – kind. There is no *one* system of realist representation, always and for ever fixed in position, from which one type of political practice, one empiricist reading of history, emanates; any more than there is one deconstructionist avant-gardism, always-for ever already inscribed in its progressive modes of seeing. Yesterday's deconstructions are often tomorrow's clichés. It depends, as always, on the way concrete practices are implemented in concrete historical conditions, the effectivity with which certain codes are constituted as 'in dominance', the struggle within the social relations of representation, at a particular conjuncture, as to whether a tendency can be articulated towards or away from the politically progressive pole. The fact is, there is no universally transhistorical 'progressive style' and the search for it is itself deeply essentialist, even when constructed under the sign of theoretical anti-essentialism. We are always and for ever in the terrain of *articulation*: linkages which can be reversed, meanings which change their sign from negative to positive as they are repositioned in the field of interdiscursivity in which ideology constantly intervenes, with its reordering, recomposing power. Hegemony is a hard taskmaster, but it really is different from the idea of the permanent and fixed ascription of an eternal dominance within any one discourse across the entire face of history.

Take, for example, the now overtypical and overtypified so-called 'documentary' shot of the man looking at the sign which reads: 'Rooms to Let. No Coloured Men'. It is in the classic documentary, re-creating-the-lived-experience, style. It constructs the black man as 'barred' and names the bar as 'discrimination': in the language of the time, the 'Colour Bar'. This representation cannot be fixed in its Truth by any Real, since it stops short before the deeper realities of 'Racism' – a phenomenon which this 'way of seeing' finds impossible to name or identify. All the same, *in its time*, this situation, which was part of the experience black migrants faced everywhere, was also systematically denied everywhere – unspoken and unspeakable. It required to be, as one might say, represented – 'documented': *of course*, within the 'social exposé' discourses of the period (how else do you represent except discursively?).

But anyone with a proper historical sense, not reading back everything with hindsight into 'pure' theoretical time (i.e. reading in a historical, not historicist, way), will know that, in this conjuncture, 'documenting it' – in the sense of putting one's finger on it, giving it an image, naming it, representing it, bringing it into the sightline (including that of other blacks who may have expected things to be different) – mattered. It registered. It was part of the politics of representation. It disturbed the 'field of vision' of its time. If it had been left unseen, unsaid, the black politics of resistance of a *later* period would have had only an empty void to build on. So there is no point in giving an account or reading of that photograph which *suppresses* time, disavows the contradiction. Things which really are contradictory are not made more 'revolutionary' by being translated into comforting theoretical simplifications . . .

Sartre once said that a 'lazy Marxism' was that which tells us only what we already know. Looking again at some of these early images, I saw something which I had not been aware of before. We have already seen how black migration was constructed in many of the news-photos as a problem. But I had forgotten how persistently in these early days, at the centre of the problem – the problem of the problem, so to speak – was the core issue of sexuality: specifically, sexual relations between different ethnic or racial groups – or, to give it its proper name, the traumatic fantasy of miscegenation. It is as if, at the centre of this whole regime of representation, there was one unrepresentable image, which nevertheless cast a silent shadow across the visual field, driving those who sensed its absent-presence crazy: the image of black sexuality figured transgressively across the boundaries of race and ethnicity. In the mirror of the imaginary – screaming to be spoken – we find figured this 'unspeakable': the traumatic inscription of black and white people, together, making love – and having children, as the proof that, against God and Nature, *something worked*. How often since, in the syntax of white racism, coiling through the Enoch Powell 'Rivers of Blood' speech, or in fantasies that drive young bullet-headed fascists or Thatcherite skinheads into an unspeakable frenzy, or in the obscene scrawls that trail their slime across the face of black people's houses and shops, or carved into the walls of public lavatories and on the sides of apartment blocks, has one 'read', hiding behind what is actually written, this great unsaid?

The *Picture Post* of 1954 had a word for it, a way of putting (representing) it: 'Would you let your daughter marry a Negro?' Typically, it is the 'sympathetic', winsome portrait of a white mother and a black child which is used to construct this representation. If we look at the contact sheets from which this particular image was selected, we find a much wider range of shots, with alternative ways of representing the white mother and black father: close, not distanced; together, or together with the child; doing things, in context – shopping, playing, walking about. The choice of a static mother-and-child image as the principal signifier of the white-family-norm-in-trouble is certainly not fortuitous, however fragile or contingent the meaning seems to be. Indeed, even through its oblique treatment here (we are once again in the negotiated discourses of *Picture Post*) we are reminded that English racism is not so much a single discourse as the interdiscursive space when several discourses are articulated together: the discourses of race, and colour, and sexuality, and patriarchy and 'Englishness' itself. 'If she was my kid,' muttered the man in overalls, 'I'd tan the backside off her.' Against this vivid, idiomatic, common-sense English 'truth' is counterposed the silent 'appeal', the sentimental eyes – playing straight to the heartstrings: 'Sometimes they say it loud enough for her to hear.'

The pull is irresistibly towards the sense of fairness, the common humanity. The *humanist* inflection is central to the *liberalism* of this whole rhetoric. The more consciously posed, formally contrasting, white couple/black couple from another Keystone agency photograph is inflected in the same direction. 'The look of the couple in front is full of scepticism. He is black – she is white', the caption in *Picture Post* reads, in case we are in any doubt. 'The other couple – bound to current traditions. Their world has to be safe, their desires are security and prosperity.' The two representations have been set up as binary opposites, mirror-images. Then comes the mediation: 'But there is one thing that they have in common: they are equivalent people with their sorrows and desires – with their hope and anxiety.' Here again, the neatly composed construction of oppositions, the 'surface' hostility, resolved by a deep, underlying, essential, oneness. The photograph as Universal Humanism. A likely story.

Each period lays its own inflections on the image. Each photograph already has a context, a set of histories within which alone it signifies. Since the photographs discussed here were taken – many now more than thirty years ago – black people in Britain have been constructed, and begun to construct themselves, as new kinds of subjects – visually, in new, different, often more challenging ways. Of course, a 'sense of history' is never confined to the past: it is always a seizure by history of the present, as Benjamin said. But it does require a delicate excavation, an archaeology, a tracing of the contradictory imprints which previous discourses have stamped, through those old images, on the iconography of popular memory.

Chapter 26

Carolyn Steedman

LANDSCAPE FOR A GOOD WOMAN [1985]

(**Source**: Steedman, Carolyn (1985) 'Landscape for a Good Woman', in Liz Heron ed. *Truth, Dare or Promise: Girls Growing Up in the 50s*, London: Virago, pp. 103–14, 118)

Editor's introduction

In this chapter (a snapshot of her 1986 book of the same name) Carolyn Steedman reclaims the complex and specific experience of class by investigating her childhood memories. Importantly it is the small lies and self-deceptions that tell a truth about social life that a mere record of social facts would miss. In this regard Steedman's work on social history shares similarities with Rancière's in that both seek to reclaim aspects of working-class identity that sit uncomfortably within the contours of traditional description. By taking a childhood dream as historical evidence Steedman might be seen as deploying a psychohistorical approach to the past. Yet her object is not to diagnose the psychopathology of class. Instead she seeks to weave desire and envy, frustration and anger, bitterness and (self) recrimination into the self-understanding of class experience. To do this requires locating class at the level of everyday life. But this is an everyday life that is never situated simply in an experiential present: the present is shot through with remembrances and aspirations. In this way her mother's manifest politics evidences a latent content that longs for the 'good life' as it struggles to reconcile the past. That this is persistently expressed in everyday life (the continual invocation of the 'other' woman, the assessment of life as permanent struggle) are clearly crucial.

Steedman's historical work has shown how important narrative is for the self-understanding of social life. In this regard the stories we can tell about ourselves (the forms of narrative that we have access to) play a constitutive role in our social consciousness. That everyday life might fall outside available narratives (for instance in its lack of 'event', or in its unheroic drudgery) is of considerable import. In her recovery of a nineteenth-century diary of a working-class soldier who went on to become a rural policeman, the effects of the absence of narratives of everyday life are vividly displayed (Steedman 1988). As the diarist moves from the adventure saga of the soldier's life to the everydayness of rural police work, the diary fragments and the social critique that had been so clear become incoherent.

Further reading: Bristow 1991; Marcus 1987; Steedman 1986, 1988; Raymond Williams 1989b.

WHEN I WAS THREE, before my sister was born, I had a dream. It remains quite clear across the years, the topography absolutely plain, so precise in details of dress that I can use them to place the dream in historical time. We were in a street, the street so wide and the houses so distant across the other side that it might not have been a street at all; and the houses lay low with gaps between them, so that the sky filled a large part of the picture. Here, at the front, on this side of the wide road, a woman hurried along, having crossed from the houses behind. The perspective of the dream must have shifted several times, for I saw her once as if from above, moving through a kind of square, or crossing place, and then again from the fixed point of the dream where I stood watching her, left forefront.

She wore the New Look, a coat of beige gaberdine which fell in two swaying, graceful pleats from her waist at the back (the swaying must have come from very high heels, but I didn't notice her shoes), a hat tipped forward from hair swept up. She hurried, something jerky about her movements, a titupping, agitated walk, glancing round at me as she moved across the foreground. Several times she turned and came some way back towards me, admonishing, shaking her finger. Encouraging me to follow in this way perhaps, but moving too fast for me to believe that she wanted me to do that, she entered a revolving door of dark polished wood, mahogany and glass, and started to go round and round, looking out at me as she turned. I wish I knew what she was doing, and what she wanted me to do.

This book is about childhood, a time when only the surroundings show, and nothing is explained. It is also about a period of recent history, the 1950s, and about the way in which those years shaped individual lives and collective ideas. But children do not possess a *social* analysis of what is happening to them, or around them, so the landscape and the pictures it presents have to remain a background, taking on meaning later, from different circumstances. Understanding of the dream built up in layers, over a long period of time. Its strange, lowered vista, for instance (which now reminds the adult more than anything else of George Herriman's *Krazy Kat*, where buildings disappear and reappear from frame to frame)[1] is an obvious representation of London in the late 1940s and 1950s: all the houses had gaps in between, because of the bombs, and the sky came closer to the ground than seemed right. I understood what I had seen in the dream when I learned the words 'gaberdine' and 'mahogany'; and I was born in the year of the New Look, understood by 1951 and the birth of my sister, that dresses needing twenty yards for a skirt were items as expensive as children – more expensive really, because after 1948 babies came relatively cheap, on tides of free milk and orange juice, but good cloth in any quantity was hard to find for a very long time.

Detail like this provides retrospective labelling, but it is not evidence about a historical period. The only *evidence* from that dream is the feeling of childhood – all childhoods, probably: the puzzlement of the child watching from the pavement, wondering what's going on, what they, the adults are up to, what they want from you, and what they expect you to do.

Worked upon and reinterpreted, the landscape becomes an historical landscape, but only through continual and active reworking. 'The essence of the historical process,' says Tamara Hareven in *Family Time and Industrial Time*,

> is the meeting between an individual's or a group's life history and the historical moment. People's responses to the historical conditions they encounter are shaped both by the point in their lives at which they encounter those conditions and by the equipment they bring with them from earlier life experiences.[2]

But children possess very little of that equipment, and in the process of acquiring it, the baggage is continually reorganised and reinterpreted. Memory simply can't resurrect those years, because it is memory itself that shapes them, long after the historical time has passed. So to present the decade through the filter of my parents' story, and my growing awareness of the odd typicality of my childhood, is the result of a decision to see the 1950s as a political moment when hope was promised, and then deferred. We rework past time to give current events meaning, and that reworking provides an understanding that the child at the time can't possess: it's only in the last few months that I've understood who the woman in the New Look coat was.

Now, later, I see the time of my childhood as a point between two worlds, an older 'during the war', 'before the war', 'in the Depression', 'then', and the place we inhabit now. The war was so palpable a presence in the first five years of my life that I still find it hard to believe that I didn't live through it. There were bombsites everywhere, prefabs on waste land, most things still rationed, my mother tearing up the ration book over my sister's pram outside the library in the High Road when meat came off points in the summer of 1951, a gesture that still fills me with the desire to do something so defiant and final; and then looking across the street at a woman wearing a full-skirted dress, and then down at the 1940s straight-skirted navy blue suit she was still wearing, and longing, irritatedly, for the New Look, and then at us, the two living barriers to twenty yards of cloth. Back home, she said, she'd be able to get it from the side door of the mill, but not here; not with you two . . . I was three in 1950, only twelve when the decade ended, just a child, a repository for other people's history; and my mother gave me her version long before my father did.

By the time my father could sit down with me in a pub, slightly drunk, tell me and my friends about Real Life, crack a joke about a Pakistani that silenced a whole table once, and talk about the farm labourer's – his grandfather's – journey up from Eye in Suffolk working on the building of the Great North Western Railway to Rawtenstall on the Lancashire–Yorkshire border, I was doing history at Sussex, and knew more than he did about the date and timing of journeys like that. My father, old but gritty, glamorous in the eyes of the class of '68, a South London wide boy with an authentic background, described his grandfather's funeral, about 1912, when a whole other family, wife, children, grandchildren, turned up out of the blue from somewhere further down the line where they'd been established on the navvy's journey north. (This was a circumstance paralleled at his own funeral, when the friends and relations of the woman he'd been living with for part of the week since the early 1960s stole the show from us, the pathetic huddle of the family of his middle years.) My mother's story on the other hand was told to me much earlier, in bits and pieces throughout the 1950s, and it wasn't delivered to entertain but rather to teach me lessons. There was a child, an eleven-year-old from a farm seven miles south of Coventry, sent off to be a maid-of-all-work in a parsonage in Burnley. She had her tin trunk, and she cried, waiting on the platform with her family seeing her off, for the through train to Manchester. They'd sent her fare, the people in Burnley; 'but think how she felt, such a little girl, she was only eleven, with nothing but her little tin box. Oh she did cry.' I cry now over accounts of childhood like this, weeping furtively over the reports of nineteenth-century commissions of inquiry into child labour, abandoning myself to the luxuriance of grief in libraries, tears staining the pages where Mayhew's little water-cress girl tells her story. The lesson was, of course, that I must never, ever cry for myself, for I was a lucky little girl; my tears should be for all the strong, brave women who gave me life. This story, which embodied fierce resentment against the unfairness of things, was carried through seventy years and three generations, and all of them, all the good women, dissolved into the figure of my mother who was, as she told us, *a good mother*. She didn't go out drinking or dancing; she didn't do as one mother she'd known (in a story of maternal neglect that I remember feeling was over the top at the time) and tie a piece of string round my big toe, dangle it through the window and down the front of the house, so that the drunken mother, returning from her carousing, could tug at it, wake the child, get the front door opened and send it down the shop for a basin of pie and peas. I still put myself to sleep by thinking about *not* lying on a cold pavement covered with newspapers. She must have told me once that I was lucky to have a warm bed to lie in at night.

What she did, in fact, the eleven-year-old who cried on Coventry station, was hate being a servant. She got out as soon as she could, and found work in the weaving sheds – 'she was a good weaver; six looms under her by the time she was sixteen' – marry, produce nine children, eight of whom emigrated to the cotton mills of Massachusetts before the First World War, managed, 'never went before the Guardians'.[3] It was much, much later that I learned from *One Hand Tied Behind Us* that four was the usual number of looms for a Lancashire weaver; Burnley weavers were not well organised, and my great-grandmother had six not because she was a good weaver but because she was exploited.[4] In 1916, when her daughter Carrie's husband was killed at the Somme, she managed that too, looking after the three-year-old, my mother, so that Carrie could go on working at the mill.

But long before the narrative fell into place, before I could dress the eleven-year-old of my imagination in the clothing of the 1870s, I knew perfectly well what that child had done, and how she had felt. She cried, because tears are cheap; and then she'd stopped, and got by, because nobody gives you anything in this world. What was given to her, passed on to all of us, was a powerful and terrible endurance, the self-destructive defiance of those doing the best they can with what life hands out to them.

From a cotton town, my mother had a heightened awareness of fabric and weave, and I can date events by the clothes I wore as a child, and the material they were made of. Post-war children had few clothes, because of rationing; but not only scarcity, rather names like barathea, worsted, gaberdine, twill, jersey . . . fix them in my mind. The dream of the New Look has to have taken place during or after the summer of

1950, because in it I wore one of my two summer dresses, one of green and one of blue gingham, that were made that year and that lasted me, with letting down, until I went to school. Sometime during 1950, I think before the summer, before the dresses were made, I was taken north to Burnley and into the sheds. My mother was visiting someone who worked there whom she'd known as a child. The woman smiled and nodded at me through the noise that made a surrounding silence. Later, my mother told me they had to lip read: they couldn't hear each other speak for the noise of the looms. But I didn't notice the noise. She wore high platform-soled black shoes that I still believe I heard click on the bright polished floor as she walked between her looms. When I hear the word 'tending' I think always of that confident attentiveness to the needs of the machines, the control over work that was unceasing, with half a mind and hands engaged but the looms always demanding attention. When I worked as a primary school teacher I sometimes retrieved that feeling with a particular clarity, walking between the tables on the hard floor, all the little looms working but needing my constant adjustment. The woman wore a dress that seemed very short when I recalled the picture through the next few years: broad shoulders, a straight skirt that hung the way it did – I know now – because it had some rayon in it. No New Look here in Burnley either. The post-war years were full of women longing for a full skirt and unable to make it. I wanted to walk like that, a short skirt, high heels, bright red lipstick, in charge of all that machinery.

It's extremely difficult for me to think of women as people who do not work; their work, moreover, is visible and comprehensible; they can explain, or show to children what they do and how – unlike men, whose process of getting money is mysterious and hidden from view. There's been recent reassessment of the traditional picture of the enforced flight from the labour force to domesticity on the part of women just after the war, and far from a flight, large-scale recruitment to the new industries in the early 1950s now seems to present a more historically accurate picture. It's probable that the memory of most children of our generation is of women as workers.[5] I had no awareness of the supposed stereotypical mother of that era – lipsticked and aproned, waiting at the door – and don't think I even encountered a picture of her, in books, comics or film, until the early 1960s.

As a teenage worker my mother had broken a recently established pattern. When she left school in 1927 she hadn't gone into the sheds. She lied to me, though, when I asked at about the age of eight what she'd done: she said she'd worked in an office, done clerical work. Ten years later, on a visit to Burnley and practising the skills of the oral historian, I talked to my grandmother, and she, puzzled, told me that Edna had never worked in any office, had in fact been apprenticed to a dry cleaning firm that did tailoring and mending. On the same visit, the first since my early childhood, I found a reference written by a local doctor for my mother, who about 1930 applied for a job as a ward maid at the local asylum, confirming that she was clean, strong, honest and intelligent. I wept over that of course, for a world where some people might doubt her – my – cleanliness. I didn't care much about the honesty, and I knew I was strong; but there are people everywhere waiting for you to slip up, to show signs of dirtiness and stupidity, so that they can send you back where you belong.

She didn't finish her apprenticeship – I deduce that, rather than know it – sometime, it must have been in 1934, came south, worked in Woolworths on the Edgware Road, spent the war years in Roehampton, a ward maid again, at the hospital where they mended fighter pilots' ruined faces. Now I can feel the deliberate vagueness in her accounts of those years: 'Where did you meet Daddy?' 'Oh, at a dance, at home.' There were no photographs. Who came to London first? I wish now I'd asked that question. He worked on the buses when he arrived, showed me a canopy in front of a hotel that he'd brought down on his first solo drive. He was too old to be called up (a lost generation of men who were too young for the first war, too old for the second). There's a photograph of him standing in front of the cabbages that he'd grown for victory wearing his Home Guard uniform. But what did he *do*? Too late to find out.

During the post-war housing shortage my father got an office job with a property company, and the flat that went with it. I was born in March 1947, at the peak of the Bulge: more babies born that month than ever before or after, and carried through the terrible winter of 1946–47. We moved to Streatham Hill in June 1951, to an estate owned by the same company, later to be taken over by Lambeth Council. A few years later, my father got what he wanted, which was to be in charge of the company's boiler maintenance. On his death certificate it says 'heating engineer'.

In the 1950s my mother took in lodgers. Streatham Hill Theatre (now a bingo hall) was on the pre-West End circuit, and we had chorus girls staying with us for weeks at a time. I was woken up in the night sometimes, the spare bed in my room being made up for someone they'd met down the Club, the other lodger's room already occupied. I like the idea of being the daughter of a theatrical landlady, but this enterprise provides my most startling and problematic memories. Did the girl from Aberdeen really say, 'Och, no, not on the table!' as my father flattened a bluebottle with his hand, and did he *really* put down a newspaper on the same table to eat his breakfast? I feel a fraud, a bit-part player in a soft and southern version of *The Road To Wigan Pier*.

I remember incidents like these, I think, because I was about seven, the age at which children start to notice social detail and social distinction, but also more particularly because the long lesson in hatred for my father had begun, and the early stages were in the traditional mode, to be found in the opening chapters of *Sons and Lovers* and Lawrence's description of the inculcated dislike of Mr Morrell, of female loathing for coarse male habits. The newspaper on the table is problematic for me because it was problematic for my mother, a symbol of all she'd hoped to escape and all she'd landed herself in. (It was at this time, I think, that she told me that her own mother, means-tested in the late 1920s, had won the sympathy of the relieving officer, who ignored the presence of the saleable piano because she kept a clean house, with a cloth on the table.)

Now, thirty years later, I feel a great regret for the father of my first four years, who took me out, and who probably loved me, irresponsibly ('it's all right for him; he doesn't have to look after you'), and I wish I could tell him now, even though he was, in my sister's words, a sod, that I'm sorry for my years of rejection and dislike. But we had to choose, early on, which side we belonged to, and children have to come down on the side that brings the food home and gets it on the table. By 1955 I was beginning to hate him – because *he* was to blame, for the lack of money, for my mother's terrible dissatisfaction at the way things were working out.

The new consumer goods came into the household slowly – because of *him*. We had the first fridge in our section of the street (he got it cheap – contacts) but were late to get a television. The vacuum cleaner was welcomed at first because it meant no longer having to do the stairs with a stiff brush. But in fact it added to my Saturday work because I was expected to clean more with the new machine. I enjoy shocking people by describing how goods were introduced into households under the guise of gifts for children: the fridge in the house of the children we played with over the road was given to the youngest as a birthday present – the last thing an eight-year-old wants. My mother laughed at this, scornfully; but in fact she gave us Christmas and birthday presents of clothes and shoes, and the record player came into the house in this way, as my eleventh birthday present. But I wasn't allowed to take it with me when I left; it wasn't really mine at all.

I remember walking up the hill from school with my mother after an open day, and asking her what class we were; or rather, I asked her if we were middle class, and she was evasive. She was smiling a pleased smile, and working things out; I think it must have been the afternoon (the only time she visited my primary school) she was told that I'd be going into the eleven-plus class and so (because everyone in the class passed the exam) would be going to grammar school. I was working out well, an investment with the promise of paying out. I answered my own question, and said that I thought we must be middle class, and reflected very precisely in that moment on my mother's black waisted coat with the astrakhan collar, and her high-heeled black suede shoes, her lipstick. She *looked* so much better than the fat, spreading South London mothers around us, that I thought we had to be middle class.

The coat and the lipstick came from her own work. 'If you want something, you have to go out and work for it. Nobody gives you anything; nothing comes free in this world.' About 1956 or 1957 she got an evening job in one of the espresso bars opening along the High Road, making sandwiches and frying eggs. She saved up enough money to take a manicuring course and in 1958 got her diploma, thus achieving a certified skill for the first time in her forty-five years. When I registered her death I was surpised to find myself giving this as her trade, because learned history implies that only the traditional ones – tailoring, weaving, joining, welding – are real. She always worked in good places, in the West End; the hands she did were in *Vogue* once. She came home with stories and imitations of her 'ladies'. When I was about twelve she told me how she'd 'flung' a sixpenny piece back at a titled woman who'd given it her as a tip: 'If you can't afford any more than that Madam, I suggest you keep it.' Wonderful! – like tearing up the ration books. From her job, supported by the magazines she brought home, and her older skill of tailoring and dressmaking, we learned how the goods of the earth might be appropriated, with a certain voice, the cut and fall of a skirt, a good winter coat; with leather shoes too, but above all by clothes, the best boundary between you and a cold world.

We weren't, I now realise by doing the sums, badly off. My father paid the rent, all the bills, gave us our pocket money, and a fixed sum of £7 a week housekeeping money – quite a lot in the late 1950s – went on being handed over every Friday until his death, even when estrangement was obvious, and he was living most of the time with someone else. My mother must have made quite big money in tips, for the records of her savings, no longer a secret, show quite fabulous sums being stored away in the early 1960s. Poverty hovered as a belief. It existed in stories of the 1930s, in a family history. Even now when a bank statement comes that shows I'm overdrawn, or the gas bill for the central heating seems enormous, my mind turns to quite inappropriate strategies, like boiling down the ends of soap, and lighting fires with candle ends and spills of screwed-up newspaper to save buying wood. I think about these things because they were domestic economies that we practised in the 1950s. We believed we were poor because we children were expensive items, and all the arrangements had been made for us. 'If it wasn't for you two,' my mother told us, 'I could be off somewhere else.' After going out manicuring she started spending Sunday afternoons in bed and we couldn't stay in the house nor play on the doorstep for fear of disturbing her. The house was full of her terrible tiredness, her terrible resentment; and I knew it was all my fault.

When I came across Kathleen Woodward's *Jipping Street*[6] I read it with the shocked amazement of one who had never seen what she knew written down before. Kathleen Woodward's mother of the 1890s was the one I knew: mothers were people who told you how long they were in labour with you, how much you hurt, how hard it was to have you ('twenty hours with you,' my mother frequently reminded me) and who told you to accept the impossible contradiction of being both desired and being a burden, and not to complain. This ungiving endurance is admired by working-class boys who grow up to write about their mothers' flinty courage. But the daughter's silence on this matter is a measure of the price you have to pay for survival. I don't think the baggage will ever lighten, for me or my sister. We were born, and had no choice in that matter; but we were burdens, expensive, never grateful enough. There was nothing we could do to pay back the debt of our existence. 'Never have children, dear,' she said. 'They ruin your life.'

Later, in 1977 after my father's death, we found out that they were never married, that we were illegitimate. In 1934 my father left his wife and two-year-old daughter in the north, and came to London. He and my mother had been together for at least ten years when I was born, and we think now that I was her hostage to fortune, the factor that might persuade him to get a divorce and marry her. But the ploy failed.

Just before my mother's death, playing around with the photographs on the bedroom mantelpiece, my niece discovered an old photograph underneath one of me at three. A woman holds a tiny baby. It's the early 1930s, a picture of the half-sister, left behind. But I think I knew about her and her mother long before I looked them both in the face, or heard about their existence; knew that the half-understood adult conversations around me, the quarrels about 'her', the litany of 'she', 'she', 'she' from behind closed doors made the figure in the New Look coat, hurrying away, wearing the clothes my mother wanted to wear, angry with me yet nervously inviting me to follow, caught finally in the revolving door. We have proper birth certificates, because my mother must have told a simple lie to the registrar, a discovery about the verisimilitude of documents that worries me a lot as a historian.

[. . .]

My mother had wanted to marry a king. That was the best of my father's stories, told in the pub in the 1960s, of how difficult it had been to live with her in 1937, during the Abdication months. Mrs Simpson was no prettier than her, no more clever than her, no better than her. It wasn't fair that a king should give up his throne for her, and not for the weaver's daughter. From a traditional Labour background, my mother rejected the politics of solidarity and communality, always voted Conservative, for the left could not embody her desire for things to be *really* fair, for a full skirt that took twenty yards of cloth, for a half-timbered cottage in the country, for the prince who did not come. My childhood was the place where, for my mother, the fairy tales failed, and through the glass of that childhood I now see that failure as part of a longer and more enduring one.

Notes

1   George Herriman's Krazy Kat cartoons, syndicated throughout the US from 1913 onwards, are reproduced in *Krazy Kat Komix*, vols 1–4, Real Free Press, Amsterdam, 1974–1975.
2   Tamara Hareven, *Family Time and Industrial Time: The Relationship Between the Family and Work in a New England Industrial Community*, Cambridge University Press, New York, 1982, p. 355.
3   That is, never applied to the Guardians of the parish for financial help under the Poor Law.
4   Jill Liddington and Jill Norris, *One Hand Tied Behind Us: The Rise of the Women's Suffrage Movement*, Virago, London, 1978, pp. 93–95.
5   See Denise Riley, *War in the Nursery*, Virago, London, 1983, pp. 145–149 for working women in the post-war years.
6   Kathleen Woodward, *Jipping Street* [1928], Virago, London, 1983.

Chapter 27

Dorothy E. Smith

A FEMINIST METHODOLOGY [1987]

(**Source**: Smith, Dorothy E. (1987) *The Everyday World as Problematic: A Feminist Sociology*, Boston, Mass.: Northeastern University Press, pp. 105–6, 132–43)

Editor's introduction

In *The Everyday World as Problematic*, Dorothy E. Smith attempts to construct a sociology that would resist turning social subjects (individual, but also social, agents) into mute objects of study. Such epistemological puzzling has a very specific goal; this sociology would be directed at reclaiming women's lives and women's voices. The argument that grounds Smith's approach is that social difference (specifically class and gender difference) is what both separates us and connects us in the everyday world. So, on the one hand, the middle-class paternalism (or condescension) that can be detected in nineteenth-century approaches to working-class women's everyday life separates the observer from the observed, the sociologist from the sociologised. The middle-class do-gooder speaks for the proletarian woman. Yet it is precisely here that Smith's argument is most interesting: although their positions might be seen as axiomatically opposed, what they share is a common actuality that saturates both their everyday lives (if only the quasi-sociologist could see it). They *share* an everyday actuality structured around class and gender differences: what separates them is also what connects them.

Rather than let this neat formulation exist as an abstraction, Smith is concerned to show how this approach might reclaim a sense of the everyday lives of those who are the objects of sociology. What is clear in her reading of the quasi-sociological text *Round about a Pound a Week* is the need to go outside the immediate frame of a specific set of everyday practices. By linking the everyday practice of washing her children to the critical (and daily) scrutiny that those children would be subjected to at school, Mrs T is connected to the interests of the writer Mrs Reeves (Mrs Reeves is similarly interested in assessing hygiene and nutrition). In this way the investigation of working-class practices exhibits the same concerns that are in operation at the school and are thereby *already* active in Mrs T's daily life (even though Mrs Reeves might be more sympathetic and less judgemental than the school teachers). Mrs T's routines (the everyday life of the one observed) are oriented to the same kind of concerns as motivate Mrs Reeves (the observer) although from distinctly different perspectives.

To make this the basis of sociology would primarily mean that sociologists would have to recognise how they are both separated from and connected to those they intend to sociologise. In effect this would require a kind of analytic self-scrutiny (and honesty) that by examining actual structural relationships would do more than simply pay lip-service to self-reflexivity by acknowledging the relatively privileged position of academics.

(**Note:** When Smith talks about 'Ones' and 'Twos' she is referring to the 'object' of sociology (the working-class mother, the sociologised) as 'One' and the sociologist as 'Two'.)

Further reading: Gardiner 2000; Haraway 1991; D.E. Smith 1999.

THE FULCRUM OF A SOCIOLOGY FOR WOMEN is the standpoint of the subject. A sociology for women preserves the presence of subjects as knowers and as actors. It does not transform subjects into the objects of study or make use of conceptual devices for eliminating the active presence of subjects. Its methods of thinking and its analytic procedures must preserve the presence of the active and experiencing subject. A sociology is a systematically developed knowledge of society and social relations. The knower who is construed in the sociological texts of a sociology for women is she whose grasp of the world *from where she stands* is enlarged thereby. For actual subjects situated in the actualities of their everyday worlds, a sociology for women offers an understanding of how those worlds are organized and determined by social relations immanent in and extending beyond them.

Methods of thinking could, I suppose, be described as 'theories', but to do so is to suggest that I am concerned with formulations that will explain phenomena, when what I am primarily concerned with is how to conceptualize or how to constitute the textuality of social phenomena. I am concerned with how to *write* the social, to make it visible in sociological texts, in ways that will explicate a problematic, the actuality of which is immanent in the everyday world. In part what is meant by methods of thinking will emerge in the course of the chapter. This is an exploration rather than an account of a destination. We are in search of conceptual practices with which to explicate the actual social relations disclosed in investigation and analysis. We are looking, in other words, for methods and principles for generating sociological texts, for selecting syntax and indexical forms preserving the presence of subjects in our accounts, in short for methods of *writing* sociology. Such methods must recognize that the subject of our sociological texts exists outside them, that, as Marx says, 'The real subject [matter] retains its autonomous existence outside the head just as before.'[1] Or perhaps we go further than Marx in insisting that both subject matter and the 'head' that theorizes it as well as its theorizing are enfolded in the existence of our subject matter. A sociology for women must be conscious of its necessary indexicality and hence that its meaning remains to be completed by a reader who is situated just as she is – a particular woman reading somewhere at a particular time amid the particularities of her everyday world — and that it is the capacity of our sociological texts, as she enlivens them, to reflect upon, to expand, and to enlarge her grasp of the world she reads in, and that is the world that completes the meaning of the text as she reads.

[. . .]

In *The German Ideology* Marx and Engels pose this question: if social relations exist only in the activities of actual individuals and individuals always start from themselves, how could those relations take on the character of forces standing over against them and overpowering their lives?[2] Marx's analysis of the commodity in *Capital* establishes the bridge over which activities pass in entering into a realm in which relations function as impersonal 'forces'. The social relations constituting commodities are distinctive. They are relations in which individuals are necessarily present and active but in which they do not appear as such. They are the relations of an economy in which money is exchanged for commodities and commodities for money. The invisibility of subjects in the commodity as a social relation is not a conceptual effect, but a feature of the particular way in which exchange relations are organized in a capitalist mode of production. The 'objectivity' of the relations is an effect of the activities of individuals concerted in determinate forms of social relations. Such a concept of social relations enables us to see how 'explanations' in terms of intentions or motives are quite insufficient as accounts of social phenomena, for the activities of individuals are articulated to and organized by the social relations that express no intention but, arising out of the multiple intentions of many, coordinate and determine (in the sense of shaping or giving determinate form to) people's intentions.

Social relations in this sense do not exist in an abstract formal space organized purely conceptually, but as determinate actual processes. Just as table takes on its specific character as people coordinate their activities in relation to it, so commodity only comes into being as such as an object is entered into the coordinated sequences of action constituting relations of exchange. Thus a commodity begins in one place as an object actually produced for sale and in the process of being exchanged for money; it is fully realized as such only at its final destination where it passes out of the commodity mode and its uses as an object come into play.[3] It takes only a little imagination to see that all such relations are present in and produced in the organization of activities at the everyday level as well as entering the everyday into relations that pass beyond the control of individual subjects. The child who goes to the corner grocery store to spend her quarter on candy or pop enters into just such a complex of relations. Her simple act and the ordinary intelligibility of the sentence describing it depend upon and are structured by that complex.

This method of thinking shows us a way of examining the actual and immediate organization of the experienced world to disclose its articulation to extended social relations. We begin with a knower, a subject, whose everyday world is determined, shaped, organized by social processes beyond her experience and arising out of the interrelations of many such experienced worlds. They are relations that coordinate and codetermine the worlds, activities, and experiences of people entered into them at different points. Their experience and knowledge of their worlds arise in their active relation to them and are necessarily various; that variety of experience and knowledge is itself organized by the complex of extended relations. The latter necessarily generate different positions and different worlds of experience. Some of these are the ineradicable differences of opposition that enter into and arise out of class struggle. The problematic of the everyday world organizes inquiry into the social relations in back of the everyday worlds in which people's experience is embedded. It opens up the possibility of exploring these relations as they really are, of discovering how they work and how they enter into the organization of the local historical settings of our work and experience and of our encounters with others. The relationships between our Ones and Twos that we tried to fit to the frame of class conceived as a set of formal categories are no longer confined to the imaginary construction of positions in a wholly conceptually structured space. Rather, we can explore the extended social relations that, even in the moment of immediate encounter between One and Two, enter into and structure it, shaping their different bases of experience within it. Working with the everyday world as problematic avoids collapsing differences in perspectives into one another by the methodologies for constructing a metaversion; rather, the object of our inquiry is the social relations establishing the matrices of such differences. And these social relations are real.

Working with the concept of social relation does not deprive subjects of activity. Class is not understood as a secret power behind our backs, determining how we think, how we understand the world, and how we act. Rather class is seen as a complex of social relations coordinating the activities of our everyday worlds with those of others with whom we are not directly connected. Such relations exist only as active practices. While we work and struggle, our everyday acts and intentions are locked into the underlying dynamic of the relations and forces of production and governed by the powers they give rise to.

Figure 27.1 shows the points linked into an intelligible structure as a cube. All at once we can grasp how they are related. The links between points represent the underlying relations determining the positions and how they stand in relation to one another. Figure 27.1 dramatizes how the mutual determination of relationships between positions can be grasped once the underlying relations are brought into view. Each point represents a matrix of the everyday world into which the individual's activities are entered and in which her experience is shaped. Those matrices of the everyday world are substructed by relations we read as relations of class. From any one of these matrices, inquiry leads back into the same set of relations. We can start anywhere and, though seen from a different perspective and experienced differently, the same complex of relations comes into view. We can see One and Two (the sociologist) within the figure, each located at different relational coordinates.

Let us explore, in a very preliminary way, such a set of extended relations as they have been crystallized in Mrs. Pember Reeves's book on the household economies of working-class mothers in London in the early twentieth century.[4] We reach back through an account that has transformed an original multivocality into one voice to a complex of relations in which different matrices of consciousness and experience are generated.

In Mrs. Reeves's study, she tells, among others, of the working day of a working-class woman she calls Mrs. T. Here then is Two, telling of One's life in a text intended for others certainly more like herself than like One. In the textual context, One is the stranger, the other whose life must be told because to the implicit 'we' of the readerly conspiracy it is not familiar (their own daily routines are not a topic). Mrs. Reeves is at

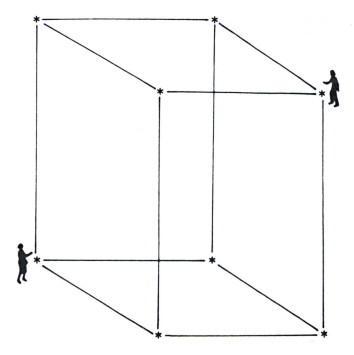

Figure 27.1

work organizing our relationship to Mrs. T., drawing us imperceptibly into the pre-suppositions of the relations that are both strangely visible but also silenced in the text. Here then we will not take the text as it appears in 'document time',[5] detached from the social relations in which it was made *and of which it formed an operative part*. It is treated rather as it gives textual presence to the actualities of the lives of working-class women in a definite and historically specific context of reading.

Much of Mrs. Pember Reeves's account of Mrs. T.'s working day is based on Mrs. T's own account, though we are not given the latter verbatim. Though Mrs. T. does not speak to us directly, she is present in the text as that subject whose experience is its necessary condition.

> *We now come to the day of a mother of six children with two rooms to keep. Mrs. T. . . . is the wife of a builder's handyman on 25s a week. The two rooms are upstairs in a small house, and, as there is no water above ground floor, Mrs. T. has a good deal of carrying of heavy pails of water both upstairs and down. She is gentle and big and slow, never lifts her voice or gets angry, but seems always tired and dragged. She is very clean and orderly. Her husband is away all day; but he dislikes the noise of a family meal and insists on having both breakfast and tea cooked specially for himself, and eats alone.*

> 6:00   *Nurses baby.*
> 6:30   *Gets up, calls five children, puts kettle on, washes 'necks' and 'backs' of all the children, dresses the little ones, does hair of three girls.*
> 7:30   *Gets husband's breakfast, cooks bloater, and makes tea.*

8:00	*Gives him breakfast alone, nurses baby while he has it, and cuts slices of bread and dripping for children.*
8:30	*He goes; gives children breakfast, sends them off to school at 8:50, and has her own.*
9:00	*Clears away and washes up breakfast things.*
9:30	*Carries down slops, and carries up water from the yard; makes beds.*
10:00	*Washes and dresses baby, nurses him, and puts him to bed.*
11:00	*Sweeps out bedroom, scrubs stairs and passage.*
12:00	*Goes out and buys food for the day. Children at home.*
12:25	*Cooks dinner; lays it.*
1:00	*Gives children dinner and nurses baby.*
1:45	*Washes hands and faces, and sees children off to school.*
2:00	*Washes up dinner things, scrubs out kitchen, cleans grate, empties dirty water, and fetches more clean from yard.*
3:00	*Nurses baby.*
3:30	*Cleans herself and begins to mend clothes.*
4:15	*Children all back.*
4:30	*Gives them tea.*
5:00	*Clears away and washes up, nurses the baby, and mends clothes till 6:30.*
6:30	*Cooks husband's tea.*
7:00	*Gives husband tea alone.*
7:30	*Puts younger children to bed.*
8:00	*Tidies up, washes husband's tea things, sweeps kitchen, mends clothes, nurses baby, puts elder children to bed.*
8:45	*Gets husband's supper; mends clothes.*
10:00	*Nurses baby, and makes him comfortable for the night.*
10:30	*Goes to bed.*[6]

The text is the product of a project undertaken by Reeves as a member of the Fabian Women's Group. It reports on a study of whether improving the nutrition of working-class women in late pregnancy and while nursing their babies improved their and the child's overall health. Its very existence is grounded in class relations, and class relations are at work in how the text is constructed as an account of the lives of working-class women *for* an 'educated' middle class. The project itself, the need for a *study* rather than hearing from the women themselves; the taken-for-granted entitlement of the visitor to inquire into the family lives and domestic work and routines of working-class women; the unmentioned quid pro quo that adds to Mrs. T.'s daily work the additional task of keeping a record of her daily routines and weekly budget; the work of editing her account into readable English (for the women Mrs. Reeves wrote about practiced, according to her, at best a phonetic spelling), and its entry into the textual discourse of early twentieth-century English socialists: all these are practices articulated to the class relations of the England of that period. This was a time in which women of the dominant classes were active in the management of the working-class family. They were involved in what we have in the past described rather contemptuously as 'charities'; they supported women's organization in trade unions; they were concerned with working-class housing, with working-class health and nutrition, with the training of working-class women for motherhood, and so forth. This text is situated in this context of an active organization of class in which women of the dominant classes played a leading role. The interests of the Fabian Women's Group in the nutrition and health of working-class mothers and their newborn children are located in a class-based concern about the health, nutrition, living conditions, and education of the working class, which first arose, in Britain, in the context of recruiting for imperialist wars that exhibited the physical inadequacies of working-class men as military 'material'.[7] This then is the site of the text and of the relevances that organize it.

Returning to the text, we can see aspects of the structuring of Mrs. T.'s work and experience and how these are organized in relations beyond her narrow domestic world. Her daily routine is powerfully structured by the employment and school schedules of her husband and children. Let us focus on the children and their relationship to school. First, school attendance is required, and the timing of the children's coming and going and its meshing with her husband's employment schedule are primary organizers of meal times and bedtimes and hence of how her domestic work has to be allocated to spaces in between the disjunctures created by the timing of their meals and the like. Her work cannot be organized in accordance with its own logic. But more is involved than cooking and scheduling meals to fit these external schedules. Mrs. T. includes in her daily routine washing the children's necks and backs, those parts of their bodies that the children themselves either cannot easily reach or see and might miss or skip. She washes them before school in the morning, and she also washes their hands and faces before they return to school after lunch. We notice that Mrs. T. must fetch water from the yard and carry it upstairs, and then she must carry the slops downstairs to dispose of. At school these children will be inspected by the teacher for their cleanliness. They are going to have the backs of their necks and their hands scrutinized. The children's cleanliness and Mrs. T.'s care to ensure they go to school clean are enforced by the school, whatever personal pride Mrs. T. may take in her children's appearance. The school's concern, enforced by the teacher, with the cleanliness of working-class children has arisen as part of the same concern as that which motivates Mrs. Reeves's study. The dominant classes have taken steps to manage the health of the working class and the working-class family, and the school is one agent through which these new managerial concerns are implemented. When we make the link between the work organization of Mrs. T.'s day and the school, the way in which the state through the school enters into that organization can be discerned in the background.

We can see thus how Mrs. T. in a curious way comes to act as an agent of this external authority vis-à-vis her children, at least in this matter. She is constrained to enforce in the home the order imposed by the school. But the relation does not appear in this way. We begin to see that the working relationships among women and men and parents and children sharing a household cannot be understood as if families formed autonomous systems. While Reeves's orientation and description isolate Mrs. T.'s work process, giving it a self-contained character, ours anchors it in the same complex of social relations in which the study arises and which the text 'expresses'.

The use of a historical example bars us forever from moving beyond the text or outside it, to talk to Mrs. T. directly. But the explication of experience as such is not the objective of this sociology for women. The use of a historical example places it in any case out of reach. Yet we see that there is a way of addressing the other side of the dissevered relationship between the women sociologist or Fabian socialist who tells the tale and those others mute but for her text who are somehow given presence in it. To take up the exploration and analysis of the social relations in which One's life is embedded is to take up the organization of her experience not as an external system but as a world, the social character of which arises in the constant ongoing intercoordination of actual activities. The reality of the relations that organize the encounter between One and Two and the ways in which Two may represent One in the texts of her discourse are an ongoing accomplishment. All the features of the world that Reeves puts before us exist (are constituted?) in social relations in which these named objects are accomplished in their quiddity.

The work of women such as Mrs. T. enters social relations such as these and is part of their formation. These relations also organize and determine their work. We understand then the reciprocal or dialectical character of social relations, for they arise in the coordering of people's work while their specific properties also organize the work process at the local historical level. Mrs. T.'s household and family are organized in determinate ways in the context of school and wage labor. They do not stand suspended as an instance of an abstract family located in an abstracted conceptual space. Rather they are clearly a work organization sustained on a daily basis by its members and continually organized and reorganized by how its members' work practices take up such material exigencies as a capitalist market in real estate and rental properties; as the enforcement of school and the authority of school authorities to examine children's cleanliness; by the specific character of the local organization of retail stores, transportation, and the like; by opportunity for additional nutritional support conditional upon allowing Mrs. Reeves and others like her to come into the home, to look about, and to approve or disapprove the housewife's dispositions. Here is the matrix of experience and an everyday world, the problematic of which we have sought to open up (in a very preliminary way). The conjunction in this book of Mrs. T.'s absent but determining experience and Mrs. Reeves's own speaking is not irrelevant. It is precisely here that we can explore the relations in which both are implicated and active and in which the account itself, *Round about a Pound a Week*, is embedded. It is precisely in these relations that we discover class and its actual character as a routine, daily accomplishment.

The sociologist inside the whale

Mrs. Reeves's study enables us to hold at a historical distance the relations we are concerned with exploring. Reaching through her work, we discover the presence of others who do not speak directly to us; through her work we have discovered the relations at work in it through which those others have been silenced. We see her text as a moment in the organization of those relations. In returning from the past to reflect upon our present, we discover our own sociological texts as moments in the organization of relations within which our work is embedded. Redesigning the relationship between sociologist and those she learns from in her investigations is not enough. Any such reconstruction still bears the determinations of the extended relations within which the encounters between sociologist and the subject are embedded. The methodology of its writing structures how it enters into the organization of the social relations that it bears.

Texts are organizers of social relations. Methods of writing them produce their capacity to organize. Sociological methods of writing texts produce accounts relating ourselves as readers to those of whom they speak in a relation of ruling. Of course we do not magically transform those relations by writing our texts in different ways. We have to recognize the real limitations of what our work can do. But a discipline such as sociology has developed powerful methods for producing texts that will operate in the extended relations of ruling. What we have focused upon here is how to produce alternatives that will go beyond the reporting of experience to the development of a knowledge of the social relations within which we work and struggle as subjects. We are seeking methods of inquiry *and* of writing sociology that organize the relation between the text and those of whom the text speaks as 'cosubjects' in a world we make – and destroy – together.

The alternative I have been developing here begins with people as subjects active in the same world as we are situated in as bodies. Subject is located at the beginning of her acts – work and other practical activities; through these she joins with others, known and unknown, in bringing into being a world that they have, but do not necessarily know, in common. The objects of our worlds, whether concrete (cigarettes, tables, horses, or microchips) or relational (commodities, gifts, capital), are accomplishments of ongoing courses of action in which many are implicated. These are actual activities; their concerting or coordering is an ongoing process.

The multiple perspectives of subjects, the multiple possible versions of the world arising in subjects' experience, create a problem for sociology only when our project is to establish a sociological version superseding theirs. It is a difficulty that arises largely from grounding sociology in 'meaning', 'interpretation', 'common understandings' and the like rather than in an ongoing coordering of actual activities accomplished in definite local historical settings. But when the latter is our ontology (the mode in which the social can be conceived as existing), then our business is to explore the ongoing socially ordered matrices differentiating experience and the extended social relations immanent in the everyday. These are actual in the simple sense that they arise in the coordering of actual activities, and they go beyond or underneath the stories people know how to tell about their lives through which what we call their experience or perspectives become part of the same world as that we are investigating. We recognize actual social relations arising in the concerting of human sensuous activity, hence objectively. Though such relations may not be already known-in-common, they may indeed be known. They may be explored, discovered, analyzed, and described.

The relation of subject to the extended relations organizing her local and immediate experience is that limned in the formulation of Marx's problematic: 'Individuals always started, and always start, from themselves. Their relations are the relations of their real life. How does it happen that their relations assume an independent existence over against them? And that the forces of their own life overpower them?'[8] As Marx developed his investigation it came to focus exclusively upon the impersonal relations in which subjects disappear as such. While he was careful to mark the shift from the concrete and 'subjective' to the constitution of the objective relations of the economy, those who have followed him have not. As his theories have been developed, subjects have been seen as totally subdued to the driving historical dynamic of capitalist forces and relations. In the thinking of some notable contemporaries they have been wholly displaced, surviving on the ontological margins, inhabiting the foxholes of functional positions, subjected to the massive on-rolling of structures lurching toward obscure destinies. Whether these are proper extensions of Marx's thinking or not is not an issue here. They are certainly totally at odds with this, perhaps any, feminist method of inquiry, for we insist on preserving the subject as active and competent and as the knower of inquiry, the knower to whom our texts should speak. We insist on recognizing our active presence as doer as well as knower and our active part in the making of relations that pass beyond the scope of our direct knowledge and power to change. I am not concerned to be faithful to Marx or to a Marxist tradition, but only to seize upon what it offers us as a means of exploring the dynamic of relations in which our lives are caught up and which are continually at work in transforming the bases and contexts of our existence and our struggles. It is only a Marxist ontology that is capable of projecting an ontology grounded in the activities of actual subjects beyond the immediately observable and known. We need such an ontological consistency if we are going to be able to move from the local matrices of experience, directly known, to extended relations beyond our direct knowledge. At the same time the standpoint of women anchors Marxist methods of thinking and inquiry. It insists that its grasp of the world be constrained not by a discourse organized for the theoretical subject tucking his own life out of sight, but for subjects situated outside discourse in the actualities of their everyday worlds. Among them, of course, is the sociological inquirer herself, a member of the same world she explores, active in the same relations as those for whom she writes.

   Like Jonah, she is inside the whale. Only of course she is one among the multiplicity of subjects whose coordered activity constitutes whale. Like the astronomer, she is of and inside the cosmos she seeks to understand. Her opportunities, her curiosities, as well as her limitations derive from just this necessary standpoint. To discover and explicate its actual character and relations depend upon recognizing that she is indeed located, that her seeing is mediated (by texts for example), that her work is located in definite social relations, that she is always and ineluctably an insider. Her own seeing arises in a context structured by the same system of social relations structuring the everyday worlds of those whose experience provides the problematic of her inquiry. Her only route to a faithful telling that does not privilege the perspectives arising in the sites of her sociological project and her participation in a sociological discourse is to commit herself to an inquiry that is ontologically faithful, faithful to the presence and activity of subjects and faithful to the actualities of the world that arises for her, for them, for all of us, in the ongoing coordering of our actual practices, both those within and those beyond our reach.

Notes

1   Karl Marx (1976) *Grundrisse: Foundations of the Critique of Political Economy*, New York: Random House.
2   Karl Marx and Friedrich Engels (1970) *The German Ideology*, New York: International Publishers.
3   See Karl Marx (1977) *Capital: A Critique of Political Economy*, New York: Vintage Books.
4   Mrs Pember Reeves (1913) *Round about a Pound a Week*, London: G. Bell & Sons.

5   Cf. Dorothy E. Smith (1974) 'The social construction of documentary reality', *Social Inquiry* 44(4): 257–68.
6   Reeves, *Round about a Pound a Week*, pp. 167–8.
7   See Anna Davin (1978) 'Imperialism and motherhood', *History Workshop: A Journal of Socialist Historians*, 5 (Spring): 9–65.
8   Karl Marx and Friedrich Engels (1973) *Feuerbach: Oppositions of the Materialist and Idealist Outlooks*, London: Lawrence & Wishart, p. 90.

Chapter 28

Paul Willis

SYMBOLIC CREATIVITY [1990]

(**Source**: Willis, Paul (1990) *Common Culture: Symbolic Work at Play in the Everyday Cultures of the Young* (with Simon Jones, Joyce Canaan and Geoff Hurd), Buckingham: Open University Press, pp. 9–13, 17–22, 26–7)

Editor's introduction

This extract is from Paul Willis's book *Common Culture: Symbolic Work at Play in the Everyday Cultures of the Young*. The book was an outcome of research into the cultural activities of young people directed by Willis and financed by the Gulbenkian Foundation in 1987–8. *Common Culture* is the result of various research projects (as Willis is the first to point out) that feed into the book, informing its theoretical agenda and providing its empirical evidence. Alongside Willis the list of researchers involved in this project reads like a virtual who's who of British cultural studies in the 1980s and 1990s: Simon Frith, Celia Lury, Angela McRobbie, Kobena Mercer, Graham Murdock and Mica Nava. While many of those named might distance themselves from Willis's optimistic rendering of youth creativity and his subsequent downplaying of the more disciplinary aspect of everyday life, Willis's work echoes a number of concerns evident within cultural studies at this time.

This extract then can (uneasily) represent a moment in cultural studies' attention to everyday life, where the everyday comes to register creativity, subversion and subcultural appropriation. This of course is not to claim that such a version of cultural studies ever understood the everyday as *always* and *only* exhibiting resistance (such an assessment would undoubtedly be fairly bizarre). Rather the orientation of Willis's work might be seen (like Michel de Certeau's) to attempt to register how people are not *reducible* to their domination. To do this Willis insists that the everyday witnesses an outpouring of activity, which although not (yet) recognised as 'art' shares the same symbolic creativity as art practices. In this Willis is not simply reclaiming the everyday as a creative realm he is (crucially) revaluing the everyday.

Where Willis might differ from de Certeau is the concern with identity. For de Certeau identity already assumes a number of operational categories that might hide more than they reveal about practices of everyday life. Perhaps Willis's privileging of identity is inevitable given that he starts out his ethnography by attending to 'identifiable' groups ('bikers', 'youth') where 'identity' is a powerful and lively currency.

Further reading: de Certeau 1984; Fiske 1989; McRobbie 1991; Willis 1977, 2000.

Necessary work and symbolic creativity

Our project is to uncover, explore and present symbolic creativity in everyday life. Apart from merely asserting its importance and, we hope, demonstrating its existence, why do we insist on the visceral connection of symbolic creativity to the everyday? At bottom, what anchors it?

We argue that symbolic creativity is not only part of everyday human activity, but also a necessary part. This is because it is an integral part of *necessary work* – that which has to be done every day, that which is not extra but essential to ensure the daily production and reproduction of human existence. It is this which actually guarantees and locks in the relevance of symbolic creativity. It is this which underlies claims that the real roots of art lie in the everyday. But of what kind of necessary work do we speak? What is the basis for including symbolic creativity in it?

Necessary work is taken usually to designate the application of human capacities through the action of tools on raw materials to produce goods and services, usually through wage labour, to satisfy physical human needs. Certainly the role of symbolic creativity in this should not be underestimated. The English radical tradition[1] has stressed the dignity of labour and has sought in different ways to unify a certain view of living art with skill in work. William Morris, of course, proposed the famous general equation art = work/pleasure. Working and writing in the 1920s and 1930s of this century Eric Gill[2] is perhaps the clearest, most trenchant and most recent exponent of this tradition.

For him art was the principle of skill in the making of useful things well. For him work was holy. The daily reproduction of our lives was holy. It was the play of symbolic creativity in these things which made them holy.

Unfortunately, it was evident in Gill's time, now overwhelming, that, despite the continuing human need for creativity in useful activity, modern industry has all but destroyed the possibility of 'art' in paid work. Machine production took the craft tool out of the craft hand. This more or less destroyed the possibilities of creativity at work. Automatic production takes hand, tool and body altogether out of the workplace! It is simply an idealism now to speak of 'holy' work. Nor will anyone pay the price of 'holy poverty' necessary to reintroduce 'holy work'.

But there is another kind of humanly necessary work – often unrecognized but equally necessary – *symbolic work*. This is the application of human capacities to and through, on and with symbolic resources and raw materials (collections of signs and symbols – for instance, the language as we inherit it as well as texts, songs, films, images and artefacts of all kinds) to produce meanings. This is broader than, logically prior to and a condition of material production, but its 'necessariness' has been forgotten.

Necessary symbolic work is necessary simply because humans are communicating as well as producing beings. Perhaps they are communicative before they are product-ive. Whilst all may not be productive, all are communicative. *All*. This is our species distinction. Nor is this a merely formal or physiological property that might lie unused in some. Only through its exercise does communication exist and all of us communi-cate. This is how we manifest and produce the social and dynamic nature of our humanity.

We argue that necessary symbolic work is spread across the whole of life. It is a condition of it, and of our daily humanity. Those who stress the separateness, the sublime and quintessential in 'art' have actually assumed and encouraged a mindlessly vulgar, materialist view of everyday life. They counterpose this to their view of 'the imaginative'. They thereby view daily life as a cultural desert. The imagined symbolic deficit of everyday life is then, in its turn, to be repaired by recourse to a free-floating 'imaginative realm', to 'useless things', to 'art for art's sake', to the 'socially redun-dant'. But this is not only circular, it's incoherent. It's like trying to make time go faster by speeding up clocks. 'Art' is taken as the *only* field of qualitative symbolic activity, the one-per-cent transcendental value that preserves humanity. As daily life is drained of its symbolic work, 'art' is grotesquely bloated till its pores leak pure imagination. And only from 'art' can come a cultural mission into the humdrum, a doomed attempt to save the masses. Again 'art' produces culture. Symbolic work starts, not ends, in separate artefacts. The imaginative is self-validating!

We insist, against this, that imagination is not extra to daily life, something to be supplied from disembodied 'art'. It is part of the necessariness of everyday symbolic and communicative work. If declared redundant here, it will certainly not be welcomed back in the finer robes of 'art'.

This point cannot be overstated: where we can't now realistically acknowledge and promote the prospect of symbolic creativity in the sinews of necessary work as material production, we can and must recognize symbolic creativity in the sinews of necessary work as symbolic production.

What are some of the basic elements of necessary symbolic work?

First, language as a practice and symbolic resource. Language is the primary instrument that we use to communicate. It is the highest ordering of our sensuous impressions of the world, and the ultimate basis of our hope and capacity to control it. It enables interaction and solidarity with others and allows us to assess our impact on others and theirs on us. It therefore allows us to see ourselves as others.

Second, the active body as a practice and symbolic resource. The body is a site of somatic knowledge as well as a set of signs and symbols. It is the source of productive and communicative activity – signing, symbolizing, feeling.

Third, drama as a practice and symbolic resource. Communicative interaction with others is not automatic. We do not communicate from head to head through wires drilled into our skulls. Communication is achieved through roles, rituals and performances that we produce with others. Dramaturgical components of the sym-bolic include a variety of non-verbal communications, as well as sensuous cultural practices and communal solidarities. These include dancing, singing, joke-making, story-telling in dynamic settings and through performance.

Fourth and most importantly, symbolic creativity. Language, the body, dramatic forms are, in a way, both raw material and tools. Symbolic creativity is more fully the practice, the making – or their essence, what all practices have in common, what drives them. This is the production of *new* (however small the shift) meanings intrinsically attached to feeling, to energy, to excitement and psychic movement. This is the basis of confidence in dynamic human capacities as realities rather than as potentials – to be made conscious, through some concrete practice or active mediation, of the quality of human consciousness and how it can further be developed through the exercise and application of vital powers. Symbolic creativity can be seen as roughly equivalent to what an all-embracing and inclusive notion of the living arts might include (counterposed, of course, to the current exclusions of 'art'.) Symbolic creativity may be individual and/or collective. It transforms what is provided and helps to produce specific forms of human identity and capacity. Being human – human be-ing-ness – means to be creative in the sense of remaking the world for ourselves as we make and find our own place and identity.

What exactly is produced by symbolic work and symbolic creativity?

First, and perhaps most important, they produce and reproduce individual identities – who and what 'I am' and could become. These may be diffuse, contradictory or decentred but they are produced through symbolic work including struggles to make meaning. Sensuous human communicative activities are also intersubjective. It is through knowing 'the other', including recognizing the self as an other for some others, that a self or selves can be known at all.

Second, symbolic work and creativity place identities in larger wholes. Identities do not stand alone above history, beyond history. They are related in time, place and things. It is symbolic work and creativity which realize the structured collectivity of individuals as well as their differences, which realize the materiality of context as well as the symbolism of self. This reminds us that locations and situations are not only *determinations* – they're also relations and resources to be discovered, explored and experienced. Memberships of race, class, gender, age and region are not only learned, they're lived and experimented with. This is so even if only by pushing up against the oppressive limits of established order and power.

Third and finally, symbolic work and especially creativity develop and affirm our active senses of our own vital capacities, the powers of the self and how they might be applied to the cultural world. This is what makes activity and identity *transitive* and specifically human. It is the dynamic and, therefore, clinching part of identity. It is the expectation of being able to apply power to the world to change it – however minutely. It is how, in the future, there is some human confidence that unities may be formed out of confusion, patterns out of irregularity. This is to be able to make judgements on who's a friend, who's an enemy, when to talk, when to hold silence, when to go, when to stop. But it's also associated with, and helps to form, overall styles of thinking which promise to make most sense of the world for you. It's also a cultural sense of what symbolic forms – languages, images, musics, haircuts, styles, clothes – 'work' most economically and creatively for the self. A culturally learned sense of the powers of the self is what makes the self in connecting it to others and to the world.

In many ways this is directly a question of cultural survival for many young people. Processes of symbolic work and symbolic creativity are very open, contested and unstable under conditions of late modernization. All young people experience one aspect or another of the contemporary 'social condition' of youth: unwilling economic dependence on parents and parental homes; uncertainty regarding future planning;

powerlessness and lack of control over immediate circumstances of life; feelings of symbolic as well as material marginality to the main society; imposed institutional and ideological constructions of 'youth' which privilege certain readings and definitions of what young people should do, feel or be.[3]

Many of the traditional resources of, and inherited bases for, social meaning, membership, security and psychic certainty have lost their legitimacy for a good proportion of young people. There is no longer a sense of a 'whole culture' with allocated places and a shared, universal value system. Organized religion, the monarchy trade unions, schools, public broadcasting, high culture and its intertwinings with public culture no longer supply ready values and models of duty and meaning to help structure the passage into settled adulthood. This is certainly partly a result of much commented-upon wider processes related to late modernization: secularization; consumerism; individualization; decollectivization; weakening respect for authority; new technologies of production and distribution. But it is also the case that these inherited traditions owe their still continuing and considerable power to the stakes they offer and seem to offer to the individual: some graspable identity within a set of relationships to other identities; some notion of citizenship within a larger whole which offers rights, satisfactions and loyalties as well as duty and submission. However, for many young people, made to feel marginal to this society, and without their own material stake in it, these merely symbolic stakes can seem very remote. These public traditions and meanings cannot make good what they offer, because they are undercut at another more basic level by unfulfilled expectations. These things are for parents and adults, for those who have an interest in and make up the civil body. For the young black British they're even more remote – they are for other people's parents. No longer can we be blind to the 'whiteness' of our major traditional public sources of identity.

Young working-class women may experience this youth condition in a special way. On the one hand they are a target consumption group for many home commodities as well as for feminine-style-and-identity products. On the other hand, and with no money recompense and no real power in the consumer market, they may be making partial, early and exploited 'transitions' (often in an imperceptible extension of childhood domestic chores 'naturally' expected of girls but not of boys) into domestic roles of care and maintenance. This may seem to be a destination of sorts and a meaningful, useful activity when labour-market opportunities are scarce or difficult, but it can often be a specific unofficial training and subjective preparation for a lifetime's future of domestic drudgery coupled with job 'opportunities' only in part-time, low-paid, insecure, usually dead-end 'female' service work.

Commodities and consumerism

The main cultural materials and resources used in the symbolic work of leisure are cultural commodities. They are supplied to the market overwhelmingly by the commercial cultural industries and media for profit. Indeed it was the market discovery, exploitation and development in the 1950s and 1960s of a newly defined affluent and expanding consumer group of young people which produced the popular conception of 'the teenager'.[4] We're currently experiencing a renewed and it seems even less caring emphasis on market forces in cultural matters. The rise of leisure we've referred to is really the rise of commercialized leisure. Does this matter? Does their production in a commercial nexus devalue cultural commodities and the contents of the cultural media?

There is a strange unanimity – and ghostly embrace of their opposites – between left and right when it comes to a condemnation of consumerism and especially of the penetration of the market into cultural matters. It is the profane in the Temple for the artistic establishment. For some left cultural analysts it constitutes a widened field of exploitation which is in and for itself unwelcome; now workers are exploited in their leisure as well as in their work. The circuit of domination is complete with no escape from market relations.

We disagree with both assessments, especially with their shared underlying pessimism. They both ignore the dynamic and living qualities of everyday culture and especially their necessary work and symbolic creativity. These things have always been in existence, though usually ignored or marginalized. They continue to be ignored even when an extraordinary development and transformation of them are in progress. For symbolic work and creativity mediate, and are simultaneously expanded and developed *by*, the uses, meanings and 'effects' of cultural commodities. Cultural commodities are catalyst, not product; a stage in, not the destination of, cultural affairs. Consumerism now has to be understood as an active, not a passive, process. Its play includes work.

If it ever existed at all, the old 'mass' has been culturally emancipated into popularly differentiated cultural citizens through exposure to a widened circle of commodity relations. These things have supplied a much widened range of usable symbolic resources for the development and emancipation of everyday culture. Certainly this emancipation has been partial and contradictory because the consumer industries have sought to provide some of the contents and certainly the forms as well as the possibilities for cultural activity. Consumerism continuously reproduces an image of, and therefore helps to encourage, selfishness and narcissism in individualized consumption and hedonism. But those tendencies are now given features of our cultural existence. It is the so far undervalued balance of development and emancipation which has to be grasped. As we shall see, the images and offers of consumerism are not always taken at face value, nor are 'individualized' forms of consciousness as socially isolated and self-regarding as the pessimists suppose. Meanwhile a whole continent of informal, everyday culture has been recognized, opened up and developed.

Capitalism and its images speak directly to desire for its own profit. But in that very process it breaks down or short-circuits limiting customs and taboos. It will do anything and supply any profane material in order to keep the cash tills ringing. But, in this, commerce discovered, *by exploiting*, the realm of necessary symbolic production within the undiscovered continent of the informal. No other agency has recognized this realm or supplied it with usable symbolic materials. And commercial entrepreneurship of the cultural field has discovered something real. For whatever self-serving reasons it was accomplished, we believe that this is an historical *recognition*. It counts and is irreversible. Commercial cultural forms have helped to produce an historical present from which we cannot now escape and in which there are many more materials – no matter what we think of them – available for necessary symbolic work than ever there were in the past.[5] Out of these come forms not dreamt of in the commercial imagination and certainly not in the official one – forms which make up common culture.

The hitherto hidden continent of the informal (including resources and practices drawn from traditional folk and working-class culture) produces, therefore, from cultural commodities much expounded, unprefigured and exciting effects – and this is why, of course, commerce keeps returning to the streets and common culture to find its next commodities. There is a fundamental and unstable contradictoriness in commercial rationality and instrumentality when it comes to consumer cultural goods. Blanket condemnations of market capitalism will never find room for it or understand it.

For our argument perhaps the basic complexity to be unravelled is this. Whereas it may be said that work relations and the drive for efficiency now hinge upon *the suppression* of informal symbolic work in most workers, the logic of the cultural and leisure industries hinges on the opposite tendency: a form of *their enablement and release*. Whereas the ideal model for the worker is the good time kept, the disciplined and empty head, the model for the good consumer is the converse – a head full of unbounded appetites for symbolic things.

Oddly and ironically, it is from capitalism's own order of priorities, roles, rules and instrumentalities *in production* (ironically, of leisure goods and services too) that informal cultures seek escape and alternatives in capitalist leisure *consumption*. Commerce appears twice in the cultural argument, as that which is to be escaped from and that which provides the means and materials for alternatives. Modern capitalism is now not only parasitic upon the puritan ethic, but also upon its instability and even its subversion.

There is a widespread view that these means and materials, the cultural media and cultural commodities, must appeal to the lowest common denominators of taste. Not only do they have no intrinsic value but, more disturbingly, they may have coded-in negative values which manipulate, cheapen, degrade and even brutalize the sensibilities of 'the masses'.

In contradiction we argue that there is no such thing as an autonomous artefact capable of printing its own intrinsic values, one way, on human sensibility. This is to put a ludicrous (actually crude Marxist) emphasis on *production* and what is held to be initially coded into artefacts.

What has been forgotten is that circumstances change cases, contexts change texts. The received view of aesthetics suggests that the aesthetic effect is internal to the text, and a universal property of its form. This places the creative impulse squarely on the material productions of the 'creative' artist, with the reception or consumption of art wholly determined by its aesthetic form, palely reflecting what is timelessly coded within the text. Against this we want to rehabilitate consumption, creative consumption, to see creative potentials in it for itself, rather than see it as the dying fall of the usual triplet: production, reproduction, reception. We are interested to explore how far 'meanings' and 'effects' can change quite decisively according to the social contexts of 'consumption', to different kinds of 'de-coding' and worked on by different forms of symbolic work and creativity. We want to explore how far *grounded* aesthetics are part, not of things, but of processes involving consumption, processes which make consumption pleasurable and vital. Viewers, listeners and readers do their own symbolic work on a text and create their own relationships to technical means of reproduction and transfer. There is a kind of cultural production all within consumption.

Young TV viewers, for instance, have become highly critical and literate in visual forms, plot conventions and cutting techniques. They listen, often highly selectively, to pop music now within a whole shared history of pop styles and genres. These knowledges clearly mediate the meanings of texts. The fact that many texts may be classified as intrinsically banal, contrived and formalistic must be put against the possibility that their living reception is the opposite of these things.

The 'productive' reception of and work on texts and artefacts can also be the start of a social process which results in its own more concrete productions, either of new forms or of recombined existing ones. Perhaps we should see the 'raw materials' of cultural life, of communications and expressions, as always intermediate. They are the products of one process as well as the raw materials for another, whose results can be, in turn, raw materials for successive groups. Why shouldn't bedroom decoration and personal styles, combinations of others' 'productions', be viewed along with creative writing or song and music composition as fields of aesthetic realization? Furthermore the grounded appropriation of new technology and new hardware may open new possibilities for expression, or recombinations of old ones, which the dominant culture misses because it does not share the same conditions and contradictory pressures of that which is to be explained or come to terms with.

Our basic point is that human consumption does not simply repeat the relations of production – and whatever cynical motives lie behind them. Interpretation, symbolic action and creativity are *part* of consumption. They're involved in the whole realm of necessary symbolic work. This work is at least as important as whatever might originally be encoded in commodities and can often produce their opposites. Indeed some aspects of 'profanity' in commercial artefacts may be liberating and progressive, introducing the possibility of the new and the socially dynamic.

It is pointless and limiting to judge artefacts *alone*, outside their social relations of consumption, with only the tutored critic's opinion of an internal aesthetic allowed to count. This is what limits the 'Official Arts' in their institutions. People bring living identities to commerce and the consumption of cultural commodities as well as being formed there. They bring experiences, feelings, social position and social memberships to their encounter with commerce. Hence they bring a necessary creative symbolic pressure, not only to make sense of cultural commodities, but partly through them also to make sense of contradiction and structure as they experience them in school, college, production, neighbourhood, and as members of certain genders, races, classes and ages. The results of this necessary symbolic work may be quite different from anything initially coded into cultural commodities.

Grounded aesthetics

As we have used the term so far, 'symbolic creativity' is an abstract concept designating a human capacity almost in general. It only exists, however, in contexts and, in particular, sensuous living processes. To identify the particular dynamic of symbolic activity and transformation in concrete named situations we propose the term 'grounded aesthetic'. This is the creative element in a process whereby meanings are attributed to symbols and practices and where symbols and practices are selected, reselected, highlighted and recomposed to resonate further appropriated and particularized meanings. Such dynamics are emotional as well as cognitive. There are as many aesthetics as there are grounds for them to operate in. Grounded aesthetics are the yeast of common culture.

We have deliberately used the term 'aesthetic' to show both the differences and the continuities of what we are trying to say with respect to the culture and arts debate. We are certainly concerned with what might be called principles of beauty, but as qualities of living symbolic activities rather than as qualities of things; as ordinary aspects of common culture, rather than as extraordinary aspects of uncommon culture. This is the sense of our clumsy but strictly accurate use of 'grounded'.

Our 'groundedness' for some will seem simply no more than the reckless destruction of flight, potting birds of paradise with sociological lead. For others the strange search for archaic aesthetics in grounded, everyday social relations will seem perverse, un-material and even mystical. We're happy to work on the assumption that 'the truth' lies somewhere, always provisionally, in between, that human be-ing-ness needs both air and earth and, in turn, makes possible our very idea of both.

Within the process of creating meanings from and within the use of symbols there may be a privileged role for texts and artefacts, but a grounded aesthetic can also be an element and a quality of everyday social relations. For instance, there is a dramaturgy and poetics of everyday life, of social presence, encounter and event. It may have become invisible in the routinized roles of adult life, but the young have much more time and they face each other with fewer or more fragile masks. They are the practical existentialists. They sometimes have no choice but to be, often too, absorbed in the moment and to ransack immediate experience for grounded aesthetics. For them some features of social life may not be about the regulation and containment of tension, but about its creation and increase. The 'aimless' life of groups and gangs may be about producing something from nothing, from 'doing nothing'. It may be about building tensions, shaping grounded aesthetics, orchestrating and shaping their release and further build-ups, so that a final 'catharsis' takes with it or changes other tensions and stresses inherent in the difficulties of their condition. Making a pattern in an induced swirl of events can produce strangely still centres of heightened awareness where time is held and unusual control and insight are possible. Grounded aesthetics are what lift and mark such moments.

Grounded aesthetics are the specifically creative and dynamic moments of a whole process of cultural life, of cultural birth and rebirth. To know the cultural world, our relationship to it, and ultimately to know ourselves, it is necessary not merely to be in it but to change – however minutely – that cultural world. This is a making specific – in relation to the social group or individual and its conditions of life – of the ways in which the received natural and social world is made human *to them* and made, to however small a degree (even if finally symbolic), controllable by them.

Against post-modernist pessimism

The much commented upon incandescence – instability, changeability, luminosity – of cultural commodities ('all that is solid melts into air')[6] is not some form of spontaneous combustion in commodities or another 'wonder' of capitalist production. It is not without or against meaning. This very incandescence passes through *necessary symbolic work*, changes and enables it. The incandescence is not simply a surface market quality. It produces, is driven by, and reproduces further forms and varieties for everyday symbolic work and creativity, some of which remain in the everyday and in common culture far longer than they do on the market.

The market is the source of a permanent and contradictory revolution in everyday culture which sweeps away old limits and dependencies. The markets' restless search to find and make new appetites raises, wholesale, the popular currency of symbolic aspiration. The currency may be debased and inflationary, but aspirations now circulate, just as do commodities. That circulation irrevocably makes or finds its own new worlds.

The style and media theorists – and terrorists – of the left and right see only market incandescence. They warn us of an immanent semiotic implosion of all that is real. They call us to a strange rejection of all that glitters and shimmers over the dark landscape, as if it *were* the landscape. But this usually metropolitan neurosis is nothing more than a bad case of idealist theorists' becoming the victims of their own nightmares. Mistaking their own metaphors for reality, they are hoist by their own semiotic petards. They are caught by – defined in professionally charting – the symbolic life on the surface of things without seeing, because not implicated in, the *necessary* everyday role of symbolic work, of how sense is made of structure and contradiction. They then coolly announce that modern culture is all surface in danger of collapse.

We must catch up with the movement of the real world. We must not be satisfied with a phantom history and demonology of its surface movement. Above all, self-deluding and complacent beliefs in aesthetic self-sufficiency and separateness, as sanctuaries in and against an imaginary history, must be firmly rejected.

Commerce and consumerism have helped to release a profane explosion of everyday symbolic life and activity. The genie of common culture is out of the bottle – let out by commercial carelessness. Not stuffing it back in, but seeing what wishes may be granted, should be the stuff of our imagination.

Notes

1   We are thinking of the line that runs through from Cobbett, Blake, Ruskin and William Morris.
2   See, for instance, *A Holy Tradition of Working*, Golgonooza Press, 1983.
3   For a full account of the 'new social condition of youth' in relation to youth unemployment, see P. Willis *et al.*, *The Youth Review*, Avebury, 1988.
4   See the first major study of youth culture in Britain, Mark Abrams, *The Teenage Consumer*, London Press Exchange, 1959.
5   We're bending the stick of argument here to emphasize how cultural products are creatively *used*, rather than passively *consumed*. We should not, of course, ignore the continuing ubiquity of forms of direct cultural production such as writing, photography and 'storying' (c.f. D. Morley and K. Worpole, *The Republic of Letters*, Comedia, 1981; S. Beszceret and P. Corrigan, *Towards a Different Image*, Comedia/Methuen, 1986; S. Yeo, *Whose Story?*, Blackwell, 1990). Equally, against élitism,

we should recall activities like knitting and gardening as combining both production and use. Our general argument here should not obscure that varieties of such 'home produce' are important fields for symbolic work and creativity.

6   The title of a book by Marshall Berman (Simon & Schuster, New York, 1982) which helped to launch the many faceted and pervasive post-modern debate.

Everyday things

INTRODUCTION TO PART FIVE

THE STUDY OF MATERIAL culture clearly has an enormous affinity with the study of everyday life. The investigation of 'things' as they are made, used, discarded, refound, loved and loathed is central to everyday life studies. Our modern life-world contains objects and material practices that connect us to a lived relationship with culture. *How* this culture is lived is a question that concerns a variety of approaches to everyday life. Modern material culture is marked by the machinations of capitalism (where exchange-value triumphs over use-value) at the same time it is also marked by our most intimate experience of the world. An item of clothing or a piece of crockery can evidence a mode of production relentlessly driven by the desire for profit, while simultaneously being a vehicle for personal memories, unfulfilled longings, or aspirational desire. A trip to the shops can be a routine task (the endless replacing of exhausted commodities) or can be filled with the kinds of ecstasy that was traditionally linked with sacred rituals.

Negotiating this ambiguity is not an easy task and the question of whether to privilege the personal, the singular, and the intimate, or the structural, the anonymous, and the institutional is a perennial problem for attending to everyday life. It is no surprise then that the kinds of attention that have been directed towards 'everyday things' are often driven by a dialectical approach that continually weaves together the particular and the general. For instance a dialectical approach can look at modern commodity culture as the promotion of individuality; yet while looking at individuality as a personal experience it can also examine the way that 'individuality' is a social process that exists at a very general level (individualism as being peddled to all). The fetish aspect of modern commodities also provides a way of negotiating between the particular and the general. To think of commodities as 'fetishes' in the way that Marx did is to recognise that they are often invested with magical properties available to all with the power to purchase. However, since Freud, the term fetish resonates with the psychic dynamics of personal histories, where 'things' are endowed with the power to ameliorate psychic trauma. In its negotiation of the large-scale structures of political economy and the small-scale (but also social) histories of intimate life, fetishism provides a useful form for attending to the material culture of everyday life.

In the chapters in Part Five, fetishism might be seen as an implicit and loose orientation. Whether it is tracing the way that modern commodities parade themselves and promise freedoms, or the way that everyday things connect you to the past, the modern commodity is always more than it seems. In this, the very materiality of everyday objects must be recognised as extending far beyond the boundaries of the designed object. It is not that the 'thing itself' cannot be separated from its context in everyday life, rather the thing itself *is* the context of everyday life in which objects and their practices exist.

Chapter 29

Georg Simmel

THE BERLIN TRADE EXHIBITION [1896]

(**Source**: Frisby, David and Featherstone, Mike eds (1997) *Simmel on Culture: Selected Writings*, London and Thousand Oaks, Calif.: Sage, pp. 255–8)

Editor's introduction

Georg Simmel (1858–1918) is one of the founders of modern sociology and sociocultural theory. Until fairly recently interest in Simmel has been eclipsed by attention to his more famous contemporaries (particularly Emile Durkheim and Max Weber), yet it is becoming clear that Simmel's approach has much to offer present-day studies of culture and society. Simmel's work is critically placed between the abstractions of philosophy and detailed empirical attention to the everyday material world. By attending to what Baudelaire called 'the ephemeral, the fugitive, the contingent' of modern life (which for Simmel included such 'trivial' phenomena as fashion and urban life) Simmel can be seen as one of the first philosophers of modernity. What also made Simmel's approach distinctly modern was his reluctance to interpret the world from the perspective of abstract theories; instead he finds philosophical generalisations within the everyday world. Meals, city living and money are Simmel's particular philosophical objects out of which he extracts the general. His approach is perhaps best described by the titles of the short essays he wrote for the journal *Jugend* – 'snapshots from the perspective of eternity' (*Momentbilder Sub Species Aeternitatis*).

In this review of the Berlin Trade Exhibition, Simmel demonstrates a number of themes that will continue to characterise his writing. First, we should note that the subject matter was hardly the kind that turn-of-the-century academics deemed worthy of consideration. Second, we see a familiar preoccupation: the everydayness of modernity wears you down and assaults your nerves. Third, and perhaps most important, is the dialectical response that qualifies any immediate assessment of modern life. So, if a description of this trade exhibition might simply suggest that it should be seen as a cause of modern existential malaise, Simmel reveals that is also one of the cultural forms adequate to the culture of modernity. Similarly the objects in the exhibition (like modern individuals) strive for uniqueness and individuality, at the same time (and for the same reasons) as they become submerged in a sea of conformity and homogeneity.

The reassessment of Simmel is clearly still in progress and is no doubt being fuelled by the evident influence he had on his students (for instance, Kracauer (Chapter 30) and Benjamin (Chapter 2). His philosophical approach to the everyday will no doubt provide a fruitful perspective for developing the study of everyday life.

Further reading: Felski 1995; Frisby 1985, 1992a, 1992b; Highmore 2002; Leck 2000; Lehmann 2000.

IN HIS *DEUTSCHE GESCHICHTE* Karl Lamprecht relates how certain medieval orders of knights gradually lost their practical purpose but continued as sociable gatherings. This is a type of sociological development that is similarly repeated in the most diverse fields. The double meaning of the word 'society' symbolizes this twin sense. Alongside the very process of sociation there is also, as a by-product, the sociable meaning of society. The latter is always a meeting-point for the most diverse formation of interest groups, thus remaining as the sole integrating force even when the original reasons for consociation have lost their effectiveness. The history of world exhibitions, which originated from annual fairs, is one of the clearest examples of this most fundamental type of human sociation. The extent to which this process can be found in the Berlin exhibition alone allows it to be placed in the category of world exhibitions. In the face of the richness and diversity of what is offered, the only unifying and colourful factor is that of amusement. The way in which the most heterogeneous industrial products are crowded together in close proximity paralyses the senses – a veritable hypnosis where only one message gets through to one's consciousness: the idea that one is here to amuse oneself. Through frequency of repetition this impression overwhelms countless no less worthy impressions, which because of their fragmentation fail to register. The sense of amusement emerges as a common denominator due to a petty but psychologically subtle arrangement: every few steps a small entry fee is charged for each special display. One's curiosity is thus constantly aroused by each new display, and the enjoyment derived from each particular display is made to seem greater and more significant. The majority of things which must be passed creates the impression that many surprises and amusements are in store. In short, the return to the main motif, amusement, is more effectively achieved by having to make a small sacrifice, which overcomes one's inhibitions to indulge, than if a higher entry price, giving unrestricted access, was charged, thereby denying that continuous small stimulation.

Every fine and sensitive feeling, however, is violated and seems deranged by the mass effect of the merchandise offered, while on the other hand it cannot be denied that the richness and variety of fleeting impressions is well suited to the need for excitement for overstimulated and tired nerves. While increasing civilization leads to ever greater specialization and to a more frequent one-sidedness of function within an evermore limited field, in no way does this differentiation on the side of production extend to consumption. Rather the opposite: it appears as though modern man's one-sided and monotonous role in the division of labour will be compensated for by consumption and enjoyment through the growing pressure of heterogeneous impressions, and the ever faster and more colourful change of excitements. The differentiation of the active side of life is apparently complemented through the extensive diversity of its passive and receiving side. The press of contradictions, the many stimuli and the diversity of consumption and enjoyment are the ways in which the human soul – that otherwise is an impatient flux of forces and denied a complete development by the differentiations within modern work – seeks to come alive. No part of modern life reveals this need as sharply as the large exhibition. Nowhere else is such a richness of different impressions brought together so that overall there seems to be an outward unity, whereas underneath a vigorous interaction produces mutual contrasts, intensification and lack of relatedness.

Now this unity of the whole creates a stronger impression and becomes more interesting when one considers the impossibility of surveying the objects produced in a single city. It is only as a floating psychological idea that this unity can be apprehended since in its origins the styles and emerging trends receive no clear expression. It is a particular attraction of world fairs that they form a momentary centre of world civilization, assembling the products of the entire world in a confined space as if in a single picture. Put the other way round, a single city has broadened into the totality of cultural production. No important product is missing, and though much of the material and samples have been brought together from the whole world they have attained a conclusive form and become part of a single whole. Thus it becomes clear what is meant by a 'world city' and that Berlin, despite everything, has become one. That is, a single city to which the whole world sends its products and where all the important styles of the present cultural world are put on display. In this sense perhaps the Berlin exhibition is unique, perhaps it has never been so apparent before how much the form of modern culture has permitted a concentration in one place, not in the mere collection of exhibits as in a world fair, but how through its own production a city can represent itself as a copy and a sample of the manufacturing forces of world culture.

It is a point of some cultural historical interest to follow how a particular style for such exhibitions has developed. The specific exhibition style is seen at its clearest in the buildings. An entirely new proportion between permanence and transience not only predominates in the hidden structure but also in the aesthetic criteria. In doing this the materials and their intrinsic properties have achieved a complete harmony in their external design, so satisfying one of the most fundamental demands of all art. The majority of the buildings, in particular the main ones, look as if they were intended for temporary purposes; because this lack of permanence is unmistakable they are absolutely ineffective as unsolid buildings. And the impression of lack of solidity works only where the temporary can claim permanence and durability. In the exhibition style the imagination of the architect is freed from the stipulation of permanence, allowing grace and dignity to be combined in their own measure. It is the conscious denial of a monumental style that has produced a new and positive shape. Elsewhere it is the meaning of art to incorporate the permanence of form in transient materials, and the ideal of architecture is to strive to give expression to the permanent, whereas here the attraction of the transient forms its own style and, even more characteristically, does this from material that doesn't appear as if it was intended for temporary use. And in fact the architects of our exhibition have succeeded in making the opposition to the historical ideal of architecture not a matter of absurdity or lack of style; rather they have taken the point last reached in architecture as their starting-point, as if only this arrangement would allow its meaning to emerge fully against a differently coloured background and yet be seen as part of a single tradition.

It is on the architectural side that this exhibition reaches its acme, demonstrating the aesthetic output of the exhibition principle. From another point of view its productivity is at least as high: and here I refer to what could be termed the shop-window quality of things, a characteristic which the exhibition accentuates. The production of goods under the regime of free competition and the normal predominance of supply over demand leads to goods having to show a tempting exterior as well as utility. Where competition no longer operates in matters of usefulness and intrinsic properties, the interest of the buyer has to be aroused by the external stimulus of the object, even the manner of its presentation. It is at the point where material interests have reached their highest level and the pressure of competition is at an extreme that the aesthetic ideal is employed. The striving to make the merely useful visually stimulating – something that was completely natural for the orientals and Romans – for us comes from the struggle to render the graceless graceful for consumers. The exhibition with its emphasis on amusement attempts a new synthesis between the principles of external stimulus and the practical functions of objects, and thereby takes this aesthetic superadditum to its highest level. The banal attempt to put things in their best light, as in the cries of the street trader, is transformed in the interesting attempt to confer a new aesthetic significance from displaying objects together – something already happening in the relationship between advertising and poster art.

Indeed it strikes one as curious that the separate objects in an exhibition show the same relationships and modifications that are made by the individual within society. On the one side, the depreciation of an otherwise qualified neighbour, on the other, accentuation at the expense of the same; on the one side, the levelling and uniformity due to an environment of the same, on the other, the individual is even more accentuated through the summation of many impressions; on the one side, the individual is only an element of the whole, only a member of a higher unity, on the other, the claim that the same individual is a whole and a unity. Thus the objective relation between social elements is reflected in the impression of things in unison within a single frame yet composed of interactively excited forces, and of contradictions, yet also their confluence. Just as in the exhibition the contours of things in their interactive effects, their moving to and fro undergoes an aesthetic exploitation, so in society the corresponding patterns allow an ethical use.

German, in particular north German, exhibitions could compete only with difficulty with French ones where the ability to accentuate by all means possible the stimulus of appearance has a much longer history and wider applicability. Nevertheless this exhibition shows the attempt, often successful, to develop aesthetic opportunities which through display can contribute to their attractiveness. Certainly the qualities of taste are mostly lacking in the individual items of the exhibition. Aside from the practical motive of Berlin's exhibition, it is to be hoped at the least that the aesthetic impulse is encouraged beyond the exhibition itself and becomes part of the way products are presented.

Chapter 30

Siegfried Kracauer

BOREDOM [1924]

(Source: Kracauer, Siegfried (1995) *The Mass Ornament: Weimar Essays,* translated by Thomas Y. Levin, Cambridge, Mass.: Harvard University Press, pp. 331–4)

Editor's introduction

While Siegfried Kracauer (1889–1966) is still probably best known for his (US) postwar writing on cinema, there is now a growing recognition of the importance of his earlier (German) work. This chapter was written for the newspaper *Frankfurter Zeitung*, a newspaper Kracauer worked on (for the most part as editor of the cultural section [*feuilleton*] of the paper) from 1921 until Hitler took power in 1933. During those Weimar years Kracauer developed a diagnostic critique of modernity that specifically took what he called 'inconspicuous surface-level expressions' as their subject matter. Here the influence of his one-time teacher Georg Simmel is vividly evident. Arguing that 'we are most deeply and continually influenced by the tiny catastrophes that make up daily life', Kracauer wrote about everyday life in Weimar Germany by attending to the new cultural forms, aimed particularly at the 'salaried masses' (shop workers, clerks and others). Best-selling novels, movie palaces, dance troupes and waiting rooms (hotel lobbies, employment exchanges and so on) supply the symptoms for Kracauer's diagnosis of the condition of modernity.

'Boredom' was written in 1924 and can be seen to anticipate his more extensive analyses of modern everyday life as a culture of distraction (a theme also explored by his friend Walter Benjamin). Here the environment of modernity is made up of commodified forms of communication (adverts, films, radio and so on) that aggressively hail and inculcate their audience. Here a world of banality inhabits the lives of people who have been left vacant by what Henri Lefebvre will call the colonisation of everyday life by the commodity. For Kracauer, in a reversal of received wisdom, boredom is not the outcome of banality, but its critical refusal. The failure to be bored in such a culture marks the success of distraction. In this he shares a slightly bizarre commonality with the Punk Rock bands of the late 1970s: to declare yourself bored is not a mark of failure but the necessary precondition for the possibility of generating the authentically new (rather than the old dressed up as the new).

What is striking in this essay is the animated agency that he gives to the world of things. In his study of white-collar culture *The Salaried Masses: Duty and Distraction in Weimar Germany* (first published in serial form in the *Frankfurter Zeitung* in 1929) he comments on the ability of a particular female filing clerk to sing along to every popular hit: 'But it is not she who knows every hit, rather the hits know her, steal up behind her and gently lay her low' (Kracauer 1998: 70). For Kracauer the designed environment of the commodity has set its designs on us.

Further reading: Giles 2000; Harootunian 2000; Katz 1999; Koch 2000; Kracauer 1995, 1998; Petro 1989.

P EOPLE TODAY WHO STILL HAVE TIME FOR BOREDOM and yet are not bored are certainly just as boring as those who never get around to being bored. For their self has vanished – the self whose presence, particularly in this so bustling world, would necessarily compel them to tarry[1] for a while without a goal, neither here nor there.

Most people, of course, do not have much leisure time. They pursue a livelihood on which they expend all their energies, simply to earn enough for the bare necessities. To make this tiresome obligation more tolerable, they have invented a work ethic that provides a moral veil for their occupation and at least affords them a certain moral[2] satisfaction. It would be exaggerated to claim that the pride in considering oneself an ethical being dispels every type of boredom. Yet the vulgar boredom of daily drudgery is not actually what is at issue here, since it neither kills people nor awakens them to new life, but merely expresses a dissatisfaction that would immediately disappear if an occupation more pleasant than the morally sanctioned one became available. Nevertheless, people whose duties occasionally make them yawn may be less boring than those who do their business by inclination. The latter, unhappy types, are pushed deeper and deeper into the hustle and bustle until eventually they no longer know where their head is, and the extraordinary, radical boredom that might be able to reunite them with their heads remains eternally distant for them.

There is no one, however, who has no leisure time at all. The office is not a permanent sanctuary, and Sundays are an institution. Thus, in principle, during those beautiful hours of free time everyone would have the opportunity to rouse himself into real boredom. But although one wants to do nothing, things are done to one: the world makes sure that one does not find oneself. And even if one perhaps isn't interested in it, the world itself is much too interested for one to find the peace and quiet necessary to be as thoroughly bored with the world as it ultimately deserves.

In the evening one saunters through the streets, replete with an unfulfillment from which a fullness could sprout. Illuminated words glide by on the rooftops, and already one is banished from one's own emptiness into the alien *advertisement*. One's body takes root in the asphalt, and, together with the enlightening revelations of the illuminations, one's spirit – which is no longer one's own – roams ceaselessly out of the night and into the night. If only it were allowed to disappear! But, like Pegasus prancing on a carousel, this spirit must run in circles and may never tire of praising to high heaven the glory of a liqueur and the merits of the best five-cent cigarette. Some sort of magic spurs that spirit relentlessly amid the thousand electric bulbs, out of which it constitutes and reconstitutes itself into glittering sentences.

Should the spirit by chance return at some point, it soon takes its leave in order to allow itself to be cranked away in various guises in a *movie theater*. It squats as a fake Chinaman in a fake opium den, transforms itself into a trained dog that performs ludicrously clever tricks to please a film diva, gathers up into a storm amid towering mountain peaks, and turns into both a circus artist and a lion at the same time. How could it resist these metamorphoses? The posters swoop into the empty space that the spirit itself would not mind pervading; they drag it in front of the silver screen, which is as barren as an emptied-out palazzo. And once the images begin to emerge one after another, there is nothing left in the world besides their evanescence. One forgets oneself in the process of gawking, and the huge dark hole is animated with the illusion of a life that belongs to no one and exhausts everyone.

Radio likewise vaporizes beings, even before they have intercepted a single spark.[3] Since many people feel compelled to broadcast, one finds oneself in a state of permanent receptivity,[4] constantly pregnant with London, the Eiffel Tower, and Berlin. Who would want to resist the invitation of those dainty headphones? They gleam in living rooms and entwine themselves around heads all by themselves; and instead of fostering cultivated conversation (which certainly can be a bore), one becomes a playground for worldwide noises that, regardless of their own potentially objective boredom, do not even grant one's modest right to personal boredom. Silent and lifeless, people sit side by side as if their souls were wandering about far away. But these souls are not wandering according to their own preference; they are badgered by the news hounds, and soon no one can tell anymore who is the hunter and who is the hunted. Even in the café, where one wants to roll up into a ball like a porcupine and become aware of one's insignificance, an imposing loudspeaker effaces every trace of private existence. The announcements it blares forth dominate the space of the concert intermissions, and the waiters (who are listening to it themselves) indignantly refuse the unreasonable requests to get rid of this gramophonic mimicry.

As one is enduring this species of antennal fate, the five *continents* are drawing ever closer. In truth, it is not we who extend ourselves out toward them; rather, it is their cultures that appropriate us in their boundless imperialism. It is as if one were having one of those dreams provoked by an empty stomach: a tiny ball rolls toward you from very far away, expands into a close-up, and finally roars right over you. You can neither stop it nor escape it, but lie there chained, a helpless little doll swept away by the giant colossus in whose ambit it expires. Flight is impossible. Should the Chinese imbroglio be tactfully disembroiled, one is sure to be harried by an American boxing match: the Occident remains omnipresent, whether one acknowledges it or not. All the world-historical events on this planet – not only the current ones but also past events, whose love of life knows no shame – have only one desire: to set up a rendezvous wherever they suppose us to be present. But the masters are not to be found in their quarters. They've gone on a trip and cannot be located, having long since ceded the empty chambers to the 'surprise party'[5] that occupies the rooms, pretending to be the masters.

But what if one refuses to allow oneself to be chased away? Then boredom becomes the only proper occupation, since it provides a kind of guarantee that one is, so to speak, still in control of one's own existence. If one were never bored, one would presumably not really be present at all and would thus be merely one more object of boredom, as was claimed at the outset. One would light up on the rooftops or spool by as a filmstrip. But if indeed one is present, one would have no choice but to be bored by the ubiquitous abstract racket that does not allow one to exist, and, at the same time, to find oneself boring for existing in it.

On a sunny afternoon when everyone is outside, one would do best to hang about in the train station or, better yet, stay at home, draw the curtains, and surrender oneself to one's boredom on the sofa. Shrouded in *tristezza*, one flirts with ideas that even become quite respectable in the process, and one considers various projects that, for no reason, pretend to be serious. Eventually one becomes content to do nothing more than be with oneself, without knowing what one actually should be doing – sympathetically touched by the mere glass grasshopper on the tabletop that cannot jump because it is made of glass and by the silliness of a little cactus plant that thinks nothing of its own whimsicality. Frivolous, like these decorative creations, one harbors only an inner restlessness without a goal, a longing that is pushed aside, and a weariness with that which exists without really being.

If, however, one has the patience, the sort of patience specific to legitimate boredom, then one experiences a kind of bliss that is almost unearthly. A landscape appears in which colorful peacocks strut about, and images of people suffused with soul come into view. And look – your own soul is likewise swelling, and in ecstasy you name what you have always lacked: the great *passion*. Were this passion – which shimmers like a comet – to descend, were it to envelop you, the others, and the world – oh, then boredom would come to an end, and everything that exists would be . . .

Yet people remain distant images, and the great passion fizzles out on the horizon. And in the boredom that refuses to abate, one hatches bagatelles that are as boring as this one.

Notes

1   Kracauer here plays with the resonance between *langweilen* ('to bore') and *lange (ver)weilen* ('to tarry' or 'to linger').

2   In the copy of this article pasted by Kracauer into his scrapbook, this adjective was crossed out in pen. It reappeared, however, when the essay was reprinted in *Das Ornament der Masse*.

3   Kracauer here plays on the resonance between *Funk*, which means 'radio', and *Funke*, which means 'spark' or 'flicker'.

4   The semantic fulcrum of this sentence is provided by the ambiguity of *Empfängnis*, which can mean both 'reception' (as in a radio broadcast) and 'conception' (the result of a sexual – as opposed to radiophonic – dissemination).

5   This English expression, rendered as 'surprising party' in the first printing of the article in the *Frankfurter Zeitung*, was subsequently corrected in the 1963 reprinting.

Chapter 31

Roland Barthes

PLASTIC [1957]

(Source: Barthes, Roland (1973) *Mythologies*, translated by Annette Lavers, London: Granada, pp. 97–9)

Editor's introduction

Roland Barthes (1915–1980) can be seen as the writer who did most to achieve semiology's goal of becoming a form of analysis that would be applicable to all aspects of life (irrespective of conventional disciplinary boundaries). In the 1950s he popularised semiology through a number of newspaper articles that 'read' everyday objects and practices. In 1957 these were collected into what is perhaps Barthes's most famous book – *Mythologies*. The 'socio-pathological' portraits that make up *Mythologies* included such everyday material as detergents, steak and chips, striptease, the new Citroën, wrestling, and plastics (reprinted here). The importance of Barthes's work does not seem to diminish with age and his contribution to cultural analysis should be crucial to everyday life studies.

'Plastic' is exemplary of Barthes's approach to everyday life at this time. By giving plastic the kind of attention that is usually reserved for the canon of literary works he recognises in the work-a-day world of plastics a cosmology of magic and myth. The reason for treating everyday materials in this way is not simply to bring them out of hiding (so to speak) but to draw attention to the way that they circulate in modern life. In the world of advertising, a perfume, for instance, is not simply a nice smelling liquid, but an 'essence of sensuality' that will cause landslides, earthquakes or, at the very least, the user to become irresistible. In capitalist culture the commodity becomes 'magical', containing properties normally bestowed on sacred objects (fetishes and gods). Thus for Barthes the everyday world contains the mythologies of a secular culture.

Barthes's post-*Mythologies* writing continued to exhibit an attraction towards the everyday. His study of fashion journalism (Barthes [1967] 1990) immersed itself in rhetorical environments that consistently echo at the level of everyday life. Even his later more 'hedonistic' writing on photography, love and himself (Barthes 1977) continually invoked the everyday as the realm in which pleasure and unease are experienced.

Further reading: Barthes [1967] 1990; Burgin 1996; Ungar 1983.

DESPITE HAVING NAMES OF GREEK SHEPHERDS (Polystyrene, Polyvinyl, Polyethylene), plastic, the products of which have just been gathered in an exhibition, is in essence the stuff of alchemy. At the entrance of the stand, the public waits in a long queue in order to witness the accomplishment of the magical operation par excellence: the transmutation of matter. An ideally-shaped machine, tubulated and oblong (a shape well suited to suggest the secret of an itinerary) effortlessly draws, out of a heap of greenish crystals, shiny and fluted dressing-room tidies. At one end, raw, telluric matter, at the other, the finished, human object; and between these two extremes, nothing; nothing but a transit, hardly watched over by an attendant in a cloth cap, half-god, half-robot.

So, more than a substance, plastic is the very idea of its infinite transformation; as its everyday name indicates, it is ubiquity made visible. And it is this, in fact, which makes it a miraculous substance: a miracle is always a sudden transformation of nature. Plastic remains impregnated throughout with this wonder: it is less a thing than the trace of a movement.

And as the movement here is almost infinite, transforming the original crystals into a multitude of more and more startling objects, plastic is, all told, a spectacle to be deciphered: the very spectacle of its end-products. At the sight of each terminal form (suitcase, brush, car-body, toy, fabric, tube, basin or paper), the mind does not cease from considering the original matter as an enigma. This is because the quick-change artistry of plastic is absolute: it can become buckets as well as jewels. Hence a perpetual amazement, the reverie of man at the sight of the proliferating forms of matter, and the connections he detects between the singular of the origin and the plural of the effects. And this amazement is a pleasurable one, since the scope of the transformations gives man the measure of his power, and since the very itinerary of plastic gives him the euphoria of a prestigious free-wheeling through Nature.

But the price to be paid for this success is that plastic, sublimated as movement, hardly exists as substance. Its reality is a negative one: neither hard nor deep, it must be content with a 'substantial' attribute which is neutral in spite of its utilitarian advantages: *resistance*, a state which merely means an absence of yielding. In the hierarchy of the major poetic substances, it figures as a disgraced material, lost between the effusiveness of rubber and the flat hardness of metal; it embodies none of the genuine produce of the mineral world: foam, fibres, strata. It is a 'shaped' substance: whatever its final state, plastic keeps a flocculent appearance, something opaque, creamy and curdled, something powerless ever to achieve the triumphant smoothness of Nature. But what best reveals it for what it is is the sound it gives, at once hollow and flat; its noise is its undoing, as are its colours, for it seems capable of retaining only the most chemical-looking ones. Of yellow, red and green, it keeps only the aggressive quality, and uses them as mere names, being able to display only concepts of colours.

The fashion for plastic highlights an evolution in the myth of 'imitation' materials.

It is well known that their use is historically bourgeois in origin (the first vestimentary postiches date back to the rise of capitalism). But until now imitation materials have always indicated pretension, they belonged to the world of appearances, not to that of actual use; they aimed at reproducing cheaply the rarest substances, diamonds, silk, feathers, furs, silver, all the luxurious brilliance of the world. Plastic has climbed down, it is a household material. It is the first magical substance which consents to be prosaic. But it is precisely because this prosaic character is a triumphant reason for its existence: for the first time, artifice aims at something common, not rare. And as an immediate consequence, the age-old function of nature is modified: it is no longer the Idea, the pure Substance to be regained or imitated: an artificial Matter, more bountiful than all the natural deposits, is about to replace her, and to determine the very invention of forms. A luxurious object is still of this earth, it still recalls, albeit in a precious mode, its mineral or animal origin, the natural theme of which it is but one actualization. Plastic is wholly swallowed up in the fact of being used: ultimately, objects will be invented for the sole pleasure of using them. The hierarchy of substances is abolished: a single one replaces them all: the whole world *can* be plasticized, and even life itself since, we are told, they are beginning to make plastic aortas.

Chapter 32

Jean Baudrillard

STRUCTURES OF INTERIOR DESIGN [1968]

(**Source**: Baudrillard, Jean (1996) *The System of Objects*, translated by James Benedict, London and New York: Verso, pp. 15–29)

Editor's introduction

The System of Objects was Jean Baudrillard's first book and can be read as a form of 'structuralist phenomenology' (see Gane 1991: 162). What this meant in practice was that Baudrillard attempted to describe the living experience of commodity culture (a kind of cultural phenomenology) via the kind of analysis afforded by structuralism. Indeed Baudrillard's work on the new designed environment can be productively compared with Roland Barthes's (1990) work on fashion in his book (published in 1967, a year before Baudrillard's) *The Fashion System* (and of course the way this echoes in the title of Baudrillard's book clearly invites such a comparison).

Both Baudrillard and Barthes are concerned not simply with the 'objects themselves' (clothes, furniture and so on) but also with the discourses that surround (and to some degree saturate) these objects. The attention to the promotional language as a *desiring* language that accompanies such objects provides the route for both authors to analyse their objects. Yet differences are also apparent. Whereas Barthes is predominantly interested in a sophisticated semiotics of a particular *moment* in fashion, Baudrillard is interested in reading the contemporary world of interior design as registering a historical shift in everyday life. On the face of it the new designed environment offers a number of evident freedoms (especially from the old spatial rigidities of a bourgeois patriarchy), yet these freedoms are limited. Indeed it might be seen that the historical shift is from a system dominated by the moral landscape of bourgeois patriarchy to a system dominated by the amoral landscape of consumption. Such a diagnosis suggests that the contemporary world of interiors primarily reveals the extent to which social subjects have become identifiable as consumers. In this he seems closest to the writing of his one-time teacher Henri Lefebvre (Chapter 22). Indeed Lefebvre's assessment of the postwar period as one that witnesses the penetration of everyday life by the commodity might be the most adequate description of Baudrillard's *System of Objects*.

Baudrillard's subsequent writing is of course much better known than this fairly 'tame' piece of analysis. Yet his more (in)famous discussions of the modern world as a simulacra obviously impacts at the level of the everyday. A study of Baudrillard's oeuvre as an articulation of the everyday would clearly be productive.

Further reading: Barthes [1967] 1990; Baudrillard 1994, 1998; Gane 1991; Genosko 1994; Kristin Ross 1995.

The traditional environment

THE ARRANGEMENT OF FURNITURE offers a faithful image of the familial and social structures of a period. The typical bourgeois interior is patriarchal; its foundation is the dining-room/bedroom combination. Although it is diversified with respect to function, the furniture is highly integrated, centring around the sideboard or the bed in the middle of the room. There is a tendency to accumulate, to fill and close off the space. The emphasis is on unifunctionality, immovability, imposing presence and hierarchical labelling. Each room has a strictly defined role corresponding to one or another of the various functions of the family unit, and each ultimately refers to a view which conceives of the individual as a balanced assemblage of distinct faculties. The pieces of furniture confront one another, jostle one another, and implicate one another in a unity that is not so much spatial as moral in character. They are ranged about an axis which ensures a regular chronology of actions; thanks to this permanent symbolization, the family is always present to itself. Within this private space each piece of furniture in turn, and each room, internalizes its own particular function and takes on the symbolic dignity pertaining to it — then the whole house puts the finishing touch to this integration of interpersonal relationships within the semi-hermetic family group.

All this constitutes an organism whose structure is the patriarchal relationship founded on tradition and authority, and whose heart is the complex affective relationship that binds all the family members together. Such a family home is a specific space which takes little account of any objective decorative requirements, because the primary function of furniture and objects here is to personify human relationships, to fill the space that they share between them, and to be inhabited by a soul.[1] The real dimension they occupy is captive to the moral dimension which it is their job to signify. They have as little autonomy in this space as the various family members enjoy in society. Human beings and objects are indeed bound together in a collusion in which the objects take on a certain density, an emotional value — what might be called a 'presence'. What gives the houses of our childhood such depth and resonance in memory is clearly this complex structure of interiority, and the objects within it serve for us as boundary markers of the symbolic configuration known as home. The caesura between inside and outside, and their formal opposition, which falls under the social sign of property and the psychological sign of the immanence of the family, make this traditional space into a closed transcendence. In their anthropomorphism the objects that furnish it become household gods, spatial incarnations of the emotional bonds and the permanence of the family group. These gods enjoyed a gentle immortality until the advent of a modern generation which has cast them aside, dispersed them – even, on occasion, reinstated them in an up-to-date nostalgia for whatever is old. As often with gods, furniture too thus gets a second chance to exist, and passes from a naïve utility into a cultural baroque.

The dining-room/bedroom pattern – an arrangement of movable property closely bound up with the house as immovable property – continues to be widely pitched by advertisers to a vast public. Department stores such as Lévitan and Galeries Barbès still titillate the collective taste with evocations of 'decorative' ensembles – despite the fact that contours are now 'stylized', despite the fact that decoration is out of favour. This furniture still sells, not because it is cheaper but because it embodies the official certainties of the group and enjoys the sanction of the bourgeoisie. A further reason is that such monumental furniture (sideboard, bed or wardrobe) and its arrangement echo the persistence of traditional family structures across broad social strata of modern society.

The modern object liberated in its function

The style of furniture changes as the individual's relationships to family and society change. Corner divans and beds, coffee tables, shelving – a plethora of new elements are now supplanting the traditional range of furniture. The organization of space changes, too, as beds become day-beds and sideboards and wardrobes give way to built-in storage. Things fold and unfold, are concealed, appear only when needed. Naturally such innovations are not due to free experiment: for the most part the greater mobility, flexibility and convenience they afford are the result of an involuntary adaptation to a shortage of space – a case of necessity being the mother of invention. Whereas the old-fashioned dining-room was heavily freighted with moral convention, 'modern' interiors, in their ingeniousness, often give the impression of being mere functional expedients. Their 'absence of style' is in the first place an absence of room, and maximum functionality is a solution of last resort whose outcome is that the dwelling-place, though remaining closed to the outside, loses its internal organization. Such a restructuring of space and the objects in it, unaccompanied by any reconversion, must in the first instance be considered an impoverishment.

The modern set of furniture, serially produced, is thus apparently destructured yet not restructured, nothing having replaced the expressive power of the old symbolic order. There is progress, nevertheless: between the individual and these objects, which are now more supple in their uses and have ceased to exercise or symbolize moral constraint, there is a much more liberal relationship, and in particular the individual is no longer strictly defined through them relative to his family.[2] Their mobility and multifunctionality allow him to organize them more freely, and this reflects a greater openness in his social relationships. This, however, is only a partial liberation. So far as the serial object is concerned, in the absence of any restructuring of space, this 'functional' development is merely an emancipation, not (to go back to the old Marxian distinction) a liberation proper, for it implies *liberation from the function of the object only, not from the object itself.* Consider a nondescript, light, foldable table or a bed without legs, frame or canopy – an absolute cipher of a bed, one might say: all such objects, with their 'pure' outlines, no longer resemble even what they are; they have been stripped down to their most primitive essence as mere apparatus and, as it were, definitively secularized. What has been liberated in them – and what, in being liberated, has liberated something in man (or rather, perhaps, what man, in liberating himself, has liberated in them) – is their function. The function is no longer obscured by the moral theatricality of the old furniture; it is emancipated now from ritual, from ceremonial, from the entire ideology which used to make our surroundings into an opaque mirror of a reified human structure. Today, at last, these objects emerge absolutely clear about the purposes they serve. They are thus indeed free as *functional objects* – that is, they have the freedom to function, and (certainly so far as serial objects are concerned) that is practically the *only* freedom they have.[3]

Now, *just so long as the object is liberated only in its function, man equally is liberated only as user of that object*. This too is progress, though not a decisive turning-point. A bed is a bed, a chair is a chair, and there is no relationship between them so long as each serves only the function it is supposed to serve. And without such a relationship there can be no space, for space exists only when it is opened up, animated, invested with rhythm and expanded by a correlation between objects and a transcendence of their functions in this new structure. In a way space is the object's true freedom, whereas its function is merely its formal freedom. The bourgeois dining-room was structured, but its structure was closed. The functional environment is more open, freer, but it is destructured, fragmented into its various functions. Somewhere between the two, in the gap between integrated psychological space and fragmented functional space, serial objects have their being, witnesses to both the one and the other – sometimes within a single interior.

The model interior

Modular components

This elusive space, which is no longer either a confined externality nor an interior refuge, this freedom, this 'style' which is indecipherable in the serial object because it is subordinated to that object's function, may nevertheless be encountered in *model interiors*, which embody a new emerging structure and a significant evolution.[4]

Leafing through such glossy magazines as *Maison Française* or *Mobilier et Décoration* [Furniture and Decoration],[5] one cannot fail to notice two alternating themes. The first reaches for the sublime, presenting houses beyond compare: old eighteenth-century mansions, miraculously well-equipped villas, Italian gardens heated by infra-red rays and populated by Etruscan statuettes – in short, the world of the unique, leaving the reader no alternative (so far as sociological generalization is concerned, at any rate) but contemplation without hope. Aristocratic models such as these, by virtue of their absolute value, are what underpin the second theme, that of modern interior decoration and furnishing. The objects and furniture proposed here, though they are high in 'status' value, do impinge on sociological reality: they are not dream creations without commercial significance but, rather, *models* in the proper sense of the word. We are no longer in a world of pure art, but in a world which (potentially, at least) is of interest to the whole of society.

These models of the home-furnishing avant-garde are organized around the basic distinction between COMPONENTS and SEATING; the practical imperative they obey is that of INTERIOR DESIGN, or syntagmatic calculation, to which may be contrasted, as seats are to components, the general concept of ATMOSPHERE.

TECMA: Extensible and interlocking components. Can be transformed or enlarged. Harmonious – they create a perfectly matching set of furniture. Functional – they answer all the needs of modern living. And they meet all your furnishing requirements – bookshelves, bar, radio, cupboards, wardrobe, desk space, cabinets, dresser, drawers, display unit, file storage, hideaway table. . . .

TECMA is available in oiled teak or finished mahogany.

OSCAR: Put your OSCAR environment together with your own hands! Exciting! Unprecedented!

The OSCAR furniturama is a set of specially pre-cut components. Discover the fun of designing a miniature three-dimensional model of your furniture, in colour and just the right size to handle! You can build your model and change it around to your heart's content – all in the comfort of your own home!

Then, with perfect confidence, order your original and personal OSCAR furniture – soon to be the pride of your household!

MONOPOLY: Every MONOPOLY ensemble is your personality's best friend. A high-quality cabinetwork system, in teak or makoré. Jointing and assembling leave no traces. Four-sided components can be put together in an infinite variety of ways – an infinite variety of genuine furniture adapted to your own particular tastes, size requirements and needs.

These are multi-combinable single-block components. You're sure to want them so that you too can give your home that refined atmosphere you've been dreaming about.

These examples reveal how the functional object is being transcended by a new kind of practical organization. Symbolic values, and along with them use values, are being supplanted by organizational values. The substance and form of the old furniture have been abandoned for good, in favour of an extremely free interplay of functions. These objects are no longer endowed with a 'soul', nor do they invade us with their symbolic presence: the relationship has become an objective one, founded on disposition and play. The value this relationship takes on is no longer of an instinctive or a psychological but, rather, of a tactical kind. What such objects embody is no longer the secret of a unique relationship but, rather, differences, and moves in a game. The former radical closure has disappeared, in parallel with a distinct change in social and interpersonal structures.

Walls and daylight

The rooms and the house themselves now transcend the traditional dividing-line of the wall, which formerly made them into spaces of refuge. Rooms open into one another, everything communicates, and space is broken up into angles, diffuse areas and mobile sectors. Rooms, in short, have been liberalized. Windows are no longer imposed upon the free influx of air and light – a light which used to come *from outside* and settle upon objects, illuminating them *as though from within*. Now there are quite simply no windows, and a freely intervening light has become a universal function of the existence of things. In the same way objects have lost the substantiality which was their basis, the form which enclosed them whereby man made them part of his self-image: it is now space which plays freely between them, and becomes the universal function of their relationships and their 'values'.

Lighting

Many significant features of this general evolution might be pointed out. The tendency for light sources to be made invisible is a case in point. 'A recessed ceiling conceals perimeter neon fixtures for general diffuse lighting.' 'Uniform lighting is ensured by neon tubes concealed in various places: the full length of the recessed ceiling above the curtains, behind and all along the top rim of the built-in units, beneath the upper row of cupboards, etc.' Everything suggests that the source of light continues to be evocative of the origin of all things: even though it no longer illuminates the family circle from the ceiling, even though it has been dispersed and made manifold, it is apparently still the sign of a privileged intimacy, still able to invest things with unique value, to create shadows and invent presences. Small wonder that a system founded on the objective manipulation of simple and homogeneous elements should strive to eliminate this last sign of internal radiance, of the symbolic envelopment of things by look or desire.

Mirrors and portraits

Another symptomatic change is the disappearance of looking-glasses and mirrors. A psycho-sociology of the mirror is overdue, especially in the wake of so much metaphysics. The traditional peasant milieu had no mirrors, perhaps even feared them as somewhat eerie. The bourgeois interior, by contrast, and what remains of that interior in present-day serially produced furniture, has mirrors in profusion, hung on the walls and incorporated into wardrobes, sideboards, cabinets or panelling. As a source of light, the mirror enjoys a special place in the room. This is the basis of the ideological role it has played, everywhere in the domestic world of the well-to-do, as redundancy, superfluity, reflection: the mirror is an opulent object which affords the self-indulgent bourgeois individual the opportunity to exercise his privilege – to reproduce his own image and revel in his possessions. In a more general sense we may say that the mirror is a symbolic object which not only reflects the characteristics of the individual but also echoes in its expansion the historical expansion of individual consciousness. It thus carries the stamp of approval of an entire social order: it is no coincidence that the century of Louis XIV is epitomized by the Hall of Mirrors at Versailles, nor that, in more recent times, the spread of mirrors in apartments coincided with the spread of the triumphal Pharisaism of bourgeois consciousness, from Napoleon III to Art Nouveau. But things have changed. There is no place in the functional ensemble for reflection for its own sake. The mirror still exists, but its most appropriate place is in the bathroom, unframed. There, dedicated to the fastidious care of the appearance that social intercourse demands, it is liberated from the graces and glories of domestic subjectivity. By the same token other objects are in turn liberated from mirrors; hence, they are no longer tempted to exist in a closed circuit with their own images. For mirrors close off space, presuppose a wall, refer back to the centre of the room. The more mirrors there are, the more glorious is the intimacy of the room, albeit more turned in upon itself. The current proliferation of openings and transparent partitions clearly represents a diametrically opposed approach. (Furthermore, all the tricks that mirrors make possible run counter to the current demand for a frank use of materials.) A chain has definitely been broken, and there is a real logic to the modern approach when it eliminates not only central or over-visible light sources but also the mirrors that used to reflect them; by thus eschewing any focus on or return to a central point, it frees space of the converging squint which gave bourgeois décor – much like bourgeois consciousness in general – such a cross-eyed view of itself.[6]

Something else, too, has disappeared in tandem with mirrors: the family portrait, the wedding photograph in the bedroom, the full-length or half-length portrait of the master of the house in the drawing-room, the framed close-ups of the children almost everywhere. All these, constituting a sort of diachronic mirror of the family, disappear along with mirrors themselves when a certain level of modernity is reached (although this has not happened as yet on any wide scale). Even works of art, whether originals or reproductions, no longer have a part to play as an absolute value, but merely in a combining mode. The success of prints as decoration in contrast to framed pictures is in part to be explained by their lower absolute value, and hence greater value in association. No object, any more than lights and mirrors, must be allowed to regain too intense a focus.

Clocks and time

Another illusion forsworn by the modern interior is the illusion of time. An essential object has vanished: the clock. It is worth recalling that although the centre of the peasant room is the fire and fireplace, the clock is nevertheless a majestic and living element therein. In the bourgeois or petty-bourgeois interior it takes the form of the clock that so often crowns the marble mantelpiece, itself usually dominated by a mirror above – the whole ensemble constituting the most extraordinary symbolic résumé of bourgeois domesticity. The clock is to time as the mirror is to space. Just as the relationship to the reflected image institutes a closure and a kind of introjection of space, so the clock stands paradoxically for the permanence and introjection of time. Country clocks are among the most sought-after of objects, precisely because they capture time and strip it of surprises within the intimacy of a piece of furniture. There is nothing in the world more reassuring. The measuring of time produces anxiety when it serves to assign us to social tasks, but it makes us feel safe when it substantializes time and cuts it into slices like an object of consumption. Everybody knows from experience how intimate a ticking clock can make a place feel; the reason is that the clock's sound assimilates the place to the inside of our own body. The clock is a mechanical heart that reassures us about our own heart. It is precisely this process of infusion or assimilation of the substance of time, this presence of duration, which is rejected, just like all other returns to inwardness, by a modern order based on externality, spatiality and objective relationships.

Towards a sociology of interior design?

It is the whole world of *Stimmung* that has disappeared, the world of 'natural' harmony between movements of the emotions and the presence of things: an internalized atmosphere as opposed to the externalized atmosphere of modern 'interiors'. Today, value resides neither in appropriation nor in intimacy but in information, in inventiveness, in control, in a continual openness to objective messages – in short, in the syntagmatic calculation which is, strictly speaking, the foundation of the discourse of the modern home-dweller.

The entire conception of decoration has changed too. Traditional good taste, which decided what was beautiful on the basis of secret affinities, no longer has any part here. That taste constituted a poetic discourse, an evocation of self-contained objects that responded to one another; today objects do not respond to one another, they communicate – they have no individual presence but merely, at best, an overall coherence attained by virtue of their simplification as components of a code and the way their relationships are calculated. An unrestricted combinatorial system enables man to use them as the elements of his structural discourse.

Advertising widely promotes this new conception of decoration: 'Create a livable and well-organized three-room flat in 30 square metres!'; 'Multiply your flat by four!' More generally, it always talks of interior decorating in terms of problems and solutions, and it is here, rather than in 'good taste', that the current direction of decoration is to be found: it is no longer a matter of setting up a theatre of objects or creating an ambience, but of solving a problem, devising the subtlest possible response to a complicated set of conditions, mobilizing a space.

In the case of serial objects, the possibilities of this functional discourse are reduced. Objects and furniture of this kind are dispersed elements whose syntactic links are not evident; to the degree that they are arranged in a calculated way, the organizing principle is penury, and the objects appear impoverished in their abstraction. This is a necessary abstraction, however, for it provides the basis, at the level of the model, for the homogeneity of the elements in functional interaction. First of all man must stop mixing himself up with things and investing them with his own image; he will then be able, beyond the utility they have for him, to project onto them his game plan, his calculations, his discourse, and invest these manoeuvres themselves with the sense of a message to others, and a message to oneself. By the time this point is reached the mode of existence of 'ambient' objects will have changed completely, and *a sociology of furnishing will perforce have given way to a sociology of interior design.*[7]

Both the images and the discourse of advertising attest to this development: the discourse, by placing the subject directly on the stage as actor and manager, in both the indicative and the imperative moods; the images, to the contrary, by leaving the subject out, for his presence would, in a way, be an anachronism. The subject is himself the order he puts into things, and this order excludes redundancy: man has simply to remove himself from the picture. His presence has accomplished its task. What man now creates is a space, not a décor, and whereas the figure of the master of the house was a normal part – indeed, the clearest connotation – of the traditional décor, a signature is thoroughly alien to any 'functional' space.

Man the interior designer

We are beginning to see what the new model of the home-dweller looks like: 'man the interior designer' is neither an owner nor a mere user – rather, he is an active engineer of atmosphere. Space is at his disposal like a kind of distributed system, and by controlling this space he holds sway over all possible reciprocal relations between the objects therein, and hence over all the roles they are capable of assuming. (It follows that he must also be 'functional' himself: he and the space in question must be homogeneous if his messages of design are to leave him and return to him success-fully.) What matters to him is neither possession nor enjoyment but responsibility, in the strict sense which implies that it is at all times possible for him to determine 'responses'. His praxis is exclusively external. This modern home-dweller does not 'consume' his objects. (Here again, 'taste' no longer has the slightest part to play, for in both its meanings it refers us back to self-contained objects whose form contains an 'edible' substance, so to speak, which makes them susceptible of internalization.) Instead of consuming objects, he dominates, controls and orders them. He discovers himself in the manipulation and tactical equilibration of a system.

There is clearly something abstract about this model of the 'functional' home-dweller. Advertising would like us to believe that modern man no longer funda-mentally *needs* his objects, that all he has to do now is operate among them as an intelligent technician of communications. Our environment, however, is a *directly experienced* mode of existence, and it is very abstract indeed to apply to it com-putational and informational models borrowed from the purely technical realm. Fur-thermore, this objectivizing approach is accompanied by a cascade of ambiguous phraseology – 'to your own taste', 'to your own measurements', 'personalization', 'the atmosphere will be yours alone', and so forth – which appears to contradict that approach but in fact covers for it. The objective game which man the interior designer is invited to play is invariably taken over by the double-dealing of advertising. Yet the game's very logic conveys with it the image of a general strategy of human relations, the image of a human project, of a *modus vivendi* for the technical age – a genuine change of civilization whose impact may be discerned even in everyday life.

Consider the object for a moment: the object as humble and receptive supporting actor, as a sort of psychological slave or confidant – the object as directly experienced in traditional daily life and illustrated throughout the history of Western art down to our own day. This object was the reflection of a total order, bound up with a well-defined conception of décor and perspective, substance and form. According to this conception, the form is an absolute dividing-line between inside and outside. Form is a rigid container, and within it is substance. Beyond their practical function, therefore, objects – and specifically objects of furniture – have a primordial function as vessels, a function that belongs to the register of the imaginary.[8] This explains their psycho-logical receptiveness. They are the reflection of a whole view of the world according to which each being is a 'vessel of inwardness' and relations between beings are transcendent correlations of substances; thus the house itself is the symbolic equivalent of the human body, whose potent organic schema is later generalized into an ideal design for the integration of social structures. All this makes up a complete mode of life whose basic ordering principle is Nature as the original substance from which value is derived. In creating or manufacturing objects, man makes himself, through the imposition of a form (i.e. through culture), into the transubstantiator of nature. It is the passing down of substances from age to age, from form to form, which supplies the archetype of creativity, namely creation *ab utero* and the whole poetic and meta-phorical symbolic system that goes with it.[9] So, with meaning and value deriving from the hereditary transmission of substances under the jurisdiction of form, the world is experienced as given (as it always is in the unconscious and in childhood), and the task is to reveal and perpetuate it. So too, with the form perfectly circumscribing the object, a portion of nature is included therein, just as in the case of the human body: the object on this view is essentially anthropomorphic. Man is thus bound to the objects around him by the same visceral intimacy, *mutatis mutandis*, that binds him to the organs of his own body, and 'ownership' of the object always tends virtually towards the appropriation of its substance by oral annexation and 'assimilation'.

What we glimpse today in modern interiors is the coming end of this order of Nature; what is appearing on the horizon, beyond the break-up of form, beyond the dissolution of the formal boundary between inside and outside and of the whole dialectic of being and appearance relating to that boundary, is a qualitatively new kind of relationship, a new kind of objective responsibility. As directly experienced, the project of a technological society implies putting the very idea of genesis into question and omitting all the origins, received meanings and 'essences' of which our old pieces of furniture remained concrete symbols; it implies practical computation and con-ceptualization on the basis of a total abstraction, the notion of a world no longer given but instead produced – mastered, manipulated, inventoried, controlled: a world, in short, that has to be *constructed*.[10]

Although it is different in kind from the traditional procreative order, this modern order nevertheless also depends on a basic symbolic system. Whereas the earlier civilization, founded on the natural order of substances, may be said to have been underpinned by oral structures, the modern order of production, calculation and functionality must be viewed as a phallic order linked to the enterprise whose goal is the supersession and transformation of the given and the opening up of new objective structures; but it is at the same time a faecal order founded on an abstraction or quintessence meant to inform a homogeneous material world, on the measuring off and division of material reality, on a great anal aggressiveness sublimated into play, discourse, ordering, classifying and placement.

The organizing of things, even when in the context of technical enterprise it has every appearance of being objective, always remains a powerful springboard for pro-jection and cathexis. The best evidence of this is the obsessiveness that lies behind so many organizational projects and (of most relevance to our present discussion) behind the will to design. Everything has to intercommunicate, everything has to be functional – no more secrets, no more mysteries, everything is organized, therefore everything is clear. This is not the old slogan of the house-proud: a place for everything and everything in its place. That obsession was moral, today's is functional – and explicable in terms of the faecal function, which requires absolute conductivity in all internal organs. Here we have the basis for a character profile of technical civilization: if hypochondria is an obsession with the circulation of substances and the functioning of the primary organs, we might well describe modern man, the cybernetician, as a mental hypochondriac, as someone obsessed with the perfect circulation of messages.

Notes

1   They may also have taste and style – or not, as the case may be.
2   We cannot help but wonder, however, whether he is not henceforward strictly defined through them relative to society at large.
3   Similarly, the bourgeois and industrial revolution gradually freed the individual from his involvement with religion, morality and family. He thus acceded to a freedom in law as an individual, but also to an actual freedom as labour-power – that is, the freedom to sell himself as labour-power. This parallel has nothing coincidental about it, for there is a profound correlation here: both the serially produced 'functional' object and the social individual are liberated in their 'functional' objectification, not in their singularity or in their totality as object or person.
4   In other words, these things happen at a privileged level. And there is a sociological and a social problem with the fact that a restricted group should have the concrete freedom to present itself, through its objects and furniture, as a model in the eyes of an entire society.
5   A glossy magazine devoted to mass-produced products is unthinkable, the only appropriate form here being a catalogue.
6   The mirror occasionally makes a comeback, but it does so in a baroque cultural mode, as a secondary object – a romantic looking-glass, say, or an antique or bull's-eye mirror. The function is no longer the same.
7   Roland Barthes describes this new stage as it affects cars:

> the uniformity of models seems to belie the very idea of technical performance, so 'normal' driving becomes the only possible field in which phantasies of power and invention can be invested. The car thus transfers its phantasied power to a specific set of practices. Since we can no longer tinker with the object itself, we are reduced to tinkering with the way it is driven . . . it is no longer the car's forms and functions that call forth human dreams but, rather, its handling, and before long, perhaps, we shall be writing not a mythology of the automobile but a mythology of driving. ('La voiture, projection de l'ego', *Réalités*, no. 213, October 1963)

8   A law of dimension also seems to come into play, however, at the level of symbolic organization: any object above a certain size, even one with phallic significance (car, rocket), becomes a receptacle, vessel or womb, while any below a particular size becomes penile, even if it is a bowl or a knick-knack.
9   Intellectual and artistic production, traditionally seen in terms of gifts, inspiration or genius, has never really been anything more than an echo of this archetype.
10   As a matter of fact this model of praxis emerges clearly only when a high technical level has been attained, or in the context of very advanced everyday objects, such as tape recorders, cars or household appliances, whose dials, dashboards or control panels bespeak the degree of mastery and coordination required to operate them. It should be noted that everyday life is still very largely governed by the traditional forms of praxis.

Chapter 33

Luce Giard

DOING COOKING [1980]

(**Source**: de Certeau, Michel, Giard, Luce and Mayol, Pierre (1998) *The Practice of Everyday Life Volume 2: Living Cooking*, translated by Timothy J. Tomasik, Minneapolis, Minn.: University of Minnesota Press, pp. 152–9)

Editor's introduction

As well as being an established historian, Luce Giard worked alongside Michel de Certeau on the project that culminated in the two volumes of *The Practice of Everyday Life* (see Chapter 6). Giard's contribution to the project needs to be seen as both an intervention in, and a continuation of, de Certeau's initial plan. Giard argued that as far as the empirical side of the investigation went little space had been given to consider that women's everyday life might feature distinct limits and pressures, and that it might also evidence specific ways of operating. Her decision to centre her research on cooking was made after watching Chantal Akerman's film *Jeanne Dielman, 23 Quai du Commerce, 1080 Bruxelles* (1975). Akerman has said of her film that it 'is a feminist film because I give space to things which were never, almost never, shown in that way, like the daily gestures of a woman' (Akerman quoted in Martin 1979: 24). In the same way Giard's descriptions of the 'art of cooking' similarly give time and space to the gestures and practices of what she calls 'Kitchen Women Nation' (*le peuple féminin des cuisines*).

Giard's approach to domestic cooking navigates between a number of perspectives. Recognising that domestic routines *are* evidence of gender inequalities, Giard nevertheless wants to both celebrate women's inventiveness in 'doing cooking' and memorialise the skills (the know-how) passed on from one generation of women to another. Memory plays a large part in this phenomenology of the cooking environment, where smells and gestures evoke places and pasts that hold out against powerful tendencies within modern life. Thus women's 'art of cooking' can evidence a tenacity that resists the packaged amnesia of nostalgia while refusing the over-modernisation promoted by the manufacturers and celebrants of the latest in (cooking) technology.

Giard's 'sociology' of cooking is purposefully intimate: her 'informants' are friends and acquaintances (rather than 'focus groups'), and their voices combine with hers in an evoca-

tion of 'doing cooking', rather than providing illustrations for an authoritative interpretation of domestic practice.

Further reading: Gullestad 1984; Highmore 2000b, 2002; Margulies 1996; Martin 1979.

O NE DAY FINALLY, when I was twenty, I got my own small apartment, apart
from school barracks, that included a rudimentary but sufficient facility in which
to prepare my meals. I discovered myself invested with the care of preparing my own
food, delighted with being able to escape from the noise and crowds of college
cafeterias and from the shuttling back and forth to face preordained menus. But how
was I to proceed? I did not know how to do anything. It was not a question of waiting
for or asking advice from the women in the family because that would have implied
returning to the maternal hearth and agreeing to slip back into that discarded feminine
model. The solution seemed obvious: just like everything else, these sorts of things
could be learned in books. All I had to do was find in a bookstore a source of
information that was 'simple', 'quick', 'modern', and 'inexpensive', according to my
then naive vocabulary. And in order to secure the means to do so (at least, so I
thought), I undertook the close study of a paperback cookbook devoid of both illustrations and 'feminine' flourishes. To my mind, this absence endowed the book with
eminent practical value and sure efficiency.

From the groping experience of my initial gestures, my trials and errors, there
remains this one surprise: I thought that I had never learned or observed anything,
having obstinately wanted to escape from the contagion of a young girl's education and
because I had always preferred my room, my books, and my silent games to the
kitchen where my mother busied herself. Yet, my childhood gaze had seen and mem-
orized certain gestures, and my sense memory had kept track of certain tastes, smells,
and colors. I already knew all the sounds: the gentle hiss of simmering water, the
sputtering of melting meat drippings, and the dull thud of the kneading hand. A recipe
or an inductive word sufficed to arouse a strange anamnesis whereby ancient knowledge and primitive experiences were reactivated in fragments of which I was the
heiress and guardian without wanting to be. I had to admit that I too had been
provided with a woman's knowledge and that it had crept into me, slipping past my
mind's surveillance. It was something that came to me from my body and that integrated me into the great corps of women of my lineage, incorporating me into their
anonymous ranks.

I discovered bit by bit not the pleasure of eating good meals (I am seldom drawn to
solitary delights), but that of manipulating raw material, of organizing, combining,
modifying, and inventing. I learned the tranquil joy of anticipated hospitality, when
one prepares a meal to share with friends in the same way in which one composes a
party tune or draws: with moving hands, careful fingers, the whole body inhabited
with the rhythm of working, and the mind awakening, freed from its own ponderous-
ness, flitting from idea to memory, finally seizing on a certain chain of thought, and
then modulating this tattered writing once again. Thus, surreptitiously and without
suspecting it, I had been invested with the secret, tenacious pleasure of *doing-cooking*.

When this became clear in my mind, it was already too late; the enemy was on the inside. It then became necessary to try to explain its nature, meaning, and manner to myself in the hopes of understanding why that particular pleasure seems so close to the 'pleasure of the text', why I twine such tight kinship ties between the writing of gestures and that of words, and if one is free to establish, as I do, a kind of reciprocity between their respective productions. Why seek to satisfy, with one as with the other, the same central need to *spend* [*dépenser*], to dedicate a part of one's lifetime to that of which the trace must be erased? Why be so avid and concerned about inscribing in gestures and words the same fidelity to the women of my lineage?

There have been women ceaselessly doomed to both housework and the creation of life, women excluded from public life and the communication of knowledge, and women educated at the time of my grandmothers' generation, of whom I would like to retain a living and true memory. Following in their footsteps, I have dreamed of practicing an impoverished writing, that of a *public writer* who has no claim to words, whose name is erased. Such writing targets its own destruction and repeats, in its own way, that humble service to others for whom these non-illustrious women (no one knows their names, strength, or courage anymore) represented for generations basic gestures always strung together and necessitated by the interminable repetition of household tasks performed in the succession of meals and days, with attention given to the body of others.

Perhaps that is exactly what I am seeking in my culinary joys: the reconstruction, through gestures, tastes, and combinations, of a *silent legend* as if, by dint of merely living in it with my hands and body, I would succeed in restoring the alchemy of such a history, in meriting its secret of language, as if, from this stubborn stomping around on Mother Earth, the truth of the word would come back to me one day. Or rather, a writing of words, reborn, that would finally achieve the expression of its wonderful debt and the impossible task of being able to return its favor. Women bereft of writing who came before me, you who passed on to me the shape of your hands or the color of your eyes, you whose wish anticipated my birth, you who carried me, and fed me like my great-grandmother blinded with age who would await my birth before succumbing to death, you whose names I mumbled in my childhood dreams, you whose beliefs and servitudes I have not preserved, I would like the slow remembrance of your gestures in the kitchen to prompt me with words that will remain faithful to you; I would like the poetry of words to translate that of gestures; I would like a writing of words and letters to correspond to your writing of recipes and tastes. As long as one of us preserves your nourishing knowledge, as long as the recipes of your tender patience are transmitted from hand to hand and from generation to generation, a fragmentary yet tenacious memory of your life itself will live on. The sophisticated ritualization of basic gestures has thus become more dear to me than the persistence of words and texts, because body techniques seem better protected from the superficiality of fashion, and also, a more profound and heavier material faithfulness is at play there, a way of being-in-the-world and making it one's home.

[. . .]

Culinary practices situate themselves at the most rudimentary level, at the most necessary and the most unrespected level. Traditionally in France, the responsibility for them falls almost exclusively on women and these tasks are the object of ambivalent feelings: the value of French cuisine is enhanced when compared to that of neighboring countries; the importance of diet in raising children and care for the family is emphasized in the media; the responsibility and role of the housewife as primary buyer and supplier for the household are stressed. At the same time, people judge this work to be repetitive and monotonous, devoid of intelligence and imagination; people exclude it from the field of knowledge by neglecting dietary education in school programs. Yet, except for residents from certain communities (convents, hospitals, prisons), almost all women are responsible for cooking, either for their own needs or in order to feed family members or their occasional guests.

In each case, *doing-cooking* is the medium for a basic, humble, and persistent practice that is repeated in time and space, rooted in the fabric of relationships to others and to one's self, marked by the 'family saga' and the history of each, bound to childhood memory just like rhythms and seasons. This women's work has them proliferate into 'gesture trees' (Rilke), into Shiva goddesses with a hundred arms who are both clever and thrifty: the rapid and jerky back and forth movement of the whisk whipping egg whites, hands that slowly knead pastry dough with a symmetrical movement, a sort of restrained tenderness. A woman's worry: 'Will the cake be moist enough?'; a woman's observation: 'These tomatoes are not very juicy, I'll have to add some water while they cook.' A transmission of knowledge: 'My mother (or aunt or grandmother) always told me to add a drop of vinegar to grilled pork ribs.' A series of techniques [*tours de main*] that one must observe before being able to imitate them: 'To loosen a crêpe, you give the pan a sharp rap, like this.' These are multi-faceted activities that people consider very simple or even a little stupid, except in the rare cases where they are carried out with a certain degree of excellence, with extreme refinement – but then it becomes the business of *great chefs*, who, of course, are men.

Yet, from the moment one becomes interested in the process of culinary production, one notices that it requires a multiple memory: a memory of apprenticeship, of witnessed gestures, and of consistencies, in order, for example, to identify the exact moment when the custard has begun to coat the back of a spoon and thus must be taken off the stove to prevent it from separating. It also calls for a programming mind: one must astutely calculate both preparation and cooking time, insert the various sequences of actions among one another, and set up the order of dishes in order to attain the desired temperature at the right moment; there is, after all, no point in the apple fritters being just right when the guests have barely started on the hors d'oeuvres. Sensory perception intervenes as well: more so than the theoretical cooking time indicated in the recipe, it is the smell coming from the oven that lets one know if the cooking is coming along and whether it might help to turn up the temperature. The creative ingenuity of cleverness also finds its place in culinary production: how can one make the most out of leftovers in a way that makes everyone believe that it is a completely new dish? Each meal demands the invention of an alternative ministrategy when one ingredient or the appropriate utensil is lacking. And when friends make a sudden, unexpected appearance right at dinnertime, one must improvise without a score and exercise one's combinatory capacities. Thus, entering into the vocation of cooking and manipulating ordinary things make one use intelligence, a subtle intelligence full of nuances and strokes of genius, a light and lively intelligence that can be perceived without exhibiting itself, in short, *a very ordinary intelligence*.

These days, when the job one has or seeks in vain is often no longer what provides social identity, when for so many people nothing remains at the end of the day except for the bitter wear and tear of so many dull hours, the preparation of a meal furnishes that rare joy of producing something oneself, of fashioning a fragment of reality, of knowing the joys of a demiurgic miniaturization, all the while securing the gratitude of those who will consume it by way of pleasant and innocent seductions. This culinary work is alleged to be devoid of mystery and grandeur, but it unfurls in a complex montage of things to be done according to a predetermined chronological sequence: planning, organizing, and shopping; preparing and serving; clearing, putting away, and tidying up. It haunts the memories of novelists, from the fabulous excesses of Rabelais's heroes, all busy eating, digesting, and relieving themselves,[1] to the 'long lists of mounds of food' of Jules Verne,[2] passing through the 'bourgeois cuisine' of Balzac's creatures,[3] the recipes of Zola, and the tasty simmering dishes of Simenon's concierges.[4]

Listen to these men's voices describing women's cooking, like Pierre Bonte's simple people, whose hearty accents [on an early morning radio talk show] used to populate city mornings with good savages:

> You see, this soup, made with beans, is what we call, of course, a bean soup, but you shouldn't think there are only beans in it. My wife made it this morning. Well, she got up at seven o'clock, her pot of water was on the wood-burning stove – she put her beans on to soak last night – then she added two leeks chopped very fine and some nice potatoes; she put all that together, and when it started boiling, she put her salt pork in. An hour before serving it to us, after three and a half to four hours of cooking, she made a fricassee for it. A fricassee is made in a pan with bacon drippings. She browns an onion in it, and when the onion is nice and golden, she makes up a nice flour roux and then puts it all in the soup.[5]

I will admit it myself: I still dream about the rice croquettes and the fritters that nice children in the Comtesse de Ségur's books used to eat for dinner as a reward for good behavior; I was less well behaved than them and these unknown dishes, which seemed to me adorned with exotic flavors, were never served at our family table. But, taken out of its literary dressing and stripped of its fleeting ennoblement, culinary work finds itself once again in dreary reality. This women's work, without schedule or salary (except to be paid off through service to others), work without added value or productivity (men have more important things to calculate), work whose success is always experienced for a limited duration (the way a soufflé just out of the oven, balancing in a subtle equilibrium, in this glorious peak, is already wavering well before it finally collapses). Yes, women's work is slow and interminable.

Notes

1   On Rabelais, Noëlle Châtelet, *Le Corps à corps culinaire* (Paris: Seuil, 1977), 55–92.

2   'This narrative, but also all the others, and this one with no exception, are interlarded with long lists of mounds of food, as in Dickens, Rabelais, Cervantes . . . For Verne, as for those writers, there is a naive and simple fantasy of feeling full, the horror of emptiness . . . nature is the mother and she provides food. She is full everywhere, as Leibniz said, and she cannot be hungry.

Man is the hole in Nature, he is the hunger of the world' (Michel Serres, *Jouvences sur Jules Verne* [Paris: Minuit, 1974], 176).

3   Robert Courtine, *Balzac à table* (Paris: Laffont, 1976).

4   Robert Courtine, *Le Cabier de recettes de Mme Maigret* (Paris: Laffont, 1974), with a preface by Georges Simenon; and *Zola à table: trois cents recettes* (Paris: Laffont, 1978).

5   Pierre Bonte, *Le Bonheur est dans le pré* (Paris: Stock, 1976), 232. See the book review by Catherine B. Clément, 'Pierre Bonte et ses philosophes du matin: le Christophe Colomb de Chavignol', *Le Monde*, 5–16 February 1976.

Chapter 34

Lynn Spigel

INSTALLING THE TELEVISION SET [1992]

(Source: Spigel, Lynn "Installing the Television Set: Popular Discourses on Television and Domestic Space, 1948–1955," *Camera Obscura* (16:1, Winter 1998). Copyright 1998. All rights reserved. Reprinted by permission of Duke University Press.

Editor's introduction

Lynn Spigel's work on television is of particular interest for the study of everyday life. If television has become a crucial element in our everyday environment, Spigel approaches it as both an everyday material object and a signifying media that continually figures and refigures this environment. So, rather than limiting herself to the analysis of television programmes as discrete texts or focusing on the empirical study of how television is received (the two dominant forms of academic attention), she instead foregrounds television as something that both reflects and constructs social relations via both discourses and material practices. By navigating across a range of texts (television programmes, adverts for television sets, popular representations of TV in the home, and so on) she reveals how television (especially in its early years) ambiguously both threatened and supported dominant familial and gendered relations.

This ambiguity of television's role in domestic life becomes clear when it is seen as a practice that both unites and divides. For early enthusiasts, TV could bring families together in the shared practice of sitting round the TV set watching 'family favourites'. But it was also clear that the practice of watching TV was as likely to divide families as it was to unite them. In particular, age and gender differences were seen as something that TV might exacerbate rather than placate. Such differentiation might be something that has been greatly extended by even more targeted programming via satellite and cable stations.

In many respects Spigel treats TV as a material practice that encompasses (in complex and often contradictory ways) a whole variety of forms that impact on everyday life. TV for Spigel is so ubiquitous and so much part of our everyday life that it extends far beyond the actual device and the programmes it transmits.

Further reading: Moores 2000; Silverstone 1994; Spigel 1991, 1992b, 2001; Walkerdine 1986.

Figure 34.1 Dumont advertisement, *House Beautiful* 91 (November 1949), p. 1

THIS ESSAY BRINGS TOGETHER a variety of popular discourses on television and domestic space which were distributed from a number of institutions – including popular books and magazines, especially middle-class women's home magazines, magazine advertisements for television which idealized a middle-class lifestyle (Figure 34.1), and early television narratives, especially family situation comedies which took the middle-class domestic interior as their principal setting.[1] In examining these discourses in connection with one another, I want to establish the ways in which representations disseminated by different media institutions converge or intersect around questions of television's place in the home. I want to look at the meanings attached to the new object and the modes of use or reception which the media advised. Although these discourses most certainly do not reflect directly the public's response to television in the postwar period, they do begin to reveal the intertextual context through which people (and here especially middle-class women) might have made sense of television and its place in everyday life.

[. . .]

Given its ability to bring 'another world' into the home, it is not surprising that television was often figured as the ultimate expression of progress in utopian statements concerning man's ability to conquer and to domesticate space. In 1946, Thomas H. Hutchinson, an early experimenter in television programming, published a popular book designed to introduce television to the general public, *Here is Television, Your Window on the World*. In his opening pages, Hutchinson wrote, 'Today we stand poised on the threshold of a future for television that no one can begin to comprehend fully. . . . We do know, however, that the outside world can be brought into the home and thus one of mankind's long-standing ambitions has been achieved.'[2] And in *Radio, Television and Society*, a general readership book of 1950, Charles Siepmann explained that, 'television provides a maximum extension of the perceived environment with a minimum of effort. Television is a form of 'going places' without even the expenditure of movement, to say nothing of money. It is bringing the world to people's doorsteps.'[3] Indeed, as this statement suggests, television meshed perfectly with the aesthetics of modern suburban architecture. It brought to the home a grand illusion of space while also fulfilling the 'easy living', minimal motion principles of functionalist housing design.

In fact, I would argue that the ideological harmony between utopian dreams for housing design and for technological solutions to distance created a joint leverage for television's rapid growth in the postwar period. Both of these utopias had been on the agenda well before television's arrival in the 1950s. As Leo Marx has suggested with reference to nineteenth-century literary utopias, the dream of eradicating distances was a central trope of America's early discourse on technology. Particularly in the post-Civil War years, it was machines of transport (especially the train) which became the rhetorical figure through which this dream was realized in popular discourse and literature.[4] By the end of the nineteenth century, communication technology had supplanted transportation. It was now the telegraph, telephone, radio – and later, television – which promised to conquer space.

In the years following World War II, this technological utopia was joined by a complementary housing utopia which was for the first time mass produced. Although the 1950s witnessed the most extreme preoccupation with the merging of indoor and outdoor space, this ideal had been part of the model for interior design in the first suburban houses of the latter nineteenth century. In their widely read book of 1869, *The American Woman's Home*, Catherine Beecher and Harriet Beecher Stowe suggested, for example, that the thrifty Victorian housewife might fashion a 'rustic [picture] frame made of branches . . . and garnish the corners with . . . a cluster of acorns', or else copy their illustration of a large window 'ornamented with a variety of these rural economical adornings.'[5] For the Beecher sisters the merging of indoor and outdoor worlds was a response to the Victorian cult of domesticity – its separation between private/female and public/male domains. Also concerned with bringing nature into the home, the architects of the late 1870s began to build bay windows or else smaller windows that were grouped together in order to form a composite view for the residents.[6] Here, the natural world was associated with the 'true woman' who was to make her home a kind of nature retreat that would counteract the signs of modernity – smokestacks, tenement buildings, crowded streets – found in the urban work centers. As the sharp gender divisions between private and public worlds became increasingly unstable at the end of the nineteenth century, the merging of outside and inside space became more important for domestic architecture, and its meaning was somewhat altered. By the early decades of the twentieth century, the nature ideal still would have been understood in terms of its association with femininity, but it also began to have the more modern meaning of an erasure between separate spheres of public and private life. The bungalow cottages built across the country began to merge inside and outside worlds with their window views and expansive porches.

The most exaggerated effort to erase spatial barriers took place in the modernist architecture movements which emerged in the 1920s in Europe. Architectural modernism, or the 'International Style' as it was also called, quickly took root on American soil, and architects working from a variety of traditions developed many of the principles of modernist design, not least of all the erasure between public and private domains. Homes ranging from Richard Neutra's classical modernist Lovell House of 1929 (a machine-like futuristic structure) to Richard Keck's almost-all-glass Crystal Palace of 1934 to Cliff May's rambling ranch-style homes of the 1940s, foregrounded the merging of indoors and outdoors with window walls, continuous living areas, and/or patio areas that appeared to extend into interior space.

Although these 'homes of tomorrow' were clearly upper-class dream-houses – too expensive or too 'unhomey' for most Americans – the public was at least to some degree familiar with architectural modernism because it was widely publicized through fairs, museum exhibitions, department stores, home magazines, and the movies.[7] In the years following World War II the spatial aesthetics established by modernists appeared in a watered down, mass-produced version when the Levittowns across the country offered their consumers large picture windows or glass walls and continuous dining-living areas, imitating the principle of merging spaces found in the architectural ideal. That this mass-market realization of utopian dreams for housing was to find its companion in television, modernity's ultimate 'space-merging' technology, is a particularly significant historical meeting.

Indeed, the ideological harmony between technological utopias and housing utopias created an ideal nesting ground for television's introduction to the public in the postwar years. Women's home magazines often displayed television sets in decorative settings which created the illusion of spatial conquests. The set was typically placed in rooms with panoramic window views, or else installed next to globes and colorful maps.[8] The image of television as a 'global village', which media critic Marshall McLuhan spoke of in the 1960s, was already suggested in the popular discourses of the postwar period.

Even the manufacturers seemed to realize the marketing potential of this new global village in a box. Advertisers for television typically used this illusion of the outside world as part of their promotional rhetoric. They placed their TV sets against scenic backgrounds suggestive of the far-off spaces which television promised to make domestic. In 1953, Arvin's advertising campaign used the Eiffel Tower and Big Ben as backdrops for its console models.[9] In that same year, Emerson TV went further than Europe. Its television set, with a picture of New York City on its screen, appeared among the planets (and note that the ad also included a smaller TV with a little girl and her poodle, thereby tying domestic meanings to the sci-fi imagery).[10]

This obsession with a view of far-away places was also registered in family sit-coms. Like the model homes in women's magazines, these TV homes incorporated an illusion of outside spaces which could be seen through large picture windows that often dominated the *mise en scène*. It was not just that these domestic interiors repeated the popular architectural ideal; they also fulfilled the expectations about television which were voiced in popular discourses of the time. That is to say, the depiction of domestic space appears to have been based in part upon those utopian predictions which promised that television would provide for its audiences a view of outside spaces. Thus, the representation of the family's private interior world was often merged with a view of public exteriors, a view which was typically a fantasy depiction of high-priced neighborhoods not readily accessible to television's less affluent audiences. Beginning with its first episode in 1950, *The Burns and Allen Show* included numerous windows and glass doors through which appeared a painted backdrop depicting George and Gracie's Beverly Hills yard. In *Make Room for Daddy*, a slightly more realistic window view of New York City dominated the *mise en scène* of the Williams's luxury penthouse. Margie Albright, the spoiled rich girl character of *My Little Margie*, was typically depicted lounging in her sprawling New York apartment – complete with a terrace view of the city skyline. In 1955, the most popular show on television, *I Love Lucy*, attempted to give the TV audience a vicarious vacation by moving its characters to Hollywood for the entire season. The Ricardo's hotel suite contained a wall of windows through which audiences were given a panoramic view of the Hollywood Hills. This travelogue motif was to become conventionalized in the sit-com form when, for example, subsequent seasons saw *Burns and Allen*'s move to New York, *I Love Lucy*'s and *The Honeymooners*' season-long European vacations, and *Make Room for Daddy*'s visit to the Grand Canyon.

This interest in bringing an illusion of the world into the home can be seen as part of a larger historical process in which the home was designed to incorporate social space. Increasingly in the twentieth century, home appliances and other luxury items replaced community facilities. In the postwar years the community activity most under question was spectatorship. According to a 1955 *Fortune* survey, even while postwar Americans were spending a phenomenal '30 billion dollars for fun' in the prosperous postwar economy, when calculated in terms of disposable income, this figure actually reflected about a 2% decline since 1947. By far, the greatest slump was in the spectator amusements – most strikingly in movie attendance, but also in base-ball, hockey, theater, and concert admissions. The *Fortune* survey concluded that American spectators had moved indoors where high fidelity sound and television promised more and better entertainment than in 'the golden age of the box-office'.[11]

Fortune's analysis indeed describes what happened to spectator amusements during the early 1950s. But its conclusion was also typical of a wider discourse which spoke of television as part of a home entertainment center which promised to privatize and domesticate the experience of spectatorship. Moreover, as in the case of the *Fortune* survey, it was primarily the movies and the movie theater which television promised to replace. In 1948, *House Beautiful* told its readers that 'looking at a television program is much like going to a movie'.[12] Advertisements variously referred to the 'family theater', the 'video theater', the 'chairside theater', the 'living room theater', and so forth. A 1953 Emerson ad went one step further by showing an oversized television set which appears on a movie theater stage as a full house views the enormous video screen. The caption reads, 'Now! A TV picture so clear, so sharp . . . you'll think you're at the movies.'[13]

The discursive refiguring of the site of theatrical exhibition was by no means a matter of simple substitution. While 'going to television' might replace going to the theater, this replacement ushered in a grave spatial problem, primarily stated as a woman's problem of spatial confinement in the home. The movie theater was not just a site of exhibition, it was also an arena in which the housewife was given access to social life in the public sphere. In 1951, a cartoon in *Better Homes and Gardens* stated the problem in graphic terms. On his way home, a husband imagines a night of television viewing while his kitchen-bound wife dreams of a night out at the movies (Figure 34.2).[14] As this cartoon suggests, the utopian discourses which promised that television would connect the home to outside spaces were met by dystopian counterparts. For even if television offered a grand illusion of the outside world with its panoramic vistas and travelogue plots, it seems likely that women were critical of this illusionism, that they recognized the discrepancy between the everyday experience of domestic

Figure 34.2 Cartoon, *Better Homes and Gardens* 29 (November 1951), p. 218

isolation perpetuated by television, and the imaginary experiences of social integration which television programming constructed.

Beyond this separation from the public sphere there were other complications for women in their new 'family theaters'. Although television was often promoted as the great instrument of family togetherness, it was just as often depicted as a divisive force. This was especially true in the case of women, who were typically shown to be isolated from the group watching television. In 1951, *American Home* showed a continuous living and dining room in which a woman supposedly was allowed to accomplish her housework among the group watching television. However, as the graphic representation shows, the woman's table-serving chores clearly isolate her from the television crowd which is pictured in the background, as the woman stands to the extreme front-right border of the frame.[15] This problem of female spatial isolation gave way to what can be called a corrective cycle of commodity purchases. Typically, in 1950, Hotpoint advertised its dishwasher by claiming that the machine would bring the woman into the living room where she could watch television with her family.[16]

The television advertisements in women's home magazines (as well as general audience magazines like *Life* and *Look*) also attempted to negotiate this conflict between women's domestic isolation and their integration into social life. Here, the television set itself was figured in the context of a night out on the town. Advertisements typically displayed glamorously dressed husbands and wives whose evenings of television took on, for example, the status of a theater date.[17] According to the logic of such ads, television turned the home into a public meeting hall in which residents could imagine that they were involved in a social occasion.

Indeed, television – at its most ideal – promised to bring to audiences not merely an illusion of reality as in the cinema, but a sense of 'being there', a kind of *hyperrealism*. Advertisers repeatedly promised that their sets would deliver picture and sound quality so real that the illusion would come alive. In 1952, Motorola promised that its 'new dimension of realism brings action right into the living room.'[18] Far exceeding the imagination of Motorola's advertising firm were the advertisers for Sparton television who produced what might be called the emblematic advertisement of this 'come to life' genre. The 1953 ad pictured a large full-color photograph of a baseball stadium. On home plate stood a Sparton TV console whose screen showed a picture of a baseball player up at bat. Out in right field (and in the foreground of the composition) stood a modern-style easy chair with baseball bats and catchers mitts placed nearby. In this way Sparton TV literally transported the living room to the baseball field.[19]

[. . .]

The arrangement of the perfect view in the home was constantly discussed in women's home magazines, which advised readers on ways to organize seating and ambient lighting so as to achieve a visually appealing effect for the spectator. In these discussions the television set was figured as a focal point in the home, with all points of vision intersecting at the screen. In 1951, *Good Housekeeping* advised its readers that 'television is theatre; and to succeed, theatre requires a comfortably placed audience with a clear view of the stage.'[20] Furniture companies like Kroehler 'TeleVue' advertised living room ensembles which were completely organized around the new TV center.

As this focal point of vision, television was often represented in terms of a spatial mathematic (or geometry) complete with charts indicating optimal formulas for visual pleasure. In 1949, *Better Homes and Gardens* suggested, 'To get a good view and avoid fatigue, sit on eye level with screen at no more than 30 degrees off to the side of screen.'[21] Even the TV networks recognized the significance of this new science. CBS in conjunction with Rutgers University studied 102 television homes in order 'to determine the distance and angle from which people watch TV under normal conditions'.[22]

This scientific management of the gaze in the home, this desire to control and to construct a perfect view, was met with a series of contradictory discourses which expressed multiple anxieties about the ability of the domestic environment to be made into a site of exhibition. The turning of the home into a theater engendered a profound crisis in vision and the positions of pleasure entailed by the organization of the gaze in domestic space. This crisis was registered on a number of levels.

Perhaps the most practical problem which television was shown to have caused was in its status as furniture. Here, television was no longer a focal point of the room; rather it was a technological eyesore, something which threatened to destabilize the unities of interior decor. Women's magazines sought ways to 'master' the machine which, at their most extreme, meant the literal camouflage of the set. In 1951, *American Home* suggested that 'television needn't change a room' so long as it was made to 'retire at your command'. Among the suggestions were hinged panels 'faced with dummy book backs so that no one would suspect, when they are closed, that this period room lives a double life with TV'.[23] In 1953, *House Beautiful* placed a TV into a cocktail table from which it 'rises for use or disappears from sight by simply pushing a button'.[24] These attempts to render the television set invisible are especially interesting in the light of critical and popular memory accounts which argue that the television set was a privileged figure of conspicuous consumption and class status for postwar Americans. This attempt to hide the receiver complicates those historical accounts because it suggests that visual pleasure was at odds with the display of wealth in the home.

It wasn't only that the television set was made inconspicuous within domestic space, it was also made invisible to the outside world. The overwhelming majority of graphics showed the television placed in a spot where it could not be seen through the windows of the room.[25] This was sometimes stated in terms of a solution for lighting and the glare cast over the screen. But there was something more profoundly troubling about being caught in the act of viewing television. The attempt to render television invisible to the outside world was imbricated in a larger obsession with privacy – an obsession which was most typically registered in statements about 'problem windows'. The magazines idealized large picture windows and sliding glass doors for the view of the outside world they provided. At the same time, however, the magazines warned that these windows had to be carefully covered with curtains, venetian blinds, or outdoor shrubbery in order to avoid the 'fish bowl' effect. In these terms, the view incorporated in domestic space had to be a one-way view.

Television would seem to hold an ideal place here because it was a 'window on the world' which could never look back. Yet, the magazines treated the television set as if it were a problem window through which residents in the home could be seen. In 1951, *American Home* juxtaposed suggestions for covering 'problem' windows with a tip on 'how to hide a TV screen'.[26] Even the design of the early television consoles, with their cabinet doors which covered the TV screen, suggested the fear of being seen by television. Perhaps, this fear was best expressed in 1949 when the *Saturday Evening Post* told its readers, 'Be Good! Television's Watching.' The article continued, 'Comes now another invasion of your privacy. . . . TV's prying eye may well record such personal frailties as the errant husband dining with his secretary'.[27] The fear here was that the television camera might record men and women unawares – and have devastating effects upon their romantic lives.

The theme of surveillance was repeated in a highly self-reflexive episode of the early 1950s science fiction anthology, *Tales of Tomorrow*. Entitled 'The Window',[28] the tale begins with a standard sci-fi drama but is soon 'interrupted' when the TV camera picks up an alien image, a completely unrelated view of a window through which we see a markedly lower-class and drunken husband, his wife and another man (played by Rod Steiger). After a brief glimpse at this domestic scene, we cut back to the studio where a seemingly confused crew attempts to explain the aberrant image, finally suggesting that it is a picture of a real event occurring simultaneously in the city and possibly 'being reflected off an ionized cloud right in the middle of our wavelength, like a mirage'. As the episode continues to alternate between the studio and the domestic scene, we learn that the wife and her male friend plan to murder the husband, and we see the lovers' passionate embrace (as well as their violent fantasies). At the end of the episode, after the murder takes place, the wife stares out the window and confesses to her lover that all night she felt as if someone were watching her. As this so well suggests, the new TV eye threatens to turn back on itself, to penetrate the private window and to monitor the eroticized fantasy life of the citizen in his or her home. That this fantasy has attached to it a violent dimension, reminds us of the more sadistic side to television technology as TV now becomes an instrument of surveillance. Indeed, this fear of surveillance was symptomatic of many statements which expressed profound anxieties about television's control over human vision in the home – especially in terms of its disruptive effects on the relationship between the couple.[29]

Television brought to the home a vision of the world which the human eye itself could never see. We might say that in popular culture there was a general obsession with the perfection of human vision through technology. This fascination of course pre-dates the period under question, with the development of machines for vision including telescopes, x-rays, photography and cinema. During the postwar period many of these devices were mass produced in the form of children's toys (including microscopes, 3-D glasses, and telescopes) and household gadgets like gas ranges with window-view ovens.

Television, the ultimate expression of this technologically improved view, was variously referred to as a 'hypnotic eye', an 'all seeing eye', a 'mind's eye', and so forth. But there was something troubling about this television eye. A 1954 documentary produced by RCA and aired on NBC suggests the problem. Entitled *The Story of Television*, this program tells the history of television through a discourse on the gaze. A voice-over narration begins the tale in the following way:

> The human eye is a miraculous instrument. Perceptive, sensitive, forever tuned to the pulsating wavelengths of life. Yet the eye cannot see over a

hillside or beyond the haze of distance. To extend the range of human eyesight, man developed miraculous and sensitive instruments.

Most prominent among these instruments was the 'electronic eye' of television.

In this RCA documentary, the discourse on the gaze was used to promote the purchase and installation of the TV set. However, even in this industry promo, there is something disturbing about the 'electronic eye' of television. For here, television inserts itself precisely at the point of a failure in human vision, a failure which is linked to the sexual relations of the couple. Accompanying this sound track is a visual narrative which represents a young couple. A woman frolics on the hillside and we cut to an extreme close-up of a man's face, a close-up which depicts a set of eyes that appear to be searching for the woman. But the couple are never able to see one another because their meeting is blocked by an alternate, and more technologically perfect view. We are shown instead the 'electronic eye' of a TV control tower which promises to see better than the eyes of the young lovers. Thus, the authority of human vision, and the power dynamics attached to the romantic exchange of looks between the couple, is somehow undermined in this technology of vision.

This failure in the authority of human vision was typically related to the man's position of power in domestic space. In 1953, *TV Guide* asked, 'What ever happened to men? Once upon a time (Before TV) a girl thought of her boyfriend or husband as her prince charming. Now having watched the antics of Ozzie Nelson and Chester A. Riley, she thinks of her man as a prime idiot.' Several paragraphs later the article relates this figure of the ineffectual male to an inability to control vision, or rather television, in the home. As the article suggests, 'Men have only a tiny voice in what programs the set is tuned to.'[30]

In a 1954 episode of *Fireside Theatre*, a filmed anthology drama, this problem is demonstrated in narrative terms. Entitled 'The Grass is Greener', the episode revolves around the purchase of a television set, a purchase which the father in the family, Bruce, adamantly opposes. Going against Bruce's wishes, the wife, Irene, makes use of the local retailer's credit plan and has a television set installed in her home. When Bruce returns home for the evening, he finds himself oddly displaced by the new center of interest. Upon entering the kitchen door, he hears music and gun shots emanating from the den. Curious about the sound source, he enters the den where he sees Irene and the children watching a TV western. Standing in the den doorway, he is literally off-center in the frame, outside the family group clustered around the TV set. When he attempts to get his family's attention, his status as outsider is further suggested. Bruce's son hushes his father with a dismissive 'Shh', after which the family resumes its fascination with the television program. Bruce then motions to Irene who finally – with a look of condescension – exits the room to join her husband in the kitchen where the couple argue over the set's installation. In her attempt to convince Bruce to keep the TV, Irene suggests that the children and even she herself will stray from the family home if he refuses to allow them the pleasure of watching TV. Television thus threatens to undermine the masculine position of power in the home to the extent that the father is disenfranchised from his family whose gaze is fastened onto an alternate, and more seductive, authority.

This crisis in vision was also registered in terms of female positions of pleasure in television. In fact, for women, pleasure in viewing television appears to have been a 'structured absence'. These representations almost never show a woman watching television by herself. Typically, the woman lounges on a sofa, perhaps reading a book, while the television remains turned off in the room.[31] Two points emerge. First, for women the continuum, visual pleasure – displeasure, was associated with interior decor and not with viewing television. In 1948, *House Beautiful* made this clear when it claimed, 'Most men want only an adequate screen. But women alone with the thing in the house all day, have to eye it as a piece of furniture.'[32] Second, while these discussions of television were often directed at women, the continuum, visual pleasure – displeasure, was not associated with her gaze at the set, but rather with her status as representation, as something to be looked at by the gaze of another.

On one level here, television was depicted as a threat to the visual appeal of the female body in domestic space. Specifically, there was something visually displeasurable about the sight of a woman operating the technology of the receiver. In 1955, Sparton Television proclaimed that 'the sight of a woman tuning a TV set with dials near the floor' was 'most unattractive'. The Sparton TV, with its tuning knob located at the top of the set, promised to maintain the visual appeal of the woman.[33] As this ad indicates, the graphic representation of the female body viewing television had to be carefully controlled; it had to be made appealing to the eye of the observer.

Beyond this specific case, there was a distinct set of aesthetic conventions formed in these years for male and female viewing postures. A 1953 advertisement for CBS-Columbia Television illustrates this well. Three alternative viewing postures are taken up by family members. A little boy stretches out on the floor, a father slumps in his easy chair, and the lower portion of a mother's outstretched body is gracefully lifted in a sleek modern chair with a seat which tilts upward.[34] Here as elsewhere, masculine viewing is characterized by a slovenly body posture. Conversely, feminine viewing posture takes on a certain visual appeal even as the female body passively reclines.

This need to maintain the 'to-be-looked at' status of the woman's body within the home might be better understood in the context of a second problem which television was shown to bring to women – namely, competition for male attention. Magazines, advertisements and television programming often depicted the figure of a man who was so fascinated with the screen image of a woman that his real life mate remained thoroughly neglected by his gaze. Thus, in terms of this exchange of looks, the television set became the 'other woman'. Even if the screen image was not literally another woman, the man's visual fascination evoked the structural relations of female competition for male attention, a point well illustrated by a cartoon in a 1952 issue of the fashionable men's magazine, *Esquire*, which depicted a newly wed couple in their honeymoon suite. The groom, transfixed by the sight of wrestling on TV, completely ignores his wife.[35] This sexual scenario was also taken up by Kotex, a feminine hygiene company with an obvious stake in female sexuality. The 1949 ad shows a woman who, by using the sanitary napkin, is able to distract her man from his TV baseball game.[36] Perhaps, the ultimate expression of female competition with television came in a 1953 episode of *I Love Lucy* entitled, 'Ricky and Fred are TV Fans'. Lucy and her best friend, Ethel Mertz, are entirely stranded by their husbands as the men watch the fights on the living room console. In a desperate attempt to attract their husbands' attention, Lucy and Ethel stand in front of the TV set, blocking the men's view of the screen. Ricky and Fred Mertz become so enraged that they begin to make violent gestures, upon which Lucy and Ethel retreat into the kitchen. Having lost their husbands to television, the women decide to go to a drugstore/soda shop. However, once in the drugstore they are unable to get service because the proprietor is likewise entranced by the TV boxing match.

But in what way could this sexual/visual competition appeal to women? A 1952 Motorola ad provides some possible answers. The graphic shows a man lounging on a chair and watching a bathing beauty on the TV screen. His wife, dressed in apron, stands in the foreground holding a shovel, and the caption reads, 'Let's go, Mr. Dreamer, that television set won't help you shovel the walk.' Television's negative effect on household chores was linked to the male's visual fascination in the televised image of another woman. This relationship drawn between the gaze and household chores only seems to underline TV's negative appeal for women; but another aspect of this ad suggests a less 'masochistic' inscription of the female consumer. The large window view and the landscape painting hung over the set suggest the illusion of the outside world and the incorporation of that world into the home. In this sense, the ad suggests that the threat of sexuality/infidelity in the outside world can be contained in the home through its representation on television. Even while the husband neglects his wife and household chores to gaze at the screen woman, the housewife is in control of his sexuality insofar as his visual pleasure is circumscribed by domestic space. The housewife's gaze in the foreground and cited commentary further illustrate this position of control.[37]

This competition for male attention between women and television also bears an interesting relationship to the construction of the female image in domestic comedies. Typically the representation of the female body was de-feminized and/or de-eroticized. The programs usually featured heroines who were either non-threatening matronly types like Molly Goldberg, middle-aged, perfect housewife types like Harriet Nelson, or else zany women like Lucy Ricardo who frequently appeared clown-like, and even grotesque.

Popular media of the postwar years illuminate some of the central tensions expressed by the mass culture at a time when spectator amusements were being transported from the public to the private sphere. At least at the level of representation, the installation of the television set was by no means a simple purchase of a pleasure machine. These popular discourses remind us that television's utopian promise was fraught with doubt. Even more importantly, they begin to reveal the complicated processes through which conventions of viewing television in the home environment and conventions of television's representational styles were formed in the early period.

Magazines, advertisements and television programming helped to establish rules for ways in which to achieve pleasure and to avoid displeasure caused by the new TV object/medium. In so doing they constructed a subject position – or a series of subject positions – for family members in the home equipped with television. Certainly, the ways in which the public took up these positions is another question. How women and men achieved pleasure from and avoided the discomforts of television is, it seems to me, an on-going and complicated historiographical problem. The popular media examined here allow us to begin to understand the attitudes and assumptions which informed the reception of television in the early period. In addition, they illustrate the aesthetic ideals of middle-class architecture and interior design into which television was placed.

As historian Carlo Ginzburg has argued, 'Reality is opaque; but there are certain points – clues, signs – which allow us to decipher it.' It is the seemingly inconsequential trace, Ginzburg claims, through which the most significant patterns of past experiences might be sought.[38] These discourses which spoke of the placement of a chair, or the design of a television set in a room, begin to suggest the details of everyday existence into which television inserted itself. They give us a clue into a history of spectators in the home – a history which is only beginning to be written.

Notes

1 This article is based on the research for my dissertation for UCLA, 'Installing the Television Set: The Social Construction of Television's Place in the Home and the Family, 1948–55'. Three leading home magazines (*House Beautiful*, *Better Homes and Gardens* and *American Home*) and one leading women's service magazine which foregrounded home economics (*Ladies' Home Journal*) were examined in entirety for the years under consideration. All of these magazines presented idealized (upper) middle-class depictions of domestic space, and were addressed to a female-housewife, middle-class reader. According to audience research studies conducted at the time, the magazines all attracted a largely female, middle-class readership. See for example, Alfred Politz Research, Inc., *The Audiences of Nine Magazines* (N.p.: Cowles Magazines, Inc., 1955). In addition to examining these publications, I used sampling techniques to analyze leading general magazines, men's magazines, and a leading women's magazine, *Good Housekeeping* (which was directed at a less affluent class). The print advertisements were found in these magazines. Finally, the paper is based upon a large number of programs from the early period including almost all episodes from *Burns and Allen*, *I Love Lucy*, and *The Honeymooners* as well as numerous episodes from *Ozzie and Harriet*, *The Goldbergs*, *Make Room For Daddy*, and *I Married Joan*. I refer to these programs as sit-coms, although it should be noted that at the time the sit-com form for television was not yet fully conventionalized.

2 Thomas H. Hutchinson, *Here is Television, Your Window on the World* (1946; New York: Hastings House, 1948), p. ix.

3 Charles Siepmann, *Radio, Television and Society* (New York: Oxford, 1950), p. 340.

4 Leo Marx, *The Machine in the Garden: Technology and the Pastoral Ideal in America* (New York: Oxford, 1964), see especially p. 193.

5 Catherine Beecher and Harriet Beecher Stowe, *The American Woman's Home* (New York: J.B. Ford and Company, 1869), pp. 91, 96.

6 Gwendolyn Wright discusses this in *Building the Dream: A Social History of Housing in America* (Cambridge, MA: MIT Press, 1981), p. 107.

7 For an interesting discussion of how modern architecture was popularized through the cinema see Donald Albrecht, *Designing Dreams: Modern Architecture in the Movies* (New York: Harper & Row, 1986).

8 See, for example, 'Home Without Compromises', *American Home* 47 (January 1952), p. 34; *Better Homes and Gardens* 33 (September 1955), p. 59; *Good Housekeeping* 133 (September 1951), p. 106.

9 *Better Homes and Gardens* 31 (October 1953), p. 48; *Better Homes and Gardens* 31 (December 1953), p. 21.

10 *Better Homes and Gardens* 33 (March 1953), p. 130.

11 *Fortune* editors, '$30. Billion for Fun', reprinted in *Mass Leisure*, ed. Eric Larrabee and Rolf Meyersohn (1955; Glencoe, IL: The Free Press, 1958), pp. 162–8.

12 *House Beautiful* 90 (November 1948), p. 230.

13 *Better Homes and Gardens* 31 (October 1953), p. 8.

14 *Better Homes and Gardens* 29 (November 1951), p. 218.

15 *American Home* 46 (September 1951), p. 27.

16 *House Beautiful* 92 (December 1950), p. 77.

17 See, for example, *Ladies' Home Journal* 67 (May 1950), p. 6; *American Home* 46 (October 1951), p. 8; *House Beautiful* 97 (November 1955), p. 126; *Colliers* 126 (9 December 1950), p. 58.

18   *Better Homes and Gardens* 30 (October 1952), p. 215. For other examples see, *Life* 34 (26 October 1953), p. 53; *Life* 35 (5 October 1953), p. 87; *House Beautiful* 91 (November 1949), p. 77.
19   *Life* 34 (27 April 1953), p. 12.
20   'Where Shall We Put the Television Set?' *Good Housekeeping* 133 (August 1951), p. 107.
21   Walter Adams and E.A. Hunferford, Jr., 'Television: Buying and Installing It is Fun; These Ideas Will Help', *Better Homes and Gardens* 28 (September 1949), p. 38.
22   Cited in 'With an Eye . . . On the Viewer', *Televiser* 7 (April 1950), p. 16.
23   'Now You See It . . . Now You Don't' *American Home* 46 (September 1951), p. 49.
24   *House Beautiful* 95 (December 1953), p. 145.
25   See, for example, *House Beautiful* 91 (October 1949), p. 167; *Better Homes and Gardens* 30 (March 1952), p. 68; *Better Homes and Gardens* 31 (December 1953), p. 71.
26   *American Home* 45 (January 1951), p. 89.
27   Robert M. Yoder, 'Be Good! Television's Watching', *Saturday Evening Post* 221 (14 May 1949), p. 29.
28   Circa 1951–53.
29   We might also imagine that television's previous use as a surveillance medium in World War II and the early plans to monitor factory workers with television sets, helped to create this fear of being seen by TV. For an interesting discussion of these early surveillance uses, and the way in which this was discussed in the popular and industry press, see Jeanne Allen, 'The Social Matrix of Television: Invention in the United States', in *Regarding Television*, ed. E. Ann Kaplan (Los Angeles: University Publications of America, Inc., 1983), pp. 109–19.
30   Bob Taylor, 'What is TV Doing to MEN?' *TV Guide* 1 (26 June–2 July 1953), p. 15.
31   See, for example, *Better Homes and Gardens* 33 (September 1955), p. 59; *Better Homes and Gardens* 31 (April 1953), p. 263; *Popular Science* 164 (February 1954), p. 211; *Ladies' Home Journal* (May 1953), p. 11.
32   W.W. Ward, 'Is It Time to Buy Television?' *House Beautiful* 90 (October 1948), p. 172.
33   *House Beautiful* 97 (May 1955), p. 131.
34   *Better Homes and Gardens* 31 (October 1953), p. 151.
35   *Esquire* 38 (July 1952), p. 87.
36   *Ladies' Home Journal* 66 (May 1949), p. 30.
37   *Better Homes and Gardens* 30 (February 1952), p. 154.
38   Carlo Ginzburg, 'Morelli, Freud and Sherlock Holmes: Clues and Scientific Method', *History Workshop* 9 (Spring 1980), p. 27.

_____

Chapter 35

Daniel Miller

MAKING LOVE IN SUPERMARKETS [1998]

(**Source**: Miller, Daniel (1998) *A Theory of Shopping*, Ithaca, NY: Cornell University Press, pp. 15–23)

Editor's introduction

Over recent years Daniel Miller has promoted the study of *material* culture as a practice that grounds the anthropology of modernity in the things that circulate in everyday life. In this section from his book on shopping, Miller is concerned with the daily shopping habits of north Londoners. Miller's approach to the performance of shopping is to look for what might be thought of as the deep structures at work in the everyday. By suggesting that shopping is an affective practice based in 'love' and 'sacrifice' Miller uses a language more familiarly used for describing sacred rights. In this insistence that an anthropological language fashioned through contact with tribal communities can 'fit' the seemingly secular and rationalised world of western-style shopping, Miller performs the classic move of 'making the familiar strange'. This defamiliarising of everyday conventions allows the mundane to be seen as a vehicle for values and meanings that might at first glance seem excessive — yet it is in precisely this way that Miller recognises a crucial feature of the everyday life of secular modernity.

From this perspective secular modernity does not simply abandon religious values, rather those values migrate and dissipate into more secular and everyday realms. Birth, death, sacrifice, guilt, all those passionate intensities that were once the province of religion, have migrated into more earthly spaces. Television, for instance, is saturated by police and medical dramas: where once we were shepherded off the earth by various envoys of the Gods, in a secular society the best we can hope for is a good-looking, sympathetic and not too desperately overworked doctor. In secular modernity the commodity fetish is quite literally a talisman invested with magical powers, a token in a cosmology of meanings and effects.

Material cultural studies as practised by Miller and others combines a range of approaches. If here the emphasis is on evidencing the sacred in the everyday (see Chapter 36 for this as well), material cultural studies is also concerned to track things as they circulate within the global networks of advancing world capitalism.

Further reading: Attfield 2000; Hollier 1988; Miller 1987.

F OR MANY PURPOSES the main division in the street where I conducted fieldwork lies between the council estates on one side and the private housing on the other. But the significance of this division cannot always be assumed. Although she lives in an owner-occupied maisonette, Mrs Wynn comes across immediately as quintessentially working class. Her husband is an electrician but has been unemployed for several months owing to an injury. She is a childminder, taking into her home other people's children while they are out working. Between his injury and the fact that someone recently ran into their car while it was parked outside their house, they were not having an easy time of it. Nevertheless, as often proved to be the case, her concerns in shopping bear little upon the contingencies of the moment, and relate more to longer-term issues surrounding the personal development of each member of the family. She was pretty fed up with the consequences of these unexpected events, but shopping as a topic drew her back to things that at one level were more mundane. But these were relationships which she cared about a great deal and was constantly thinking about and forming strategies to deal with. In conversation she notes:

A[1] My husband is quite fussy vegetable wise and he's a big meat eater, but yes I've been doing a lot of stir fries because I found I could get him to eat a lot more vegetables if I do stir fries, and he likes Chinese. He likes spicy stuff. He's got a lot better than when I first met him because his mum's Irish and overcooked everything and was pretty basic and he's got so much better in the years.
Q Do the kids eat the same as him?
A No. Jack my son's got very fussy, definitely in the last year. I would say he's a good vegetable and fruit eater but he's the basic chips and burger and I'm afraid so.
Q Do you cook separately for them?
A Pasta he loves pasta. Yes, and separate times as well.

Later on in the same conversation she notes:

A I try not to buy a lot of convenience [foods]. I do buy meat that is marinated and stuff like that and then think what can I do with it, but now and again I will sit down and get my books out and have a look. I did it last week just because I was getting a bit tired of things. But also what I will do is buy the sauces and the stir-fry things, stuff like that, and then just add it to everything so it makes a bit of difference, but I seem to get stuck doing the same things over and over again. So, every now and then, I've got to get my books out to remind myself or think of some new things.
Q Is it you that's bored?
A No. He will say as well, we've had this a bit too much. I'm a great chicken eater and he says chicken again!

Later still she starts discussing the purchase of clothing for the family, making it clear that she buys her husband's clothes. She notes that out of preference he would just wear some old T-shirts, and often would then go on to use these as cloths during his work. It's not just his clothing she buys. In practice she prefers not to let him do any of the shopping. She feels that if she lets him shop, then he misses things on the list she has made, or buys himself things like biscuits on a whim.

A So it's more hard work. I'd rather him stay here and look after the children and I'll do it. Then it's a break for me and you know.

These views were reiterated when we were out shopping in a local supermarket. She again noted the problems with getting her children to eat what she wants them to eat rather than what they would choose for themselves. She claimed to be quite strict with the children that she was paid to look after, but with respect to her own children, she tended to be much more lenient – 'anything for a bit of peace and quiet.' Again and again her actual purchases are related back to household preferences. When she buys mint-flavoured lamb at the butcher's she notes in passing that this had gone down really well the week before and that she had been asked to get it again. Equally, some jam tarts purchased previously because they were under offer (going cheap) had been well received. The only exceptions to this orientation to the household in her shopping come with the purchase of some bread rolls and frankfurters for a friend who will be coming round for tea. Also at another point in our expedition she buys a fancy ice cream called Vienetta which she declares is 'a treat for herself'.

By no means all the shoppers I accompanied were like Mrs Wynn, but she is representative of a core of households. She should anyway be quite a familiar figure from many previous feminist studies of the housewife. [. . .] Many researchers have acknowledged that which would be clearly evident here. However oppressive the outside observer might find this subsumption of the individual to her husband and children, the housewife herself insists that she merely expresses thereby a series of responsibilities and concerns with which she strongly identifies and of which she is generally proud.

Mrs Wynn acknowledges that she is constantly monitoring, even researching, the desires and preferences of her household. These include both foundational goods which are expected to be constantly present and available in the house, but also transient desires which arise from a preference for at least a subsidiary element of change and innovation. But she would by no means regard herself as merely the passive representative of these desires. Indeed if she merely bought what the other members of her household asked for, shopping would be relatively easy. The problem is that she wishes to influence and change her husband and children in quite a number of ways. She is constantly concerned that they should eat healthier foods than those they would choose for themselves. By the same token she wants them to wear either better quality or at least more respectable clothes than those they prefer. She sees her role as selecting goods which are intended to be educative, uplifting and in a rather vague sense morally superior. It is precisely their unwillingness to be uplifted by her shopping choices that creates the anxieties and battles of shopping. In vindicating their decisions, such housewives often lay claim to a wider perspective than that of other family members. They see themselves as having the foresight to prevent the embarrassment and disdain that others might feel if they let their families dress as they choose, or determine their own food choices.

Of course, all these efforts could be reduced to her interests. It could be argued that she is buying better clothes because she feels she will be made to suffer the opprobrium of criticism by others if she doesn't. She buys healthier foods because she would have to look after the person who otherwise becomes ill. But for us to try to figure out whether the constant hassle of arguing with her family, in order to persuade them to adopt her preferences, actually pays some kind of long-term dividend is the kind of daft calculation we may safely leave to economists, socio-biologists and their ilk. There is no reason to suppose that Mrs Wynn engages in any such weighing up of cost or benefit. As far as she is concerned, the reasons that she researches their preferences and equally that she then tries to improve upon them are the same. Both are assumed by her to represent the outcome of a responsibility so basic that it does not need to be made explicit or reflected upon. In short, her shopping is primarily an act of love, that in its daily conscientiousness becomes one of the primary means by which relationships of love and care are constituted by practice. That it is to say, shopping does not merely reflect love, but is a major form in which this love is manifested and reproduced. This is what I mean to imply when I say that shopping in supermarkets is commonly an act of making love.

One could use other terms than love. Care, concern, obligation, responsibility and habit play their roles in these relationships. So also may resentment, frustration and even hatred. Can these latter be the ingredients of something we may properly term love? As long as it is clear that we understand by this term 'love' a normative ideology manifested largely as a practice within long-term relationships and not just some romantic vision of an idealized moment of courtship, then the term is entirely appropriate. Love as a practice is quite compatible with feelings of obligation and responsibility. As Parker (1996) has noted, love for infants is inevitably accompanied by hatred and resentment, and this is perhaps rather more evident for partnerships. The term is certainly justified by ethnography in as much as these shoppers would be horrified by the suggestion that they did not love the members of their family or that there was not a bedrock of love as the foundation of their care and concern, though they might well acknowledge some of these other attributes as well.

I never knew Mrs Wynn well enough to be able to gain a sense of the more intimate moments within her household. I don't know how free she felt about expressing her love in explicit forms. In general, a reticence with regard to more overt expressions of emotion is regarded as a typically British characteristic, and was commented upon by those born elsewhere. But this reticence about love need not imply its absence, so much as its being essentialized as so natural that it becomes embarrassing to feel the need to express it. One consequence of this reticence is that love has come to be primarily objectified through everyday practices of concern, care and a particular sensitivity to others, within which shopping plays a central role.

During the course of this essay the term 'love', which first appears here as the common term by which relationships are legitimated will become used to represent a value that leads us towards the problems of cosmology and transcendence. These terms are not intended to obfuscate or make complex some simple phenomenon. They merely remind us that within a largely secular society almost all of us still see ourselves as living lives directed to goals and values which remain in some sense higher than the mere dictates of instrumentality. Daily decisions are constantly weighed in terms of moral questions about good and bad action indicated in traits such as sensitivity as against style, or generosity as against jealousy. Though these may not be made explicit, the accounts we use to understand each others' actions depend on the continued existence of cosmology as a realm of transcendent value.

The terms 'cosmology' and 'transcendent' suggest values that are long lasting and opposed to the contingency of everyday life. They are intended to imply that although we focus upon the particular persons, children, partners and friends who occupy our concerns at a given moment of time, the way we relate to them is much influenced by more general beliefs about what social relations should look like and how they should be carried out. At one level then, love is a model of one particular type of identification and attachment. It is one we are socialized into and constantly informed about. This ideal is then triggered by an individual, such as a family member who makes it manifest. A relationship then builds its own specificity and nuance which (sometimes) goes well beyond the transcendent model with which we started. When the term 'love' is used, as here, in a more general sense, actual relationships are found to develop on the basis of much wider norms and expectations which pre-exist and remain after the relationship itself.

The term 'love' then indicates more than a claim to affection made during courtship. It stands for a much wider field of that to which life is seen as properly devoted. In later parts of this essay it will be more closely related back to devotional practices in which the term 'cosmology' is more obviously appropriate since the context is more clearly that of religion. The ethnography suggested that just as devotion is the taken-for-granted backdrop to the carrying out of religious rites in other times and places, so in North London love remains as a powerful taken-for-granted foundation for acts of shopping which will be argued to constitute devotional rites whose purpose is to create desiring subjects.

I would call Mrs Wynn a housewife, even though for the present she is the sole wage-earner of the family, because, for her, housewifery is her principal *raison d'être*. As feminist research has made clear, a person such as Mrs Wynn is more likely to view her earnings as simply part of her housewifery than as a job equivalent to that which her husband would be engaged in were he fit. As someone who identifies with being a housewife, the requests made by her family for particular foods are not viewed with resentment but are in fact desired by her. This is made quite explicit in another conversation with a working-class Cypriot woman.

Q Do you enjoy cooking?
A Yes I do, I'm afraid I do.
Q Does your family appreciate it?
A Oh yes, they do they love the food, my daughter when she comes home she says 'Oh mum food', she opens the fridge as soon as she comes in.
Q Is your husband particular?
A Oh he doesn't like very hot, very spicy food, but no he just eats what he's given really.
Q Does he make any requests?
A Oh I wish he would! No he doesn't.

Here, as is so often the case, there is no evident resentment at being identified unambiguously with housewifery. On the other hand, there is a considerable desire that this should be appreciated by the family members, and not taken for granted. A specific request for an item when shopping is taken as a kind of bringing into consciousness of the role played by the shopper and is most often viewed positively, even if it becomes a cause of contention. The subsequent argument is itself an opportunity for the housewife to demonstrate that she is only contradicting the request because of how much she cares for the person and therefore the consequences of what she buys. In general, the problem many housewives expressed was the lack of valorization, most particularly of the moral, educative and provisioning roles that housewives see as of immense importance. They would not normally use the term 'love' for such concerns, but it is clear from what they do say, that it is love alone that can satisfactorily legitimate their devotion to this work. It is also clear that to be satisfactory the subjects of love should desire and acknowledge that which the housewife sees as her ordinary devotional duty.

In the [1980s and 1990s] we have become far better informed about the work involved in keeping a home going and activities such as shopping. This is almost entirely thanks to a series of important empirical studies of housework inspired by the feminist critique of housewifery as unvalorized labour. Within a short time a normative pattern was uncovered and well documented which suggested that women tended to be largely responsible for the basic provisioning of the household, while men tended to be responsible mainly for extra items that were of particular interest to themselves, but were relatively unimportant in, for example, provisioning for children. Male work outside the home was found to be fully acknowledged through wages and through an endorsement of its centrality to the maintenance of the home as in the phrase 'bringing home the bacon'. By contrast, women's work in the home was not only unpaid but even the homeworker tended to downplay the sheer weight of labour involved in keeping house. This degree of exploitation and the asymmetry of power was reinforced rather than redressed in consumption, where housewives were found to give the best of their labour in meals and comforts to others while often denying themselves the pleasure they strove to create for others.[2]

In general, our fieldwork revealed similar patterns to those uncovered in this previous work, and merely demonstrates that these generalizations still largely hold for the 1990s in this area of North London. Our research thereby also confirms the main conclusion of these other studies as to the basic asymmetry of housework and the exploitation of female labour. By the same token these previous studies provide the bulk evidence for the centrality of love and care as the ideology behind mundane domestic activities such as shopping, to which this case study becomes merely an additional exemplification. The primary examples are these highly conventional expressions of care and concern within households. But there is a wide range of other ways in which love is expressed. Examples include love within egalitarian couples, by the elderly, between friends, siblings and a gamut of other relationships. Even if love is extended to this degree, however, I am obviously not claiming it is ubiquitous. Not every shopping practice is about love; there are others that relate more to selfishness, hedonism, tradition and a range of other factors. What I will claim, however, is that love is not only normative but easily dominant as the context and motivation for the bulk of actual shopping practice.

Notes

1   Throughout this essay 'A' is the informant's answer to a question and 'Q' is the question asked. The speech is reported verbatim and I have not tried to convert it into formal grammar or 'accepted' words.

2   Examples for Britain start with Oakley (1976), and a good selection of the genre may be found collected together in Jackson and Moores (1995). Feminist research is complemented by other genres of sociological research of which Finch (1989) is a particularly important representative and whose results have largely confirmed the centrality of woman as carer and worker within the family.

Chapter 36

_____

Steven Connor

ROUGH MAGIC: BAGS [2000]

(**Source**: first broadcast as part of the series 'Rough Magic' on BBC Radio 3, 9 January 2000, with a transcript made available at http://www.bbk.ac.uk/eh/eng/skc/magic/bags.htm)

Editor's introduction

This chapter is an expanded transcript of what was originally one of a series of radio talks by Steven Connor offering 'philosophical adventures in the everyday'. This series, called 'Rough Magic', exemplifies an approach to material culture based on the fairly modest project of 'thinking through things rather than thinking them through' (Connor 2000a: 4). Initially these forays into the 'magic' of everyday things might bare comparison with Michel Leiris's surreal ethnography in 'The Sacred in Everyday Life' (Leiris [1938] 1988). Yet while Leiris is interested in what constitutes the sacred for him, Connor has a much more cultural and therefore communal project in mind.

The term that Connor uses to describe his approach to the material world is 'cultural phenomenology', and it is the qualification of 'phenomenology' by the term 'cultural' (and vice versa) that suggests its pertinence for approaching the everyday. For Connor:

> Cultural phenomenology would aim to enlarge, diversify and particularise the study of culture. Instead of readings of abstract structures, functions and dynamics, it would be interested in substances, habits, organs, rituals, obsessions, pathologies, processes and patterns of feeling. Such interests would be at once philosophical and poetic, explanatory and exploratory, analytic and evocative. Above all, whatever interpreting and explication cultural phenomenology managed to pull off would be achieved by the manner in which it got amid a given subject or problem, not by the degree to which it got on top of it.
>
> (Connor 1999: 18)

The things examined in 'Rough Magic' (bags, wires, screens and sweets) implicitly suggest the fruitfulness of recovering a perspective on everyday life that navigates across and between the anthropological and the psychoanalytic, the structural and the phenomenological.

Further reading: Clucas 2000; Connor 1999, 2000b; Merleau-Ponty 1962; Trotter 2000a.

T HESE PROGRAMMES are about the role in contemporary lives of certain, very mundane, but at the same time quite magical things. The more abstract, placeless and bodiless our existences, the more we come to live beside ourselves, and encounter the world and each other at a distance and through various kinds of remote control, the odder and lovelier things can become, and the greater the importance in our lives can be of objects that we can lay hands on, manipulate, transform and do things with. Human beings are such incorrigible fidgets, such manipulators of objects, of things we can touch and handle, or think of touching and handling, that it is scarcely possible for us to think, dream and imagine without things exerting their shaping force upon us. We think with shapes and weights and scales and textures. We literally keep ourselves in shape by the ways in which we heft and press and handle things. 'One does not think', Gilles Deleuze and Félix Guattari have written, 'without becoming something else, something that does not think – an animal, a molecule, a particle – and that comes back to thought and revives it.'[1] The effort to prolong this way of thinking through things is what constitutes the group of writings assembled here under the title of *Rough Magic* [only 'Bags' is included here].

The essence of a magical object is that it is more than an object. We can do whatever we like to objects; but magical objects are things that we allow and expect to do things back to us. All magical objects surpass themselves. There is no more magical object than a ball. The first magical objects are probably the blankets, rattles and teddies that young children use for comfort and security, and to ease the growth of the knowledge that the world is full of things that are not them. Children know that their blankets, rattles and teddy-bears are not them, but are nevertheless theirs. Magical objects are for doing magic with; but we use the magical objects in which I am most interested to do magic, not so much on others as on ourselves. These objects have the powers to arouse, absorb, stabilise, seduce, disturb, soothe, succour and drug. They have a life of their own: a life we give them, and give back to ourselves through them, thereby giving rise anew to ourselves. Some of the magical objects about which I talk are ancient, some belong to the world of contemporary technology. All of them are strangely anachronistic.

Bags

If you were to arrive on this earth from another planet, what would be the thing that would strike you most about humans, compared with other species? It would not, I think, be the possession of language, the capacity to laugh, or to remember, or to use tools, or any of these more traditional prerogatives human beings like to accord to themselves. It would be our need, apparently unshared by any other species, to carry things around with us. We are not homo erectus, or homo sapiens, but homo ferens. If we like retrievers and gundogs, it is because we have taught them to share our tenderness about the act of carrying things.

On the isle of Laputa, Swift's Lemuel Gulliver encounters a people who are so mistrustful of language that they carry around in a sack all the objects to which they may need to make reference during the day, producing and displaying them as the occasion arises. Human beings have evolved a fantastic and still-expanding set of ways of dispensing with having to carry our worlds around with us, language being the most important of them. Yet the need persists to bear the weight of things around with us. I am a light traveller by preference; my heart droops at the thought of having to cram my possessions into bags that I will then have to lug around with me wherever I go. I look forward to the day when I can step off the aeroplane in shorts and trainers, have my security details scanned via subcutaneous barcode and walk straight out of the airport. And yet, like everybody else, I also find travelling without luggage intolerable. We are beings apt to feel unbearably light without 'our things'. We don't seem to be able to transport ourselves without transporting things with us. Bags mean this possibility. Bags mean ownership, identity, self-possession. They are memory, the weight of all we have been. Bags I! children used to say. That's not my bag, as jazzmen and hippies had it.

Human beings are given to conceiving of themselves in terms of bags and receptacles. The mother's breast is perhaps at the origin of the sense of promise and secret goodness attaching to bags, and embodied in Santa's bulging sack. Our stories are full of the excitement of delicious and dangerous powers hidden away in bags; letting the cat out of the bag is a dangerous and exciting proceeding, as is letting the winds out of the bag of Aeolus. Sausages and saveloys were sometimes known in the nineteenth century as 'bags of mystery'.

Because they are in essence such fleshly or bodily things, bags enact as nothing else does our sense of the relation between inside and outside. We are creatures who find it easy and pleasurable to imagine living on the inside of another body; we ourselves come into independent existence very slowly, being carried, like bags, for long enough to come to know this intermediate condition intimately, and never to be able to forget it. Independence literally means not hanging. Human beings make the world into bags, because holding things together, holding things up, and being ourselves held and held up, is so important to us. Infant human beings are carried for longer than any other creature. For no other creature, it seems, are carrying and being carried so inextricably a part of one's identity. This is indicated clearly enough in the many different senses in which carrying and carriage are threaded through our language. Carrying things is important for how we carry ourselves. The fact that we understand so well what it is to be carried, what it is to be in a bag, or to be like one, accounts for our concern for and even tenderness towards bags. We carry bags, but we design them also to be able to cling on to us, our shoulders, or the crooks of our arms, or even to hang at our waists. When we give bags handles, we give them hands. Bags are the little people we once were and still are. We love portable property because we were it. Since the months I spent carrying my babies in slings, I have been unable to see or hold a bag without tenderness. Bags must be treated with care, because of the life there is in them. It is impossible to be wholly without grace when carrying a bag.

Bags join space to time. We do indeed, in every sense, 'bear children'. Both 'bearing' and 'carrying' conjoin in the same way the meanings of holding up and holding out: of supporting, holding and transporting through space, and enduring or lasting out through time. You bear an ordeal, or carry out a task, or hold on through suffering, as though time were something we experienced as a kind of weight. 'Time', we say, 'hangs heavy'. To bear, to carry, means to endure, to last out; to carry and to carry on, to carry over, to endure: weight means time: so weight means waiting. Samuel Beckett puns lengthily on the two different kinds of wait in his play *Waiting for Godot*, which contains a memorable bag-carrier in the person of Lucky, the slave of the tyrant Pozzo, who spends most of the play encumbered by his master's enormous bags. Because he is kept at the end of a long rope tied around his neck, Lucky is himself a kind of bag, more or less. Estragon, one of the two tramps who meet Pozzo and Lucky in the indeterminate landscape of the play, is tormented by the question 'Why doesn't he put down his bags?', asking it again and again.[2] The question itself holds up the action, which in this play of ultimate inaction, actually means keeping it going. When eventually Lucky does put down his bags, in order to start incomprehensibly thinking out loud, the others find his monologue intolerable, and beat him to the ground. Carrying not only weighs us down, it also, it appears, keeps us up.

And is not Beckett the great, hitherto uncelebrated dramatist of bags? In his play *Happy Days*, the first act of which is the monologue of a woman buried up to her waist in a mound of earth, the action is punctuated and parcelled out by Winnie's plunges and sallies into her bag – for lipstick, toothpaste, mirror, medicine, and all the possibilities they bury of beguiling the vicious time they embody. ('Perhaps just one quick dip', she says, as a boozer to his tipple.)[3] When, in the second act, she is inhumed up to her neck, the horror of her situation is signalled most of all by the bag which lies on the mound, tauntingly gaping just in sight and to hand, though for the handless Winnie now unreachable; as though all the resources of life and memory and history were held inaccessibly in it.

Lives are full of bags. Bags are full of lives.

Bags are female seeming objects, and have strong associations with female experience in many cultures. Few women are able to bear the horror of male fingers rummaging in their handbags; there is no man who has never itched to do this. In Britain and America, subtle, untaught but unbreachable rules still govern the kind of bags that men and women can feel comfortable holding or carrying. One of the rules seems to be that the floppier the bag, the less male it seems. Another bizarre rule concerns the length of the handle. The longer the handles of a bag, the more effeminate the bag, perhaps because the more handle there is attached to a bag, the more it can appear to be something hanging on to you, rather than something that you are actively holding. And then, for reasons which I cannot easily explain, a man's masculinity seems more compromised by a string bag than any other kind. But then why do women, whom men delight in imagining to be made up almost entirely of dark recesses and hidden cavities, usually have no pockets? My father used to say that somebody or something was 'as useless as a pocket in a singlet'. But such a thing has only to be named for me to be able to imagine its marsupial comfort and utility. I would willingly wear a singlet in secret if only to have such a thing close to me.

In every household I know, there is a special place where plastic carrier bags are hoarded. A drawer, or a box, or, nine times out of ten, a bag of bags. What is it for? What is the meaning of this? Perhaps because there is always something ruthless or insulting about simply throwing away a bag. In our cellar, we have an even more marvellous contrivance. It is a luggage nest. On the outside, there is a large, firm, capacious suitcase, snapped shut with latches. Inside that, there is a slightly smaller suitcase; unzip that, and there is an aptly-named holdall, clasped tightly round a vanity case, and then a series of ever flimsier, but more tightly-budded pouches, purses and something I cannot forbear calling a reticule, though I do not know what this is. And round the whole thing, holding together the whole bursting, visceral contraption, there is a sheet of polythene against the dust, swollen skin-tight. It is a body we have got down there, a cannibal organism that binges on and breeds itself. I have just remembered that, when I was at school, the girls used to bring in anatomical dolls, that you could fold open to reveal their inner organs. Kneeling in front of our luggage nest, my hand plunging through the layers, groping for the little overnight bag I want right in the last level, I am doing the same play-surgery as they did in the playground.

If bags irresistibly suggest wombs, bellies and breasts, and may suggest an identification with women in their containing function, they have some distinctively male ingredients, too. For the shape of bags is rhythmic. Bags are defined by a rhythm of alternation between rigidity and collapse. Held, or worn, or carried, bags come into their own, assume and hold their own shapes. Put down, bags sag and crumple, their rigidity and definition ebbing from them. And bags offer quickening excitement in the contrast between hard and soft shapes; the pillow-case on Christmas morning, jutting with exciting knobs, elbows and corners, or the inverse, the impermeable outer casing containing folded softness.

You can think of bags as concrete meditations on the nature of human weight and shape. The principle of a bag is that it runs from the skimpiest form, which does nothing but wrap its contents, through to the sturdiest skeleton, which gives no clue as to the size or shape or weight of what lies inside. It is the operative difference between men, who may think of themselves as impermeable and undentable, but who nevertheless know, perhaps even more intimately than women, the bag-like rhythm of tumescence and collapse, and women, who cannot give birth without having to change their shapes. Bagmakers and bag users relish the jokes this contrast allows: a lock on a floppy bag is the most lovely futility imaginable.

How we carry bags is important. Bags are carried in the hand, in the crook of the arm, over the shoulder, on the back. In the form of pockets, bags can blister out on chests, thighs and hips. Our care for baggage extends to our means of transport, which have bags attached to them, from saddlebags to the boots of coaches and cars. We carry bags on our fronts, on our heads, to the side, on our backs. Bags are a way of keeping and displaying connections between our fronts and other parts of us, less visible, more vulnerable. A couple of years ago, do you remember, girls took to wearing tiny, exquisitely functionless little rucksacks, like a ganglion in the middle of their backs. It was as though they had a third eye, or a little growing homunculus clinging to them. Bags are our most intimate selves, even when we wear them most casually strung around our necks or on our backs.

Just as we sleep in sleeping bags, we have a need to restore ourselves to bags and sacks when we die, just as we come from bags and sacks in getting born. This is why we find the idea of putting a body straight into the ground so difficult to do, and why bags and sacks are associated with death just as much with life. Nineteenth-century resurrectionists, who dug up newly-buried bodies for the purposes of medical dissection, were known as 'sack 'em up men'. The more like bags we become, the more we sag and dangle, the more we are weighed down with ourselves, rather than carrying ourselves, the closer we are to death. War means servicemen coming home in body-bags. The First World War poet Isaac Rosenberg refers to the body of a soldier about to be reduced vilely to mere matter as the 'soul's sack'.

So, as well as goodness and wealth and plump incipience, bags are also the sign of indigence and indignity. Uselessness, indignity and superannuation. Giving somebody the sack derives from the phrase 'to give someone the bag to hold' common in the eighteenth and nineteenth centuries. A woman who left a man at a dance to flirt with another would give him the metaphorical bag to hold, the idea being, I suppose, that to be left holding somebody's bag, left uselessly hanging on, or hanging around, you have been reduced to the condition of a bag. Holding her bag, the jiltee would have become it. Similarly, to be given the sack and made useless is to become a sack. No beggar so poor as to be unaccommodated with a bag of some kind; in the late sixteenth century, to 'turn to bag and wallet' meant to become a beggar. Tramps and bag ladies need bags to make the nothing they have and are into a kind of portable property.

Bags are antique and aging things. You can call someone an old bag, but it would be ridiculous to call someone a young bag. We carry more and more bags about our persons, which themselves become more and more baglike, as we age. Clothes enact our relationship to this ageing into the state of baggage, rags, luggage. Our very clothes keep us clear of death and age only as long as they hold us, the function of clothes not at all being to cover, but to contain and sustain. Is there a grimmer witness to our good riddance than our clothes when they are emptied of us – a flung sock, or a tangled brassière?

The absurd uselessness of baggage at the approach of death identifies baggage with death's ultimate beggary. Perhaps this is why packing, even in the midst of life, is always a bit like picking over and putting away the possessions of the newly dead.

Notes

1   Gilles Deleuze and Félix Guattari (1994) *What Is Philosophy?*, translated by Hugh Tomlinson and Graham Burchill, London: Verso, p. 42.
2   Samuel Beckett (1986) *Waiting for Godot, Complete Dramatic Works*, London: Faber & Faber, pp. 28–9.
3   Samuel Beckett (1986) *Happy Days, Complete Dramatic Works*, London: Faber & Faber, p. 151.

Bibliography

Adair, Gilbert (1993) 'The Eleventh Day: Perec and the Infra-ordinary', *Review of Contemporary Fiction*, 13(1): 98–107.

Adorno, Theodor (1991) 'Free Time', in *The Culture Industry: Selected Essays on Mass Culture*, London and New York: Routledge.

—— (1994) *The Stars Down to Earth and Other Essays on the Irrational in Culture*, London and New York: Routledge.

Ahearne, Jeremy (1995) *Michel de Certeau: Interpretation and its Other*, Cambridge: Polity Press.

Althusser, Louis and Balibar, Etienne ([1968] 1979) *Reading Capital*, London: Verso.

Anderson, Perry (1979) *Considerations of Western Marxism*, London: Verso.

—— (1992a) *A Zone of Engagement*, London: Verso.

—— (1992b) *English Question*, London: Verso.

Ang, Ien (1996) *Living Room Wars: Rethinking Media Audiences for a Postmodern World*, London and New York: Routledge.

Appadurai, Arjun (ed.) (1986) *The Social Life of Things: Commodities in Cultural Perspective*, Cambridge: Cambridge University Press.

Aragon, Louis ([1926] 1987) *Paris Peasant*, translated by Simon Watson Taylor, London: Picador.

Armstrong, Tim (1998) *Modernism, Technology and the Body: A Cultural Study*, Cambridge: Cambridge University Press.

Arvatov, Boris ([1925] 1997) 'Everyday Life and the Culture of the Thing (Towards a Formulation of the Question)', translated by Christina Kiaer, *October*, 81: 119–28.

Asad, Talal (ed.) (1973) *Anthropology and the Colonial Encounter*, New York: Humanities Press.

Attfield, Judy (2000) *Wild Things: The Material Culture of Everyday Life*, Oxford and New York: Berg.

Attfield, Judy and Kirkham, Pat (eds) (1995) *A View from the Interior: Women and Design*, London: The Women's Press.

Augé, Marc (1995) *Non-Places: Introduction to an Anthropology of Supermodernity*, translated by John Howe, London: Verso.

—— (1998) *A Sense for the Other: The Timeliness and Relevance of Anthropology*, translated by Amy Jacobs, Stanford, Calif.: Stanford University Press.

—— (1999a) *An Anthropology for Contemporaneous Worlds*, translated by Amy Jacobs, Stanford, Calif.: Stanford University Press.

—— (1999b) *The War of Dreams: Studies in Ethno Fiction*, translated by Liz Heron, London: Pluto Press.

Bakhtin, Mikhail (1981) *The Dialogic Imagination*, translated by Caryl Emerson and Michael Holquist, Austin, Tex.: University of Texas Press.

—— (1984) *Rabelais and his World*, translated by Hélène Iswolsky, Bloomington, Ind.: Indiana University Press.

Barthes, Roland ([1957] 1973) *Mythologies*, translated by Annette Lavers, London: Granada.

—— (1977) *Roland Barthes by Roland Barthes*, translated by Richard Howard, New York: Hill & Wang.

—— ([1966] 1987) *Criticism and Truth*, translated by Katrine Pilcher Keuneman, London: Athlone Press.

—— ([1967] 1990) *The Fashion System*, translated by Matthew Ward and Richard Howard, Berkeley, Calif. and London: University of California Press.

Bassnett, Susan (1986) *Feminist Experiences: The Women's Movement in Four Cultures*, London: Allen & Unwin.

Bataille, Georges (1985) *Visions of Excess: Selected Writing 1927–1939*, translated by Allan Stoekl, Manchester: Manchester University Press.

Bataille, Georges, Leiris, Michel *et al.* (1995) *Encyclopaedia Acephalica*, London: Atlas.

Baudelaire, Charles (1964) *The Painter of Modern Life and Other Essays*, translated by Jonathan Mayne, New York: Da Capo.

Baudrillard, Jean ([1981] 1994) *Simulacra and Simulation*, translated by Sheila Faria Glaser, Ann Arbor, Mich.: University of Michigan Press.

—— ([1968] 1996) *The System of Objects*, translated by James Benedict, London and New York: Verso.

—— ([1970] 1998) *The Consumer Society: Myths and Structures*, London and Thousand Oaks, Calif.: Sage.

Baxandall, Rosalyn and Ewen, Elizabeth (2000) *Picture Windows: How the Suburbs Happened*, New York: Basic Books.

Bellos, David (1999) *Georges Perec: A Life in Words*, London: Collins Harvill.

Bellour, Raymond (ed.) (1992) *Jean-Luc Godard: Son + Image 1974–1991*, New York: Museum of Modern Art, Harry N. Abrams.

Benedict, Ruth ([1934] 1989) *Patterns of Culture*, Boston, Mass.: Houghton Mifflin.

Benjamin, Walter (1982a) *Illuminations*, translated by Harry Zohn, London: Fontana.

—— (1982b) 'The Work of Art in the Age of Mechanical Reproduction', in *Illuminations*, translated by Harry Zohn, London: Fontana.

—— (1983) *Charles Baudelaire: A Lyric Poet in the Era of High Capitalism*, translated by Harry Zohn, London: Verso.

—— (1996) *Selected Writings Volume 1: 1913–1926*, Cambridge, Mass. and London: Harvard University Press.

—— (1999a) *Selected Writings Volume 2: 1927–1934*, Cambridge, Mass. and London: Harvard University Press.

—— (1999b) *The Arcades Project*, translated by Howard Eiland and Kevin McLaughlin, Cambridge, Mass. and London: Harvard University Press.

Bennett, Tony (1998) *Culture: A Reformer's Science*, London: Sage.

Bentley, Nancy (1995) *The Ethnography of Manners: Hawthorne, James and Wharton*, Cambridge: Cambridge University Press.

Berger, John and Mohr, Jean (1982) *A Seventh Man: A Book of Images and Words about the Experience of Migrant Workers in Europe*, London and New York: Writers and Readers.

Berger, Peter and Luckmann, Thomas ([1966] 1991) *The Social Construction of Reality: A Treatise in the Sociology of Knowledge*, Harmondsworth: Penguin.

Berlant, Lauren (1991) *The Anatomy of National Fantasy: Hawthorne, Utopia, and Everyday Life*, Chicago: University of Chicago Press.

Berman, Marshall (1983) *All that is Solid Melts into Air: The Experience of Modernity*, London: Verso.

Blanchot, Maurice ([1959] 1987) 'Everyday Speech', translated by Susan Hanson, *Yale French Studies*, 73: 12–20.

Bonnett, Alastair (1992) 'Art, Ideology and Everyday Space: Subversive Tendencies from Dada to Postmodernism', *Environment and Planning D: Society and Space*, 10: 69–86.

Bourdieu, Pierre ([1972] 1977) *Outline of a Theory of Practice*, translated by Richard Nice, Cambridge: Cambridge University Press.

—— ([1979] 1989) *Distinction: A Social Critique of the Judgement of Taste*, translated by Richard Nice, London and New York: Routledge.

—— (1990) *In Other Words: Essays towards a Reflexive Sociology*, translated by Matthew Adamson, Cambridge: Polity Press.

—— (1992) *The Logic of Practice*, translated by Richard Nice, Cambridge: Polity Press.

Bourdieu, Pierre, *et al.* (1999) *The Weight of the World: Social Suffering in Contemporary Society*, translated by Priscilla Ferguson, Cambridge: Polity Press.

Bowlby, Rachel (2000) *Carried Away: The Invention of Modern Shopping*, London: Faber & Faber.

Boym, Svetlana (1994) *Common Places: Mythologies of Everyday Life in Russia*, Cambridge, Mass.: Harvard University Press.

Braudel, Fernand (1985) *The Structures of Everyday Life: The Limits of the Possible. Volume One of Civilization and Capitalism 15th–18th Century*, translated by Siân Reynolds, London: Fontana.

Brecht, Bertolt (1964) *Brecht on Theatre: The Development of an Aesthetic*, translated and edited by John Willett, London: Methuen.

Breton, André (1960) *Nadja*, translated by Richard Howard, New York: Grove Press.

Bristow, Joseph (1991) 'Life Stories: Carolyn Steedman's History Writing', *New Formations*, 13: 113–31.

Brown, Bruce (1973) *Marx, Freud, and the Critique of Everyday Life: Toward a Permanent Cultural Revolution*, New York: Monthly Review Press.

Bruner, Jerome (1987) 'Life as Narrative', *Social Research*, 54(1): 11–32.

Buchanan, Ian (1996) 'De Certeau and Cultural Studies', *New Formations*, 31: 175–88.

—— (2000) *Michel de Certeau: Cultural Theorist*, London and Thousand Oaks, Calif.: Sage.

Buchloh, Benjamin H. D. and Rodenbeck, Judith F. (2000) *Experiments in the Everyday: Allan Kaprow and Robert Watts – Events, Objects, Documents*, New York: Wallach Art Gallery, Columbia University.

Buck-Morss, Susan (1986) 'The Flâneur, the Sandwichman and the Whore: The Politics of Loitering', *New German Critique*, 39: 99–140.

—— (1989) *The Dialectics of Seeing: Walter Benjamin and the Arcades Project*, Cambridge, Mass.: MIT Press.

Burgin, Victor (1996) *In/Different Spaces: Place and Memory in Visual Culture*, Berkeley, Calif. and London: University of California Press.

Burke, Peter (1990) *The French Historical Revolution: The Annales School 1929–89*, Cambridge: Polity Press.

—— ed. (1991) *New Perspectives on Historical Writing*, Cambridge: Polity Press.

Burns, Tom (1992) *Erving Goffman*, London and New York: Routledge.

Caillois, Roger (1959) *Man and the Sacred*, translated by Meyer Barash, Glencoe, NY: Free Press.

Calder, Angus and Sheridan, Dorothy (eds) (1985) *Speak for Yourself: A Mass-Observation Anthology 1937–1949*, Oxford: Oxford University Press.

Carrard, Philippe (1995) 'Theory of a Practice: Historical Enunciation and the *Annales* School', in Frank Ankersmit and Hans Kellner (eds) *A New Philosophy of History*, London: Reaktion.

Castoriadis, Cornelius ([1975] 1997) *The Imaginary Institution of Society*, translated by Kathleen Blamey, Cambridge: Polity Press.

Cavell, Stanley (1994) *In Quest of the Ordinary: Lines of Skepticism and Romanticism*, Chicago and London: University of Chicago Press.

Chant, Colin ed. (1988) *Sources for the Study of Science, Technology and Everyday Life 1870–1950 – Volume 2: A Secondary Reader*, London: Hodder & Stoughton.

Charney, Leo and Schwartz, Vanessa R. (eds) (1995) *Cinema and the Invention of Modern Life*, Berkeley, Calif.: University of California Press.

Chartier, Roger (1988) *Cultural History: Between Practices and Representations*, translated by Lydia G. Cochrane, Cambridge: Polity Press.

Chatterjee, Partha (1993) *The Nation and its Fragments: Colonial and Postcolonial Histories*, Princeton, NJ: Princeton University Press.

Chaturvedi, Vinayak (ed.) (2000) *Mapping Subaltern Studies and the Postcolonial*, London and New York: Verso.

Chow, Rey (1995) *Primitive Passions: Visuality, Sexuality, Ethnography, and Contemporary Chinese Cinema*, New York: Columbia University Press.

Clark, T. J. (1985a) *The Painting of Modern Life: Paris in the Art of Manet and his Followers*, London: Thames & Hudson.

—— (1985b) 'Clement Greenberg's Theory of Art', in Francis Frascina ed. *Pollock and After: The Critical Debate*, London: Harper & Row.

Clarke, John, Critcher, Chas and Johnson, Richard (eds) (1979) *Working Class Culture: Studies in History and Theory*, London: Hutchinson.

Clifford, James (1988) *The Predicament of Culture: Twentieth-Century Ethnography, Literature, and Art*, Cambridge, Mass.: Harvard University Press.

Clifford, James and Marcus, George E. (eds) (1986) *Writing Culture: The Poetics and Politics of Ethnography*, Berkeley, Calif.: University of California Press.

Clucas, Stephen (2000) 'Cultural Phenomenology and the Everyday', *Critical Quarterly*, 42(1): 8–34.

Cohen, Margaret (1993) *Profane Illumination: Walter Benjamin and the Paris of Surrealist Revolution*, Berkeley, Calif.: University of California Press.

Cohen, Stanley and Taylor, Laurie ([1976] 1992) *Escape Attempts: The Theory and Practice of Resistance to Everyday Life*, London and New York: Routledge.

Connor, Steven (1999) 'CP: or, a Few Don'ts by a Cultural Phenomenologist', *Parallax*, 11: 17–31.

—— (2000a) 'Making an Issue of Cultural Phenomenology', *Critical Quarterly*, 42(1): 2–6.

—— (2000b) *Dumbstruck: A Cultural History of Ventriloquism*, Oxford: Oxford University Press.

Cowan, Ruth Schwartz (1989) *More Work for Mother: The Ironies of Household Technology from the Open Hearth to the Microwave*, London: Free Association Books.

Crook, S (1998) 'Minatours and Other Monsters: "Everyday Life" in Recent Social Theory', *Sociology*, 32(3): 523–40.

Cross, Gary (ed.) (1990) *Worktowners at Blackpool: Mass-Observation and Popular Leisure in the 1930s*, London and New York: Routledge.

Dant, Tim (1999) *Material Culture in the Social World*, Buckingham: Open University Press.

Davidoff, Leonore (1995) *Worlds Between: Historical Perspectives on Gender and Class*, Cambridge: Polity Press.

Davies, Margery W. (1982) *Woman's Place is at the Typewriter: Office Work and Office Workers 1870–1930*, Philadelphia, Pa: Temple University Press.

de Beauvoir, Simone ([1949] 1993) *The Second Sex*, translated by H. M. Parshley, London: Campbell.

Debord, Guy (1983) *Society of the Spectacle*, Detroit, Ill.: Black and Red.

de Certeau, Michel (1984) *The Practice of Everyday Life*, translated by Steven Rendall, Berkeley, Calif.: University of California Press.

—— (1997a) *The Capture of Speech and Other Political Writings*, translated by Tom Conley, Minneapolis, Minn.: University of Minnesota Press.

—— (1997b) *Culture in the Plural*, translated by Tom Conley, Minneapolis, Minn.: University of Minnesota Press.

de Certeau, Michel, Giard, Luce and Mayol, Pierre (1998) *The Practice of Everyday Life Volume 2: Living Cooking*, translated by Timothy J. Tomasik, Minneapolis, Minn.: University of Minnesota Press.

Delany, Samuel R. (1993) *The Motion of Light in Water: Sex and Science Fiction Writing in the East Village*, New York: Richard Kasak.

de Man, Paul (1986) *The Resistance to Theory*, Manchester: Manchester University Press.

Dent, Gina (ed.) (1992) *Black Popular Culture (A Project by Michele Wallace)*, Seattle, Wash.: Bay Press.

Devereaux, Leslie and Hillman, Roger (eds) (1995) *Fields of Vision: Essays in Film Studies, Visual Anthropology and Photography*, Berkeley, Calif.: University of California Press.

Dirlik, Arif and Zhang, Xudong (eds) (2000) *Postmodernism and China*, Durham, NC and London: Duke University Press.

Donzelot, Jacques (1997) *The Policing of Families*, translated by Robert Hurley, Baltimore, Md and London: Johns Hopkins University Press.

Drotner, Kirsten (1994) 'Ethnographic Enigmas: "The Everyday" in Recent Media Studies', *Cultural Studies*, 8(2): 341–57.

Eagleton, Terry (1986) *Against the Grain: Selected Essays*, London: Verso.

—— (1990) *The Ideology of the Aesthetic*, Oxford: Blackwell.

Edwards, Stephen (1984) 'Disastrous Documents', *Ten-8*, 15: 12–23.

Eldridge, John and Eldridge, Lizzie (1994) *Raymond Williams: Making Connections*, London and New York: Routledge.

Fabian, Johannes (1983) *Time and the Other: How Anthropology Makes its Object*, New York: Columbia University Press.

Fanon, Frantz (1986) *Black Skin, White Masks*, translated by Charles Lam Markmann, London: Pluto Press.

Featherstone, Mike (1992) 'Postmodernism and the Aestheticization of Everyday Life', in Scott Lash and Jonathan Friedman (eds) *Modernity and Identity*, Oxford: Blackwell.

—— (1995) 'The Heroic Life and Everyday Life', in *Undoing Culture: Globalization, Postmodernism and Identity*, London: Sage.

Featherstone, Mike, Hepworth, Mike and Turner, Bryan S. (eds) (1991) *The Body: Social Process and Cultural Theory*, London: Sage.

Felski, Rita (1995) *The Gender of Modernity*, Cambridge, Mass.: Harvard University Press.

Ferguson, Harvie (1996) *The Lure of Dreams: Sigmund Freud and the Construction of Modernity*, London and New York: Routledge.

Finch, Janet (1989) *Family Obligations and Social Change*, Cambridge: Polity Press.

Fiske, John (1989) *Understanding Popular Culture*, London and New York: Routledge.

—— (1992) 'Cultural Studies and the Culture of Everyday Life', in Lawrence Grossberg, Cary Nelson and Paula Treichler (eds) *Cultural Studies*, New York and London: Routledge.

Fitzpatrick, Sheila (2000) *Everyday Stalinism – Ordinary Life in Extraordinary Times: Soviet Russia in the 1930s*, Oxford: Oxford University Press.

Foucault, Michel (1971) *Madness and Civilization: A History of Insanity in the Age of Reason*, translated by Richard Howard, London: Tavistock.

—— (1976) *The Birth of the Clinic*, translated by A. M. Sheridan, London: Tavistock.

—— (1977) *Language, Counter-Memory, Practice: Selected Essays and Interviews*, translated Donald F. Bouchard, New York: Cornell University Press.

—— (1980a) *Power/Knowledge: Selected Interviews and Other Writings, 1972–1977*, translated by Colin Gordon, New York: Pantheon.

—— (1980b) *Herculine Barbin: Being the Recently Discovered Memoirs of a Nineteenth-Century French Hermaphrodite*, translated by Richard McDougall, New York: Pantheon.

—— (1982) *Discipline and Punish: The Birth of the Prison*, translated by Alan Sheridan, Harmondsworth: Penguin.

—— (1984) *The History of Sexuality, Volume One: An Introduction*, translated by Robert Hurley, Harmondsworth: Penguin.

Fowler, Bridget (ed.) (2000) *Reading Bourdieu on Society and Culture*, Oxford: Blackwell.

Frascina, Francis and Harris, Jonathan (eds) (1992) *Art in Modern Culture: An Anthology of Critical Texts*, London: Phaidon.

Freud, Sigmund ([1901] 1975) *The Psychopathology of Everyday Life*, translated by Alan Tyson, Harmondsworth: Penguin.

Friedan, Betty ([1963] 1965) *The Feminine Mystique*, Harmondsworth: Penguin.

Frisby, David (1984) *Georg Simmel*, London: Methuen.

—— (1985) *Fragments of Modernity: Theories of Modernity in the Work of Simmel, Kracauer and Benjamin*, Cambridge: Polity Press.

—— (1992a) *Sociological Impressionism: A Reassessment of Georg Simmel's Social Theory*, London and New York: Routledge.

—— (1992b) *Simmel and Since: Essays on Georg Simmel's Social Theory*, London and New York: Routledge.

Gane, Mike (1991) *Baudrillard's Bestiary: Baudrillard and Culture*, London and New York: Routledge.

Ganguly, Keya (2001) *States of Exception: Everyday Life and Postcolonial Identity*, Minneapolis, Minn.: University of Minnesota Press.

Garber, Marjorie (2000) *Bisexuality and the Eroticism of Everyday Life*, London and New York: Routledge.

Gardiner, Michael E. (2000) *Critiques of Everyday Life*, London and New York: Routledge.

Garfinkel, Harold ([1967] 1987) *Studies in Ethnomethodology*, Cambridge: Polity Press.

Garson, Barbara (1994) *All the Livelong Day: The Meaning and Demeaning of Routine Work*, Harmondsworth: Penguin.

Gates, Henry Louis (1995) *Colored People*, Harmondsworth: Penguin.

Geertz, Clifford (1973) *The Interpretation of Cultures: Selected Essays*, London: Fontana.

—— (1993) *Local Knowledge*, London: Fontana.

Genosko, Gary (1994) *Baudrillard and Signs: Signification Ablaze*, London and New York: Routledge.

Gibian, Peter (ed.) (1997) *Mass Culture and Everyday Life*, London and New York: Routledge.

Giedion, Siegfried (1969) *Mechanization takes Command: A Contribution to Anonymous History*, New York: Norton.

Giles, Steve (2000) 'Cracking the Cultural Code: Methodological Reflections on Kracauer's "The Mass Ornament"', *Radical Philosophy*, 99: 31–9.

Gilloch, Graeme (1996) *Myth and Metropolis: Walter Benjamin and the City*, Cambridge: Polity Press.

Gilroy, Paul (1987) *There Ain't No Black in the Union Jack: The Cultural Politics of Race and Nation*, London: Hutchinson.

—— (1993) *The Black Atlantic: Modernity and Double Consciousness*, London and New York: Verso.

Goffman, Erving (1974) *Frame Analysis*, London: Harper & Row.

—— ([1959] 1990) *The Presentation of Self in Everyday Life*, Harmondsworth: Penguin.

Goldberg, Jim (1986) *Rich and Poor*, New York: Random House.

Grossberg, Lawrence (1992) *We Gotta Get Out of this Place: Popular Conservatism and Postmodern Culture*, New York and London: Routledge.

—— (1997a) *Bringing it All Back Home: Essays on Cultural Studies*, Durham, NC and London: Duke University Press.

—— (1997b) *Dancing in Spite of Myself: Essays on Popular Culture*, Durham, NC and London: Duke University Press.

Gullestad, Marianne (1984) *Kitchen-Table Society: A Case Study of the Family Life and Friendships of Young Working-class Mothers in Urban Norway*, Oslo: Universitetsforlaget.

—— (1992) *The Art of Social Relations: Essays on Culture, Social Action and Everyday Life in Modern Norway*, Oslo: Universitetsforlaget.

Gumpert, Lynn (ed.) (1997) *The Art of the Everyday: The Quotidian in Postwar French Culture*, New York: New York University Press.

Hall, Stuart (1984) 'Reconstruction Work: Images of Post War Black Settlement', *Ten–8*, 16: 2–9.

—— (1993) 'Culture, Community, Nation', *Cultural Studies*, 7(3): 349–63.

—— (1995) 'Negotiating Caribbean Identities', *New Left Review*, 209: 3–14.

—— (1996) *Critical Dialogues in Cultural Studies*, London and New York: Routledge.

Hall, Stuart and Jefferson, Tony (eds) (1976) *Resistance through Rituals: Youth Subculture in Post-War Britain*, London: Hutchinson.

Hamper, Ben (1992) *Rivethead: Tales from the Assembly Line*, London: Fourth Estate.

Hannerz, Ulf (1980) *Exploring the City: Inquiries toward an Urban Anthropology*, New York: Columbia University Press.

Haraway, Donna J. (1991) 'Situated Knowledges: The Science Question in Feminism and Privilege of Partial Perspective', in *Simians, Cyborgs, and Women: The Reinvention of Nature*, London: Free Association Press.

Harootunian, Harry (2000a) *History's Disquiet: Modernity, Cultural Practice, and the Question of Everyday Life*, New York: Columbia University Press.

—— (2000b) *Overcome by Modernity: History, Culture, and Community in Interwar Japan*, Princeton, NJ and Oxford: Princeton University Press.

Harris, Steven and Berke Deborah (eds) (1997) *Architecture of the Everyday*, New York: Princeton Architectural Press.

Harrisson, Tom (1942) 'Notes on Class Consciousness and Class Unconsciousness', *Sociological Review*, 34(3–4): 147–64.

Heath, Stephen (1986) 'Joan Riviere and the Masquerade', in Victor Burgin, James Donald and Cora Kaplan (eds) *Formations of Fantasy*, London: Methuen.

Hebdige, Dick (1976) 'The Meaning of Mod', in Stuart Hall and Tony Jefferson (eds) *Resistance through Rituals: Youth Subculture in Post-War Britain*, London: Hutchinson.

—— (1979) *Subculture: The Meaning of Style*, London and New York: Methuen.

—— (1987) 'The Impossible Object: Towards a Sociology of the Sublime', *New Formations*, 1: 47–76.

—— (1988) *Hiding in the Light: On Images and Things*, London and New York: Routledge.

Hermes, Joke (1993) 'Media, Meaning and Everyday Life', *Cultural Studies*, 7(3): 493–506.

Highmore, Ben (2000a) '"Opaque, Stubborn Life": Everyday Life and Resistance in the Work of Michel de Certeau', *XCP – Cross-Cultural Poetics*, 7: 90–101.

—— (2000b) 'Dwelling on the Daily: On the Term Everyday Life as used by Henri Lefebvre and Michel de Certeau', 'The Everyday', *Daidalos: Architecture, Art, Culture*, 75: 38–43.

—— (2002) *Everyday Life and Cultural Theory: An Introduction*, London and New York: Routledge.

Hine, Thomas (1987) *Populuxe*, London: Bloomsbury.

Hirsch, Marianne (1997) *Family Frames: Photography, Narrative and Postmemory*, Cambridge, Mass. and London: Harvard University Press.

Hitchcock, Peter (1993) *Dialogics of the Oppressed*, Minneapolis, Minn.: University of Minnesota Press.

Hollier, Denis (ed.) (1988) *The College of Sociology 1937–39*, translated by Betsy Wing, Minneapolis, Minn.: University of Minnesota Press.

—— (1993) 'While the City Sleeps: Mene, Mene, Tekel, Upharsin', *October* 64: 3–15.

Horowitz, Daniel (1998) *Betty Friedan and the Making of* The Feminine Mystique: *The American Left, The Cold War, and Modern Feminism*, Amherst, Mass.: University of Massachusetts Press.

Iverson, Margaret, Crimp, Douglas and Bhabha, Homi K. (1997) *Mary Kelly*, London: Phaidon

Jackson, Stevi and Moores, Shaun (eds) (1995) *The Politics of Domestic Consumption: Critical Readings*, London: Harvester Wheatsheaf.

Jameson, Fredric (1991) *Postmodernism, or the Cultural Logic of Late Capitalism*, London: Verso.

—— (1998) *Brecht and Method*, London: Verso.

Jappe, Anselm (1999) *Guy Debord*, translated by Donald Nicholson-Smith, Berkeley, Calif. and London: University of California Press.

Jay, Martin (1984) *Marxism and Totality: The Adventures of a Concept from Lukács to Habermas*, Cambridge: Polity Press.

—— (1998) 'Songs of Experience: Reflections on the Debate over *Alltagsgeschichte*', in *Cultural Semantics: Keywords of our Time*, Amherst, Mass.: University of Massachusetts Press.

Jeffrey, Tom (1978) 'Mass-Observation: A Short History', *Occasional Paper, Centre for Contemporary Cultural Studies*, University of Birmingham.

Jenkins, Henry (1992) *Textual Poachers: Television Fans and Participatory Culture*, London and New York: Routledge.

Jenkins, Richard (1992) *Pierre Bourdieu*, London and New York: Routledge.

Joyce, James ([1922] 1969) *Ulysses*, Harmondsworth: Penguin.

Kaplan, Alice (1993) *French Lessons: A Memoir*, Chicago and London: University of Chicago Press.

Kaplan, Alice and Ross, Kristin (eds) (1987) 'Introduction', *Everyday Life: Yale French Studies*, 73: 1–4.

Kaprow, Allan (1996) *Essays on the Blurring of Art and Life*, Berkeley, Calif. and London: University of California Press.

Kasson, John F. (1990) *Rudeness and Civility: Manners in Nineteenth-Century Urban America*, New York: Hill & Wang.

Katsiaficas, George (1997) *The Subversion of Politics: European Autonomous Social Movements and the Decolonization of Everyday Life*, Atlantic Highlands, NJ: Humanities Press.

Katz, Marc (1999) 'The Hotel Kracauer', *Differences: A Journal of Feminist Cultural Studies*, 11(2): 134–51.

Kelly, Mary (1983) *Post-Partum Document*, London: Routledge & Kegan Paul.

—— (1986) *Interim*, Edinburgh, Cambridge and London: Fruitmarket Gallery, Kettle's Yard and Riverside Studios.

Kern, Steven (1983) *The Culture of Time and Space 1880–1918*, Cambridge, Mass.: Harvard University Press.

Kinser, Samuel (1992) 'Everyday Ordinary', *diacritics*, 22(2): 70–82.

Klevan, Andrew (2000) *Disclosure of the Everyday: Undramatic Achievement in Narrative Film*, Trowbridge: Flick.

Knabb, Ken (ed.) (1981) *Situationist International Anthology*, Berkeley, Calif.: Bureau of Public Secrets.

Koch, Gertrud (2000) *Siegfried Kracauer: An Introduction*, Princeton, NJ: Princeton University Press.

Kofman, Myron (1996) *Edgar Morin: From Big Brother to Fraternity*, London: Pluto Press.

Kracauer, Siegfried (1972) *Orpheus in Paris: Offenbach and the Paris of his Time*, translated by Gwenda Davis and Eric Mosbacher, New York: Vienna House.

—— (1995) *The Mass Ornament: Weimar Essays*, translated by Thomas Y. Levin, Cambridge, Mass.: Harvard University Press.

—— (1998) *The Salaried Masses: Duty and Distraction in Weimar Germany*, translated by Quintin Hoare, London: Verso.

Kramarae, Cheris (ed.) (1988) *Technology and Women's Voices: Keeping in Touch*, London: Routledge & Kegan Paul.

Kuhn, Annette (1995) *Family Secrets: Acts of Memory and Imagination*, London: Verso.

Kuisel, Richard (1993) *Seducing the French: The Dilemma of Americanization*, Berkeley, Calif. and London: University of California Press.

Kuper, Adam (1996) *Anthropology and Anthropologists: The Modern British School*, 3rd edn, London and New York: Routledge.

Langbauer, Laurie (1992) 'Cultural Studies and the Politics of the Everyday', *diacritics*, 22(1): 47–65.

—— (1999) *Novels of Everyday Life: The Series in English Fiction 1850–1930*, Ithaca, NY and London: Cornell University Press.

Leck, Ralph M. (2000) *Georg Simmel and Avant-Garde Sociology: The Birth of Modernity, 1880–1920*, New York: Humanity Books.

Lee, Leo Ou-fan (1999) *Shanghai Modern: The Flowering of a New Urban Culture in China 1930–45*, Cambridge, Mass.: Harvard University Press.

Lefebvre, Henri ([1968] 1984) *Everyday Life in the Modern World*, translated by Sacha Rabinovitch, New Brunswick, NJ: Transaction.

—— ([1947/1958] 1991) *Critique of Everyday Life: Volume 1*, translated by John Moore, London: Verso.

Lefebvre, Henri ([1962] 1995) *Introduction to Modernity*, translated by John Moore, London: Verso.

Lehmann, Ulrich (2000) *Tigersprung: Fashion in Modernity*, Cambridge, Mass. and London: MIT Press.

Leiris, Michel ([1938] 1988) 'The Sacred in Everyday Life', in Denis Hollier (ed.) *The College of Sociology 1937–39*, translated by Betsy Wing, Minneapolis, Minn.: University of Minnesota Press.

—— ([1939] 1992) *Manhood: A Journey from Childhood into the Fierce Order of Virility*, translated by Richard Howard, Chicago: University of Chicago Press.

Leonard, George J. (1994) *Into the Light of Things: The Art of the Commonplace from Wordsworth to John Cage*, Chicago: University of Chicago Press.

Linhart, Robert (1981) *The Assembly Line*, translated by Margaret Crosland, London: John Calder.

Loizos, Peter (1993) *Innovation in Ethnographic Film*, Manchester: Manchester University Press.

Lüdtke, Alf (ed.) (1995) *The History of Everyday Life: Reconstructing Historical Experiences and Ways of Life*, translated by William Templer, Princeton, NJ: Princeton University Press.

—— (2000) 'People Working: Everyday Life and German Fascism', *History Workshop Journal*, 50: 75–92.

Lynd, Robert S. and Lynd, Helen Merrel (1929) *Middletown: A Study in Modern American Culture*, New York: Harvest.

Lyon, David (2001) *Surveillance Society: Monitoring Everyday Life*, Buckingham: Open University Press.

Lyotard, Jean-François ([1979] 1986) *The Postmodern Condition: A Report on Knowledge*, translated by Geoff Bennington and Brian Massumi, Manchester: Manchester University Press.

MacAloon, John (ed.) (1984) *Rite, Drama, Festival, Spectacle: Rehearsals toward a Theory of Cultural Performance*, Philadelphia, Pa: Institute for the Study of Human Issues.

MacCabe, Colin (1980) *Godard: Images, Sounds, Politics*, London: British Film Institute and Macmillan.

McDonough, Thomas F. (1994) 'Situationist Space', *October*, 67: 59–77.

MacDougall, David (1998) *Transcultural Cinema*, Princeton, NJ: Princeton University Press.

Mackay, Hugh (ed.) (1997) *Consumption and Everyday Life*, London and Thousand Oaks, Calif.: Sage.

McRobbie, Angela (1991) *Feminism and Youth Culture: From Jackie to Just Seventeen*, London: Macmillan.

—— (ed.) (1997) *Back to Reality? Social Experience and Cultural Studies*, Manchester: Manchester University Press.

Madge, Charles (1976) 'The Birth of Mass-Observation', *Times Literary Supplement*, November: 1395.

Maffesoli, Michel (1996) *Ordinary Knowledge: An Introduction to Interpretative Sociology*, translated by David Macey, Cambridge: Polity Press.

Malinowski, Bronislaw (1922) *Argonauts of the Western Pacific*, London: G. Routledge & Sons.

—— (1967) *A Diary in the Strict Sense of the Term*, New York: Harcourt, Brace.

Mandel, Ernest (1979) *Trotsky: A Study in the Dynamic of his Thought*, London: New Left Books.

Manning, Philip (1993) *Erving Goffman and Modern Sociology*, Cambridge: Polity Press.

Marcus, Laura (1987) '"Enough about You, Let's Talk about Me": Recent Autobiographical Writing', *New Formations*, 1: 77–94.

Margulies, Ivone (1996) *Nothing Happens: Chantal Akerman's Hyperrealist Everyday*, Durham, NC: Duke University Press.

Martin, Angela (1979) 'Chantal Akerman's Films: A Dossier', *Feminist Review*, 3: 24–47.

Marx, Karl (1852) 'The Eighteenth Brumaire of Louis Bonaparte', in Karl Marx and Frederick Engels (1968) *Selected Works in One Volume*, London: Lawrence & Wishart.

Marx, Karl and Engels, Frederick ([1848] 1973) *Manifesto of the Communist Party*, Beijing: Foreign Language Press.

—— ([1846] 1985) *The German Ideology*, edited by C. J. Arthur, London: Lawrence & Wishart.

Maspero, Francois (1994) *Roissy Express: A Journey through the Paris Suburbs*, translated by Paul Jones, London: Verso.

Mass-Observation (1937a) *Mass Observation*, introduction by Julian Huxley, London: Fredrick Muller.

—— (1937b) *May 12th Mass-Observation Day Surveys*, edited by Humphrey Jennings and Charles Madge, London: Faber & Faber.

—— (1937c) 'They Speak for Themselves: Mass-Observation and Social Narrative', *Life and Letters*, 17: 37–42.

—— (1937d) 'Poetic Description and Mass-Observation', *New Verse*, 24: 1–6.

—— (1938) *First Year's Work 1937–38*, edited by Charles Madge and Tom Harrisson, London: Lindsay Drummond.

—— (1939) *Britain*, Harmondsworth: Penguin.

Mathews, Harry and Brotchie, Alastair (eds) (1998) *Oulipo Compendium*, London: Atlas Press.

Matich, Olga (1996) 'Remaking the Bed: Utopia in Daily Life', in John E. Bowlt and Olga Matich (eds) *Laboratory of Dreams: The Russian Avant-Garde and Cultural Experiment*, Stanford, Calif.: Stanford University Press.

Mercer, Kobena (1994) *Welcome to the Jungle: New Positions in Black Cultural Studies*, New York and London: Routledge.

Merleau-Ponty, Maurice (1962) *The Phenomenology of Perception*, translated by Colin Smith, London: Routledge & Kegan Paul.

Miller, Daniel (1987) *Material Culture and Mass Consumption*, Oxford: Blackwell.

—— (1994) *Modernity: An Ethnographic Approach*, Oxford: Berg.

—— (1997) *Capitalism: An Ethnographic Approach*, Oxford: Berg.

—— (1998) *A Theory of Shopping*, Cambridge: Polity Press.

Miller, Toby and McHoul, Alec (1998) *Popular Culture and Everyday Life*, London: Sage.

Mizuta, Kazuo (1993) *The Structures of Everyday Life in Japan in the Last Decade of the Twentieth Century*, Lewiston, NY: Edwin Mellen.

Molesworth, Helen (1998) 'Work Avoidance: The Everyday Life of Marcel Duchamp's Readymades', *Art Journal*, 57(4): 51–61.

—— (2000) 'House Work and Art Work', *October*, 92: 71–97.

Moores, Shaun (1996) *Satellite Television in Everyday Life*, Luton: University of Luton Press.

—— (2000) *Media and Everyday Life in Modern Society*, Edinburgh: Edinburgh University Press.

Morin, Edgar (1971a) *Plodémet: Report from a French Village*, translated by A. M. Sheridan-Smith, London: Allen Lane.

—— (1971b) *Rumour in Orleans*, translated by Peter Green, London: Anthony Blond.

Morris, Meaghan (1990) 'Banality in Cultural Studies', in Patricia Mellencamp (ed.) *The Logics of Television: Essays in Cultural Criticism*, Bloomington, Ind.: Indiana University Press.

—— (1998) *Too Soon, Too Late: History in Popular Culture*, Bloomington, Ind.: Indiana University Press.

Mort, Frank (1989) 'The Politics of Consumption', in Stuart Hall and Martin Jacques (eds) *New Times: The Changing Face of Politics in the 1990s*, London: Lawrence & Wishart.

Mukerji, Chandra and Schudson, Michael (eds) (1991) *Rethinking Popular Culture: Contemporary Perspectives in Cultural Studies*, Berkeley, Calif.: University of California Press.

Mulhern, Francis (2000) *Culture/Metaculture*, London and New York: Routledge.

Nasaw, David (1999) *Going Out: The Rise and Fall of Public Amusements*, Cambridge, Mass. and London: Harvard University Press.

Nichols, Bill (1994) *Blurred Boundaries: Questions of Meaning in Contemporary Culture*, Bloomington, Ind.: Indiana University Press.

Oakley, Ann (1976) *Housewife*, Harmondsworth: Penguin.

Osborne, Peter (1995) *The Politics of Time: Modernity and Avant-Garde*, London: Verso.

Parker, Rozsika (1996) *Torn in Two: The Experience of Maternal Ambivalence*, London: Virago.

Penley, Constance (1982) 'Les Enfants de la Patrie', *Camera Obscura*, 8–9–10: 33–58.

Perec, Georges ([1978] 1987) *Life: A User's Manual*, translated by David Bellos, London: Collins Harvill.

Perec, Georges (1997) *Species of Spaces and Other Pieces*, translated by John Sturrock, Harmondsworth: Penguin.

Pessoa, Fernando ([1916–32] 1998) *The Book of Disquiet*, translated by Alfred Mac Adam, Boston, Mass.: Exact Change.

Petro, Patrice (1989) *Joyless Streets: Women and Melodramatic Representation in Weimar Germany*, Princeton, NJ: Princeton University Press.

—— (1993) 'After Shock/Between Boredom and History', *Discourse: Journal of Theoretical Studies in Media and Culture*, 16(2): 77–99.

Phillips, Adam (1993) *On Kissing, Tickling and Being Bored: Psychoanalytic Essays on the Unexamined Life*, London: Faber & Faber.

Phillips, Tom (2000) *The Postcard Century: Cards and their Messages, 1900–2000*, London and New York: Thames & Hudson.

Pickering, Michael (1997) *History, Experience and Cultural Studies*, London: Macmillan.

Pickering, Michael and Chaney, David (1986) 'Democracy and Communication: Mass-Observation 1937–1943', *Journal of Communication*, 36(1): 41–56.

Pile, Steve (1996) *The Body and the City: Psychoanalysis, Space and Subjectivity*, London and New York: Routledge.

Plant, Sadie (1992) *The Most Radical Gesture: The Situationist International in a Postmodern Age*, London: Routledge.

Plummer, Ken (1995) *Telling Sexual Stories: Power, Change and Social Worlds*, London and New York: Routledge.

Pollock, Griselda (1988a) 'Screening the Seventies: Sexuality and Representation in Feminist Practice – a Brechtian Perspective', in *Vision and Difference: Femininity, Feminism and the Histories of Art*, London and New York: Routledge.

—— (1988b) 'Modernity and the Spaces of Femininity', in *Vision and Difference: Femininity, Feminism and the Histories of Art*, London and New York: Routledge.

Poster, Mark (1976) *Existential Marxism in Postwar France: Sartre to Althusser*, Princeton, NJ: Princeton University Press.

—— (1978) *Critical Theory of the Family*, New York and London: Pluto Press.

—— (1997) *Cultural History and Postmodernity: Disciplinary Readings and Challenges*, New York: Columbia University Press.

Pred, Allan (1990) *Lost Words and Lost Worlds: Modernity and the Language of Everyday Life in Late 19th Century Stockholm,* Cambridge: Cambridge University Press.

Probyn, Elspeth (1993) *Sexing the Self: Gendered Positions in Cultural Studies*, London and New York: Routledge.

—— (2000) *Carnal Appetites: FoodSexIdentities*, London and New York: Routledge.

Pullin, Faith and Colebrook, Claire (1993) 'The New Feminist Dispensation: from Betty Friedan to Madonna', in A. Robert Lee (ed.) *A Permanent Etcetera: Cross-Cultural Perspectives on Post-War America*, London: Pluto Press.

Quinn, Malcolm (1997) 'Re-thinking the Unthinkable: Ventriloquy, the Quotidian and Intellectual Work', *Third Text*, 40: 13–20.

Quinney, Richard (1998) *For the Time Being: Ethnography and Everyday Life*, New York: State University of New York Press.

Rabinbach, Anson (1992) *The Human Motor: Energy, Fatigue, and the Origins of Modernity*, Berkeley, Calif: University of California Press.

Rabinovitz, Lauren (1998) *For the Love of Pleasure: Women, Movies, and Culture in Turn-of-the-Century Chicago*, Princeton, NJ: Princeton University Press.

Rakow, Lana (1992) *Gender on the Line: Women, the Telephone, and Community Life*, Urbana, Ill.: University of Illinois Press.

Rancière, Jacques (1989) *The Nights of Labor: The Worker's Dream in Nineteenth Century France*, translated by John Drury, Philadelphia, Pa: Temple University Press.

—— (1994) *The Names of History: On the Poetics of Knowledge*, translated by Hassan Melehy, Minneapolis, Minn. and London: University of Minnesota Press.

Rappaport, Erika Diane (2000) *Shopping for Pleasure: Women in the Making of London's West End*, Princeton, NJ: Princeton University Press.

Rattansi, Ali (ed.) (1989) *Ideology, Method and Marx*, London and New York: Routledge.

Read, Alan (1993) *Theatre and Everyday Life: An Ethics of Performance*, London and New York: Routledge.

Revel, Jacques and Hunt, Lynn (1995) *Histories – French Constructions of the Past: Postwar French Thought Volume 1*, New York: The New Press.

Rifkin, Adrian (1993) *Street Noises: Parisian Pleasure 1900–40*, Manchester: Manchester University Press.

Rifkin, Adrian and Thomas, Roger (eds) (1988) *Voices of the People: The Social Life of 'La Sociale' at the End of the Second Empire*, translated by John Moore, London: Routledge & Kegan Paul.

Rigby, Brian (1991) *Popular Culture in Modern France: A Study of Cultural Discourse*, London and New York: Routledge.

Riviere, Joan ([1929] 1986) 'Womanliness as a Masquerade', in Victor Burgin, James Donald and Cora Kaplan (eds) *Formations of Fantasy*, London: Methuen.

Robbins, Derek (1999) *Bourdieu and Culture*, London and Thousand Oaks, Calif.: Sage.

Roberts, John (1998) *The Art of Interruption: Realism, Photography and the Everyday*, Manchester: Manchester University Press.

—— (1999) 'Philosophizing the Everyday: The Philosophy of Praxis and the Fate of Cultural Studies', *Radical Philosophy*, 98: 16–29.

Ross, David A. (ed.) (2000) *Quotidiana: The Continuity of the Everyday*, Milan: Charta.

Ross, Kristin (1988) *The Emergence of Social Space: Rimbaud and the Paris Commune*, London: Macmillan.

—— (1992) 'Watching the Detectives', in Francis Barker, Peter Hulme and Margaret Iversen (eds) *Postmodernism and the Re-reading of Modernity*, Manchester: Manchester University Press.

—— (1995) *Fast Cars, Clean Bodies: Decolonization and the Reordering of French Culture*, Cambridge, Mass.: and London: MIT Press.

—— (1996) 'Streetwise: The French Invention of Everyday Life', *Parallax*, 2: 67–71.

—— (1997) 'Lefebvre on the Situationists: An Interview', *October*, 79: 69–83.

Russell, Catherine (1999) *Experimental Ethnography: The Work of Film in the Age of Video*, Durham, NC and London: Duke University Press.

Sadler, Simon (1998) *The Situationist City*, Cambridge, Mass. and London: MIT Press.

Scannell, Paddy (1996) *Radio, Television and Modern Life*, Oxford: Blackwell.

Schirato, Tony (1993) 'My Space or Yours? De Certeau, Frow and the Meaning of Popular Culture', *Cultural Studies*, 7(2): 282–91.

Schivelbusch, Wolfgang (1977) *The Railway Journey: The Industrialization of Time and Space in the 19th Century*, New York: Berg.

—— (1988) *Disenchanted Night: The Industrialization of Light in the Nineteenth Century*, translated by Angela Davies, Berkeley, Calif. and London: University of California Press.

Schor, Naomi (1992) 'Cartes Postales: Representing Paris 1900', *Critical Inquiry*, 18: 188–241.

Schutz, Alfred (1967) *The Phenomenology of the Social World*, Evanston, Ill.: Northwestern University Press.

Schwartz, Vanessa R. (1999) *Spectacular Realities: Early Mass Culture in Fin-de-Siècle Paris*, Berkeley, Calif.: University of California Press.

Scott, James C. (1987) *Weapons of the Weak: Everyday Forms of Peasant Resistance*, New Haven, Conn.: Yale University Press.

Serres, Michel and Latour, Bruno (1995) *Conversations on Science, Culture, and Time*, translated by Roxanne Lapidus, Ann Arbor, Mich.: University of Michigan Press.

Sheringham, Michael (1995) 'Marc Augé and the Ethno-analysis of Contemporary Life', *Paragraph*, 18(2): 210–22.

Shields, Rob (1999) *Lefebvre, Love and Struggle: Spatial Dialectics*, London and New York: Routledge.

Shotter, John (1993) *Cultural Politics of Everyday Life: Social Constructionism and Knowing of the Third Kind*, Toronto: University of Toronto Press.

Silverman, Kaja and Farocki, Harun (1998) *Speaking about Godard*, New York and London: New York University Press.

Silverstone, Roger (1994) *Television and Everyday Life*, London and New York: Routledge.

—— (ed.) (1996) *Visions of Suburbia*, London and New York: Routledge.

Simmel, Georg (1971) *On Individuality and Social Forms*, edited by Donald N. Levine, Chicago: University of Chicago Press.

—— ([1900/1907] 1991) *The Philosophy of Money*, translated by Tom Bottomore and David Frisby, London and New York: Routledge.

—— (1997) *Simmel on Culture*, edited by David Frisby and Mike Featherstone, London: Sage.

Smith, Dorothy E. (1987) *The Everyday World as Problematic: A Feminist Sociology*, Boston, Mass.: Northeastern University Press.

—— (1999) *Writing the Social: Critique, Theory and Investigations*, Toronto: University of Toronto Press.

Smith, Gary (ed.) (1989) *Benjamin: Philosophy, Aesthetics, History*, Chicago: University of Chicago Press.

Spacks, Patricia Meyer (1995) *Boredom: The Literary History of a State of Mind*, Chicago: University of Chicago Press.

Spigel, Lynn (1991) 'From Domestic Space to Outer Space: The 1960s Fantastic Family Sitcom', in Constance Penley, Elisabeth Lyon, Lynn Spigel and Janet Bergstrom (eds) *Close Encounters: Film, Feminism, and Science Fiction*, Minneapolis, Minn.: University of Minnesota Press.

—— (1992a) 'Installing the Television Set: Popular Discourses on Television and Domestic Space, 1948–1955', in Lynn Spigel and Denise Mann (eds) *Private Screenings: Television and the Female Consumer*, Minneapolis, Minn.: University of Minnesota Press.

—— (1992b) *Make Room for TV: Television and the Family Ideal in Postwar America*, Chicago and London: University of Chicago Press.

—— (2001) *Welcome to the Dreamhouse: Popular Media and Postwar Suburbs*, Durham, NC and London: Duke University Press.

Spigel, Lynn and Mann, Denise (eds) (1992) *Private Screenings: Television and the Female Consumer*, Minneapolis, Minn.: University of Minnesota Press.

Stanley, Liz (1990) 'The Archeology of a 1930s Mass-Observation Project', *Sociology: Occasional Paper* 27, Manchester: University of Manchester.

Steedman, Carolyn (1986) *Landscape for a Good Woman: The Story of Two Lives*, London: Virago.

—— (1988) *The Radical Soldier's Tale: John Pearman, 1819–1908*, London and New York: Routledge.

Stelarc (1997) 'From Psycho to Cyber Strategies: Prosthetics, Robotics and Remote Existence', *Cultural Values* 1(2): 241–9.

Sterritt, David (ed.) (1998) *Jean-Luc Godard Interviews*, Jackson, Miss.: University Press of Mississippi.

Stewart, Susan (1993) *On Longing: Narratives of the Miniature, the Gigantic, the Souvenir, the Collection*, Durham, NC and London: Duke University Press.

Stocking, George W. Jr (1996) *After Tylor: British Social Anthropology 1888–1951*, London: Athlone Press.

Strathern, Marilyn (1981) *Kinship at the Core: An Anthropology of Elmdon a Village in North-west Essex in the Nineteen-sixties*, Cambridge: Cambridge University Press.

Tang, Xiaobing (2000) *Chinese Modern: The Heroic and the Quotidian*, Durham, NC and London: Duke University Press.

Taussig, Michael (1992) *The Nervous System*, New York and London: Routledge.

—— (1993) *Mimesis and Alterity: A Particular History of the Senses*, New York and London: Routledge.

—— (1997) *The Magic of the State*, New York and London: Routledge.

Terry, Jennifer and Calvert, Melodie (eds) (1997) *Processed Lives: Gender and Technology in Everyday Life*, London and New York: Routledge.

Tobin, Joseph J. (ed.) (1992) *Re-Made in Japan: Everyday Life and Consumer Taste in a Changing Society*, New Haven, Conn.: Yale University Press.

Trinh T. Minh-ha (1992) *Framer Framed*, New York and London: Routledge.

—— (1999) *Cinema Interval*, New York and London: Routledge.

Trotsky, Leon (1973) *Problems of Everyday Life and Other Writings on Culture and Science*, New York: Monad Press.

Trotter, David (2000a) *Cooking with Mud: The Idea of Mess in Nineteenth-Century Art and Fiction*, Oxford: Oxford University Press.

—— (2000b) 'The New Historicism and the Psychopathology of Everyday Modern Life', *Critical Quarterly*, 42(1): 36–58.

Turner, Graeme (1992) *British Cultural Studies: An Introduction*, New York and London: Routledge.

Turner, Victor (1974) *Dramas, Fields, and Metaphors: Symbolic Action in Human Society*, Ithaca, NY: Cornell University Press.

Turner, Victor and Brunner, Edward (eds) (1986) *The Anthropology of Experience*, Urbana, Ill.: University of Illinois Press.

Ungar, Steven (1983) *Roland Barthes: The Professor of Desire*, Lincoln, Nebr.: University of Nebraska Press.

Veeser, H. Aram (ed.) (1989) *The New Historicism*, New York and London: Routledge.

Vlastos, Stephen (ed.) (1998) *Mirror of Modernity: Invented Traditions of Modern Japan*, Berkeley, Calif. and London: University of California Press.

Walkerdine, Valerie (1986) 'Video Replay: Families, Films and Fantasy', in Victor Burgin, James Donald and Cora Kaplan (eds) *Formations of Fantasy*, London: Methuen.

—— (1997) *Daddy's Girl*, Basingstoke and New York: Palgrave.

Warf, B. (1986) 'Ideology, Everyday Life and Emancipatory Phenomenology', *Antipode*, 18(3): 268–83.

Waters, Chris (1999) 'Representations of Everyday Life: L. S. Lowry and the Landscape of Memory in Postwar Britain', *Representations*, 65: 121–50.

Watkins, Evan (1993) *Throwaways: Work Culture and Consumer Education*, Stanford, Calif.: Stanford University Press.

Wellman, David (1994) 'Constituting Ethnographic Authority: The Work Process of Field Research, an Ethnographic Account', *Cultural Studies*, 8(3): 569–83.

White, Hayden (1973) *Metahistory: The Historical Imagination in Nineteenth-Century Europe*, Baltimore, Md and London: Johns Hopkins University Press.

Willemen, Paul (1994) 'An Avant-Garde for the 90s', in *Looks and Frictions: Essays in Cultural Studies and Film Theory*, London: British Film Institute.

Williams, Raymond (1960) *Border Country*, London: Chatto & Windus.

—— ([1958] 1989a) 'Culture is Ordinary', *Resources of Hope: Culture, Democracy, Socialism*, London: Verso.

—— (1989b) *What I Came to Say*, London: Hutchinson Radius.

—— ([1961] 1992) *The Long Revolution*, London: Hogarth Press.

Williams, Rosalind H. (1982) *Dream Worlds: Mass Consumption in Late Nineteenth-Century France*, Berkeley, Calif.: University of California Press.

Willis, Paul (1977) *Learning to Labour: How Working Class Kids Get Working Class Jobs*, London: Saxon House.

—— (1978) *Profane Culture*, London: Routledge & Kegan Paul.

—— (1990) *Common Culture: Symbolic Work at Play in the Everyday Cultures of the Young* (with Simon Jones, Joyce Canaan and Geoff Hurd), Buckingham: Open University Press.

—— (2000) *The Ethnographic Imagination*, Cambridge: Polity Press.

Willis, Susan (1991) *A Primer for Daily Life*, London and New York: Routledge.

Winnicott, D. W. (1985) *Playing and Reality*, Harmondsworth: Penguin.

Wolin, Richard (1987) 'Agnes Heller on Everyday Life', *Theory and Society*, 16: 295–304.

Wollen, Peter (1993) *Raiding the Icebox: Reflections on Twentieth-Century Culture*, London: Verso.

Woodham, Jonathan M. (1997) *Twentieth-Century Design*, Oxford and New York: Oxford University Press.

Woolf, Virginia ([1925] 1992) *Mrs Dalloway*, Oxford: Oxford University Press.

Zhang, Yingjin (1996) *The City in Modern Chinese Literature and Film: Configurations of Space, Time, and Gender*, Stanford, Calif.: Stanford University Press.

Index

Abrams, M. 291
Adair, G. 176, 177
Adams, W. and Hunferford, E.A. Jr 338
Adorno, T. 9–10
advertizing 108, 113, 302–3
Aglietta, M. 111, 116
Ailing, Z. 134, 135
Akerman, C. 319
Albrecht, D. 337
Algeria 108, 112, 161–2
alienation 123, 231–2, 233–5, 239, 243
alphabet 180–2; graphic examples 184–98
Althusser, L. 246
Ambrose, S.E. 107
American Exhibition (Moscow 1959) 102–7
Annales School 47, 114
anthropology 139–40; need for 146–7
Aragon, L. 176
Archibald, K. 56
art 24–8, 179–80, 229–30, 282, 283–4, 285
Arvatov, B. 120, 124
Asad, T. 33
assembly line work 44
Association of Writers and Revolutionary Artists
  (AEAR) 226
Atsuyoshi, M. 121
Attfield, J. and Kirkham, P. 16
Augé, M. 8, 33
authenticity 119, 130, 237

bags, as antique/aging 351; associated with
  death 350–1; carrying 350; as female objects

349, 350; hoarding 349–50; meanings of
  348–9; as sign of indigence/indignity 351;
  sleeping in 350; weight/shape of 350
Balibar, E. 117
Balzac, H. de 109, 110, 115
Barel, Y. 75
Barthes, R. 20, 71, 111, 116, 305–6, 309, 318
Bataille, G. 21, 22–3
Baudelaire, C. 15, 26, 45
Baudrillard, J. 75, 111, 308–9
Beauvoir, S. de 16, 53, 57, 110, 116
Beckett, S. 351
Beecher, C. and Stowe, H.B. 337
Belinsky, V. 90
Bell, C. 94
Bellos, D. 177
Bellour, R. 202
Benedict, R. 9
Benjamin, W. 44–5, 119
Bennett, T. 34
Benveniste, E. 74
Berlin Trade Exhibition (1896) 297, 298–300
Bernstein, R.J. 67, 74
Besant, W. 56
Beszceret, S. and Corrigan, P. 291
Black immigrants, photographic portrayals of
  252–61
Blanchot, M. 14, 18, 111
Boerne, L. 88, 90
Boissevain, J. 67
Bonte, P. 324
boredom 302–4